Professional and Practice-based Learning

Volume 30

Professional and practice-based learning brings together international research on the individual development of professionals and the organisation of professional life and educational experiences. It complements the Springer journal *Vocations and Learning: Studies in vocational and professional education.*

Professional learning, and the practice-based processes that often support it, are the subject of increased interest and attention in the fields of educational, psychological, sociological, and business management research, and also by governments, employer organisations and unions. This professional learning goes beyond, what is often termed professional education, as it includes learning processes and experiences outside of educational institutions in both the initial and ongoing learning for the professional practice. Changes in these workplaces requirements usually manifest themselves in the everyday work tasks, professional development provisions in educational institution decrease in their salience, and learning and development during professional activities increase in their salience.

There are a range of scientific challenges and important focuses within the field of professional learning. These include:

- understanding and making explicit the complex and massive knowledge that is required for professional practice and identifying ways in which this knowledge can best be initially learnt and developed further throughout professional life.
- analytical explications of those processes that support learning at an individual and an organisational level.
- understanding how learning experiences and educational processes might best be aligned or integrated to support professional learning.

The series integrates research from different disciplines: education, sociology, psychology, amongst others. The series is comprehensive in scope as it not only focuses on professional learning of teachers and those in schools, colleges and universities, but all professional development within organisations.

Please contact Grace Ma at grace.ma@springer.com if you wish to discuss a book proposal.

More information about this series at https://link.springer.com/bookseries/8383

Simon Flandin • Christine Vidal-Gomel
Raquel Becerril Ortega
Editors

Simulation Training through the Lens of Experience and Activity Analysis

Healthcare, Victim Rescue and Population Protection

Springer

Editors
Simon Flandin
Faculty of Psychology and Educational Sciences
University of Geneva
Geneva, Switzerland

Christine Vidal-Gomel
Centre de Recherches en Education de Nantes
University of Nantes
Nantes, France

Raquel Becerril Ortega
Adult Education
University of Lille
Lille, France

ISSN 2210-5549 ISSN 2210-5557 (electronic)
Professional and Practice-based Learning
ISBN 978-3-030-89566-2 ISBN 978-3-030-89567-9 (eBook)
https://doi.org/10.1007/978-3-030-89567-9

This Springer imprint is published by the registered company Springer Nature Switzerland AG
The registered company address is: Gewerbestrasse 11, 6330 Cham, Switzerland

Series Editors' Foreword

A key goal of the Professional and Practice-based Learning book series is to contribute to discussions about and processes for improving the enactment of occupational capacities through practice-based learning experiences for both the initial learning of those capacities and their ongoing development. A related goal is associated with understanding and enhancing the contributions that different kinds of experiences can make to the formation and continuity of those occupational practices and from different conceptual and methodological orientations. To date, the volumes in this series have contributed a range of perspectives, approaches and outcomes to these discussions. This volume continues that tradition through its focus on simulation training and from a Francophone orientation and through detailed and grounded analyses of how simulation experiences can be designed, organised, enacted and engaged with.

The authors argue that the demands of work and work requirements have become more complex, interrelated and, perhaps, less easy to be taught and learnt. However, to date, the focuses on the use of simulation training have been often quite specifically focused and narrow. It follows then that their volume seeks to redress this issue. It does this through providing detailed descriptions of the learning potential of simulation training through considerations of its strengths and limitations; identify how it can be used to achieve strong learning outcomes within occupational preparation and ongoing development, and, also inform further how practice based approaches to learning can be effectively harnessed. Given that the learning of occupations where risk is high to both the practitioners and those who are serviced by them, the ability to provide experiences through simulations but avoid harm to either and offer scenarios, options and ways of representing occupationally based experiences that can be adapted to either performance requirements or learners' needs brings with it enormous potential. The question is how these simulations can be most effectively designed, implemented and experienced by learners.

In responding to these challenges, a particular feature of this volume is that it adopts a Francophone approach that focuses upon activities and experience as an analytical and procedural orientation. This includes engaging the readership in a consideration of ergonomics from a cognitive and activity perspective that is central to the Francophone approach. In doing so, it draws upon illustrations from and appraisals of simulation training activities occurring within a range of sectors including healthcare, firefighting, security, policing and civil security. The discussion within the volume acknowledges the issues arising from the significant advance in electronic and digital technology that has occurred rapidly and continues to do so thereby opening up a whole range of ways in which experiences can be provided and activities organised and enacted as learning experiences. Within this development is the ongoing focus on addressing fidelity of experiences and validity of their learning potential. The grounded orientation to understanding occupational practice and learning that is central to the Francophone approach is well suited to illuminate and appraise issues of validity and fidelity.

The organisation of the volume is structured in ways that outlined these key concerns and issues within the contributions in the initial part, followed by parts that provide empirical and methodological contributions that explore these facets, with two summarising chapters comprising the final part. In this way, both individually and collectively, the contributions to this volume do much to advance understandings about the conceptual premises through which the design, organisation and enactment of simulation training might progress, and sets of procedural considerations to realise its contributions and secure efficacy.

In these ways, the volume makes a significant contribution to the field of professional practice-based learning and addresses an important gap both conceptually and procedurally about the ways in which experiences can be provided to achieve learning and developmental outcomes that go beyond what would be permissible, could be achievable and possibly engage with by learners, in so doing.

University of Paderborn Christian Harteis
Paderborn, Germany

University of Regensburg Hans Gruber
Regensburg, Germany

Griffith University Stephen Billett
Brisbane, Australia
August 2021

Keywords

Simulation-based learning in healthcare
Psychological validity of training simulations
Role-playing-games
Virtual simulation environment
Training of healthcare professionals in geriatrics
Situated cognition approaches
Civil security crisis simulations
Simulation training and risk management
Urban fire simulation
High-intensity simulated training
Activity-based training design
Use-of-force simulation-based training
Decision-making in police training facilities

Contents

Part II Empirical Lessons from Experience and Activity-Based Approaches to Simulation Training

Part III Promising Avenues for Simulation Training Design and Research

About the Authors

Simon Flandin is a researcher in the CRAFT lab in the Faculty of Psychology and Educational Sciences at the University of Geneva. His research consists of analysing the occupational and training activity of professionals in order to determine the best methods of generating transformations that improve performance, health, and development. His research approach is grounded in French-speaking Ergonomics and in Enaction theory, and his main fieldworks are video and simulation uses in various contexts of vocational education and professional development. Since 2016, his research agenda is polarised by safety and crisis management training. In 2019, he was the first educational scientist to obtain a SNSF (Swiss National Science Foundation) Ambizione Fellowship.

Christine Vidal-Gomel is Full Professor of Educational and Training Sciences. She is affiliated with the Centre de Recherche en Éducation de Nantes (CREN) at the University of Nantes (France). Her research approach consists of analysing the activity and development of professionals from the theoretical and methodological frameworks of French-speaking Ergonomics and Professional Didactics. She works on the design of 'enabling' training situations, integrating professional development and occupational health and safety. She carries out field studies in different domains, such as healthcare, building and civil engineering, and autonomous vehicle driving.

Raquel Becerril Ortega is an industrial engineer and Associated Professor of Educational Sciences in the CIREL laboratory (University of Lille, France). Her work consists of analysing occupational and training activity in order to design and develop adult training courses using simulation. She teaches to both academic and professional audiences. Her main interests are theories of adult learning and training, training design, simulation, and occupational activity analysis. In 2018, she obtained a research fellowship from the French National Institute for Research in Digital Science and Technology to contribute to a research and development programme on simulation training at the University of Santiago, Chile.

An Introduction to Simulation Training Through the Lens of Experience and Activity Analysis

Simon Flandin, Christine Vidal-Gomel, and Raquel Becerril Ortega

Abstract: This opening chapter offers an overview of the conditions under which experience and activity can be fruitful objects for examining what occurs in simulation training, understanding participants' learning and development processes, and deriving robust design principles. It is argued that this approach is particularly useful in the field of simulation training, especially when achieving high standards of operational performance is complicated by critical issues (health, safety, security, protection, etc.) and difficult working environments (dynamic, uncertain, high-risk, etc.). We show that this approach is able to integrate authentic, embodied, and embedded practice experiences with domain-related or cross-cutting learning content. We also provide key concepts that can guide readers in understanding how simulation-enhanced learning and development processes are studied and how the different ways of enabling trainees to construct usable knowledge in verisimilar contexts are derived from these studies. The organization of the book sections and chapters are then presented. In sum, this opening chapter introduces the purpose of the book, explains why the research presented here fills an important knowledge gap, and suggests ways that readers might profitably engage with its contents.

Keywords Simulation training · Vocational training · Training design · Experience · Activity analysis · Ergonomics

---

S. Flandin (✉)
Faculty of Psychology and Educational Sciences, University of Geneva, Geneva, Switzerland
e-mail: simon.flandin@unige.ch

C. Vidal-Gomel
Centre de Recherches en Education de Nantes, University of Nantes, Nantes, France
e-mail: christine.vidal-gomel@univ-nantes.fr

R. B. Ortega
Centre Interuniversitaire de Recherche en Éducation de Lille, University of Lille & INRIA [French National Institute for Research in Digital Science and Technology], Lille, France
e-mail: raquel.becerril-ortega@univ-lille.fr

S. Flandin et al. (eds.), *Simulation Training through the Lens of Experience and Activity Analysis*, Professional and Practice-based Learning 30,
https://doi.org/10.1007/978-3-030-89567-9_1

1 Addressing Major Contemporary Challenges for Vocational Education and Training Through Research-Informed Simulation Practice

In today's world, professionals everywhere are facing rapid and massive technical, social, economic, and organizational changes. The domain of vocational education and training has been impacted, and it is now facing new challenges, with the expectation that it will promote approaches based on good/evidence-based practices and respond to growing demands for training in nontechnical/transversal/soft skills (e.g., leadership, communication, situation awareness, stress management) and the imperative of improved performances in the short term. Simulation training is a highly rated means to quickly reach very specific professional learning objectives. But often and overall, simulation training programs seem to struggle to obtain satisfying, long-lasting, and measurable outcomes. It might be assumed that the main reason for this is that, in these programs, the complex human factors of performance tend to disintegrate into skills that are "extracted" from work for organizational purposes. Yet, although human factors are much more "manageable" as skills units, it then becomes very difficult to "reunify" the skills units into a balanced professionalism.

Nevertheless, dividing professionalism into skills units is an increasingly common way of sequencing what needs to be developed and trained for among professionals. The most common division currently distinguishes the technical skills that relate to a specific type of work and the nontechnical skills that relate to work in general, a professional field, and even all professions. This division has certain advantages for managing, without which it would not have established itself in the cultures of human resources, management, and *education and training*. The popularity of the concept of nontechnical skills/soft skills and its now widespread use in work and training organizations is no coincidence either. By providing a conceptual basis and vocabulary, it fits into a much broader trend that has become essential in the contemporary world of work: the specialization of professional functions. Yet, this trend can be harmful when it generates two deviations in particular. The first is when nontechnical skills become disarticulated from technical skills, as this makes it difficult for professionals to develop the capacity to intervene in ways that integrate all the components of real work. The second is when skills become artificialized, which occurs when the situational anchoring has been forgotten and the risk is thus high that the skills become meaningless.

The specialization of professional functions can nevertheless be beneficial when it facilitates the pooling of advances produced in professional fields showing strong similarities, such as in the fields covered in this book: health care, victim rescue, and civil protection. This pooling can contribute to both enhanced performances and improved ways to help professionals achieve better performances, in particular through *vocational education and training*.

It is important to bear in mind that when skills are considered transversally and are not specific to a type of work, they are difficult to define, operationalize, and evaluate, and these are crucial tasks of training design and implementation. Defining training objectives in ways that go beyond the classic domain-related approaches is necessary to draw on the cross-cutting principles for training design. However, definition is difficult because if it is too general, the instructional value remains low, and if it is too specific, the cross-cutting outcomes may not be achieved.

How can contemporary organizational and vocational expectations be met without losing instructional ambition? Given that simulation training is a suitable framework for situated, embodied, and embedded experimentation, we are convinced that this type of training has much to offer. The research on simulation training to date has nevertheless mainly focused on understanding performance improvements in very compartmented domains of skills or professions. Educational approaches that focus on experience, activity, learning, development, and practice changes do not appear to be sufficiently integrated. A particular problem is that the research evidence often remains domain-related (medical health care, fire rescue, civil protection, police intervention, military missions, etc.) and offers simulation trainers very few robust inputs to build programs oriented by cross-cutting principles, even though these professional domains share very similar issues and challenges.

The aim of this book is to present a comprehensive account of the various ways in which the analysis of experience and activity in the context of simulation training (i) helps identify learning affordances and obstacles and provides a detailed description of the learning process and outcomes, (ii) points toward promising design orientations for simulation-based vocational education and training, and (iii) contributes to the overall understanding of practice-based professional learning. Accordingly, the objectives of the book are:

- To describe and discuss the theoretical, methodological, and/or practical issues related to trainees' experiences and activities in simulation training
- To provide evidence of how the conditions under which lived experience in simulation can foster or hinder learning
- To identify the conceptual bases and empirical applications and implications of this approach to learning through simulation-based experimentation
- To contribute to both domain-related and generic orientations for simulation design

Herein, we thus present the research on various simulation training programs in the domains of health care, victim rescue, and population protection, involving healthcare workers (5 chapters), firemen (2 chapters), policemen (2 chapters), servicemen (2 chapters), and civil security leaders (1 chapter).

This opening chapter offers an overview of the conditions under which experience and activity can be fruitful objects for examining what occurs in simulation training, understanding participants' learning and development processes, and deriving robust design principles. It is argued that this approach is particularly useful in the field of simulation training, especially when achieving high standards of operational performance is complicated by critical issues (health, safety, security, protection, etc.) and difficult working environments (dynamic, uncertain, high risk, etc.). We show that this approach is able to integrate authentic, embodied, and embedded practice experiences with domain-related or cross-cutting learning content. We also provide key concepts that can guide readers in understanding how simulation-enhanced learning and development processes are studied and how the different ways of enabling trainees to construct usable knowledge in verisimilar contexts are derived from these studies. The organization of the book sections and chapters is then presented. In sum, this opening chapter introduces the purpose of the book, explains why the research presented here fills an important knowledge gap, and suggests ways that readers might profitably engage with its contents.

2 Theoretical Background: A Francophone Research Tradition in Cognitive Ergonomics and Vocational Education and Training

2.1 Cognitive Ergonomics and Educational Research Traditions in Simulation Training

The chapters of this book present studies at the interface of several research traditions, notably cognitive ergonomics and "the ergonomics of activity." Since the 1980s, cognitive ergonomics has focused on the design and improvement of "information technologies" – and more recently on digital resources – by including training in its line of research questions, whereas the ergonomics of activity has been integrated into the sciences of education and training. Much of the research presented here has drawn on these two traditions in particular and sought to contribute to a deeper understanding of simulation as a support for the development of what Chernikova, Heitzmann, Stadler, Holzberger and Seidel (2020) call "complex skills": "Critical thinking, problem solving, communication, and collaboration seem to be the most relevant skills[1] that [...] should [be acquired], in addition to domain-specific knowledge and skills, to be able to make professional decisions and implement solutions" (op. cit., p. 501). However, unlike these authors, the researchers presented here are not necessarily concerned with initial training or higher education. The studies often focus on a set of professionals from different fields and with different levels of initial training who nevertheless all need to acquire and develop complex skills in order to perform quality work in every day or more exceptional situations.

Simulation training experienced a real boom in the twentieth century with the development of computing resources, computers, and digital technology (Rosen, 2013). Cognitive ergonomics, which first emerged in the 1950s, has been interested in simulation since the 1960s, mainly conducting studies in the fields of the military, nuclear power plants, and maintenance tasks (Patrick, 1992). In the 1980s, with the

[1] The notion of skill is used here to highlight the characteristics of the tasks to be performed, and this usage is different from that found later in this introduction.

spread of new computing tools, simulation training expanded to other industrial and at-risk fields (Norros, 1989). During this period, the research focused on the design and improvement of simulators and simulations for teaching, certification, and training. The validity and reliability of the simulators and simulation situations in comparison with "real work" situations have been widely debated, and these issues continue to receive attention (e.g., Drews & Bakdash, 2013; Persson, 2017). At the same time, the research carried out in the sciences of education and training in French-speaking countries since the mid-1990s has tended to focus on the professions of service relations (education and training, health care, etc.) in which the interventions relate to another human (particularly with education, development, and health objectives). In these professional sectors, the contributions of digital technology are more recent than in industry, and some have touted digital resources for training as the means to achieve major improvements. These arguments recall those that Leplat (1989) and Patrick (1992) pointed to concerning other major contributions that were expected to improve the world of work, when in fact some indeed made real contributions and some were revealed to be limited and/or "naive."

In the 1990s, the debates began to move in other directions. For example, some focused on the interest and limitations of microworlds designed for in vitro experiments (Brehmer & Dorner, 1993). These works underscored the complexity of fidelity: Microworlds are artificial situations that are not faithful to "natural" situations, although they retain certain features. Two types of problems were thus raised: that of ecological validity, which can be defined as "the possibility to generalize the conclusion obtained by the study of an artificial situation to a class of natural situation" (Hoc, 2001, p. 284), and that of fidelity. Physical fidelity, or the resemblance to reality (Patrick, 1992), is differentiated from functional fidelity, or "the degree to which a simulator acts like the real equipment" (Grau et al., 1998, p. 370), and from "psychological fidelity," which refers to the determination of the psychological dimensions mobilized in the simulated situation that are hypothesized to be equivalent to those at work in a "natural" situation (Baker & Marshall, 1989; Patrick, 1992). Patrick reformulated it in these terms: "The simulation has to represent the task to the trainee in such a way that the psychological or skill requirements of the task are not changed significantly. The trainee should have to deploy the same cognitive activities in performing the simulated task as the actual task" (1992, p. 495). It has thus been well established that physical fidelity is not necessary when the objective of training is the acquisition of procedures or the mastery of tasks for which the cognitive dimensions of the activity are important.

Rogalski (1995) suggested that these problems might be better understood and even resolved by analyzing the tasks to be performed at a cognitive and conceptual level and by modeling the development of professional skills[2] (the KEOPS model). This implies designing simulation situations while retaining or transforming "task

[2] The notion of professional competence used in French, which is often translated by the term "skill" in English, refers to the dimensions of activity mobilized to carry out tasks, to accomplish a mission. Bainbridge and Ruiz Quintanilla (1989) discussed the different meanings of the term skill in English and French cognitive ergonomics.

functionalities" for a learning and development objective. "The term task functionality refers, on the one hand, to the properties of the deep structure of the task, involving cognitive requirements, and, on the other hand, to the properties of what is often seen as context which are in fact closely tied to the task and have strong effects on operators' behavior when performing a task" (op. cit., p. 127). From this perspective, the model takes into account the situational and organizational characteristics that affect activity and require the development of specific skills by individuals and groups in order to achieve mastery of these situations and obtain the desired results.

2.2 *Simulation Training Through the Lens of Experience and Activity*

The debates on validity and fidelity have continued with one example being in the health sector, which tends to favor high-fidelity simulations, thus creating confusion between fidelity and its many components and the "reproduction of the real." In the research world, authors like Persson (2017) and Hamstra, Brydges, and Hatala et al. (2014) have suggested dropping the term "fidelity." Persson (op. cit.) pointed out that this term tends to center the debate on technological advances and a resemblance to "real" situations, rather than on the relevance of simulation for learning. Béguin and Pastré (2002) suggested going beyond questions of validity and fidelity in exploring the functions of the simulated situation by putting the focus on trainees' activity and the meanings that the simulation takes on for them. This viewpoint is quite close to that of Rogalski (op. cit.) in that it emphasizes the importance of how trainees interpret a situation, and it may be an important dimension of the skills that need to be acquired.

During this period, the issues surrounding simulations for professional training came to the attention of researchers working within the cognitive ergonomic framework (i) regarding the characterization of expertise and "skills" and the development and learning processes, as in Bainbridge and Ruiz Quintanilla's book (1995) titled "Developing skills with information technology," and (ii) from a training perspective, as in Patrick's (1992) work: "Training: Research and practice." Along the same lines, Hoc, Cacciabue, and Hollnagel's book (1995) included a section of four chapters that focused on characterizing expertise and its consequences for training, skill development through simulation, and the limits of operational knowledge acquired on the job and by transmission within a group of peers, as well as how it can be completed through training.

This type of research has intensified in high-risk sectors. As studies have highlighted the importance of collective functioning to ensure the efficiency and safety of work systems, this theme has also emerged in research on the use of simulation in training (Salas & Cannon-Bowers, 2001; Salas et al., 2012). In the 2000s, training simulations developed beyond these professional environments in response to societal demands, notably in healthcare environments where such rules as "never for the first time on a patient" are unquestioned. They also proliferated because the costs of simulation devices have decreased with technological advances (web 2.0, etc.). Yet, despite this growing body of research, it is regrettable that certain aspects of training simulations, such as the activity of trainers – who are crucial to training effectiveness – have been little explored, with few exceptions (Rogalski et al., 2002).

In the 1990s, the education and training sciences of the French-speaking world seized upon a set of theoretical frameworks that mobilized the concept of activity. Fillietaz and Billet (2015) gave a detailed account of this period. Thus, alongside the work in cognitive ergonomics, aspects of which we have noted because of their contributions to simulation training, other orientations developed. This particularly concerned the research carried out from the "ergonomics of activity"[3] perspective, whose researchers have been critical of cognitive psychology, as have "course-of-action" researchers (Durant & Poizat, 2015). These two approaches to "human factors," for example, can be distinguished from the traditional approaches by the place given to the concept of activity and the systemic point of view that is defended (Daniellou, 2005; Rabardel & Daniellou, 2005; Vidal-Gomel et al., 2019).

Thus, Durand and Poizat (op. cit., p. 223) specified the framework of the "course of action," which defines activity as "what a given actor does as a living, cultural and reflexive unit engaged in a social practice (in this case, work). A here-and-now activity refers to a time point or state in the history of dynamic exchanges between this living unit and its environment." This approach integrates contributions from Maturana (1988), particularly by taking into account "the living unit as autopoietic," which means that the unit of analysis is defined as a unit–environment coupling. The definition of coupling within this research stream differs markedly from that of other approaches to activity: "Activity is, thus, taken to be the set of ongoing interactions of a living unit and its environment, and it is further assumed that these interactions produce the very structure of this unit and its environment and are in no way the mere response of a predetermined unit reacting to stimuli or adapting to constraints from a world that is itself predetermined. During these interactions, the unit and its environment are in a relationship of co-definition. They define each other. But, this co-definition is asymmetric in that only the living unit specifies what in the environment is meaningful for it (and not the reverse)" (op. cit., p. 226).

Other researchers working within the framework of the ergonomics of activity are closer to the community conducting research based on Russian psychology. The cultural–historical activity theory (CHAT) of Leontiev (1978) and Vygotsky (1934/1978) presents some of the best-known ideas from Russian psychology. Engestrom's model (1987), which was built on an interpretation of CHAT, has been widely disseminated. However, other models, such as the model of Norros (2005, 2014), are less well-known, as are a range of other studies based on Russian psychology (Daniellou & Rabardel, 2005). It is notable that the ergonomics of activity

[3] Many authors use the term "French-speaking ergonomists" to designate this line of research. In order to avoid overlooking a large part of our colleagues who contribute and enrich this approach, we prefer the term "ergonomics of activity."

community and the community that has drawn on Russian psychology and its developments continue to interact in events organized regularly for the triennial Congress of the International Ergonomics Association. They are identified under the title "Activity theory for work analysis and design."

In a historical analysis of the development of activity ergonomics, Daniellou (2005) noted how the translation of Leontiev's work into French in 1975 influenced researchers in what was not yet called "the ergonomics of activity." He explained how the concept of activity was incorporated into research that mobilized "psychological analyses of work," replacing the concept of "conduct" that had been used up to that point. In this regard, Daniellou quotes Leplat and Cuny (1977, in Daniellou, op. cit., p. 411): "the central object of psychological analysis is the worker's conduct or in other words, the human operator's conduct. We will sometimes use the word 'activity' as being synonymous with conduct. (…) When analyzing work, we must differentiate the analysis of conduct from the analysis of the requirements or conditions to which this conduct is subjected and to which it replies." This quotation is striking for underlining the reconciliation of the viewpoints of the two communities. Daniellou and Rabardel (2005, p. 355) also recalled a set of viewpoints shared by the ergonomics of activity and Russian psychology-based research on the subject of activity, which we recall here very schematically:

- "Activity is finalized. Activity is object-oriented in order to attain one or more goals, which are not always evident, and which the analyst may have trouble identifying.
- The relation between the subject and object is mediated by technical devices, psychological schemes and organization […] These activity mediators are socially and culturally constructed as well as historically situated.
- Activity is always unique. It is specific to given subjects in a given context […].
- Activity bears traces of its past. Activity […] is affected by the subject's life experience and is, thus, constantly revised and reinvested […].
- Activity is not only a relationship between a subject and an object. It is also a relationship with other subjects, who may be physically present or present via instruments and tools, sign systems […].
- The analyst's approach to activity is intrinsic: he/she seeks to understand 'from within' how the subject constructs his/her activity to attain the object, given the resources and constraints at their disposal […].
- Activity is integrational. It is constructed at the crossroads of the subject's motives and goals […] and several determinants, which may be clearly connected to the workstation layout or apparently unrelated (the subject's history, the company's sales policy)."

One of the peculiarities of Francophone ergonomics is precisely its interest in these determinants from a systemic approach, that is, "the point of view that is adopted to jointly take into account a set of dimensions of human activity (biological, psychological, cognitive, social) and that also seeks to highlight a set of determinants of operators' activity, depending on the problem addressed" (Vidal-Gomel et al., 2019, p. 234). Leplat's model (1997), which is shared by many researchers in the ergonomics of activity (Daniellou, 2005), provides a framework for such an analysis. It differentiates:

- The factors that determine activity (characteristics of workers, means of work and tasks)
- The characteristics of the activity in the situations being analyzed
- The effects (in terms of health or skill development) and results (in terms of productive efficiency)
- Last, given the dynamics of the situated action in the short, medium, or longer term, the effects that transform the determining factors in a transitory or more lasting way

This approach has been widely used in the field of professional training, highlighting, for example, (i) the interest of not limiting the scope of activity analysis to the work activities to be trained for; (ii) the need to take into account the work activities of both trainers and trainees and, in some situations, colleagues that are not directly concerned but will have to help new entrants; (iii) the interest of an approach that seeks to understand work situations rather than only the tasks that must be mastered by the end of a training program; and (iv) the importance of subjective engagement at work (Vidal-Gomel et al., op. cit.).

Professional didactics is an heir to both cognitive ergonomics and the ergonomics of activity with regard to understanding work, as well as to a theory of adult cognitive development that considers "conceptualization in action" (Vergnaud, 2009) and seeks to develop a pedagogy of situations for training (Mayen, 2015; Tourmen et al., 2017).

These currents of thought, all based on the concept of activity but sometimes approaching it from different angles, run through this book to varying degrees. We would like to point out that they also share a number of epistemological, theoretical, and methodological orientations. We note the following points:

- The actual work (as it is performed in the situation) is differentiated from the work prescribed by those who order its execution orally or via job descriptions.
- The work expected and planned for by the work organization or the workers themselves is different from the actual work.
- Analyzing work cannot be reduced to analyzing the tasks that need to be done. The analysis must take into account the results of the work (results prescribed, expected, and recognized in the company or institution, as well as the various viewpoints on the results) and the consequences for individuals, collectives, and the work organization. Also, the analysis takes on its full meaning only with the analysis of activity, which starts from the situated action of an individual or a group and is apprehended through its dynamics as the situation unfolds (action carried out or action prevented).
- The activity is understood to depend jointly on the characteristics of the situation and those of the individual.
- Primacy is given to the analysis of in vivo activity and the ecological validity of the results.

- Intervention is an important dimension of the research carried out using these approaches: The research aims to transform work and training environments with the objective of developing the actors.

Among the viewpoints shared by these schools of thought, some relate more specifically to professional training. In particular, it is acknowledged that scientific and technical knowledge is necessary but insufficient to perform work, and it must therefore be supplemented by knowledge about action based on professional experience to ensure optimal preparation for work: "the operator's knowledge comes from basic education, training, and direct experience in working with the system. Through basic education, the operator learns the physical laws underlying the process, the principles of functioning for the components, and the principles that govern the behavior of complex systems. It is, however, only through training and experience that the operator becomes acquainted with how the plant or the process conducts itself in normal and abnormal conditions" (Hoc et al., 1995, p. 13).

When the initial training involves many years devoted to knowledge acquisition (typically higher education), the confrontation with professional situations or simulation situations leads to a restructuring of this knowledge, as well as its articulation with the characteristics of the encountered situations and the knowledge acquired in the course of processing these situations. Thus, Boshuizen and Schmidt (Schmidt et al., 1988; Boshuizen et al., 1995; Van de Wiel et al., 2000) focused on the initial training of doctors and showed that as doctors acquire experience with the situation of dealing with clinical cases, they develop concepts that encapsulate the theoretical knowledge that they have acquired thus far: "the networks of biomedical knowledge acquired in initial training are included in higher-level clinical concepts," which means that "the networks of knowledge about the pathophysiological mechanisms linking the causes and consequences of a disease are 'captured' [i.e., encapsulated] by clinical concepts" drawn from situated action (Van de Wiel et al., 2000, p. 328). Biomedical knowledge is mobilized when the clinical knowledge is insufficient, and for students with little or no experience, this is often the case, while for more experienced physicians it only occurs in rare or complex situations. Pastré (2005) made a similar observation by examining the activity of engineers learning to operate a nuclear power plant on a simulator after high-level scientific and technical training. He hypothesized that during training on simulators, a "semantics of action" is constituted in the confrontation with the situation. This semantics articulates the indices present in in the situation and the concepts (scientific and technical or resulting from action in a simulated situation and interactions with peers) that give them meaning and allow for an interpretation of the situation – and ultimately the categorization of situations. Thus, categories of problems and situations are developed in a process he calls "pragmatization," wherein theoretical concepts are transformed.

However, such processes do not emphasize the variety and the diversity of knowledge necessary for the work, but rather on central invariant dimensions of these knowledge. A part of this knowledge includes knowledge of particular cases and different types of experience of dealing with risk and the unforeseen events that punctuate the daily job or constitute exceptional situations – even "crisis situations." In fact, the types of training that interest us here are non-curricular.

2.3 *Applications to Health Care, Victim Rescue, and Population Protection*

Based on this common grounding, the book chapters focus on the use of simulation in training in several areas of activity, particularly the management of typical, deteriorating, or even critical situations in contexts of health and safety. These are areas in which simulation is a necessity because it is impossible and/or unacceptable to learn on the job. It is impossible because of the rarity of crises or disasters and unacceptable because of the risks involved for the professionals and those they serve.

These domains of intervention are all "dynamic environments: It is characteristic of a dynamic system that it may evolve without operator intervention. Thus, even if the operator does not interact with the system, for instance, when he is trying to diagnose or plan, the state of the system may change" (Hoc et al., 1995, p. 4). The situation variables may change at different tempos, and their effects may intersect at possibly different moments. The sequences of reasoning required to understand what is happening and to act may thus progress through "several steps."

The characteristics of such work situations have consequences for the skills that need to be acquired: "Working with a dynamic system not only means that time may be limited, but it also means that the mental representation of the system must be continuously updated. The choice of a specific action is based on the operator's understanding of the current state of the system and the expectations of what the action will accomplish. If the understanding is incomplete or incorrect, the actions may fail to achieve their purpose" (op. cit., p. 5).

Among these dynamic work situations, some can immediately be qualified as "crisis management" situations, whereas others drift toward crisis – that is, "an event, in general unexpected, whose consequences may develop with very rapid dynamics, producing significant risks that exceed the pre-existing resources in terms of action procedures" (Rogalski, 2004, p. 531). We might underline that crises have serious consequences. They create "significant and widespread human, material, economic and or environmental losses that exceed the ability of the affected community or society to cope within its own resources [...] The development of events following the sudden onset is so rapid that it exceeds the ability to respond [...] Events often develop in unexpected directions, thus challenging the readiness and resources of the responding organizations" (Hollnagel, 2012[4]).

Crises thus pose recurring problems, but the shift into crisis cannot be analyzed in the same way across these fields of activity: "disasters are 'normal' in the activity of firefighters, which is not the case for most other systems. Therefore, a variety of

[4] Unpaged document.

resources are already associated with different types of disasters, the organization of which (actors and resources) has been extensively planned for [...] The difference in disaster management by emergency service actors is the relocation of system functions and the overwhelming of pre-existing resources" (Rogalski, 2004, p. 531).

Yet, there are also substantial points in common for these areas of intervention that justify our choice to have brought them together in this book: All these professionals have to deal with risky situations that are not always predictable, despite the planning efforts of their respective professional communities. Thus, in disaster management or at another scale of crisis management, the appropriate response to the situation rarely comes from the application of standardized procedures. They must be at the very least adjusted to the situation, which requires the operators to have a detailed understanding of the situation and the procedures in question. In the field of health care with relationships with patients and caregiving, "care" itself cannot be reduced to techniques and procedures that can be applied systematically. Thus, training is not merely a matter of imitation or reproduction. These are, of course, usable training methods, but they must lead to understanding, the construction of meaning, and conceptualization on individual and collective levels. Moreover, these areas are all affected by uncertainty and surprise, which are therefore important characteristics that operators must be prepared for through training.

These are interesting areas for professional training because learning in these contexts is difficult: It is difficult to relate an action that has been carried out to its effects on the situation, especially with the rapid changes in dynamics and entangled variables; it is impossible to go back and learn by repetition; and it is necessary to anticipate (which constitutes one of the difficulties of beginners) in a situation that is uncertain, poses multiple risks, cannot be fully understood, and presents phenomena that may never before been encountered. Indeed, we do not have sufficient scientific models for these contexts, which also underlines the importance of experiential knowledge even though these fields can be very codified, standardized, and procedural, sometimes leaving little room for the actor's experience.

Focusing attention on "fields of activity" can contribute to the construction of knowledge about the characteristics of situations and of the activity in these situations, which can facilitate the identification of relevant training situations. Fields of activity in fact call upon sets of activities, objects, and tasks, which, at a certain level, can be defined as characteristics, as having common traits (Rabardel & Samurçay, 2004). Thus, we know that the control of dynamic environments, which are characteristic of these situations, requires anticipation, a characteristic of activity. Activity cannot be reduced to this trait, but it encompasses it. Therefore, characterizing fields of activity can help guide the design of simulation situations.

From this perspective, the jobs of firefighters, police officers, and healthcare professionals fall within fields of activity that differ in terms of the objectives they pursue, the resources they can access, and the organization of the work and value systems.

In these fields, however, although scientific and technical knowledge is necessary, it is insufficient to produce quality work. Knowledge is not always well stabilized, and the knowledge that professionals acquire over the course of their experience often remains implicit, poorly understood, and little disseminated and discussed. The contributions of the professional community can therefore be important, although they often need to be discussed and debated to identify their limits. The contributions for training can then be distributed among peers and trainers who may differ in their opinions, particularly because there is rarely a single good response to a situation but rather a set of acceptable solutions, which need to be evaluated according to different types of criteria. In the field of health care and crisis management, it may be a question of stabilizing the situation by limiting the consequences of risks according to the resources that are available at time "t." A debriefing can then provide opportunities for debate to examine the chosen solutions and identify their advantages and limitations (Mollo & Nascimento, 2014). Last, in these fields, the experience acquired by the professionals is not always sufficient as they may need to be prepared for new situations: The interest of simulation is precisely that it offers "the possibility of extrapolating and creating a knowledge base starting from bounded experience" (Hoc et al., 1995, p. 13).

In any case, trainees are not considered as having "received" knowledge transmitted by trainers. Simulation situations are designed to give trainees experience, letting them live an experience that can then be analyzed individually and collectively after the fact. This kind of a posteriori analysis, removed from the heat of the moment, is an opportunity for professional development.

The training simulations presented in this book also suggest a set of ethical questions: Is it acceptable to put professionals in difficulty in front of their colleagues? How far can they be pushed to confront difficult and stressful situations? What are the consequences for them?

3 Simulation Training as a Controlled Space for Experimentation in Practice-Based Learning

Simulations grew out of the demand from work organizations to take real activity into account in training situations (Ughetto et al., 2018) by giving individuals the possibility of experiencing or reliving past or current situations (realized or not) and future situations in order to think or rethink more productively about them and better act in them (Bobillier Chaumon et al., 2018). Simulations can be understood as putting activity into perspective, leading to a form of detachment from reality. In this book, simulation is considered a pedagogical and didactic approach to promote experimentation in training that can be configured in different ways, depending on the objectives noted in the research presented in each chapter.

3.1 Simulation, an Educational Process

The history of simulation as a method of acquiring professional skills (Singh et al., 2013) sheds light on this educational issue. Simulation training drew inspiration from simulations in avionic safety systems and military training, which were then transposed to other professional systems, such as health care (Rosen, 2013) or civil security. Simulations in avionics focus on error and action and prevention strategies, with a pedagogical corollary being to "do the experiment without causing damage": without physical damage to self and others, without material damage, and thus without ecological damage. In the military, the simulation tradition aims to make the combat experience more up-close and intimate in order to build the military experience needed for success in theaters of operation (Hill & Tolk, 2017). Here, simulations are used to develop and test action protocols and train soldiers to implement them.

Thus, this educational approach places the person "in a situation" *to experiment* in order to learn or question practices. It is based on experimentation with ordinary, complex, and even critical situations. Different educational configurations can be used, depending on the knowledge targeted, the trainees qualities, the objectives to be achieved (learning, assessment, certification), the technologies available, etc.

On the assumption that experimentation is a continuous elaboration of experience, two cognitive dispositions can be mobilized according to different temporalities. First, regarding the immediacy of action, experimentation is understood as a reworking of the experience *in situ*. This occurs, for example, when a professional in the situation constructs guiding and corrective hypotheses related to action strategies, depending on the context. Second, with regard to long-term experience as a reservoir of available actions inscribed in the biographical or life story, actions are geared toward the success of a project. Experimentation, here understood as a sifting through of experience, is activated to face new situations, thereby contributing to the anticipation and management of future problems.

3.2 Simulation, a Didactic Approach

The history of simulation also teaches us that its development goes hand in hand with the new possibilities offered by simulators (Rosen, 2013), which are the technical support for simulations (Vadcard, 2022). In the military field, for example, board games were used to develop strategies, then life-size simulations were used to train soldiers (Hill & Tolk, 2017). In the field of medicine, simulation methods can be supported by biological equipment, as in animal experimentation, cadaver use, standardized patients, role plays, etc.; synthetic equipment, like patient or procedural simulators; and electronic equipment, like virtual or augmented reality and 3D environments (Betz et al., 2014).

Thus, beyond the representativeness and fidelity of the simulation to the situation it represents, the didactic approach is concerned with the design of the training situation. Simulators support preconceived simulation situations, most of which are designed from real field situations (military, aviation, clinical cases, etc.). These simulation situations are part of the training system or meet a specific training need. An epistemological vigilance that is specific to this didactic approach consists in identifying the technical constraints that the simulator imposes on the simulation – for example, by limiting the possible actions – and by doing so, it identifies the possibilities of developing new knowledge and skills. This epistemological vigilance also consists in controlling the epistemic network mobilized during the simulation, and not only that of the representation provided by the simulator from the start. Thus, the technical constraints and possibilities of simulations constitute one dimension among others, largely influenced, moreover, by the knowledge and skills brought into play by the trainees and trainers.

Simulation as a didactic approach offers a space for experimentation to elaborate or re-elaborate knowledge. It assumes the elaboration of knowledge from action – on the assumption that this elaboration results in novelty compared to the state of knowledge previously available – and the gradual stabilization of a repertoire of action structures to act effectively and deal with the unforeseen – which presupposes adaptation to the context.

3.3 Simulation, a Controlled Experimentation Space

In this book, simulation is seen as part of a constructivist perspective on learning, heir to major trends in the psychology of learning and development (Piaget, 1947). It has been grouped by some under the term experiential learning (Yardley et al., 2012), which also includes Vygotsky's socioconstructivist perspective. Dewey, for example, argued that experience implies a connection between the action and its consequence for the subject: if the active phase, action, is separated from the passive phase of experience, the reflection carried on about this action, real meaning is destroyed (Dewey, 1934, p. 298). For Piaget (1947), on the other hand, experience is not a primary fact: it must be organized by the subject and presupposes an activity. It is therefore quite different from a system of exogenous associations. Any experience is an experiment in the sense of the subject's organization of a question posed to nature or a situation in which he or she is engaged, which must respond with yes or no. Experimentation is active and cannot be reduced to experience in the ordinary sense of everyday experience – that is, simple perceptual contact with events taking place in the external environment.

Simulation, as an educational and didactic process, is constituted as a controlled space for experimentation: experimentation with risks, unforeseen events, or the vagaries of new or known situations, in the aim of elaborating or re-elaborating knowledge. Simulation helps to define the dimensions of a context of anticipation and freedom, so that this context can be assumed by professionals during training.

4 Introducing the Contributions to Simulation Training

The contributors to this book have empirically or conceptually analyzed the characteristics and effects of simulation training programs, mainly in the dimensions of the activity deployed and/or the experience lived by the trainees, as explained above. Doing so has enabled them to evaluate the design principles that might fruitfully be generalized and/or to improve their effectiveness for both trainers and trainees. These simulation systems involve one or more categories of professionals in the fields of health care, victim rescue, or civil protection, and are all finalized by the improvement of performance, defined through a wide spectrum of generic factors (e.g., crisis management) or factors specific to the field of practice (e.g., a technical nursing act).

The contributions bring together:

- Empirical reports based on the study of programs either designed by the researchers or identified in the field as having characteristics of particular interest (innovative goals, original principles, unprecedented attempts, etc.)
- Conceptual reports based on the analysis of current trends and research results in simulation, underlining and criticizing, promoting, and/or deriving new keys for comprehension or new design principles

This broad scope of analysis has resulted in chapters that describe, analyze, critique, and contribute to improving a vast set of simulation practices in the fields of health care, victim rescue, and population protection and that more broadly offer insights into professional learning by practice in simulation training.

The book is structured into three sections.

4.1 Experience- and Activity-Based Conceptualizations of Simulation Design and Outcomes

This first section examines activity as unfolding and experience as meaningful lived episodes during contrasted simulation training situations. It contributes to a deeper understanding of simulation design (objectives, format, tasks, animation, perturbations, facilitation, etc.) and outcomes (from very specific technical gestures to wide and multidimensional dispositions).

4.1.1 Conceptual Contributions for the Design of Activity-Led Simulation Training

The chapters of this subsection (2–4) provide insights from empirical and conceptual research about simulation training outcomes and design principles in the domains of health care and interprofessional management of civil safety.

Chapter "Simulation-Based Learning for Technical Gestures in Health Care: What Kind of Experience Is Required?", authored by Lucile Vadcard, provides an analysis of simulation-based learning in medicine from a wide range of simulation practices, from mock-ups to virtual reality. In this chapter, she explains what type of experience is provided, depending on the learning objectives, and develops the example of technical gestures in surgery and the Socratic method. Vadcard (i) questions the taken-for-granted quest for realism in simulation, (ii) advocates for strong didactic principles to enable the development of the conceptualization processes needed for technical learning, and (iii) proposes a tool for the analysis and design of promising simulation situations.

In Chapter "Four Lines of Analysis for Civil Security Crisis Simulations: Insights for Training Design", Simon Flandin also analyzes the conditions under which learning and development can occur through simulation. In his chapter, he describes how civil security leaders develop and reinforce dispositions to act efficiently during crisis management situations through the various features of interprofessional simulation training. Inductively deriving four dimensions for understanding and transforming individual and collective activity, Flandin contributes to the state of knowledge in the fields of collective performance in civil security crisis management and interprofessional simulation design.

This ambition to contribute to a conceptual renewal in the field of simulation training is shared by Zoya Horcik, who explains how a (re-)consideration of the situated cognition approach could prove fruitful for simulation in the medical field. Specifically, she defines three "missed appointments" between medical simulation and situated cognition. Chapter "Renewing the Tools for Simulation-Based Training in Medical Education: How Situated Cognition Approaches Can Help Us?" thus aims to encourage global reflection on the relationships between theoretical frameworks and design principles by analyzing the links between how learning is conceptualized and how simulation-based training programs are implemented.

4.1.2 Insights from Design-Based Research in Simulation Training

The chapters of the next subsection (5–7) provide design-based research accounts regarding three simulation programs: care gestures in health care, patient management in geriatrics, and "mass casualty event" management.

Chapter "The Psychological Validity of Training Simulations: Analysis of a Simulation with Role-Playing Games to Experiment the Gesture of "Relational Touch", authored by Christine Vidal-Gomel, addresses the notion of psychological validity by reflecting on the dimensions of work activity that are brought into play in simulation. In this chapter, she analyzes the activity of healthcare professionals in a simulation co-designed by the researcher and a trainer, finalized by the acquisition of a technical gesture: the gesture of "relational touch." In doing so, Vidal-Gomel contributes to our understanding of the conditions under which simulation promotes the learning of "professional" gestures through practice, here seen (i) as the "transformation of schemas" and (ii) through the lens of the subjective engagement of actors in situation and with their relationship to the profession.

Also in the field of health care, the research reported by Raquel Becerril Ortega and colleagues was aimed at developing a virtual simulation training tool for caregivers in geriatrics. Chapter "Design Process for a Virtual Simulation Environment for Training Healthcare Professionals in Geriatrics" thus describes the whole process of developing this tool, from identifying the training needs (through observations and interviews) to analyzing testers' activity and the "figurations" produced through simulation training. This design-based research account explores innovative avenues for the design of virtual simulation tools addressing difficult healthcare challenges like communicating with patients with Alzheimer's disease or other forms of dementia.

The last chapter in this subsection, from Vincent Boccara, Renauld Delmas, and Françoise Darses, is also part of the design-based research paradigm. In Chapter "Ergo-Scripting in Activity-Based Training Design: An Illustration from the Design of a Virtual Environment", the authors thus promote a methodological approach they call "ergo-scripting." This method is based on the argument that the design of learning scenarios must be supported by both ergonomic and didactic analyses of work. Boccara and his colleagues explain how to implement this approach and illustrate it through a concrete example: the design of a virtual training environment to train medical leaders as they acquire and develop the skills needed to cope with a mass casualty event (attack, external operation, etc.).

4.2 Empirical Lessons from Experience- and Activity-Based Approaches to Simulation Training

The second section is devoted to empirical accounts of the activity and experience of professionals through the study of work-as-done in simulation training programs. It informs the field of simulation with original and acute findings on professional engagement and performance in simulation training and offers relevant guidelines for simulation design.

4.2.1 Empirical Lessons from the Analysis of Trainees' Activity in Simulation Training

The chapters of this subsection (8–10) present activity studies of professionals' actions, decisions, communications, interactions, and configurations as they deal with urgent and/or critical events (firemen and policemen).

Chapter "Simulation to Experiment and Develop Risk Management in Exceptional Crisis Situations: The Case of the Casualty Extraction", authored by Laurie-Anna Dubois, Sylvie Vandestrate, and Agnès Van Daele, presents a study on how firefighters belonging to a "Casualty Extraction Team" manage and learn to manage high risks in a simulated exceptional crisis situation (post-attack crisis). In this chapter, they analyze the activity of both the trainees and trainers in simulation from audio–video recordings. The relevance of the simulation training under study vis-à-vis the skills targeted for acquisition is assessed through the study of transformations in the trainees' activity. The results contribute to the state of knowledge on preparing for the management of high-risk relief situations.

The second chapter in this subsection also analyzes the activity of firefighters during full-scale simulated rescue situations. Cyril Bossard, Yohann Cardin, Magali Prost, and Gilles Kermarrec studied the construction of collective meaning in intervention during an urban fire simulation. Using subjective video data and resituating interviews, the analysis presented in Chapter "Analyzing the Collective Activity of Firefighters During Urban Fire Simulation" allowed them to model six typical collective configurations. This contribution informs both the work of firefighters in this type of intervention and the design of simulation training likely to favor the processes of collective meaning construction, which is a crucial dimension of performance in this type of rescue.

The methods that use subjective video data and resituating interviews are particularly suited to very fine-grained analysis of the activity of professionals, particularly when they are engaged in very intense interventions. Sophie Le Bellu, Saadi Lahlou, Joshua M. Phelps, and Jan Aandal also used these methods in their documentation of the decision-making processes of police officers during training simulations. In Chapter "Subjective Evidence-Based Ethnography: An Alternative to Debriefing for Large-Scale Simulation-Based Training?", they propose a method that can be used for both research purposes and training: subjective evidence-based ethnography. This method uses contextualized, constructed, and guided debriefings to make better use of the simulation situation, with benefits to learning and reflexivity for the trainees.

4.2.2 Empirical Lessons from the Analysis of Trainees' Lived Experience in Simulation Training

The chapters of this subsection (11–13) present fine-grained explorations of the lived experience, concerns, sensemaking and situational dispositions of individual policemen, servicemen, and healthcare workers facing complex and potentially – physically and mentally – intense simulated occupational configurations.

Chapter "A Study of Police Cadets' Activity During Use-of-Force Simulation-Based Training: Empirical Lessons and Insights for Training Design", authored by Rachel Boembeke, Laurane De Carvalho, and Germain Poizat, examines the full-scale simulation training of police officers in intervention techniques and tactics. In this chapter, they document the lived experience of the trainees, particularly (i) their typical concerns, (ii) the nature of their involvement in the situation, and (iii) their methods of knowledge building. The analyses contribute to a better understanding of the optimal conditions for ensuring the effectiveness of high-fidelity simulations and point to the design principles to be favored.

Full-scale high-fidelity simulations offer particularly interesting training opportunities for trainers aiming for a high degree of ecological validity. In the following chapter, Hervé de Bisschop and Serge Leblanc show how simulated situations that are physically and mentally "overly demanding" are able to transform the way in which army officer cadets mobilize, maintain, and preserve the resources and capacities needed to fulfill their mission. In Chapter "How Do Simulated High-Intensity Situations Train Leaders to Maintain Their Ability to Act in Unfamiliar, Unforeseen or Uncertain Environments?", they thus point out the need for disruptive and long-lasting simulations so that the trainees develop "conservatory" arrangements allowing them to "hold on" in the face of critical adversity.

Critical situations are not always at the heart of professional activity. Elodie Ciccone, Lucie Cuvelier, Anne Bationo-Tillon, and Françoise Decortis were interested in simulation preparation for healthcare professionals who need to communicate with the families of patients, particularly when bad news is announced. In Chapter "On Care and the Sensitive Experience of Caregiver Activity in Simulation Situations: A Possible Model for Encounters Between Health Practitioners and Their Patients to Enhance Communication Training", they examine the role of the sensitive dimensions of experience in the simulation training process. In an original and fertile approach, these authors trace the development of highly specific caring skills that are often reduced in the scientific literature to "relational" or "nontechnical" dimensions.

4.3 Promising Avenues for Simulation Training Design and Research

The third and last section is a prospective discussion and extension to the preceding chapters. Scholars having broad international expertise in simulation and vocational learning have been invited to react to the preceding chapters, present complementary views, and/or establish the connections between the evidence provided in each chapter and its implications for simulation training design.

In the first chapter, entitled "New Questions for Interventions and Research in Simulation Training Based on Actors' Activity", Janine Rogalski considers the book from two perspectives: French-language ergonomics and professional didactics. She first presents her reflections on the studies – particularly French-language – which seem to her to have a structuring role in the field of simulation training for professionals. She then focuses particularly on the examples in the health field to present several promising avenues for future research to both expand our current understanding and enhance effective simulation design.

In the second chapter, entitled "Simulation in Healthcare, a Resource in Times of Crisis. A Look Back and a Look Forward", Eliana Escudero suggests taking a step back and reflecting both retrospectively and prospectively on the challenges and progress related to the use of simulation for healthcare training. She develops her expert point of view on simulation as a means of improving healthcare performance and patient safety by including an analysis concerning a crisis unprecedented in modern history: the Covid-19 pandemic.

References

Bainbridge, L., & Ruiz Quintanilla, S. A. (Eds.). (1989). *Developing skills with information technology*. John Wiley and Sons Ltd.

Baker, S., & Marshall, E. (1989). Simulators for training and the evaluation of operator performance. In L. Bainbridge & S. A. Ruiz Quintanilla (Eds.), *Developing skills with information technology* (pp. 293–312). John Wiley and Sons Ltd.

Béguin, P., & Pastré, P. (2002). Working, learning and designing through simulation. In S. Bagnara, S. Pozzi, A. Rizzo, & P. Wright (Eds.), *Proceedings of the 11th European Conference on Cognitive Ergonomics (ECCE'11): «Cognition, culture and design»* (pp. 5–13). CNR, Istituto di Scienze e technologie della cognizione.

Bobillier Chaumon, M.-E., Rouat, S., Laneyrie, E., & Cuvillier, B. (2018). De l'activité DE simulation à l'activité EN simulation: simuler pour stimuler. *Activités*, 15–11.

Boshuizen, H. P. A., Schmidt, H. G., Custers, J. F. M., & Van de Wiel, M. W. (1995). Knowledge development and restructuring in the domaine of medicine: The role of theory and practice. *Learn Instr, 24*(4), 269–289.

Brehmer, B., & Dörner, D. (1993). Experiment with computer simulated micro worlds: Escaping both the narrow starts of the laboratory and the deep blue see of the field study. *Comput Hum Behav, 9*, 171–184.

Chernikova, O., Heitzmann, N., Stadler, M., Holzberger, D., Seidel, T., & Fischer, F. (2020). Simulation-based learning in higher education: A meta-analysis. *Rev Educ Res, 90*(4), 499–541. https://doi.org/10.3102/0034654320933544

Danielllou, F. (2005). The French-speaking ergonomists' approach to work activity: Cross-influences of field intervention and conceptual models. *Theor Issues Ergon Sci, 6*(5), 409–427. https://doi.org/10.1080/14639220500078252

Daniellou, F., & Rabardel, P. (2005). Activity-oriented approaches to ergonomics: Some traditions and communities. *Theor Issues Ergon Sci, 6*(5), 353–357. https://doi.org/10.1080/14639220500078351

Drews, F. A., & Bakdash, J. Z. (2013). Simulation training in health care. *Reviews of Human Factors and Ergonomics, 8*, 191–234.

Durand, M., & Poizat, G. (2015). *An activity-centered approach to work analysis and the Design of Vocational*. Springer.

Filliettaz, L., & Billett, S. (Eds.). (2015). *Francophone perspectives of learning through work: Conceptions, traditions and practices* (pp. 221–240). Springer.

Filliettaz, L., Billett, S., Bourgeois, E., Durand, M., & Poizat, G. (2015). Conceptualising and connecting francophone perspectives on learning through and for work. In L. Filliettaz & S. Billett (Eds.), *Francophone perspectives of learning through work: Conceptions, traditions and practices* (pp. 19–48). Springer.

Hamstra, S., Brydges, R., Hatala, R., Zendejas, B., & Cook, D. (2014). Reconsidering fidelity in simulation-based training. *Acad Med, 89*(3), 387–392. https://doi.org/10.1097/ACM.0000000000000130

Hoc, J.-M. (2001). Toward ecological validity of research in cognitive ergonomics. *Theor Issues Ergon Sci, 2*, 278–288.

Hoc, J.-M., Cacciabue, P. C., & Hollnagel, E. (Eds.). (1995). *Expertise and technology: Cognition & humancomputer cooperation*. Lawrence Erlbaum Associates.
Hill., R-R. & Tolk., A. (2017). A history of military computer simulation. In A. Tolk, J. Fowler, G. Shao, & E. Yücesan (Eds.), *Advances in Modeling and simulation, simulation foundations, methods and applications* (pp. 277–296). Springer International Publishing AG.
Hollnagel, E. (2012). *Resilience engineering and crisis management*. https://gnssn.iaea.org/NSNI/SC/TMMtU/Presentations/Mr%20Hollnagel%27s%20Presentation%202.pdf
Leplat, J. (1989). Simulation and simulators in training: Some comments. In L. Bainbridge & S. A. Ruiz Quintanilla (Eds.), *Developing skills with information technology* (pp. 277–292). John Wiley and Sons Ltd.
Norros, L. (1989). Simulation in industrial work and training. In L. Bainbridge & S. A. Ruiz Quintanilla (Eds.), *Developing skills with information technology* (pp. 315–327). John Wiley and Sons Ltd.
Norros, L. (2005). The concept of habit in the analysis of situated actions. *Theor Issues Ergon Sci, 6*(5), 385–407. https://doi.org/10.1080/14639220500076520
Norros, L. (2014). Developing human factors/ergonomics as a design discipline. *Appl Ergon, 45*, 61–71.
Ouellet, S., & Vézina, N. (2015). Activity analysis and workplace training: An ergonomic perspective. In L. Filliettaz & S. Billett (Eds.), *Francophone perspectives of learning through work: Conceptions, traditions and practices* (pp. 241–256). Springer.
Patrick, J. (1992). *Training, Research & practice*. Academic press.
Rogalski, J. (1995). From real situations to training situations: Conserving the functionalities. In J.-M. Hoc, P. C. Cacciabue, & E. Hollnagel (Eds.), *Expertise and technology: Cognition & human-computer cooperation* (pp. 125–139). Laurence Erlbaum Associate.
Pastré, P. (2005). La conception de situations didactiques à la lumière de la théorie de la conceptualisation dans l'action. In D. P. Rabardel & P. Pastré (Eds.), *Modèles du sujet pour la conception. Dialectiques activité développement* (pp. 73–107). Octarès.
Persson, J. (2017). A review of the design and development processes of simulation for training in healthcare. A technology-centered versus human-centered perspective. *Appl Ergon, 58*, 314–326.
Rogalski, J., Plat, M., & Antolin-Glenn, P. (2002). Training for collective competence in rare and unpredictable situations. In N. Boreham, R. Samurçay, & M. Fischer (Eds.), *Work process knowledge* (pp. 134–147). Routledge.
Rosen, K. (2013). The history of simulation. In A. I. Levine, S. DeMaria, A. D. Schwartz, & A. J. Sim (Eds.), *The comprehensive textbook of healthcare simulation* (pp. 5–49). Springer. https://doi.org/10.1007/978-1-4614-5993-4_2
Salas, E., & Cannon-Bowers, J. A. (2001). The science of training: A decade of Progress. *Annu Rev Psychol, 52*, 471–499.
Salas, E., Tannenbaum, S. I., Kraiger, K., & Smith-Jentsch, K. A. (2012). The science of training and development in organizations: What matters in practice. *Psychol Sci Public Interest, 13*(2), 74–101.
Schmidt, H. G., Boshuizen, H. P. A., & Hobus, P. P. M. (1988). Transitorily stages in the development of médical expertise: The «intermediate effect» in clinical case representation studies. In *Proceedings of the cognitive science society meeting*. Lawrence Erlbaum.
Teiger, C., & Lacomblez, M. (Eds.). (2013). *(Se) Former pour transformer le travail: Dynamiques de construction d'une analyse critique du travail*. Presses Universitaires de Laval & European Trade Union Institute.
Tourmen, C., Holgado, O., Métral, J., et al. (2017). The Piagetian Schème: A framework to study professional learning through conceptualization. *Vocat Learn, 10*(3), 343–364. https://doi.org/10.1007/s12186-017-9174-y
Ughetto, P., Haradji, Y., & Van Belleghem, L. (2018). Introduction au dossier "mettre en scène l'activité: les nouvelles figures de la simulation". *Activités, 15*, 1.
Vadcard, L. (2022). *Gestes techniques et formation. Un point de vue didactique*. PUG.

Van Daele, A. (1997). Contribution de la simulation à l'étude de l'activité de l'opérateur en situation dynamique. In P. Beguin & A. Weill-Fassina (Eds.), *La simulation en ergonomie: connaître, agir et interagir* (pp. 29–38). Octarès.

Van de Wiel, M. W. J., Boshuizen, H. P. A., & Schmidt, H. G. (2000). Knowledge restructuring in expertise development: Evidence from pathophysiological representations of clinical cases by students and physicians. *Eur J Cogn Psychol, 12*(3), 323–355.

Vergnaud, G. (2009). The theory of conceptual fields. *Hum Dev, 52*, 83–94. https://doi.org/10.1159/000202727

Vidal-Gomel, C., Boccara, V., Delgoulet, C., & Cau-Bareille, D. (2019). How holistic approaches of activity analysis in ergonomics renew training design? In D. S. Bagnara, R. Tartaglia, S. Albolino, T. Alexander, & Y. Fujita (Eds.), *Proceedings of the 20th congress of the International Ergonomics Association (IEA 2018). Volume IV: Organizational Design and Management (ODAM), Professional Affairs* (pp. 233–241). Springer. https://doi.org/10.1007/978-3-319-96080-727

Vygotski, L. (1928–1931/2014). Histoire du développement des fonctions psychiques supérieures. La Dispute.

Vygotsky, L. S. (1934/1978). *Mind in society: The development of higher psychological processes*. Harvard University Press.

Yardley, S., Teunissen, P.-W., & Dornan, T. (2012). Experiential learning: AMEE guide n° 63. *Med Teacher, 34*, 102–115.

Part I
Experience and Activity-Based Conceptualizations of Simulation Design and Outcomes

This part examines activity as unfolding and experience as meaningful lived episodes during contrasted simulation training situations. It contributes to the understanding of simulation design (objectives, format, tasks, animation, perturbation, facilitation…) and outcomes (from very specific technical gestures to wide and multidimensional dispositions).

Chapters 2, 3 and 4 provide insights from empirical and conceptual research about simulation training outcomes and design principles in the domains of healthcare and interprofessional management of civil safety.

Chapters 5, 6 and 7 provide design-based research accounts regarding three different simulation programs: technical gesture in nursing, patient management in geriatrics, and "mass casualty event" management in military rescue.

Simulation-Based Learning for Technical Gestures in Health Care: What Kind of Experience Is Required?

Lucile Vadcard

Abstract Simulation is a widespread, interesting and promising learning approach in healthcare. It can allow students to acquire minimal ease before being confronted to patients. The development of simulation largely focuses on the quest of realism, i.e. fidelity with real situations. In this chapter, we question the relevance of such an approach in the case of learning technical gestures in healthcare. We first define the notion of technical gesture in a way that is suitable for reflection on learning. We highlight its structuring dimension, which completes its motor and functional ones. We then expose a design process of learning environments that take into account this deep interaction between movements and knowledge. This approach is more centred on interaction between the students and the simulator than on the realism of this latter. Based on vocational didactics approach, it necessitates a deep analysis of learning objective and introduces the notion of conflict and contradiction as fruitful leverages for learning. We exemplify this design process with environments dedicated to the learning of blind gestures in orthopaedics and maieutics.

Keywords Simulation · Healthcare · Gesture · Didactics · Constructivism · Realism

Technical gestures are key components of numerous professional occupations. Concerning health care, they are obviously a crucial part of activity: One expects that they are correctly performed, with respect for patients and in compliance with the "rules of art." Therefore, training technical gestures is clearly an extremely important topic. Important, but not so simple, as early practical training on patient is both recognized as essential and unacceptable. Simulation is considered as the current and future solution to this paradox. It is, obviously, highly promising. However, in order to go beyond the institutional and commercial discourses, which

L. Vadcard (✉)
Université Grenoble Alpes, Grenoble, France
e-mail: lucile.vadcard@univ-grenoble-alpes.fr

S. Flandin et al. (eds.), *Simulation Training through the Lens of Experience and Activity Analysis*, Professional and Practice-based Learning 30,
https://doi.org/10.1007/978-3-030-89567-9_2

extol the virtues of this learning modality, we intend to examine it more precisely. To what extent do such environments allow students to experience and draw from this experience the elements focused by the training and relevant for the occupation?

We thus examine in this chapter if and how simulation-based environments can participate in relevant experiences for learning technical gestures in health care. Simulation-based training in health care is now widely spread. It is intended to provide various and efficient learning experiences. From Resusci Anne in the 1960s to recent virtual reality systems, a long way has been traveled. For now about 20 years, evolutions of technologies (concerning digital but also material, electronic, etc.) have accelerated the production of simulators. Currently, a lot of different devices have been gathered behind the terms "simulation" and "simulator" (Gallagher & O'Sullivan, 2012; Persson, 2017). Each kind of device is dedicated to some aspect of training: movements, procedures, team collaboration, emergency decisions, etc. This diversity is, however, driven by one common feature, named realism, fidelity, or authenticity. Some authors and commercial distributors claim that the more realistic a simulator is, the more efficient for learning it will be. Others try to nuance this approach by using variations of realism in terms of fidelities (Liu et al., 2009). The approach is interesting but finally remains based on the same hypothesis: The better the resemblance with reality is, the better the learning will be. In this text, we propose to discuss and go beyond these approaches. From a theoretical point of view, we base on a constructivist approach, which highlights the value of conflicting experiences for learning (Brousseau, 1997). From a methodological point of view, we elaborate on the notion of epistemological domain of validity, initially developed by Balacheff and Sutherland (1994). We show that this notion complements the approaches based on realism and fidelities by providing systematic analysis tools of learning potential and by considering the interaction of learner with the device, instead of the device only. Thus, we will see that, as features that are more than often put forward are the ones that make simulation looks like reality (skin elasticity, thorax movements, etc.) and provide "authentic experiences," they are perhaps not always the more relevant to provide efficient learning.

Regarding this topic, the question of the learning goal is obviously a central one: What is relevant for one learning goal should be useless or even disabling for another one. Moreover, one learning goal can contain several dimensions, each being acquired more efficiently by different features of simulation. In this chapter, we concentrate on learning technical gestures in health care.

1 Simulation in Health Care

1.1 Issue and Current State

Acquisition of technical gestures in professional fields has always been a crucial aspect of apprenticeship. Each professional sector manages this issue according to its constraints and inheritance. In craft industry, transmission in situ allows the progressive acquisition of gestures by apprentices (Sennett, 2008). In industry, school workshops within factories enable apprentices to develop skills without damaging production. In vocational schools, workshops are equipped with material quite similar to that of companies, in order that students acquire the basics of professional gestures. Internships complete training by providing immersion in professional environments. Students are invited to carry out gestures in autonomy, gradually and as far as possible. Articulation of these different pedagogical modalities raises specific problems and interesting questions: definitions and links between theory and practice and between particular cases and general case, characterization of hybrid spaces, and role of tutors (Billett, 2010; Veillard, 2015).

Learning technical gestures in health care is also a key issue, whatever the specialties. As in other professions, training methods are varied: internships, practical work on mannequins and cadavers, etc. The access to the body has always been a crucial question regarding training. Historically, there have been public demonstrations of care and dissections, more or less official training on cadavers, training on living or dead animals, and tinkered models to train or demonstrate, like dummies sewn by the midwife Madame du Coudray in the eighteenth century (Sakka, 1997; Dachez, 2008; Sage Pranchère, 2017). Observations during practical sessions completed this training. In France, at the beginning of the nineteenth century, the creation of the medical internship has provided students a greater access to patient care during their studies. It has increased opportunities to train technical gestures in situ. Currently, in all specialties and at all levels these periods play the role of acculturation and training ground. However, the delicate nature of the acquisition of gestures on the patient remains. Students then also practice on animals, on cadavers, on mock-ups, and increasingly on simulators, which technical features evolve along with their promises of training success.

Indeed, since the 1960s and the first dummy Rescusi Ann, technical evolutions (properties of plastics, digital coupling, etc.) have led to major achievements concerning industrial production of training devices. These technical evolutions meet a professional environment, which is more and more reluctant to entrust patients to non-expert hands and brains. As a result, there is currently a widespread use of simulation for training in health care, and a large hope on its efficacy. Hospitals, health faculties, and schools equip themselves to avoid problems when students will act for "the first time on patient." Numerous devices exist, from the more basic ones to the more sophisticated ones. Some are very expansive, some other are less. In literature and manuals, one can find almost the same typologies (Gallagher & O'Sullivan, 2012; Granry & Moll, 2012). Authors distinguish biologic, synthetic, numeric, and hybrid devices. Biologic devices are based on humans or animals, are whole or part, and are dead or alive. Principally, these can be actors, animal or human bench-top models, cadavers, and live animals. Synthetic devices can be bench-top models, dedicated to particular gesture (suture, knee arthroscopy, breast palpation, needle insertion, etc.) or full-scale mannequins that can be used alone (e.g., for first-aid procedures) or coupled with software (and thus become high-fidelity human patient simulators, which belong to the hybrid category). Numeric devices are scarcely simple software and are most often coupled with haptic devices and/or synthetic models. They can be rather basic or very sophisticated, like high-fidelity virtual reality simulations (in dental implantology, see Cormier et al., 2011; see also 3D system corporation for other examples). In addition to numeric coupling, hybrid devices include human and synthetic coupling: A professional uses a synthetic model to act a scene (e.g., delivery). All these devices are now widely used in schools and hospitals.

These developments are in line with current training recommendations: never the first time on the patient. Indeed, it seems obvious that it is no longer acceptable in our societies for a student to practice on a patient. However, there is and there always will be a first time on the patient. Nowadays, without questioning the pedagogical interest of the previous devices, this "first time" remains problematic: Sometimes, it's the students who encounter difficulties and apprehension to engage in gesture; sometimes it's their instructors who still consider them too far from self-sufficiency to confide gestures. To some extent this is not surprising: to grasp gesture at the same time as its context and its responsibility is a major and unavoidable difficulty. A reasonable objective is therefore not to seek to eliminate it, but to make it manageable and not dangerous for patients.

Current answer to this objective is to further increase technological developments, hoping to replicate working conditions as closely as possible. Actually, regardless of the nature of the training devices, it can be seen that important efforts are done to improve their realism. In this chapter, we discuss this approach. Is the race for realism the right solution to improve students' confidence in their ability to perform a gesture for the first time, while ensuring sanitary efficiency? Is realism sufficient to characterize learning experiences that simulation devices can support? Isn't it time for a breakthrough in learning healthcare technical gesture?

1.2 From Realism to Epistemological Domain of Validity[1]

The realism or authenticity of simulation devices is widely emphasized in commercial speeches, and also in numerous research papers. It is naturally considered to be a determining factor in the effectiveness of training. For many authors, there is no doubt that simulation will soon become more and more realistic thanks to technological advances—particularly those of virtual reality. According to them, the massive diffusion of such devices will be accompanied by complete learning success, and obstacles to this massive distribution can only be economic. In fact, the link between realism and learning effectiveness is rarely studied. When it is, the correlation is not always observed (Nyssen et al., 2002; Scerbo et al., 2006; Aggarwal et al., 2010). There are thus a few authors who question this strong trend. For Gallagher and O'Sullivan (2012), "face validity" is a trap for physicians, who

[1] Some ideas exposed here are extracted from a book to be published in French, in which they are more developed.

"mistakenly believe that a simulator that looks like real patient anatomy is a good simulator" (p. 34).

Limits of the realism approach led different authors to propose a more fine-grained analysis of simulation for learning. Since the late 1980s, these authors have been working on an operational differentiation of realism (among the first were Alessi, 1988; Grau et al., 1998). They have introduced the notion of fidelity, which they have declined in several dimensions. They often distinguish physical, functional, and psychological fidelities. Physical fidelity relates to the visual resemblance; functional fidelity indicates the extent to which the simulator acts and reacts likes reality. An environment has a high psychological fidelity if "it generates psychological characteristics of real operations in terms of complexity, perceptual abilities, decision making or stress" (Grau et al., 1998, p. 370). To better distinguish the emotional side from the cognitive one, we proposed to define the epistemic fidelity, which relates to knowledge. A learning environment has epistemic fidelity if knowledge requires to interact with it is consistent with knowledge requires in a work situation.

Other authors have proposed additional reflections. In medicine, Scerbo and Dawson (2007) propose to distinguish physical, semantic, and phenomenal fidelities. According to the Haute Autorité de Santé in France, one may distinguish psychological, equipment, environment, and temporal fidelities (HAS, 2012, p. 12). Finally, for Liu et al. (2009) "fidelity is an umbrella term" (p. 62). Authors and sellers now have at their disposal a panel of dimensions that are supposed to cover what was previously too generally described as "realism." Indeed, fidelities' approach is still the same techno-centered approach as realism: It is a matter of reproducing part of the work environment and to put apprentices in front of it. Moreover, fidelities are also not very useful concepts for the design of environments. They seem to be more effective for sales, as manufacturers minimize deviations to perfect realism by highlighting the most successful dimensions of their products. Some authors then propose to stop using the term fidelity, as it continues to focus attention on resemblance rather than relevance in terms of learning and transfer (Hamstra et al., 2014). They call for more human-centered approaches, which focus on student–device interaction (Horcik et al., 2014; Vadcard, 2017). Indeed, from a training perspective, we argue that it can be more interesting to consider first the subject who is learning; and the technical objects with which he or she is led to interact, solely with regard to the objectives of the training and the nature of the subject him(her)self.

The scientific domain of vocational didactics (Pastré, 2005; Mayen, 2015) has made important steps forward in the reflection on vocational training based on simulation. For Pastré, training should not be defined only according to the work situation but according to interactions between the learner and the situation. This approach relies on theoretical developments about conceptualization (Vergnaud, 1996; Tourmen et al., 2017). It introduces the idea that training situations are crucially different from work situations: "we invert the relationship of subordination between productive and constructive activity" (Pastré, 2006, pp. 110–111). According to him, it is by finding out what is problematic at work that one could be able to develop relevant training situations. These problematic situations can be staged in technical devices, which are called "problem-solving simulators."

This is an interesting approach which some authors have followed to design learning environments for professional gestures in health care (Luengo et al., 2009): dental implantology (Cormier et al., 2011), mini-invasive orthopedic surgery (Chieu et al., 2010), prostate biopsies (Fiard et al., 2014), maieutics (Zara et al., 2014), and infant's respiratory physiotherapy (Maréchal et al., 2012), for example. In these studies, authors identified on which key component gesture relies and designed a learning environment that focuses on it. More to the point, they also identified what is the problem of learners concerning understanding and control of gesture. Doing so, they are more centered on interaction between the students and the simulator than on the realism of this latter. We'll give some details further on orthopedics and maieutics learning environments.

2 Learning Technical Gestures

Technical gestures in health care are a crucial aspect of profession and training. Some are really specialized and linked to professional innovations, and some other are more elementary ones but remain essential. Acquiring gestures is sometimes considered as taken for granted and sometimes considered as being a complex objective. In any case, we argue that first of all, the very notion of gesture is perhaps not clear enough to make scientific advances in the field of its learning design. We then argue that acquisition of gesture is more than often focused on its physical aspect. Doing so, the strong relationship it has with conceptualization is too much neglected.

2.1 What Is a Technical Gesture?

Actually, gesture is often affected by a lack of clear definition. A preliminary classification is that some gestures are dedicated to communication (e.g., communication between pilot and tarmac during take-off preparation, communication between underwater divers—and to some extent artistic body gestures), some others are dedicated to production that can be either intrinsic (like sports gestures) or extrinsic. Leplat (2013) calls them sign gestures (for communication) and action gestures (for production). In this text, we focus on professional extrinsic production gestures. A second clarification relates to its extent. Sometimes, gesture is considered as a whole action (e.g., delivery gesture); sometimes, it is considered as a single physical movement (e.g., gripping gesture). As a matter of fact, gesture and action share a same objective, and gesture involves movements. But gesture is neither action nor movement. Although physical movement is the manifest dimension of gesture, this is not the only one and perhaps not the more important one, especially regarding learning. Let's thus make a point on the complex nature of gesture.

Gesture consists of movements and body posture: This is its motor dimension, which is the more evident one. It is also the more studied aspect of gesture, especially in the field of sports and biomechanics. But gesture is also linked to the environment and the goal of action: This is its functional dimension. Technical gestures can be oriented toward transforming material (e.g., surgery suture) or toward picking information (e.g., medical palpation). This aspect is mainly studied by anthropologists (Goodwin, 2003; Biryukova & Bril, 2008). Then, gesture is also the answer that one person gives to an encountered situation. For that, gesture is based on the subject's knowledge and, in turn, enables him/her to acquire some. We propose to call this process the structuring dimension of gesture. This third dimension is crucial for learning. Yet, it is less evident and much less studied. It concerns the constructive effects of gesture for the subject: Gesture relies on subject's knowledge and at the same time makes him/her develop and structure knowledge (Piaget, 1974). The "intelligence of gesture" (de Montmollin, 1984; Sennett, 2008) is then linked to the capacities of the subject to adapt gesture to the particularities of the environment and circumstances. Thus, performing a gesture is closely linked to cognitive processes like information taking, decision making, anticipation, and regulation (Berthoz, 1997; Bril, 2015).

This strong relationship between gesture and knowledge is particularly well illustrated in the case of "blind gestures" in health care. These are gestures that are realized with no direct sight of the treatment area. Some of these gestures have been developed a long time ago (in physiotherapy and midwifery, for example). Some others emerge from more recent care techniques (mini-invasive surgery, ultrasound biopsies). The visible part of these gestures seems relatively simple: hammer a pin and operate a screwdriver, handle a probe and pull a trigger, and press a thorax with hands, for example. It therefore seems obvious that the difficulty of these gestures largely lies in the articulation with knowledge. It is, in particular, the characteristics of the environments in which gestures are carried out, the capacity of subjects to dynamically appreciate the effects of their own action on these environments. For this, subjects coordinate a collection of relevant information that they gradually build. Thus, behind an apparent motor simplicity, these gestures embed complex processes.

Moreover, this emphasis on interaction implies that learning gesture is a very personal matter. It develops by each subject according to the situations encountered. One major issue of vocational education is thus to decide what situations for what subjects will be able to allow them to develop efficient knowledge and consequently, efficient gestures.

2.2 How Do We Learn Gesture?

On this basis, we can now examine what kind of learning experiences is relevant for gesture acquisition. Existing literature from various fields identifies different key factors of learning professional gesture.

Authors working on handicrafts, often anthropologists or sociologists, identify imitation as the fundamental process of acquisition. Following Mauss (Mauss, 1950; Schlanger, 2019), they describe "top-notch imitation." Natural talent is also pointed as being influent. These elements are key aspects of traditional transmission of knowledge. They partly operate during internships. Unfortunately, they have little analytical value for the design of training environments. For their part, ergonomists often work in production companies. They focused on decomposition of gesture. According to them, it is by describing steps of gesture and criteria for success that acquisition occurs. Their objective is that the operators carry out efficient gestures while preserving their health. Finally for some other researchers working in the field of physiology and biomechanics, the key process of gesture acquisition is rehearsal. Most often, these authors deal about non-productive gestures like sports or rehabilitation care.

Each of these approaches focuses mainly on some of the dimensions we have identified above. Repetition focuses on the motor one, imitation on the functional one, and decomposition on both. They also touch a little on the structuring dimension but mainly indirectly. Consequently, as motor and functional dimensions of technical gestures are well represented in actual simulators, the last one seems neglected. Is it possible to do otherwise and to restore a balance between the three characters of gestures? Could knowledge be considered as primary in the design of training for gesture? How to implement such an approach?

We advocate the idea that a didactical approach of learning (Brousseau, 1997; Mayen, 2015; Tourmen et al., 2017), largely based on constructivist theories, can be applied to acquisition of gestures. Piaget's work gives prominence to knowledge and conceptualization in motor skill acquisition processes. According to him, the progressive understanding of the objects and the environment properties fully participate in the physical efficiency (see Piaget, 1974). It is then by exploring the properties of the environment through action that the subject will gradually progress in the conceptualization of its constraints and opportunities. Conceptualization progressively enables these properties to be taken into account before action. This is the mechanism of programming the action and anticipating its effects. During this development process, contradiction plays a crucial role.

The scientific domain of didactics takes this as a basis and makes some theoretical and methodological developments concerning the design of learning environments. A particularly important element for our purpose is the "milieu," which designates the antagonist learning environment. It is what causes resistance to the subject during the learning process (Brousseau, 1997, p. 57). It relies on the fundamental basic idea that learning occurs when subjects are confronted with some opposition: To face limitations of our current knowledge is the better way to improve it. This implies to define training situations that can adequately "resist" to students, in order to make them understand and acquire properties of their environment and their actions. Learning experiences must be conflicting; i.e., they should give evidence to learners of the existence of a discrepancy between expectation and observation. They must also be constructive; i.e., they should let learners build an understanding of this discrepancy—and fill the gap.

So what kind of experience is likely to generate such reactions for the learning of gesture?

2.3 *What Simulators to Learn Gesture?*

Bench-top models—mock-ups—are the most often used training devices for technical gestures. Baby dolls, arms, legs, and so on are largely employed to train newborn care, first-aid measures, venous accesses, injections, etc. According to the realism approach discussed above, one can argue that these are realistic, even if partial (and even though no one would be fooled). But this approach is not really helpful regarding the analysis of learning. As we developed above, the fidelities' approach is a little more specific. Let's take the example of a pediatric forearm for venous access. It can be agreed that it has a correct level regarding physical fidelity and a low level regarding psychological fidelity: It doesn't cause students to feel emotion like the fear of inserting the needle in a child's arm. Concerning functional fidelity (does the mock-up operate like a real arm?), the analysis gets harder: In one way, it works, but not in the other. As students can insert needle, action is possible. But reaction is missing: Is the gesture adequate, failed, or dangerous? Is the needle well positioned or does it puncture the vein? In fact, one main problem is that these materials reproduce some static states and are not able to reproduce processes. Concerning epistemic fidelity, the analysis is quite similar: As students have to mobilize some knowledge to act, they cannot benefit from feedback to appreciate the validity or invalidity of their knowledge according to the consequences of their action. We conclude that these materials are probably appropriated to help advanced students to acquire some motor automatisms by drill. However, according to the definition of gesture we developed above, these are not fully adequate for learning. More realistic feedback is probably possible, and some researchers are working hard on it (see Delpech et al., 2017, who impulse blood circulation in cadavers). Complex systems are thus developed, which are often very high-cost devices. Although they can be efficient for some dimensions of gestures, they do not avoid inaptness of the realistic techno-centric approach that will appear soon or later.

In our view, it is possible and useful to adopt a different approach, with lower cost technical developments and positive results on learning. This implies to change our point of view on simulation: to move from a mainly material approach to a more human-centered approach. This leads us to consider interactions between the student and the learning environment. For each learning environment project, in-depth analysis of learning objectives and learners is necessary to identify relevant knowledge on which to design the interaction—that should offer proper feedback to learners. A learning environment should bring learners to discover the properties (rules, constraints, etc.) they will face in real professional situations. To this end, realism is not necessarily the right choice. In our own work, we participated in the design and development of learning environments, which were very basic according to the likeness with physical reality but were efficient to make learners understand some crucial properties of the professional situation. Such an understanding consequently improves their professional gestures.

In a methodological perspective, we present here details about the tool we use for the design of such learning environments. Our objective is to go beyond discourses about resemblance, reality, or fidelities of simulators that focus mainly on the technical device, and neglect the subject–device interaction and the specificities of learning objective. To that end, we elaborate on—and in a sense we rehabilitate—the notion of epistemological domain of validity of learning environments. This tool was initially dedicated to software design and analysis in mathematics education (Balacheff & Sutherland, 1994). It puts the emphasis on validity processes and allows to rationalize learning activity. It "refers to the knowledge and relation to knowledge which is allowed by a software" (p. 137). It thus deals with the meaning that the interaction with a learning environment can provide, according to the learning objective. This is a valuable tool to analyze and design learning environments, even those that are not based on software. It is composed of four elements that we present here with our own adaptation:

- The set of problems the environment allows to be proposed, i.e., what is being asked to students
- The nature of the information gathering and material operations the environment makes available to the user, i.e., what is available to solve the problem
- The nature of the tools and objects provided by its formal structure, i.e., what kind of "depth" lies behind the visible interface (e.g., a simple plastic baby doll can be empty or be filled with electronic components)
- The kind of control the environment makes available to the user and the feedback provided, i.e., what are the dynamic processes allowed and produced by the formal structure

To conclude this chapter, we give details of two learning environments designed with this methodological tool.

2.4 *Designing Conflicting Experiences for Learning—Two Examples*

Our first example is a rather ancient software learning environment for mini-invasive orthopedics surgery. It has been developed in the early 2000 in the context of the VOEU, then TELEOS projects (Virtual Orthopaedics European University—IST-1999-13079 & Technology Enhanced Learning for Orthopaedic Surgery—see

Luengo et al., 2006). Our second example is an underdevelopment hybrid environment (mock-up coupled to software) for maieutics. It has been initiated in the context of the SAGA project (simulators for the learning of birth delivery gestures—see Zara et al., 2014). Both concern blind gestures. As defined above, these gestures deal with information gathering, coordinating, and extrapolating. Indeed, processes of validation are based on the correct appreciation of the current state and the efficiency of its dynamic time-based projection. This shows the importance of the last component of our methodological tool: Tools for control and feedback provided are crucial regarding this dimension. In both cases, the design focuses on making contradiction occurs between what students primarily consider as correct and what they observe consequently to their actions. Learning environments disrupt learners and offer a fertile ground to positive re-equilibration (Piaget, 1970). Such a design previously necessitates to identify possible discrepancies and—above all—the reasons why.

It is not the place to describe here the entire design process of such environments. Concisely, we led joint analysis of work and training, involving field studies with observation and inquiry methods. This is a classical process in the field of vocational didactics (see Mayen, 2015). Some elements of these analysis outcomes are detailed below.

In the case of blind gestures, a key aspect of work and learning is linked to the coordination of different indicators—signs—for the understanding of the situation and the planification of action. In mini-invasive orthopedic surgery, these can be external landmarks (bone reliefs), haptic sensations (bone resistance), and X-rays. In the case of examination in midwifery, these can be digital sensations, fetal heart rate and uterine contractions, diagrams, graphs, and codes. As we discussed above, collecting and coordinating relevant information is a really important objective concerning learning gestures, which should be supported by simulators. This objective can in turn influence positively the realization of gesture. Concerning orthopedic surgery, observations in operating theater show that although interns often correctly interpret X-rays, they often fail to properly correct their trajectory. For example, if the pin is too "high" on one X-ray they put it lower in the body. Due to complex links between body position and X-ray projections, the consequence is that the pin is even higher on the X-ray—thus worse positioned. The software we designed offers a relevant learning experience by providing evidence of this contradiction to interns, and by giving them time to explore these complex links. Evaluation of this software showed its benefit for interns: Fewer attempts were needed to put the pin in a right position (Tonetti et al., 2009). Concerning midwifery, digital examination of fetal presentation is a complex gesture to acquire. Digital sensations are difficult to apprehend and interpret. Facing this difficulty during internships, students tend to rely on experts or on ultrasound device. Yet, it is important that they assume responsibility of this gesture. This requires that they ensure their perceptions and decisions. The role of the ongoing process of the fetal descent is often neglected in this apprenticeship. In fact, as numerous positions of the fetal head are possible, the position at a time "t" is partly determined by the previous positions. As what we know influences what we feel, we design a learning environment that invites students to couple their haptic acquisitions with the analysis of the fetal descent process. We hypothesize that a better understanding and consideration of the previous fetal positions will help students to interpret digital sensations and even more help them guide their digital paths for diagnosis.

Concerning the very design process of learning environments, it is obviously dependent of authors' learning hypothesis. In the francophone field of vocational training, one can observe two major trends. Some authors, mainly ergonomist and occupational psychologists, base their work on an exposure approach of learning. They design learning environments that help learners, by providing decomposition of gestures, explanations on processes, etc. Some other authors, from educational sciences, are influenced by the approach of didactics, of semiotics and interactionist approaches. They base their learning environments on the notions of problem, obstacle, or disruption (Mellet-d'Huart, 2006; Poizat et al., 2016). As we discussed above, we belong to this category and fully endorse the francophone didactical approach of learning (Brousseau, 1997). We now give some details of the design process of the learning environments we participate to elaborate, by making our methodological tool operate.

The set of problems the environment allows to be proposed, i.e. *what is being asked to students.*

In both cases, assignment is clear and simple. In the case of orthopedics, students are asked to insert a pin in the sacral bone, through the iliac wing. In the case of maieutics, the system is dedicated to the identification of the fetal presentation by vaginal examination on a mock-up.

The nature of the information gathering and material operations the environment makes available to the user, i.e. *what is available to solve the problem.*

In orthopedics, the software provides a crude representation of part of a body, with landmarks (the same as those that are marked on patients' skin by surgeons at the beginning of the intervention). It provides possibility of taking X-rays (with the same orientations that are used during interventions). These X-rays are somehow realistic because they include user's pin position. They are also somehow not realistic as they are based on a commercial plastic bone. A first consequence is that bone structure is perfectly visible, which is not the case in reality. A second one is that bone structure is a theoretical structure (it represents an abstract general case of bone). The material operations available are to choose an entry point for the pin and to orientate it, and to push it through the body representation and to take X-rays. In a first version, all these operations were available through a simple mouse, and in a second version, we integrated an haptic device, while we integrated haptic recognition in our learning objectives.

In maieutics, students are first confronted to a mock-up, which consists of a fetal plastic head inserted in a plastic device that reveals just a part of it. They do a vaginal examination and express what they feel in the software, by manipulating graphic representations of fetal head positions. In a second step, a partograph is provided, which represents different steps of the fetal descent process. Students are invited to re-examine the fetal head and to confirm or adjust their choice.

The nature of the tools and objects provided by its formal structure, i.e. *what kind of "depth" lies behind the visible interface* (e.g. *a simple plastic baby doll can be empty or be filled with electronic components).*

In the orthopedic software, the interface crude representation of a portion of body is linked to a 3D modelization of the bone and nervous structures. This allows to calculate user's pin position in order to 1/display it on X-rays when user takes some and 2/to evaluate user's pin position in relation to body structures (proximity of nerves, extra- or intra-osseous trajectory).

In maieutics, we base the production of partographs on fetal descents that are generated by a numeric simulation developed in the SAGA project (Buttin et al., 2013). These fetal descents are non-deterministic and relevant according to the modeled features.

The kind of control the environment makes available to the user and the feedback provided, i.e. *what are the dynamic processes allowed and produced by the formal structure.*

At this step of the design description, it is interesting to distinguish two kinds of feedback and some associated learning hypothesis. Informative feedback is available during the activity. It provides information, which is entirely linked to the domain: X-ray, partograph, etc. Evaluative feedback is available at the end of the activity—after user's validation of choices. It provides indication relative to the learning objective. It can include assessment criteria that should be based on relevance according to the domain, and not only on the comparison with the expert best practice.

Concerning the orthopedic learning environment, controls of action are solely provided by X-rays that users can take when they feel it necessary. Feedback is of two kinds: During users' insertion, it is non-evaluative and consists of a dynamic calculus of pin's position on X-rays; at the end of users' action (when they validate their trial), evaluative feedback gives a message concerning intra- or extra-osseous trajectory and potential dangerousness. It also gives possibility to erase tissues to visualize pin's trajectory.

Concerning the maieutic learning environment, the two kinds of feedback are used. The first one is the partograph, which is an ongoing informative feedback, intended to provoke conceptualization among students and to make gesture evolve. The second kind of feedback is given after the validation of the second choice: visualization of the fetal head position and possibility to "play" the scene of the entire fetal descent. In a further version, we intend to instrument the fetal head (or the gloves) to allow visualization of digital paths of students' examination trials.

3 Conclusion

Constructivist approach of learning is based on the idea that conflict and contradiction are very fruitful leverages for learning. This is a rather well-known and developed approach in school contexts but less common in vocational training contexts.

We adopt this approach in the case of learning blind gestures in health care. This implies to put forward the structuring aspect of gesture, that is, knowledge on which gesture is based and that it allows to elaborate.

This requires to investigate properly what should cause problem to students, to be able to design learning environments that will provide them conflicting experiences. Generally speaking, simulation is dedicated to exploration and could benefit from realism. By contrast, we argued that simulators for learning are specific devices that should be designed to provoke planned contradiction by students. To this end, they have to reduce the complexity of the real world to focus on relevant aspects; sometimes, they even have to distort reality to reach their objectives.

The domain of epistemological validity initially defined by Balacheff and Sutherland is a relevant methodological tool to analyze and develop such learning environments. It allows to go beyond classical discourses on realism and fidelities of simulators and helps to characterize learning experiences that can be provided by such devices. We have shown its relevance in the case of technical gestures. Even if we are not specialist of other skills that are concerned by simulation, we suppose that the approach can be generalized in a beneficial and relevant way.

We have shown that each learning project necessitates a deep analysis of learning objective in order to design learning environments that are really focused on students' needs. Otherwise, environments are more than often solely dedicated to the reproduction of part of the work environment. These are really nice, but they miss the specificity of the learning objective and learning process. In consequence, the experiences they provide are not sufficiently meaningful regarding knowledge. Particularly, technical gestures rely on a deep interaction between movements and knowledge that is not taken into account in most simulators. We thus have proposed a new way of thinking the design of simulators for the learning of technical gestures in health care.

References

Aggarwal, R., Mytton, O. T., Derbrew, M., Hananel, D., Heydenburg, M., Issenberg, B., MacAulay, C., Mancini, M. E., Morimoto, T., Soper, N., Ziv, A., & Reznick, R. (2010). Training and simulation for patient safety. *Quality & Safety in Health Care, 19*(Suppl 2), i34–i43. https://doi.org/10.1136/qshc.2009.038562

Alessi, S. M. (1988). Fidelity in the design of instructional simulations. *Journal of Computer-Based Instruction, 15*(2), 40–47.

Balacheff N., & Sutherland R. (1994). Epistemological domain of validity of microworlds, the case of Logo and Cabri-géomètre. In R. Lewis & P. Mendelshon (Eds), *Proceedings of the IFIP TC3/WG3.3: Lessons from learning* (pp. 137–150). Amsterdam, North-Holland.

Berthoz, A. (1997). *Le sens du mouvement*. Odile Jacob.

Billett, S. (2010). *Learning through practice. Models, traditions, orientations and approaches*. Springer.

Biryukova, L., & Bril, B. (2008). Organization of goal directed action at a high-level of motor skill: The case of stone knapping in India. *Motor Control, 12*, 181–209.

Bril, B. (2015). Learning to use tools: A functional approach to action. In L. Filliettaz & S. Billett (Eds.), *Francophone perspectives of learning through work conceptions, traditions and practices* (pp. 95–118). Springer.

Brousseau G. (1997). *Theory of didactical situations* (N. Balacheff, M. Cooper, R. Sutherland, & V. Warfield, Edition and Transl.). Kluwer Academic Publishers.

Buttin, R., Zara, F., Shariat, B., Redarce, T., & Grangé, G. (2013). Biomechanical simulation of the fetal descent without imposed theoretical trajectory. *Computer Methods and Programs in Biomedicine, 111*(2), 389–401. https://doi.org/10.1016/j.cmpb.2013.04.005

Chieu, V. M., Luengo, V., Vadcard, L., & Tonetti, J. (2010). Student modeling in orthopedic surgery training: Exploiting symbiosis between temporal Bayesian networks and fine-grained didactic analysis. *International Journal of Artificial Intelligence in Education, 20*(3), 269–301.

Cormier, J., Pasco, D., Syllebranque, C., & Querrec, R. (2011). VirTeasy a haptic simulator for dental education. In *Proceedings of the 6th International Conference on Virtual Learning ICVL* (pp. 62–69).

Dachez, R. (2008). *Histoire de la médecine de l'Antiquité au XXe siècle*. Tallandier.

De Montmollin, M. (1984). *L'intelligence de la tâche. Eléments d'ergonomie cognitive*. Peter Lang.

Delpech, P. O., Danion, J., Oriota, D., Richer, J. P., Breque, C., & Faure, J. P. (2017). SimLife a new model of simulation using a pulsated revascularized and reventilated cadaver for surgical education. *Journal of Visceral Surgery, 154*(1), 15–20.

Fiard, G., Selmi, S. Y., Promayon, E., Vadcard, L., Descotes, J.-L., & Troccaz, J. (2014). Initial validation of a virtual-reality learning environment for prostate biopsies: Realism matters! *Journal of Endourology, 28*(4), 453–458.

Gallagher, A., & O'Sullivan, G. (2012). *Fundamentals of surgical simulation: Principles and practice*. Springer.

Goodwin, C. (2003). The body in action. In J. Coupland & R. Gwyn (Eds.), *Discourse, the body, and identity* (pp. 19–42). Palgrave Macmillan.

Granry, J.-C., & Moll, M.-C. (2012). *État de l'art (national et international) en matière de pratiques de simulation dans le domaine de la santé* [Rapport de mission pour la Haute Autorité de Santé]. HAS. http://www.has-sante.fr/portail/upload/docs/application/pdf/2012-01/simulation_en_sante_-_rapport.pdf.

Grau, J.-Y., Doireau, P., & Poisson, R. (1998). Conception et utilisation de la simulation pour la formation: pratiques actuelles dans le domaine militaire. *Le Travail Humain, 61*(4), 361–385.

Hamstra, S. J., Brydges, R., Hatala, R., Zendejas, B., & Cook, D. A. (2014). Reconsidering fidelity in simulation-based training. *Academic Medicine, 89*(3), 387–392.

HAS – Haute Autorité de Santé. (2012). *Guide de bonnes pratiques en matière de simulation en santé*.

Horcik, Z., Savoldelli, G., Poizat, G., & Durand, M. (2014). A phenomenological approach to novice nurse anesthetists' experience during simulation-based training sessions. *Simulation in Healthcare, 9*, 94–101.

Leplat, J. (2013). Les gestes dans l'activité en situation de travail. Aperçu de quelques problèmes d'analyse. *Pistes, 15*(1), 1–23.

Liu, D., Macchiarella, N. D., & Vincenzi, D. A. (2009). Simulation fidelity. In D. Vincenzi, J. Wise, M. Mouloua, & P. Hancock (Eds.), *Human factors in simulation and training* (pp. 61–73). CRC Press.

Luengo, V., Vadcard, L., Dubois, M., Mufti-Alchawafa, D. (2006). TELEOS: de l'analyse de l'activité professionnelle à la formalisation des connaissances pour un environnement d'apprentissage. In M. Harzallah, J. Charlet, N. Aussenac-Gilles. *17e journées francophones d'ingénierie des connaissances IC'2006*, Nantes, France. hal-00190719.

Luengo, V., Aboulafia, A., Blavier, A., Shorten, G., Vadcard, L., & Zottmann, J. (2009). Novel technology for learning in medicine. In N. Balacheff et al. (Eds.), *Technology-enhanced learning* (pp. 105–120). Springer.

Maréchal, L., Barthod, C., Goujon, L., & Büssing, T. (2012). Design and development of a mechatronic infant torso simulator for respiratory physiotherapy learning. *Mechatronics, 22*, 55–64.

Mauss, M. (1950/2013). Sociologie et anthropologie. Presses Universitaires de France.

Mayen, P. (2015). Vocational didactics: Work, learning, and conceptualization. In L. Filliettaz & S. Billett (Eds.), *Francophone perspectives of learning through work conceptions, traditions and practices* (pp. 201–219). Springer.

Mellet-d'Huart. (2006). A model of (en) action to approach embodiment: A cornerstone for the design of virtual environments for learning virtual reality. *Journal of Virtual Reality, 10*(3–4), 253–269.

Nyssen, A.-S., Larbuisson, R., Janssens, M., Pendeville, P., & Mayné, A. (2002). A comparison of the training value of two types of anesthesia simulators: Computer screen-based and mannequin-based simulators. *Anesthesia and Analgesia, 94*(6), 1560–1565.

Pastré, P. (2005). *Apprendre par la simulation : de l'analyse du travail aux apprentissages professionnels*. Octarès.

Pastré, P. (2006). Apprendre à faire. In E. Bourgeois & G. Chapelle (Eds.), *Apprendre et faire apprendre* (pp. 109–121). Presses Universitaires de France.

Persson, J. (2017). A review of the design and development processes of simulation for training in healthcare - A technology-centered versus a human-centered perspective. *Applied Ergonomics, 58*, 314–326.

Piaget, J. (1970). *Genetic epistemology*. Columbia University Press.

Piaget, J. (1974). *Réussir et Comprendre*. Presses Universitaires de France [*Success and understanding*; Transl. from the French by Arnold J. Pomerans. Routledge and Kegan Paul, 1978].

Poizat, G., Durand, M., & Theureau, J. (2016). Challenges of activity analysis oriented towards professional training. *Le Travail Humain, 79*, 233–258.

Sage Pranchère, N. (2017). *L'école des sages-femmes. Naissance d'un corps professionnel – 1786–1917*. Presses Universitaires François-Rabelais.

Sakka, M. (1997). *Histoire de l'anatomie humaine*. PUF, coll. Que sais-je ?.

Scerbo, M. W., & Dawson, S. (2007). High fidelity, high performance? *Simulation in Healthcare, 2*(4), 224–230.

Scerbo, M. W., Schmidt, E. A., & Bliss, J. P. (2006). Comparison of a virtual reality simulator and simulated limbs for phlebotomy training. *Journal of Infusion Nursing, 29*, 214–224.

Schlanger, N. (2019). Marcel Mauss (1872–1950): Socializing the body through techniques. *History of Humanities, 4*(2). https://doi.org/10.1086/704847

Sennett, R. (2008). *The craftsman*. Allen Lane.

Tonetti, J., Vadcard, L., Girard, P., Dubois, M., Merloz, P., & Troccaz, J. (2009). Assessment of a percutaneous iliosacral screw insertion simulator. *Orthopaedics & Traumatology: Surgery & Research, 95*(7), 471–477.

Tourmen, C., Holgado, O., Métral, J., Mayen, P., & Olry, P. (2017). The Piagetian *Schème*: A framework to study professional learning through conceptualization. *Vocations and Learning, 10*, 343–364.

Vadcard, L. (2017). Réflexions à propos de la conception d'environnements de formation par la simulation. Le cas de la formation médico-chirurgicale. *Raisons Educatives, 21*, 83–96.

Veillard, L. (2015). University-corporate partnerships for designing workplace curriculum: Alternance training course in tertiary education. In L. Filliettaz & S. Billett (Eds.), *Francophone perspectives of learning through work conceptions, traditions and practices* (pp. 257–278). Springer.

Vergnaud, G. (1996). Some of Piaget's fundamental ideas concerning didactics. *Prospects, XXVI*(1), 183–194.

Zara, F., Vadcard, L., & Redarce, T. (2014). Le développement de nouvelles technologies de formation aux gestes médico-chirurgicaux. *Réalités industrielles, 4*, 30–35.

Four Lines of Analysis for Civil Security Crisis Simulations: Insights for Training Design

Simon Flandin

Abstract Crisis simulation training is a common organizational tool to improve civil security preparedness. Although nowadays its overall benefits can't be denied, the conditions under which these simulations offer improvement opportunities remain often unclear. The aim of this chapter is to derive new lines of analysis from a study conducted in a crisis simulation training program based on two principles: (i) confrontation of the trainees to stressful, complex, dynamic, and verisimilar situations and (ii) testing modalities of action and organization that were not prescribed, or only partially. Ergonomics methods (direct observations, field notes, interviews, and self-confrontation interviews) were used to document and analyze protection, rescue, and care stakeholders, and decision makers' experience and actions during two crisis simulations in operational command posts. The results are developed along four lines: (i) enactment-reenactment, (ii) curriculum-discovery, (iii) perturbation-reassurance, and (iv) trust-mistrust. They allow us to precise the link between (i) typical simulation-based training experiences, (ii) actors' dispositions to crisis management, and (iii) simulation training design principles likely to provide promising learning affordances in authentic settings.

Keywords Simulation · Vocational training · Training design · Crisis management · Civil security

Simon Flandin would like to thank the Foundation for an Industrial Safety Culture (FONCSI - project n°AO-2017-02) and the Swiss National Science Foundation (SNSF - project n°PZ00P1_185903/1) for having funded parts of his research reported in this book.

S. Flandin (✉)
Faculty of Psychology and Educational Sciences, University of Geneva, Genève, Switzerland
e-mail: simon.flandin@unige.ch

S. Flandin et al. (eds.), *Simulation Training through the Lens of Experience and Activity Analysis*, Professional and Practice-based Learning 30,
https://doi.org/10.1007/978-3-030-89567-9_3

1 Simulate to Prepare Professionals for Crisis Management

In the field of crisis management, it is generally acknowledged that a crisis is a system disruption (technical, human, or organizational) before it is perceived as an object that can be "managed"—that is, contained, controlled, and little by little overcome by a set of appropriate actions. Reactivity in the face of disruptive events is therefore a crucial dimension of crisis management. We here examine all the factors—in this case, what professionals individually and collectively do—that contribute to bouncing back following a significant disruption. In this context, we take "bouncing back" to mean "recovering a capacity for interpretation and action and the means for projecting into the future" (Flandin et al., 2021).

Improving crisis management skills involves developing the capacity to respond quickly and effectively to disruptions that may well be extraordinary and even critical to life. This capacity to respond is inextricably linked to (i) a capacity to make sense of the situation, which research in the humanities and social sciences has already widely investigated, notably using the concepts of *sensemaking* (e.g., Weick, 1993), *situational awareness* (e.g., Stanton et al., 2001), and *decision-making* (e.g., Klein, 2015), and (ii) an ability to reorganize the available resources and means of action, even finding new ones, which has notably been investigated in studies drawing on the concepts of *adaptability* (e.g., Maynard et al., 2015) and *abduction* (e.g., Pettersen, 2013). Given these factors that make up effective crisis management, it seems clear that managing a crisis cannot be strictly speaking taught, even though in certain fields and with regard to certain well-defined problems, knowledge about effective interventions in crisis situations is available and can be presented in curricular form for training interventions. Samurçay and Rogalski (1998) analyzed the contribution of simulation to training in crisis situations, notably underlining that didactic approaches are limited when the relevance of conceptual variables and the variety of indices available in target situations are reduced. Citing Weick (1993), they referred to the "cosmological episode" in which "the universe no longer appears rational" as the archetype of a crisis before which any curricular approach is powerless (p. 345).

Yet, if crisis management cannot be taught, under what conditions can it nevertheless be made an object of learning and development? This would imply designing simulations not aimed at the transmission of knowledge presumably relevant to target situations, but at developing the capacity to interpret and (re)act in highly stressful, complex, and indeterminate situations (e.g., Bergström et al., 2011; Flandin et al., 2018; Fornette et al., 2015; Kouabenan et al., 2007). For the design of such simulations, it would be necessary to assume the relevance of training methods based on triggering significant experiences (striking, decisive) for civil security professionals. Such experiences bring about an evolution in their culture (understood as everything that they might mobilize at any moment to give meaning to, take decisions about, and act in a situation) and have an impact on their professional situations, especially in crisis management. Essentially, such designs "capitalize" on the opportunities offered by *practice-based learning* (e.g., Billett et al., 2014), *workplace learning* (Billett, 2020), and *experiential learning* (e.g., Fenwick, 2003). Simulations in training situations that are close to actual target situations provide these professionals with the opportunity to experience crisis situations in practice and thus to develop their capacity to react and new modalities of interpretation, action, and collective configuration.

Based on our understanding of the research in the field, the objective of programs to train and prepare for crisis situations should be twofold:

1. Enrich the "reservoirs of meaning" (Weick, 1993) by training professionals to apprehend the novel and even the unthinkable. Confronting professionals with new and ill-defined problems in simulation increases the chances that traits of familiarity will appear to them later in a real crisis situation and that they will connect what they are experiencing in the crisis (often at first in an unprecedented and indeterminate way) with their lived experiences in simulation. Traits of familiarity can be very strong: Actors experience the situation as familiar or even identical to others that are part of their culture. They are then able to very quickly remobilize modalities of interpretation and action that have already been positively tested (or "typified," according to Varela et al., 1991). Conversely, traits of familiarity can be very tenuous: Actors then experience feelings of vague resemblance, but this nevertheless prompts a set of provisional hypotheses that can be useful for producing meaning during the course of action. In both cases, enriching the "reservoirs of meaning" is crucial to guard against the "collapse of sensemaking" (Weick, 1993), in which confusion and even stupefaction can be paralyzing for professionals and nullify any possibility of crisis management.
2. Train individual and collective capacities to appropriately reorganize activity (resources, roles, and means of action) in order to produce the adjustments needed to rapidly return to a determined and controlled situation following disruptions of different types, including those that have never been seen and are massive. Notably, this can result in bifurcations in the modalities of operation and cooperation, the invention and adoption of new channels of communication, and the reconfiguration of roles among the professionals. Some of the research conducted in the field of "team training" from a dynamic systems approach (e.g., Gorman et al., 2010) has conceptualized and mobilized disruption as a means for designing simulations. They hypothesize that the reconfigurations of collective activities provoked in crisis simulations tend to materialize in real crisis situations under certain conditions (especially partial similarities or family resemblances between the training conditions and the actual work).

The conditions for meeting these objectives are unevenly contained in crisis management simulations, whether or not they are explicitly pursued by the designers and facilitators. In general, the organizational dimension of implementing these simulations poses a set of problems that limits the learning and development opportunities that have just been described, particularly in the field of civil security.

2 Limitations of Crisis Management Simulations for Civil Security Professionals

Civil security crisis simulations are often designed primarily as operational tests for organizational learning (the targeted transformations relate to the rules and procedures that govern professional work). They are less often designed—and sometimes not at all—for training aimed at transforming the culture and the repertoire of meanings and actions of these professionals (Borodzicz & Van Haperen, 2002). Even when the simulations integrate training objectives, their structure and organization do not seem to encourage learning and development for three main reasons.

The first reason is that when simulations are designed to test and continuously improve procedures and methods—as is often the case in civil security—the scenarios test the relevance of the organization of crisis response itself, its appropriability by the professionals, and/or the ability of these professionals to implement it. This aim is good in itself, but it cannot help professionals learn to intervene in the face of crises that escape the organization of a response. Thus, the aim tends more toward stabilizing organizational routines (Anderson & Adey, 2011), and generally, these routines can be very effective for dealing with difficult events that are not far removed from those already encountered. Yet, they can prove to be rigid and even paralyzing in completely new situations that are far from what has been prefigured and tested beforehand.

The second reason is that as the simulations often fulfill an evaluative, certifying, or policy function, the organizers and participants tend to be reluctant to acknowledge deviations, obvious errors, and failures in response organization. This has two consequences.

The first is that simulations that have been designed within the same framework, with the same scripting, often have scenarios that tend to become uniform. The problem is that this may reify crisis management in the participants' experience, whereas the essence of crisis is intangible, dynamic, uncertain, and evolving: It cannot be reduced or enclosed as an object with well-defined contours. By making crisis a part of routine thinking and action, it may become a "well-structured" problem, which could prove to be of no help, or even counterproductive, during events hitherto unimaginable. This trend thus presents the risk of normalization (Borraz & Gisquet, 2019), which must be guarded against.

In addition, such simulations prompt the tendency to hide errors and adapt to fictitious resolutions of the scripted problems (the participants speculatively agree that the problem has been solved) by eliminating overly complex or undesirable aspects. Most often, a scenario is played out in such a way that it gradually prescribes a positive exit that is more or less independent of the participants' activity. Under these conditions, the exercise is in no way an educational space in which errors and misunderstandings are examined and dealt with, thus constituting a lever for learning and development, but are instead masked (Flandin et al., 2019). Moreover, these simulations are often designed and implemented by professionals who have little experience or skill in training.

The third reason is that crisis management simulations are often costly (in terms of time, money, and skill), which is why in the absence of a formalized offer (which is more likely to be found in the medical field) they are organized infrequently and for limited times (half a day, typically). Moreover, crisis management simulations very rarely integrate notions of disruption, the unforeseen, the never before seen, and the unthinkable—however promising for training—because at a practical level doing so is unfeasible (Flandin et al., 2018). We thus once again encounter the problem of standardized scenarios because of the constraints to design and implementation, to which a certain regulatory rigidity is sometimes added.

According to Wright-Maley (2015), simulation tends to provide developmental opportunities if it is featured by dynamism and outcome variability, making unscripted and unexpected activities possible. This design principle demands and enhances a high degree of human agency (Duchatelet et al., 2019), which should be further investigated to understand how to strengthen the developmental function of simulations.

From this analysis, it seems clear that further research in simulation and civil security, and more generally protection, rescue, and emergency care, has become imperative. We need to better understand how to design simulations that are both efficient with respect to the above-defined objectives and appropriable by the organizations despite the many constraints. Our contribution to addressing this need was an examination of an exemplary simulation program that met the following aims: an interprofessional simulation based on the confrontation with an uncontrolled crisis situation and the organization of a crisis response that is only partially prescribed.

3 Simulate to Bring About and Experience Critical Situations in Training: A Qualitative Study in a Real-Life Context

3.1 Theoretical Background

Consistent with the foregoing analysis, the hypothesis underlying the study presented here is the following: Simulation can be an effective training tool in civil security crisis management if it is designed according to modalities that (i) exploit the properties of autonomy, self-organization, and resilience in human activity, which are particularly evident in cases of overcoming critical situations (e.g., Flandin et al., 2021), and (ii) develop a disposition to act in situations of uncertainty rather than focusing on the acquisition of predefined knowledge (Flandin et al., 2018). This hypothesis is also congruent with an enactive conception of human activity and cognition: Activity is characterized by indeterminate dynamics that cannot be conceptualized as rule following, and cognition is not a representation of a world predetermined by a predetermined mind. Rather, it is the enaction of a world and a consciousness based on the history of their relations—that is, the history of the actions and experiences lived by the actor (Varela et al., 1991). This hypothesis contrasts with those in which behavior is described as a mechanical reaction to events that would occur uniformly for any actor (Daniellou & Rabardel, 2005; Klein, 2015). It also has strong implications for the understanding and design of performance-promoting environments (e.g., Récopé et al., 2019) and, of course, education and training (e.g., Durand & Poizat, 2015). Therefore, research from this perspective cannot consist only of collecting and analyzing extrinsic data on professional activity, but also requires data "from within" on how actors organize their activity to give it meaning and be able to act taking into account the resources and constraints in play.

This has led to a "design-based" research program in the field of crisis management simulation training. This program consists of examining original and/or remarkable simulation programs with a focus on the participants' training activity, particularly the dynamics of meaning production. The aims are to acquire scientific knowledge and derive sound principles for simulation designs.

The study consisted of first identifying a simulation training program designed, not according to a didactic approach finalized by the acquisition of predefined knowledge, but according to a principle of confronting trainees with a stressful, complex, and dynamic situation and finalized by testing the modalities of action and organization that were not predefined, or only in part. This type of simulation training can be thought of as "development-oriented participation in an interactive system" (Berlin & Carlström, 2015).

3.2 *Field for Study*

We chose an interprofessional civil security simulation program (professionals working in defense, justice, interior, and health services) to train professionals in chemical, biological, radiological, nuclear, and high-yield explosive (CBRNE) crisis management. The main objective of this program is to test joint intervention procedures (which may imply that the participants override them) and thus to train those working in decision-making (operation management by the local authority), rescue (particularly fire brigades), first aid (particularly emergency medical services), civil order (police and gendarmerie), and defense (army) services to deal with a CBRNE accident or attack. The simulation was designed as a "guided game"—that is, based on a scenario introducing multiple elements and interactions with the facilitators. It was deployed "in the field" for "operational" actions and in the operational command post (OCP) for decision and command actions. Our study focused specifically on crisis simulation for decision-makers and commanders in OCPs, and we studied two occurrences. These simulations were designed as "crisis cells" (a single room equipped with a central table and telecommunications means bringing together a team of a dozen stakeholders playing their own role).

Although minimally theorized by the program's design team, the design principle of a "test" underlying this simulation was consistent with the simulation modalities noted and discussed above. We were particularly interested in determining to what extent the activity encouraged by this program would contribute to the participants' developing new dispositions to act in critical situations.

3.3 *Method*

The method used to study the simulations articulated an observatory of the context and organizational issues (constraints and effects of training) with an observatory of in situ activity, to which primacy was granted.

3.3.1 Observatory of the Constraints and Effects of Training

This observatory aimed to study the constraints, which were (i) all the elements that participated in delimiting the perimeter of action in which the participants were evolving (type of organization; prescriptions, norms, and rules; habits; spontaneous statements and interactions between the participants; etc.) and the effects, which were (ii) all the elements brought into existence or transformed by the participants' activity (their own activity, that of others, the organization, etc.).

Depending on the authorizations and opportunities for access to practices, documents, and participants, the method combined (i) direct observation of training situations with note-taking, (ii) documentary study of various activity traces (postings on site, working documents, reference documents, circulars, email exchanges, etc.), and (iii) informal exchanges with the participants.

3.3.2 Observatory of Training Activity

The analysis of the participants' activity during the guided games constituted the hardcore of the study. The activity was documented in its observable dimension (participants' behaviors captured in terms of gestures, positioning, movements, attitudes, statements, interactions, etc.) and in an unobservable dimension that was nevertheless accessible to the consciousness of the participants (concerns, intentions, expectations, perceptions, attentions, emotions, knowledge, etc.). This dimension of activity was documented at two levels: (i) reflexive consciousness, which was expressed in ordinary exchanges with the researcher, and (ii) pre-reflexive consciousness, which was expressed under specific conditions of exchanges based on the situational analysis of the actor.

Here again, the method combined (i) direct observation of training situations with note-taking, (ii) deferred observation using photos and video recordings of various kinds (onboard cameras, wide shots, and 360° format), and (iii) an interview modality that articulated phases of experience description through self-confrontation, and comprehensive and reflexive phases built on the basis of a prior reenactment of the situation. Self-confrontation (Rix-Lièvre & Lièvre, 2009; Theureau, 2003) consisted of retrospectively confronting participants with video recordings of the situations studied, and in particular of their behavior, in order to promote an embodied speech position.

3.3.3 Data Processing

Two occurrences of the program were studied. The data collection is summarized in Table 1.

The processing consisted of identifying the significant elements in the corpus of observation and interview data with regard to the research question, that is, those elements indicating modifications in the participants' disposition to act. We then evaluated the gradients of typicality in these elements. Typicality was assessed by: (i) statements by the participants on the recurring nature of a perceived element (a configuration, a situation, an action, a feeling, a communication, an interpretation, etc.), (ii) the frequency of occurrence of an element in the verbatims and/or the behavior of the same actor, and (iii) the identification of similar documentation in the verbatims and/or behaviors of several participants related to the same element. These elements were then progressively assigned to provisional categories with the aim of ordering them exhaustively. We regularly assessed these categories and their ability to saturate and order the variability of the significant elements: The four lines we present here result from this analysis.

Table 1 Summary of data collection

Simulation	Theme and duration	Type and volume of collected data
Simulation 1	Radiological attack	Informal exchanges
	150 minutes	Note-taking
		Photos (16)
		Video recording (170 minutes)
		Interviews (4 participants, total: 320 minutes)
		Diverse documents
Simulation 2	Chemical attack	Informal exchanges
	150 minutes	Note-taking
		Photos (20)
		Video recording (160 minutes)
		Interviews (4 participants, total: 363 minutes)
		Diverse documents

3.4 *Results: Four Lines of Insight on Activity and Its Transformation in Crisis Simulation*

The empirical analysis revealed four lines of insight into activity and its transformation in crisis simulation. Each of these lines of analysis shows the tension between categories having the same theme but that are polarized, even opposite at times, with the exception of line 1: enactment–reenactment.

3.4.1 Enactment–Reenactment

Enactment–reenactment concerned the immediate experiences of the participants in the simulated context. Enactment refers to the way in which each participant brought out and experienced real situations in the fictional scenario. Reenactment refers to an experience already lived by a participant that re-emerged and was thus reexperienced by him or her because of a strong proximity and resemblance between a situation currently being experienced in the simulation and a situation previously experienced (at work or in another simulation).

3.4.1.1 Enactment

Through the simulation process, it was possible to bring about situations whose rarity made them uncertain and difficult for the professionals to grasp. It is important here to differentiate between two cases. First, when the situations were somewhat familiar, could be sized up as to their extent, and were foreseeable despite being rare, the simulations allowed the participants to experience them in a concrete and plausible way even though what was at stake was of course fictitious. When these situations were made to occur in the realm of the participants' concrete experience—that is, within their field of attention but also in their bodies—they were able to gain a sense of "what it can be" and "what it can do" to be faced with a civil security crisis. Second, when the situations were largely new and out of the ordinary, the simulations allowed the participants to test their capacities for interpretation and action in highly stressful and uncertain conditions, thus also prompting them to extend their understanding (the domain of possible meanings) and develop the disposition to act in crisis situations (the repertoire of possible and desirable actions). By living out these extraordinary situations in simulation, the participants were also able to experience the feeling of vulnerability that arose from the mismatch between the means for interpretation and available action and the demands of the situation that needed to be managed.

At the end of Simulation 1, the Judicial Police Commissioner commented:

> After the training I thought, "Wow, there were a lot of things we should have known how to do that didn't work the way they should have. Things that we need to review without the other departments. So we organized a morning of additional in-house training to 'bring us up to speed'".

3.4.1.2 Reenactment

When the rare, simulated situations had a "family resemblance" with one or more situations the participants had already experienced (in real intervention or during a previous simulation), the simulations allowed them to re-do the experience in a new way. When the participants experienced reenactment, they mobilized, dramatized, and revitalized events, episodes, and even atmospheres from the past (Daugbjerg et al., 2014). This then contributed to a dual "circulation of experiences": between events that were chronologically distant and between people who were present but were not the same in the past and present situations. Reenacted under different conditions, the meanings initially produced were reworked according to modes of strengthening, weakening, and/or relativizing their validity (Rosch, 1978), a process that tended to enrich the participants' "reservoirs of meaning" (Weick, 1993) and thus their capacity for interpretation.

At the end of simulation 2, the Emergency Operations Commander commented:

> "I realized that I had too much of a tendency to be overbearing in these inter-service situations, even to 'spill over' a little into a scope of action that is not my own. And that this was likely to irritate some colleagues. This is a point of vigilance that emerged for me at the end of the training, and in retrospect it sheds new light on a real crisis management situation that did not go ideally, perhaps in part for this reason."

3.4.2 Curriculum–Discovery

Curriculum–discovery concerned the processes by which the participants benefited from the simulations with regard to the demands of a crisis situation. This benefit occurred because of the entire body of knowledge already established for managing a CBRNE crisis (the curriculum), the utility of which was felt from time to time as problems arose. It also occurred because of the practical confrontation with the demands of the crisis and the activity it typically encouraged from the participants, which resulted in frequent discoveries.

3.4.2.1 Curriculum

The participants were expected to have mastered a body of knowledge on CBRNE crisis management before the simulation program, which was designed to prepare them to put this knowledge into action. In this sense, the simulation program was a high point of the professional curriculum on crisis management situations. Nevertheless, we noted that the participants showed wide differences in their mastery of the "expected" knowledge or rather the knowledge generally accepted as useful for managing CBRNE crises. This difference is usually manifested by the tendency to pose questions to those participants perceived as being likely to know the answer. This sometimes gave rise to forms of "spontaneous tutoring" between the participants, during which the transmission of knowledge could range from simple information sharing to more in-depth explanations on a topic. Thus, the simulations during the guided games were frequently punctuated by "instructive parentheses" that were both timely and ephemeral: a participant (more experienced on a given topic at instant *t*) filled in a colleague's knowledge gap. This could be related to any number of topics: an acronym, a procedure, a legal question, a geographic, professional or organizational specificity, etc., and was dealt with by a short explanation given in a natural and "fluid" way during the simulation without interrupting the unfolding of the scenario.

During Simulation 2, the young Medical Director asks the more experienced Rescue Commander as an aside:

- *What is the "RCI"?*
- *It's the Rescue Centre for the Involved.*
- *But aren't we supposed to call it the "RCTI"?*
- *That's what we used to say; "RCI" is an acronymic simplification.*
- *Okay! Thanks for your help.*

3.4.2.2 Discovery

Although the simulation was an opportunity to put into action a predefined curriculum, it was also the occasion for many experiences of imitation, learning, or reciprocal adaptation for the participants as they interacted with their counterparts from other professions and services, and therefore other cultures. This "reciprocal acculturation" was not the only means of discovery. Confronting the scenario created multiple opportunities for imagination (formulating and prioritizing explanatory hypotheses on the basis of rare, imprecise, or even potentially false information), invention (inventing new modes of action), and improvisation (finding resources in an environment that was a priori devoid of them in order to be able to act), etc. All this was possible because of the participants' engagement, which had been provoked and sustained by the dynamic nature of the simulation. This sustained engagement was thus accompanied by the "training of attention," which simultaneously encompassed vigilance to the various aspects of the threat, a necessary attention to detail, and attention to oneself and others in the situation—in such a way that the participants developed a special disposition for attentiveness as an aide to crisis management.

At the conclusion of Simulation 1, one firefighter officer comments:

> I learned a lot about the needs and concerns of medical rescue colleagues in this type of situation. I also understood why our colleagues from the police department are bothering us with certain procedures related to the investigation.

3.4.3 Disruption–Reassurance

Disruption–reassurance concerned two opposing modes of preparation for crisis management. Disruption consisted of prompting responsiveness by bringing about situations that shook up the participants' expectations in order to test the robustness of their modalities of interpretation, action, and collective configuration, and/or to encourage the development of new modalities. Conversely, reassurance consisted of encouraging the success of the participants through scripting effects, either on an ad hoc basis or overall. The idea was that succeeding together helps the team, even in a simulated context, to increase the feeling of competence and preparation in the face of a major crisis.

3.4.3.1 Disruption

The simulation included "injects," events aimed at iteratively creating disruptions in the course of crisis management. These disruptions could play a simple role of focusing attention and/or concretizing the variability of events that can occur during an actual crisis. They could also play a more decisive role that ranged from calling into question the culture of action or profession to provoking surprise, shock, and dissatisfaction—even to the point of rendering the participants' activity "insufficient" to address the emerging problems. This type of disruption may lead to a major bifurcation in a participant's developmental trajectory. More broadly, disruption can encourage not only the reorganization of actions and resources, but also the imagination of new possibilities for interpretation and action. The configurations of collective activities tested in simulations tend to materialize in real crisis situations when certain conditions are present (particularly partial resemblances or family resemblances between the conditions of training and those of real work).

At the beginning of Simulation 2, the Police Commissioner is missing. The Director of Emergency Operations then entrusts the command of Police and Gendarmerie Operations to the Captain of the Gendarmerie, a responsibility that he has no experience in and that his rank normally does not allow him to take. The beginning of the simulation was very difficult for the captain, who received a great deal of information and requests that he tried to process as best he could. After about 20 minutes, his superior (who was training in another room) comes to replace him so that the command is assured by a qualified officer. This double change in roles experienced by the captain proved to be very disturbing for him, but useful and constructive in allowing him to foreshadow a possible scenario. Indeed, in crisis management, a hazard can make it necessary to substitute roles. This is why it is worthwhile to train in order to achieve the best possible fluidity.

3.4.3.2 Reassurance

Although the simulations were designed to disrupt the participants' activity for the purposes of training, learning, and development, the scripting and debriefing procedures systematically led to a finding of "relative success": The simulation was generally successful (because in a guided game, the problems to be solved are reasonably sized and the facilitators intervene if needed to help the participants to solve them), but points for improvement in crisis management were always identified. One might question this "always happy" ending from the perspective of training evaluation. However, it fulfilled an important function of collective reassurance, helping the participants to see (or believe) that they were ready and capable and would know how to cope in a real situation. This function fueled the feeling of individual and collective competence and to unite these professionals as members of a "winning team."

At the conclusion of Simulation 2, a firefighter comments:

> We still think that if it were to happen, we would not be lost. There are always things to improve, but overall, I think we managed the events well. It's important to feel capable of dealing with this kind of situation, because the risk of something like this happening is real.

3.4.4 Trust–Distrust

Trust–distrust concerned the nature of the social relationships that were established explicitly or implicitly between the participants. Crisis management requires mechanisms to reduce complexity, and knowing how to determine who to count on (trust) and who not to count on (distrust) in a given type of situation is one such mechanism.

3.4.4.1 Trust

We saw that reassurance was based on a sense of individual and collective competence when a simulated crisis was effectively managed. Reassurance thus refers to a feeling of confidence in oneself and others, and it can be diffuse or, on the contrary, it can stem from very specific significant experiences of competence and/or reliability being demonstrated to another participant or to everyone. This was particularly common in interactive episodes in which a participant sought the assistance of a third party perceived on that occasion as relevant and effective. This significant experience tended to be typified (taking on a value that goes beyond the situation in which it was experienced), and it can be expected that it will be echoed in similar situations in the future. This experience of trust thus constituted a resource for action, which can be summed up in the formula "this person/this group of people is reliable in this type of situation."

At the conclusion of Simulation 2, a Gendarmerie Officer commented:

> It's important to know who you can count on when the situation starts to get out of hand. And it's true that with these colleagues, we work together on a daily basis [...], we train together in complicated situations like this one, and that creates bonds between us. Bonds of trust that reassure us that we can count on each other.

3.4.4.2 Distrust

Although simulated crisis management is particularly favorable for building benchmarks, especially social and organizational, it should be noted that social benchmarks are not limited to establishing relationships of trust, but also relationships of distrust. Although it seems counterintuitive, relationships of distrust can be resources for action. This meaningful experience also tended to be typified, and it may be expected that it will be echoed in similar situations in the future. The experience of distrust thus constituted a resource for action, which can be summed up in the formula "this person/this group of people is not reliable in this type of situation." Distrust arose mainly from conflicts of objectives, methods, and standards between different services or professionals engaged in the same task. A notable limitation of the simulation, in this regard, is that it provided very little framework for discussion and debate, with action and organization oriented toward solving immediate and urgent problems.

At the end of simulation 2, a Gendarmerie Officer comments:

> It's tricky to say but it's true that there are people or even services with whom we don't get along well, which doesn't facilitate cooperation. We see this in the simulation, but it's not surprising because in reality it happens in the same way with them, that is to say badly. Often we have to deal with them, but if we can do without them, we do it...

4 Conclusion

Civil security crisis simulations, such as we have seen, script and animate situations likely to provoke significant experiences of not only surprise, uncertainty, distrust, and discomfort, but also complicity, solidarity, reassurance, and even pride, depending on the moment and the participants. Without these experiences, CBRNE crisis management would remain virtual and very abstract, and the participants would have to wait until they were actually confronted with a crisis to develop their capacity to deal with it. Thus, the crisis simulation can be a "controlled space for experimentation" (Becerril Ortega et al., 2022) during which participants experience a crisis in a controlled manner. This type of program encourages a form of exploratory activity from which multiple learning and development opportunities can emerge (whether or not linked to the body of knowledge predefined as being relevant), such as those we have described along these four analytical lines.

The dimension of reenactment was added to that of enactment, the interest of which we have explained. Reenactment episodes are re-presentifications of past events (Tutt & Hindmarsh, 2011) in which the present and past coexist on the basis of a resemblance (from the perspective of lived experience), the past being the object of vivification (Nichols, 2008). This immediate relationship between significant past and present experiences can constitute a powerful vector for reconfiguring the relationship maintained between the participant and the significant event at the origin of the process (e.g., Drakos et al., 2021). This reconfiguration can potentially be actualized in all dimensions of the event and can even "migrate" through meaningful sharing among multiple participants. Indeed, in addition to contributing to a form of "sharing in action" between participants, one of the interests of simulation training resides in (i) the possibility of physically experiencing the power "to act" together in a way that exceeds the individual capacity for action of the various participants, and (ii) the creation of a "community of activity" in which inter-service interactions are gradually mingled with ordinary modalities of intervention.

Crisis management simulations constructively exploit collective activity beyond simply familiarizing trainees with collective techniques and procedures (acquisition, stabilization, automation, coordination of the practical actions of the various actors in the field). Although familiarization remains important with regard to the gestures and procedures to be mastered in primary intervention (technical and organizational resources directly available and activatable), the part of crisis intervention that requires sensitivity and its deployment in the collective seems to be an essential aspect of learning and development that occurs in crisis simulation. These simulations encourage in the participants the emergence, testing, and strengthening of dispositions to "see," "perceive," "feel," "act," "imagine," and "interact" in a crisis. This "dispositional" perspective (Muller & Plazaola Giger, 2014) makes it possible to think about and account for the transformations of activity in simulation while maintaining a certain distance from the basic notions of training (techniques, procedures, etc.). Simulation can then be understood as a space not only for training personnel, but also for creating effective collective activity configurations, underpinned by what we call dispositions. The four lines of analysis presented here seem useful for enhancing our understanding of the conditions under which training can encourage the development of dispositions to act in a crisis situation (reorganization of available resources, creation of new resources, rebound capacity, etc.).

We noted the paradox in crisis simulations, which consists in seeking to disrupt the participants' activity to meet training, learning, and development objectives, all the while ensuring that the scripting and the modalities of debriefing create the conditions for a "positive outcome." To this end, we observed that the disruptions and problems to be solved were always reasonably sized and the simulation facilitators always intervened as needed to help the participants resolve them. Nevertheless, simulating disruptive events (outside the known framework, without the possibility of assessing the size of the disruption or its danger, where all seems to escape "understanding") seems to be crucial for preparing professionals to manage real and more extreme crisis situations and not just what some participants have called "ordinary crises." Yet conceptually and operationally, much is still lacking that would equip facilitators to design and implement ways to exit from more extreme crisis simulations—that is, with disruptions that offer the participants "desirable difficulties" (Bjork, 2013) likely to improve their performance.

Professionals in fields that concern issues of security and threats of crisis face a wide range of challenges: automating first-line actions and procedures (technical and organizational resources that are directly available and activatable) without compromising the ability to adapt to the unforeseen or even the unthinkable (events outside the framework, whose size cannot be assessed); strengthening individual and collective feelings of competence ("if it happens, we'll be able to cope") without creating the illusion of ultimate control ("losing control, that can't happen to us…"); and developing both proactivity, i.e., the ability to maintain a level of safety or halt the escalation of a threat, and reactivity, i.e., the ability to bounce back from critical organizational destabilization. A crisis is an event of powerful intensity that also offers the conditions for major transformations. We contend that crisis management training should exploit the characteristics of the crises for which trainees are preparing (accidents, cyberattacks, terrorist attacks, etc.) as a means of creating the conditions for individual and organizational development. Simulation offers the opportunity for empirical investigation in a research direction that seems highly innovative in this sense: the development of a technology for using perturbation as a tool for training (Flandin et al., 2018; Gorman et al., 2010; Schot et al., 2019). Other innovative and ambitious research programs are needed, particularly to enrich our understanding of the concrete effects of training and training exercises on real-life interventions (in terms of learning and development, repercussions, and the improvement of intervention practices). This would make it possible to establish a compelling link between training design and implementation principles on the one hand, and what is empirically documentable in the field on the other hand.

References

Anderson, B., & Adey, P. (2011). Affect and security: Exercising emergency in 'UK civil contingencies'. *Environment and Planning D: Society and Space, 29*(6), 1092–1109.

Becerril Ortega, R., Vanderstichel, H., Petit, L., Urbiolagallegos, M.-J., Schoch, J., Dacunha, S., Benamara, A., Ravenet, B., Zagdoun, J., & Chaby, L. (2022). Design Process for a Virtual Simulation Environment for Training Healthcare Professionals in Geriatrics. In S. Flandin, C. Vidal-Gomel, & R. Becerril Ortega (Eds.), *Simulation training through the lens of experience and activity analysis: Healthcare, victim rescue and population protection* (Professional and practice-based learning series). Springer.

Bergström, J., Henriqson, E., & Dahlström, N. (2011). From crew resource management to operational resilience. In *Proceedings of the 4th Resilience Engineering Symposium*, 8–10 June 2011, Sophia Antipolis, France.

Berlin, J. M., & Carlström, E. D. (2015). Collaboration exercises: What do they contribute? – A study of learning and usefulness. *Journal of Contingencies and Crisis Management, 23*(1), 11–23.

Billett, S. (2020). *Learning in the workplace: Strategies for effective practice*. Routledge.

Billett, S., Harteis, C., & Gruber, H. (Eds.). (2014). *International handbook of research in professional and practice-based learning*. Springer.

Bjork, R. A. (2013). Desirable difficulties perspective on learning. *Encyclopedia of the Mind, 4*, 134–146.

Borodzicz, E., & Van Haperen, K. (2002). Individual and group learning in crisis simulations. *Journal of Contingencies and Crisis Management, 10*(3), 139–147.

Borraz, O., & Gisquet, E. (2019). L'extension du domaine de la crise ? Les exercices de gestion de crise dans la gouvernance de la filière nucléaire française. *Critique internationale, 4*, 43–61.

Daniellou, F., & Rabardel, P. (2005). Activity-oriented approaches to ergonomics: Some traditions and communities. *Theoretical Issues in Ergonomics Science, 6*(5), 353–357.

Daugbjerg, M., Eisner, R., & Knudsen, B. T. (2014). Re-enacting the past: Vivifying heritage 'again'. *International Journal of Heritage Studies, 20*, 681–687.

Drakos, A., Flandin, S., Filippi, G., Palaci, F., Veyrunes, P., & Poizat, G. (2021). From exploration to re-enactment: Instructional uses of a desktop virtual environment for training nuclear plant field operators. *Vocations and Learning, 14*, 327–352.

Duchatelet, D., Gijbels, D., Bursens, P., Donche, V., & Spooren, P. (2019). Looking at role-play simulations of political decision-making in higher education through a contextual lens: A state-of-the-art. *Educational Research Review, 27*, 126–139.

Durand, M., & Poizat, G. (2015). An activity-centred approach to work analysis and the design of vocational training situations. In L. Filliettaz & S. Billett (Eds.), *Francophone perspectives of learning through work* (pp. 221–224). Springer.

Fenwick, T. (2003). Reclaiming and re-embodying experiential learning through complexity science. *Studies in the Education of Adults, 35*, 123–141.

Flandin, S., Poizat, G., & Durand, M. (2018). Improving resilience in high-risk organizations. Principles for the design of innovative training situations. *Development and Learning in Organizations: An International Journal, 32*(2), 9–12.

Flandin, S., Poizat, G., & Perinet, R. (2019). Contribuer à l'amélioration de la sécurité industrielle « par le facteur humain » : Un regard pour aider à (re)penser la formation. *Collection Regards sur la sécurité industrielle.* : FONCSI.

Flandin, S., Salini, D., Drakos, A., & Poizat, G. (2021). Concevoir des formations facilitant l'émergence de nouvelles significations face à des évènements inédits et critiques. *Activités, 18*(1).

Fornette, M. P., Darses, F., & Bourgy, M. (2015). How to improve training programs for the management of complex and unforeseen situations. In *Proceedings of the Human Factors and Ergonomics Society Europe* (pp. 217–224).

Gorman, J. C., Cooke, N. J., & Amazeen, P. G. (2010). Training adaptive teams. *Human Factors, 52*(2), 295–307.

Klein, G. (2015). Whose fallacies? *Journal of Cognitive Engineering and Decision Making, 9*(1), 55–58.

Kouabenan, D. R., Cadet, B., Hermand, D., & Muñoz Sastre, M. T. (2007). *Psychologie du risque*. De Boeck.

Maynard, M. T., Kennedy, D. M., & Sommer, S. A. (2015). Team adaptation: A fifteen-year synthesis (1998–2013) and framework for how this literature needs to "adapt" going forward. *European Journal of Work and Organizational Psychology, 24*(5), 652–677.

Muller, A., & Plazaola Giger, I. (2014). *Dispositions à agir, travail et formation*. Octarès.

Nichols, B. (2008). Reenactment and the fantasmatic subject. *Critical Inquiry, 35*, 72–89.

Pettersen, K. (2013). Acknowledging the role of abductive thinking: A way out of proceduralization for safety management and oversight? In C. Bieder & M. Bourrier (Eds.), *Trapping safety into rules* (pp. 107–117). Ashgate.

Récopé, M., Fache, H., Beaujouan, J., Coutarel, F., & Rix-Lièvre, G. (2019). A study of the individual activity of professional volleyball players: Situation assessment and sensemaking under time pressure. *Applied ergonomics, 80*, 226–237.

Rix-Lièvre, G., & Lièvre, P. (2009). Self-confrontation. In A. Mills, G. Durepos, & E. Wiebe (Eds.), *Encyclopedia of case study research* (pp. 847–849). Sage.
Rosch, E. (1978). Principles of categorization. In E. Rosch & B. B. Lloyd (Eds.), *Cognition and categorization* (pp. 27–48). Lawrence Erlbaum.
Samurçay, R., & Rogalski, J. (1998). Exploitation didactique des situations de simulation. *Le travail humain, 61*(4), 333–359.
Schot, S., Flandin, S., Goudeaux, A., Seferdjeli, L., & Poizat, G. (2019). Formation basée sur la perturbation: preuve de concept par la conception d'un environnement numérique de formation en radiologie médicale. *Activités, 16*(2).
Stanton, N. A., Chambers, P. R., & Piggott, J. (2001). Situational awareness and safety. *Safety Science, 39*(3), 189–204.
Theureau, J. (2003). Course-of-action analysis and course-of-action centered design. In H. Mahwah (Ed.), *Handbook of cognitive task design* (pp. 55–81). Lawrence Erlbaum Associates.
Tutt, D., & Hindmarsh, J. (2011). Reenactments at work: Demonstrating conduct in data sessions. *Research on Language & Social Interaction, 44*, 211–236.
Varela, F. J., Thompson, E., & Rosch, E. (1991). *The embodied mind. Cognitive science and human experience*. MIT Press.
Weick, K. E. (1993). The collapse of sensemaking: The Mann Gulf disaster. *Administrative Science Quarterly, 38*, 62.
Wright-Maley, C. (2015). Beyond the "Babel problem": Defining simulations for the social studies. *The Journal of Social Studies Research, 39*(2), 63–77.

Renewing the Tools for Simulation-Based Training in Medical Education: How Situated Cognition Approaches Can Help Us?

Zoya Horcik

Abstract This chapter aims to contribute to a global reflection on the relationships between theoretical frameworks and design principles by analysing the links between how learning is conceptualized and how simulation-based training programs are implemented. For research in education, learning theories circumscribe the phenomena that are examined. They have a substantial impact on methods, data analysis and interpretations of the results. We believe that the same goes for the design of training sessions in adult education, especially for simulation-based training, which often articulates several learning methods in complex training environments.

The situated cognition approaches are strongly linked to simulation-based training by definition. We take a look at the theoretical roots of these approaches and question their translation to design principles for simulation-based training sessions. Our goal is to go beyond the design principles that are frequently used in the literature about simulation-based training and contribute to their actualisation.

We believe that a strong point of view about how learning occurs, in addition to a precise knowledge of theoretical frameworks in adult education, can provide some advantages in design and clarity about learning objectives, goals and methods to achieve it.

Keywords Situated cognition · Simulation-based training · Theoretical frameworks · Pedagogical design · Learning theories · Adult education

---

Z. Horcik (✉)
Équipe CRAFT, University of Geneva, Genève, Switzerland
e-mail: horcik.zoya@t-l.ch

S. Flandin et al. (eds.), *Simulation Training through the Lens of Experience and Activity Analysis*, Professional and Practice-based Learning 30,
https://doi.org/10.1007/978-3-030-89567-9_4

1 Introduction

The purpose of this book is to present the evolutions of the research field about simulation-based training and the development of various methods to analyze these educational programs as they are today widely used in many professional areas. It contributes to a reflection for innovative training design principles and is meant for professionals involved in pedagogical design or in a reflection upon simulation-based practices. The works gathered in this book, and this chapter is no exception, are mostly related to the activity analysis's point of view and more specifically the French-speaking ergonomic approach which the English-speaking audience is perhaps less familiar with.

This particular chapter aims to contribute to a global reflection on the relationships between theoretical frameworks and design principles by analyzing the links between how learning is conceptualized and how simulation-based training programs are implemented (Dennick, 2016). For research programs in education, learning theories circumscribe the phenomena that are examined. Learning theories have a substantial impact on methods, data analysis, and interpretations of the results. We believe that the same goes for the design of training sessions in adult education, especially for simulation-based training that often articulates several learning methods in complex training environments.

The situated cognition approaches[1] are strongly linked to simulation-based training by definition. We would like to take a look at the theoretical roots of these approaches and question their translation to design principles for simulation-based training sessions. Our goal is to go beyond the design principles that are frequently used in the literature about simulation-based training and contribute to their actualization.

We believe that a strong point of view about how learning occurs, in addition to a precise knowledge of theoretical frameworks in adult education, can provide some advantages in design and clarity about learning objectives, goals, and methods to achieve it. Therefore, it can be a useful tool for professionals dealing with training design sessions.

1.1 Multiple Practices in a Changing Context

Simulation-based training has been integrated into medical and nursing programs in both vocational education and continuing education for several years now by training policies in medical education. The spread of these methods and the expansion of practices have opened up various themes and areas of development, such as training in interprofessional collaboration (Peeters et al., 2017) for technical and

[1] We define those approaches as a gathering of non-unified research, or research programs in various scientific disciplines that are bound by one or multiple common hypotheses.

nontechnical skills or the investigation upon the notion of professionalism (Birden et al., 2013; Bracq et al., 2019; Yucel et al., 2020), role model (Johnson et al., 2012), or deliberate practice (Ju et al., 2019).

These methods are now being challenged by the growing development of distancial training programs and digital learning methods such as serious games, online content, and collaborative work platforms, which are permanently modifying the relationship between professionals and training. Until recently, professional training has been dominated by so-called face-to-face training programs, delimited by a so-called synchronous framework. It has been well reported that simulation-based training is particularly costly in terms of time and resources (Walsh & Jaye, 2012); (Maloney & Haines, 2016). The cost–benefit ratio of the implementation of these training programs is today strongly questioned by multiple digital devices such as smartphones, laptops, or tactile tablets.

This trend is part of a general development of new training technologies that offers ready-to-use devices more or less adaptable to the professional problems. The role of those in charge of training and development management is therefore currently to manage adequacy between the current offers and the "in-house" design of training according to the needs of the field. We think that this reflection and these choices can be nurtured by a detailed knowledge of learning theories and their implications in terms of training program design (identification of goal situations, which professions are involved, etc.). Simulation in health care has now been practiced for several decades and is in the process of losing its hegemony. This implies a tightening of the understanding of the learning phenomena at work to make it more relevant and effective in a global context of reduced resources in order to make good use of the plasticity of this type of device.

1.2 The Various Approaches of Situated Cognition

The situated cognition approaches postulate that learning is context-related. It is in part on this postulate that current simulation training programs are based. By reproducing the ecological context or area of a work environment in a secure setting, those training programs have put in their center the relationship skill's acquisition (technical, clinical, or teamwork) and the professional context (Kneebone, 2005, 2010; Østergaard et al., 2011). These programs aim to develop and enhance learning for a vast number of professional areas, especially healthcare professions. By focusing on the concrete aspects of a professional situation—reproducing a specific dynamic, recreating parts or the whole of a work environment—simulated training allows the learner to build strong contextual knowledge that can be further analyzed, which will enable them to validate or invalidate the efficient and inefficient aspects of their work routine. Even though the format of such simulated training can vary considerably from one to another depending on the goal (part task trainers, high fidelity simulators, crisis scenario, basic and usual task training), the situated cognition premise is, by nature, at the root of any simulation-based training.

First of all, it should be mentioned that this stream of research is not a unified theory unit but includes several currents that are not always unified, which makes it complex to refer to a single paradigm or a specific theory. Numerous disciplines such as linguistics, psychology, and ergonomics each have different notions, notably notions of situation and different focuses toward the objects of study.[2]

1.3 Plan of the Chapter

Of course there is also a multiplicity of practices and work areas that are using simulation. We will deliberately stay at a very general level. Simulation for learning purposes is an extremely broad field. The challenge is not to focus exclusively on one type of program while remaining precise enough to provide the reader with relevant information. We will focus on face-to-face programs involving one or several learners and one or several instructors accompanying the session by piloting or not the simulator and followed or not by didactic sequences of debriefing or mixed type.

In the rest of this chapter, we will try to synthesize the main topics of the approaches to situated and embodied cognition: its origins and the main trends and disciplines where the topics about cognition, learning, the body, and its environment are central. We will also refer to research work that falls within this approach. We will then make the link with a brief review of the literature on simulation in the medical field and its links with situated cognition. The objective of this part will be to show what conceptual links tie simulation training programs and this stream. Finally, we would like to suggest design principles and examples that have emerged from the different chapters of this book and can be useful to rethink simulation-based training with a "situated approach's point of view."

In order to carry out the literature review of point 3, we have focused on the main publications dealing with situated cognition in the field of simulation-based training by prioritizing articles exposing the theoretical foundations of these programs and recent publications (<10 years) (keywords "Situated cognition"; "simulation based training"; "incarnated cognition"; "embodied cognition"; "experiential learning").

[2] Translated by the author.

2 Situated and Embodied Cognition: What Specificities for Learning?

As mentioned before, it would be difficult to track the evolution of the situated cognition field as having a single trajectory or a steady given number of scientific disciplines. This group of theories brings together a multiplicity of research fields, programs, and convergent hypotheses from various disciplines (anthropology, sociology, cognitive sciences, psychology, etc.) whose dialogue is particularly fruitful for the development of pedagogical design. We deliberately choose this chapter to address the group of research, which seems to bring a certain number of elements of understanding and promises of development for training design. Well aware that this selection is necessarily reductive and influenced by the approach in which we conduct our researches and professional activities (an ergonomic approach to training based on the postulate of enaction), our goal is to bring a view that we hope will help to give a voice to other theoretical aspects than those generally called for in medical education research.

The main idea that unites these approaches is that cognition is linked to the characteristics of an actor and his environment in permanent co-construction according to the statuses and variations of these two "poles." These approaches, which focus their research on the situation's characteristics, or psychological, social, cultural processes, are opposed to the idea that cognition results from a selection of stimuli that are perceived by the perceptual system in a given environment, thus making learning as an information processing system.

We can gather four different themes that are enlightened by the research from these approaches: (a) an individual/action and situation conception that cannot be dissociated; (b) the role of experience in cognition; (c) embodied cognition; and (d) cognition and culture.

2.1 *Individual/Action and Environment*

The beginning of the cognition stream is generally identified with the work of Lucy Suchman (1987, 1993), who showed the distributed and opportunistic nature of learning in relation to the dominant paradigm in cognitive psychology that has been cognitivism, where learning is primarily a symbolic and individual internal process (Paige & Daley, 2009). Research from the cognitivist paradigm conceptualizes learning as a symbolic information processing system such as computers: selecting stimuli from the situation that are relevant to the action to be taken. Lucy Suchman's work (Theureau, 2004b) has highlighted a new way of conceptualizing the notion of situation (resulting from a "bundle of hypotheses" already put forward a few years earlier in response to the paradigm of cognition as an information processing system, as explained in Theureau (2004b), and more specifically the stream of cognitive anthropology (Corcuff, 2008; Hutchins, 1995) and a new reading of Vygotsky's psychological work. In summary: "cognition is not located in the head, but in an in-between, between the actor and the situation, to which the other actors belong. Consequently, on the one hand, the relevant cognitive phenomena mainly concerns perception and action, and on the other hand, the essential place of their study is the work situation itself, because if one tries to study them by moving from a work situation to a laboratory situation, one risks losing them all[3]" (Theureau, 2004b, p. 7). Cognition is therefore not conceptualized as having elements existing outside the actor but is inseparable from his interaction with the world.

Hutchins' work develops the notion of distributed cognition. His famous study on aircraft piloting simulators (Hutchins, 1995) highlights the statement that "cognition is distributed between actors and material supports that together constitute a 'system of distributed cognition' (or 'cognitive ecology unit')" (Theureau, 2019). In other words, cognitive processes are inseparable from the material but also sociocultural environment in which they are deployed. Studying or being interested in cognitive processes thus implies understanding and a unit of analysis including an individual/action/environment system.

It is the dynamic that the actor maintains in a work situation mediated by his activity (a "situation" must be understood as the set of constraints that influences the actor's action) that is the subject of researches resulting from the French-speaking ergonomic approach (Ombredane & Faverge, 1955). This research field aims to improve human relations to work. The notion of activity is crucial here because it is the product of (a) the state of the subject (the individual known as the actor), (b) the situation in which it takes place, and (c) whose results lead back to changes in the actor and the situation. The action then becomes the revealer of the cognitive processes underlying the interpretation of a situation by an actor in (a) a specific state, (b) with a given intention, and (c) provides anchors for the future action's development.

An action is therefore the result of a form of a situation's interpretation by an actor and is concomitant with the sensorimotor processes.

Research in professional didactics (Pastré, 2011; Pastré et al., 2006) has strongly contributed to the development of professional training programs based on activity analysis and cognitive processes resulting from the relationship of the actor to the situation. To sum up, the activity is organized by a certain number of pragmatic concepts that allow the professional to both diagnose the state of the situation, to understand what is happening, and to act on its progress in an efficient way: These concepts are never evoked as such by professionals but inhabit formal and informal exchanges. The main idea of professional didactics has been to identify these concepts in the activity (see the work of Pastré on the activity of injection molding machines) (Pastré et al., 2009) and to transpose them (in the manner of the didactics of disciplines in teaching) to professional training. These trainings are therefore based on the real activity of the operators and the pragmatic concepts relating to class situations useful for a given professional field.

[3] Translated by the author.

2.2 The Role of Experience

If the hypothesis of the activity as it is described in particular by French-speaking ergonomic research is taken seriously, then the actor's activity produces an immediate experience (as in "to experiment"), which aggregates and organizes the actor's future knowledge (as in the expression: "having experience"). Experiential learning carried out by researchers such as Kolb (1984) and Schön (1983) focuses on how concrete experience is transformed into a more general and abstract experience that can be mobilized in a wide variety of situations.

For Kolb (1984), learning proceeds from concrete experimentation by the actor, followed by a reflexive process that feeds into the construction of abstractions that are then explored in new concrete experiments. This verification leads to new hypotheses, new questions, thus leading to a new cycle. This learning cycle shows the importance for Kolb of the relationship between the three factors involved in this process: the experience as subjectively lived by the actor in singular situations (he experiences and takes part in an experience), the understanding of this situation, and the construction of knowledge from this context. Kolb has also developed a classification of "learner" styles characterized by the pre-eminence of one or the other of these stages of the cycle (Kolb, 1999). Simulation-based training is generally designed according to an alternation of three phases (simulated briefing–scenario–debriefing). It is mainly oriented toward a reflexive approach to learning, which is characterized by the importance given to the debriefing phase compared to the realization of the simulated scenario (Horcik, 2014).

The notion of experience is also mobilized in research on the embodied dimension of cognition, which is part of a phenomenological perspective of action in that it can only be known through the actor's point of view (Sartre, 1956) (Merleau-Ponty, 1962) and more particularly on the paradigm of enaction.

2.3 Embodied Cognition

Embodied cognition is centered on the relationship between cognition and its "embodied" dimension (Shapiro, 2014). It emerged in the 1990s initiated by Varela Thompson and Rosch (F. Varela et al., 1991) and then Maturana and Varela (1992).

The research stream is based on the postulate of autopoiesis developed by Maturana and Varela (Maturana & Varela, 1992) and Varela, Thompson, and Rosch (1991). This paradigm postulates cognition as the result of autopoiesis: the property of a living system to produce itself despite disturbances and from disturbances. These disturbances may come from the environment but also from the system itself. The dynamics of the interactions between the system (called actor) and its environment is called structural coupling. This coupling is said to be asymmetrical insofar as it is the structure of the actor that selects the disturbances of the environment impacting its own organization. Understanding the history of coupling (the interactions between the actor and the environment) is therefore a matter of cognition.

Cognition is constantly accompanying action: as making a world relevant for an action to emerge or enact a world also known as the "own world." The notion of own world does not correspond to an objective world "already there" to which the coupling adapts but corresponds to a set of disturbances relevant for the actor at a given moment. Coupling is, for example, determined not only by the sensory-motor capacities of the system but also by its concerns or intentions (such as concerns related to nutrition or protection). The actor's world is thus inseparably linked to the action. In this paradigm, acting is equivalent to knowing, thus expressing knowledge already assimilated and under construction. Cognition does not therefore result from an adaptive intention of the system but from an essential and inherent dynamic of life: "By using the term embodied we mean to highlight two points: first, that cognition depends upon the kinds of experience that come from having a body with various sensorimotor capacities, and second, that these individual sensorimotor capacities are themselves embedded in a more encompassing biological, psychological and cultural context" (Varela et al., 1999, pp. 172–173).

The notion of "own world" is close to the notion of Umwelt by Von Uexküll (1965), who in the framework of his research in biology put forward the hypothesis that each living species has its own world, which is simultaneously defined by its perceptive capacities and the elements determining its survival from its environment.

To take into account the coupling for the study of human activity means to analyze the actor's own world and to simultaneously consider cognition, action, and environment as indissociable elements of a dynamic.

According to Maturana and Varela (1992), the surface effect of the dynamics of the structural coupling of an actor and his environment could be the subject of a symbolic description admissible in the framework of the human sciences. This surface effect is associated by Theureau (2004a, 2006) with the concept of pre-reflective consciousness developed by Sartre (1956) that allows one to build a methodology to access this surface effect in professional situations.

Let us also mention Lakoff and Johnson (Lakoff & Johnson, 1980; Lakoff, 2012) and their work in cognitive linguistics that highlight the crucial role of our human, physical condition in the construction of language metaphors that shape our relationship with knowledge. Positive elements, happiness and unhappiness, the relationship with time, and cause and effect relationships are conceptualized by means of sensory metaphors (time through movement, happiness through a vertical station) derived from our sensory experience. Locating these metaphors is particularly interesting for understanding cognition and how the actor conceptualizes the world.

2.4 Cognition and Culture

As we have seen, the principles resulting from situated cognition give primacy to the point of view of the system constituted by the interactions of the actor with his environment. However, as we have mentioned, this environment/situation is made up of a given cultural anchoring resulting from a common history, shared practices that influence the action, perception, and cognitive processes of the actor (Theureau, 2004a). It is the actor's participation in these social practices (professional or not) that will shape the understanding of the situations. A fundamental notion of this current is the notion of community of practice.

This notion developed by Lave et Wenger (Lave & Wenger, 1991) concerns the positioning of the actor who is inserted in a context defined with its rules, principles, and specific roles and fields of action that are attributed to him/her in the framework of his/her activity.

This theory highlights the existing dynamics between newcomers (beginners, or people integrating teams) and old-timers (experts, people already integrated in the socio-professional context) working together on a certain number of common tasks. To summarize briefly, beginners integrating a new activity are first entrusted with a series of peripheral tasks that do not correspond to the core activity. Gradually, as they become part of the team, they are given tasks of increasing importance in the form of coaching supervised by an old-timer until they become professionals themselves, recognized by their community and independent, thus developing an identity specific to the community.

This theory corresponds to the apprenticeship systems used in traditional training courses where a master trains an apprentice, but the vocational and continuing training systems have also developed principles derived from community of practice, in particular the notion of the role model, and the identification processes of experts in the field, but also in the creation of groups of students to reinforce the students' sense of belonging to a company, a profession, or a social role. This notion is nowadays exploited in project management insofar as the development of means of communication facilitates the pooling of different actors that have common practices.

For training design, this means that the actor's relationship with the world is constantly creating meanings that can be partially shared. The preliminary study of the activity, which consists of the actor's relationship with the world, the meaning he gives to his action, and his perception of the world in which he participates, using observation and interview methods, allows the modeling of work situations and the possibility to design training courses focused on the key aspects of the targeted activity (Flandin & Ria, 2014; Olry & Vidal-Gomel, 2011; Ria & Leblanc, 2011). Research in French-speaking ergonomics also mentions that the analysis of the training activity is also a source of development and learning (Durand, 2008).

In actual practices of simulation-based training design in the medical field, these dimensions seem relatively absent to us insofar as the situations serving as a basis for the scenarios seem to take little account of the actors' point of view and the construction of their activity. In the following section, we will detail the points that we believe are crucial to address in order to take into account the principles of cognition in simulation.

3 Three Missed Appointments Between Medical Simulation and Situated Cognition

We identify three major focus points for the development of simulation-based training session on taking the paradigm of situated cognition as a design guide. The first one concerns the building of scenarios based on situations and real practices. The second concerns the relationship with the learning situation as a provider of affordances, anchors relevant to the participant (Durning & Artino, 2011). The third theme is the transfer of knowledge acquired within a group (a community of practice) to an individual and from the individual to his or her daily practice (Paige & Daley, 2009). In this part, we are talking about three missed appointments insofar because, after studying the recent literature, three major references to the current state of situated cognition structure the conceptualization of simulation-based training programs: (a) building scenarios from situations and practices; (b) the bodily dimension of learning; and (c) the primacy of the participant's sense of action.

We believe that some of the elements mentioned in the previous section may allow for an extension of the design principles in simulation-based training or may reorient some design strategies. After a brief summary of the state of the literature on the three topics, we will successively make some conceptual propositions in order to show a broader side of the situated cognition approach for training design.

3.1 Building Scenarios from Situations and Practices

Training programs using simulation focus on specific occupations and scenarios centered on particular professions. The interdisciplinary simulation trends that are currently undergoing strong development are also based on the notion of community of practice in the sense that the scenarios seek to integrate the cultural and socio-professional context of the targeted activity, thus questioning the functional link between the different professional fields. The objective is to foster cohesion between the different members of the same profession. Reflection and exchanges are promoted and facilitated by the trainer (Onda, 2012).

3.1.1 Taking into Account Simulation as a Cultural Practice

One of the difficulties of the concept of community of practice applied to training design is that the place of "cultural" practices in the design is today dominated by the vocabulary of training policies and human resources policies obliterating real practices in the field. The problem is therefore in the constitutions of curricula, which are today in medicine mainly based on "evidence-based" research, incident reports, or emblematic cases. This raises questions about the purpose of training systems in medical institutions. Should they adapt to field practices (or adapt existing practices that can be improved) or follow the principles of harmonization of training systems induced by the globalized research trends currently at work in medical education research and development?

A crucial point raised by the work of Dieckmann et al. (2007) is that the simulator and more broadly simulation-based training constitute specific social practices with their own codes that must also be integrated by the learners. Dieckmann et al. (2007) submit an analysis of simulation programs using Goffmann's framework theory of experience (Goffmann, 1974) and show that these cultural practices and norms play a very important role in the design of simulation training either as constraining the activity of the trainers or as having a poorly evaluated impact on the activity of the participants during the simulated sequences and thus potentially on the learning that takes place there.

Mc Niesh (2015) also shows that the simulated scenarios are the subject of constant negotiation between the trainers, producing a scenario and implementing a certain number of instructions, and the activity of the students constantly "altering" or challenging these elements individually and collectively. These include familiarization of the context by the students, simulating the role of an experienced nurse (the study focuses on nurses in training), learning to work by making mistakes within the simulator, practicing an activity while being observed and evaluated, learning to consider the dummy as a real patient in order to perform an adequate activity in simulation, and learning collectively and anticipating the debriefing. These different elements allow us to re-evaluate the notion that simulated scenarios are a mirror of the targeted professional activity.

The right balance is thus to be requested by the designers of this type of program. What is the importance given to individual learning vs. group learning vs. learning about the standards of the profession? To what extent do training systems tolerate the presence of practices that sometimes deviate from the norm that originate in the field? We believe that "practical" and "cultural" learning is mainly taught in the field on a day-to-day basis and that the challenge of simulation-based training is to determine the status of daily practice and its sometimes marginal practices in teaching. To this, cultural dimension of learning is added the concept of simulation as a social practice, which is not explicitly addressed in terms of design (Glavin, 2009).

3.1.2 Developing Non-curricular Training Programs

One of our suggestions follows Flandin's (in this book), which is that simulation-based training in the medical field could add risk management models to their design principles. Of course, simulation in health care has a long practice of training for risk situations, especially with the development of training content related to CRM (Gross et al., 2019), but this particular method is based on a curriculum that includes safety training, but also communication techniques and situation awareness. We think that this type of training could also benefit from approaches that do not directly use curriculum-based design principles.

De Bisschop and Leblanc in this book mention the three modalities for training, namely transmissive, training, and developmental. We believe that developmental training opens up the prospect of non-curricular type training (i.e., not referring to a precise pedagogical content but rather to a type of situations). Our previous work on the training of novice nurse anesthetists consisted in maintaining the anesthesia procedure in a critical situation (incidental situation) (Horcik et al., 2014). As such, we believe that many simulator-based training courses in the medical field do not specifically make this distinction and combine curricular content (derived from evidence-based research guidelines) and developmental training aimed at maintaining an activity in a variety of situations. This type of training seems interesting insofar as it allows focusing the design more on situations and their characteristics rather than on a content of knowledge or procedures to master. They are halfway between training of the transmissive type and training of the training type and allow nuancing the mastery of these situations (constitution of knowledge on situations given by novices, for example, has regular training of skills by more expert participants). Van Daele in this book mentions the idea that a good balance between interpersonal trust between the participants allows flexibility in reacting to the hazards of the situation and distrust/vigilance/maintenance of safe procedures, which are of course essential in risk areas.

Flandin in this book also proposes four axes, which can lead to simulation-based design principles: "enactment/reenactment," "curriculum/discovery," "disturbance/reassurance," and "trust/distrust." If these four dimensions are taken into account in the training design, they then allow to work on the notion of situation while taking into account the notion of experience. Boccara, Delmas, and Darses in this book specify the notion of situation and present a method for designing scenarios based on the analysis of work situations. This proposal complements the construction of scenarios based on typical skills or procedures.

Schot, Flandin, and Goudeaux (2019) have designed a training program on a non-curricular approach based on the principle of disruption. By creating trainings that shock, or disrupt the actor's activity, it is hoped that the latter will modify his understanding in order to restore a state of equilibrium. Once again, the phases of indeterminacy of the actor's activity are hoped to bring about development.

If the culturally anchored dimension of the activity and the primacy of the meaning allocated by the actor to his activity are taken seriously in simulation-based design, it seems essential to us to think about the developmental potential of the situations and the activity itself. The dynamic dimension of knowledge building allows strong exploitation of the trainee's experience as long as the trainers are familiar with the specific interview and questioning methods and the participants are also familiar with the expression of their activity (see Becceril and Ortega in this book on concomitant verbalizations). We believe that training based on this experience without a prior curriculum could be a powerful lever for professional development in the health professions.

3.2 Relationship with the Learning Situation

3.2.1 Bodily Dimension of Learning and Sensitive Experience

The literature on simulation-based training mentions the importance of the bodily dimension of learning. This is also frequently related to the dimensions of situated learning as integrating the whole body as a means of cognition. Simulation-based training that emphasizes the active participation of learners is therefore based on this principle. However, to our knowledge this dimension is not translated as design principles for simulation-based training. The fundamental principle of simulation-based training programs is the proximity of activity and experience of situations with reality, but the dimension of the body as mediating learning is little explored.

Surgical training has traditionally developed part task trainers, focused on a specific procedure to be mastered by the trainees. These simulation training techniques have also profoundly modified the way surgery training is delivered (Okuda et al., 2009).

Pediatrics also makes a wide use of standardized patients for the work of confrontations with families. This discipline also uses simulation to test the development of guidelines in relation to neonatal resuscitation. The importance of authentic activities and situations/tools is therefore a founding principle of the design (Okuda et al., 2009).

Kneebone's work (Kneebone, 2016, 2020; Kneebone & Woods, 2014) after focusing on the development of simulators for surgical teams focuses on the "sensitive" "unteachable" dimension of surgical learning. It also uses the practice of surgery to explore the links with different professions whether they are direct (tailor, dressmaker) or indirect such as the performance of an activity under stress (restaurant services, musicians, etc.). This work focuses on analogies between various professional practices and surgery. This research postulates the transferability of skills through the identification of similar skills, allowing a step aside. It should also be noted that other of his research also focuses on the question of points of view, in particular the documentation of the practices of experienced surgeons who are now retired and who practice old procedures on a simulator with young surgeons in training to encourage verbalization. Beyond the objectives pursued by this work, it is very interesting insofar as it voluntarily and stereotypically brings into play the communities of practice and the links between old-timers and newcomers whose relationships are mediated by an old practice that sheds light on the current progress of the discipline.

According to Onda (2012), much research on simulation focuses on the evaluation of training and its effectiveness on the attitude and perception of students rather than on an actual measurement of skill acquisition. For nursing, the links between body-related skill acquisition and simulation-based training programs are not yet clear.

3.2.2 Mimetic Experience

Research on experience, and particularly research on embodied cognition, has also shown that some learning is linked to a metaphorical dimension (Lakoff & Johnson, 1980). Kneebone's work that we have already cited above focuses on this question. What are the occupations, the activities that may be related to the surgical activity and how these apprenticeships are carried out? What can these different environments teach to the learning of surgery? This lever is powerful because it opens up to other types of environments and goes beyond the notion of goal situation. In short, it allows for innovation. As an example, let us mention the research that aimed to produce a tissue simulator, produced by a lacemaker for surgery (R. Kneebone et al., 2019). This metaphor of human tissues and textiles allows a new and low-cost exploration of the delicacy of the gestures to be performed to suture two pieces of tissue without breaking and tearing them.

We mentioned that simulation training is based on the actor's experience and the construction of meaning. Our research has shown the specificity of the experience during simulation-based training sessions as being complex and constantly oscillating between commitments oriented toward the training program ("what do the trainers expect from me?") and the target activity ("what do I have to do to solve the situation?"). We refer to this specific experience as "mimetic" as it is not the same experience than the goal activity it mimics. As a result, part of the design is somehow beyond the control of the designing trainer as he cannot influence the totality of this experience. By taking seriously, the complexity of this experience and its elusive aspect would allow a refocusing of the scenarios questioning trainers and tracking of knowledge construction processes (Horcik, 2014). This also raises the question of training the trainers to identify and verbalize the participants' experience.

Another point raised by the research of Harder et al. (2013) shows that there is an interest in simulation-based training that is frequently explored, which is the role change between different medical professions. It shows that these role changes are not sufficiently thought out and scripted to have a real impact on learning. However, we believe that this shift can also promote mimetic experience and the relationship with one's own profession.

3.3 Skills Transfer

The issue of learning transfer is linked to the ability of learners to reuse the training content in their workplace. Numerous studies have focused on this issue, and simulation-based training is a tool that is particularly well suited to the transfer of complex situations through training or the development of potentially fruitful anchors for work in real-life situations. This question is strongly linked to the topic of meaning that is given to the actor in his action and his understanding of the context.

3.3.1 Primacy of Actor's Meaning

Research on situated cognition and simulation emphasizes the fact that the learner uses the context available to him according to his experience and his interpretation of the situation to act efficiently. Simulated scenarios as they are widely used today are based on the strong principle that they feed the debriefing in order to enhance learner's awareness by means of a reflective debriefing, which allows coupling reflection on action with reflection in action and guides this process of creating meaning: Within the setting of simulation, perhaps the most obvious form of reflection is reflection on action. This typically occurs via a debriefing process after the conclusion of the scenario. Debriefing is a "period of self-reflection about what just took place. The overall purpose is to uncover the cognitive frame that was operating during the experience and make sense of external stimuli through internal cognitive frames" (Kuiper et al., 2008, p. 2). Ideally, reflective discussions revolve around the issues of the way in which clinical problems were identified and solved and the effectiveness of attempted interventions. This process allows for the formation of abstractions and, it is hoped, leads to the development of self-correcting practice habits when faculty can help students recognize and resolve clinical and behavioral dilemmas that occurred during the simulation (Horcik et al., 2014; Onda, 2012; Rudolph et al., 2006). Our research's results showed that the reflexive aspects during debriefings are often overused comparatively to the simulated situations the trainees were put in, creating a gap between the lived experience in the simulator and the debriefing. This often leads to leaving the scenario as background noise, reducing the simulation to any other theoretical lesson. This leads, through a progressive drift effect, emptying of meaning of certain sequences of a pedagogical program or, in any case, not to question them in terms of the objectives pursued (Horcik et al., 2014).

A second problematic aspect would be to deprive designers of potential future orientations and developments for the design of training courses that could be partly creatively based on principles derived from learning theories. If this principle of primacy of the learner's point of view is taken seriously in the design, it is at the heart of training for beginners, which is intended to train their interpretation of contexts and actions by making them intelligible. This is the object of the work of the current professional didactics (Pastré, 2011) and of the work of Ria et al. (Flandin & Ria, 2014; Ria & Leblanc, 2011). In the literature on medical education, the importance of mentors is paramount insofar as they make sure that the requirements of professional practices and mastery of standards are met. As we mentioned before, it is interesting to note that there is research that allows participants to explore roles other than their own at the time of training by playing the role of other professionals. This has shown mixed results (Harder et al., 2013). This aspect is used more often to occupy participants who are not the "primary" roles targeted by the training. Harder especially insists on the fact that this element could be potentiated if the scenarios strongly include work on these roles in truly interprofessional systems.

Durning and Artino (2011) mention that situated cognition theories allow training designers to think of content as more than just training. The role of the designer/trainer must therefore take into account and organize the teaching according to the environment from the perspective of the learners in addition to the content of the course. These questions show that teaching in medical education is still struggling to fully grasp the environment as fully affordant (Billett, 2010). Traditionally, the part between "teaching" and facilitation with students is determined according to their level. The more experienced professionals the participants are, the less teaching part is required and the more facilitation part is important (Rudolph et al., 2007). Durning and Artino (2011) reintroduce a planning aspect into the trainer's role as facilitator, also informing this notion of role model or expert often referred to in the medical literature.

It is also interesting to note that there is a great temptation for the designer/trainer to start piloting situations rather than the training sessions themselves. Simulation-based training allows many possibilities for trainers to modulate the learning context. But in doing so, is it possible that the main focus of these sessions slowly drifted from a focalization on learning to a focus on the situation itself?

"The teacher should not only spend time on drafting discussion points for the session, he should consider, for example, learner perspectives and preparation, potential group dynamics, tools available in the teaching environment (artifacts) to assist the learner and how to best optimize them, and authenticity of the instructional format (how close to actual practice are the materials). Situativity theory would argue that it all matters and though the instructional designer cannot control how the different factors interact, explicitly paying attention to (and adjusting, as much as is possible for the teacher) the components of the factors and their interactions can optimize learning. This model also provides a scaffold for changing instruction by encouraging teachers to focus on not only the content, but also on these other factors and how they play out in the session." (Durning & Artino, 2011, p. 196).

Working with the trainees' experience as a fundamental principle of scenario design therefore partly helps to move away from the idea that reflexive learning is the only way to make trainees learn. By analyzing situations beforehand in terms of the actors' perception of their situation and activity (whether novice or not) and consciously transposing them into a simulated scenario, it seems easier to confront experience and activity from different points of view and expertise and thus promote their transfer.

3.3.2 Toward a Positive Conception of Risk and Doubt

One of the key aspects of simulation training is learning procedures or ways of acting in common or degraded situations. The hoped-for challenge here is to learn ways to manage the crisis in a real situation. Simulation-based training frequently mentions the characteristic of these trainings to constitute a "protected space" where the error can be fully experienced. Our research as well as that of other authors qualifies these assertions insofar as they have shown that the experience of participants in these trainings is complex and oriented toward an expectation of problematic elements (Dieckmann et al., 2007; Horcik et al., 2014). Moreover, the collective and artificial dimension of this environment makes the experiences of error particularly salient despite the efforts of trainers to make these experiences constructive.

The work of De Bisshop and Leblanc in this book shows training for leaders in the high-intensity military environment, in an environment where participants are forced to organize their activity to deal with the different eventualities threatening their integrity and that of their group. One of the key points of this research is that risk is here thought as a component of action and not as an object to be avoided or controlled exogenously. This seems to us to be a complete break with simulation training in the medical field where risk is essentially addressed to be controlled by means of procedures and cases resulting from evidence-based research. By designing high-intensity training courses based on the disruption of the trainees' activity and exploiting the doubt or wanderings of the participants as a learning vector (see Flandin and Bombeke in this book) for the medical field, we believe that this could open up the development of attentional and reactive capacities in the event of a crisis.

It can be assumed that the practices initiated with the development of simulation-based training are not simply pedagogical and theoretical quarrels "off the ground." They are part of research and the development of programs in tension with related training methods and programs, training policies, and hospital management. Thus, it can be assumed that the assimilation of new safety standards has somehow taken precedence over the exploratory aspect of professional practices via simulation and a real turning point in the way of thinking about professional practices in the medical field.

4 Conclusion

We believe that a large part of the systems currently deployed in training institutions are partly based on these presuppositions, but in a more or less conscious way. What we are trying to argue is that a conscious endorsement of these principles by designers–trainers may open up to a clarification of the design steps. As Flandin mentions in this book, the relationship between analysis and design may need to be rethought in a more detailed way concerning simulation-based training. Is the analysis at the level of the work situation, the learner's activity within the simulation, or the conduct of the simulation? A fine analysis of the reference activity as described in the other chapters of this book can allow for the precision of the contents and to take into account the sociocultural aspects of the activity in which the actors are involved, their level of mastery of the activity, and to work on the design of scenarios.

We also think it is important to take into account that training programs including simulation training are nowadays governed by training policies and academic circles. In this sense, we realize that these design changes in the daily activity can be a source of difficulty in challenging traditional design principles such as the idea of a non-competitive design of training or to promote the experience of the trainees without the transmission of previously established procedures.

This chapter invites us to consider the design of simulation training in the medical field in the light of theories from the field of situated cognition. This imprecise and biased account is intended more as an appeal to consider these theories as the foundations of the design of simulation training programs than as an exhaustive review of theory and literature.

References

Billett, S. (2010). The practices of learning through occupations. In S. Billett (Éd.), *Learning through practice* (pp. 59–81). Springer Netherlands.

Birden, H., Glass, N., Wilson, I., Harrison, M., & Usherwood, T. (2013). Teaching professionalism in medical education : A best evidence medical education (BEME) systematic review. *Medical Teacher, 35*(7), 1252–1266.

Bracq, M.-S., Michinov, E., & Jannin, P. (2019). Virtual reality simulation in nontechnical skills training for healthcare professionals a systematic review. *Simulation in Healthcare: Journal of the Society for Simulation in Healthcare, 14*(3), 188–194.

Corcuff, P. (2008). Aaron V. Cicourel : De l'ethnométhodologie au problème micro/macro en sciences sociales. *SociologieS [online]*. http://journals.openedition.org/sociologies/2382.

Dennick, R. (2016). Constructivism : Reflections on twenty five years teaching the constructivist approach in medical education. *International Journal of Medical Education, 25*(7), 200–205.

Dieckmann, P., Gaba, D., & Rall, M. (2007). Deepening the theoretical foundations of patient simulation as social practice. *Simulation in Healthcare: Journal of the Society for Simulation in Healthcare, 2*(3), 183–193.

Durand, M. (2008). Un programme de recherche technologique en formation des adultes. *Éducation et Didactique, 2*(3), 97–121.

Durning, S., & Artino, A. (2011). Situativity theory : A perspective on how participants and the environment can interact : AMEE Guide no. 52. *Medical Teacher, 33*(3), 188–199.

Flandin, S., & Ria, L. (2014). Un programme technologique basé sur l'analyse de l'activité réelle des enseignants débutants au travail et en vidéoformation. *Activités [online], 11*(2).

Glavin, R. (2009). Using simulations for education, training, and research. *Simulation in Healthcare: Journal of the Society for Simulation in Healthcare, 4*(3), 184.

Goffmann, E. (1974). *Frame analysis : An essay on the organization of experience*. Harvard University Press.

Gross, B., Rusin, L., Kiesewetter, J., Zottmann, J. M., Fischer, M. M., Prückner, S., & Zech, A. (2019). Crew resource management training in healthcare : A systematic review of intervention design, training conditions and evaluation. *BMJ Open, 9*(2), 1–13.

Harder, N., Ross, C., & Paul, P. (2013). Student perspective of roles assignment in high-fidelity simulation : An ethnographic study. *Clinical Simulation in Nursing, 9*, 329–334.

Horcik, Z. (2014). *Former par la simulation : De l'analyse de l'expérience des participants à la conception de formations par simulation.* Phd thesis, University of Geneva [online]. https://archive-ouverte.unige.ch/unige:4083.

Horcik, Z., Savoldelli, G., & Durand, M. (2014). A phenomenological approach to novice nurse anesthetists' experience during simulation-based training sessions. *Simulation in Healthcare: Journal of the Society for Simulation in Healthcare, 9*(2), 94–101.

Hutchins, E. (1995). How a cockpit remembers its speeds. *Cognitive Science, 19*(3), 265–288.

Johnson, E., Lasater, K., Hodson-Carlton, K., Siktberg, L., Sideras, S., & Dilliard, N. (2012). Geriatrics in simulation : Role modeling and clinical judgment effect. *Nursing Education Perspectives, 33*(3), 176–180.

Ju, L., Xue, L., Linlin, G., Rui, Z., Zhao, R., Cai, Q., Lu, Y., Wang, H., Meng, Q., & Wei, H. (2019). Effects of simulation-based deliberate practice on nursing students' communication, empathy, and self-efficacy. *Journal of Nursing Education, 58*(12), 681–689.

Kneebone, R. (2005). Evaluation in clinical simulation for learning procedural skills : A theory-based approach. *Academic Medicine, 80*(6), 549–553.

Kneebone, R. (2010). Simulation, safety and surgery. *Quality and Safety in Health Care, 19*, 147–152.

Kneebone, R. (2016). Simulation reframed. *Advances in Simulation, 1*(27). https://doi.org/10.1186/s41077-016-0028-8

Kneebone, R. (2020). *Expert : Understanding the path to mastery*. Viking.

Kneebone, R., & Woods, A. (2014). Recapturing the history of surgical practice through simulation-based re-enactment. *Medical History, 58*(1), 106–121.

Kneebone, R., Oakes, F., & Bicknell, C. (2019). Reframing surgical simulation : The textile body as metaphor. *The Lancet, 393*(10166), 22–23.

Kolb, D. (1984). *Experiential learning : Experience as the source of learning and development.* Prentice-Hall.

Kolb, D. (1999). *The Kolb learning style inventory, version 3*. Hay Group.

Kuiper, R. A., Heinrich, C., Matthias, A., Graham, M., & Bell-Kotwall, L. (2008). Debriefing with the OPT model of clinical reasoning during high Fidelity patient simulation. *International Journal of Nursing Education Scholarship, 5*(1), 1–14.

Lakoff, G. (2012). Explaining embodied cognition results. *Topics in Cognitive Science, 4*(4), 773–785.

Lakoff, G., & Johnson, M. (1980). *Metaphors we live by*. University of Chicago Press.

Lave, J., & Wenger, E. (1991). *Situated learning : Legitimate peripheral participation*. Cambridge University Press.

Maloney, S., & Haines, T. (2016). Issues of cost-benefit and cost-effectiveness for simulation in health professions education. *Advances in Simulation, 1*(13). https://doi.org/10.1186/s41077-016-0020-3

Maturana, H., & Varela, F. (1992). *The tree of knowledge*. Shambhala Publications.

Mc Niesh, S. (2015). Cultural norms of clinical simulation in undergraduate nursing education. *Global Qualitative Nursing Research*, 1–10. https://doi.org/10.1177/2333393615571361

Merleau-Ponty, M. (1962). *Phenomenology of perception*. Routledge.

Okuda, Y., Bryson, E., De Maria, S., Jacobson, L., Quinones, J., Shen, B., & Levine, A. (2009). The utility of simulation in medical education : What is the evidence? *Mt Sinai Journal of Medicine, 76*(4), 330–343.

Olry, P., & Vidal-Gomel, C. (2011). Conception de formation professionnelle continue : Tensions croisées et apports de l'ergonomie, de la didactique professionnelle et des pratiques d'ingénierie. *Activités, 8*(2). https://doi.org/10.4000/activites.2604

Ombredane, A., & Faverge, J.-M. (1955). *L'analyse du travail*. PUF.
Onda, E. (2012). Situated cognition : Its relationship to simulation in nursing education. *Clinical Simulation in Nursing, 8*, 273–280.
Østergaard, D., Dieckmann, P., & Lippert, A. (2011). Simulation and CRM: Best practice & research. *Clinical Anaesthesiology, 25*(2), 239–249.
Paige, J., & Daley, B. (2009). Situated cognition : A learning framework to support and guide high-fidelity simulation. *Clinical Simulation in Nursing, 5*, 97–103.
Pastré, P. (2011). *La didactique professionnelle : Approche anthropologique du développement chez les adultes*. PUF.
Pastré, P., Mayen, P., & Vergnaud, G. (2006). La didactique professionnelle. Revue française de pédagogie. *Recherches en éducation, 154*, 145–198.
Pastré, P., Parage, P., Richard, J.-F., Sander, E., Labat, J.-M., & Futtersack, M. (2009). La résolution de problèmes professionnels sur simulateur. *Activités, 6*(1), 3–27.
Peeters, M., Sexton, M., Metz, A., & Hasbrouck, C. (2017). A team-based interprofessional education course for first-year health professions students. *Currents in Pharmacy Teaching and Learning, 9*(6), 1099–1110.
Ria, L., & Leblanc, S. (2011). Conception de la plateforme de formation Néopass@ction à partir d'un observatoire de l'activité des enseignants débutants : Enjeux et processus. *Activités, 8*(12), 151–172.
Rudolph, J. W., Simon, R., Dufresne, R., & Raemer, D. (2006). There's no such thing as "nonjudgmental" debriefing : A theory and method for debriefing with good judgment. *Simulation in Healthcare: Journal of the Society for Simulation in Healthcare, 1*(1), 49–55.
Rudolph, J., Simon, R., Rivard, P., Dufresne, R., & Raemer, D. (2007). Debriefing with good judgment : Combining rigorous feedback with genuine inquiry. *Anesthesiology Clinics*. https://doi.org/10.1016/j.anclin.2007.03.007
Sartre, J.-P. (1956). *Being and nothingness : An essay on phenomenological ontology*. Kensington Publishing.
Schön, D. (1983). *The reflexive practitioner : How professionals think in action*. Basic Books.
Schot, S., Flandin, S., Goudeaux, A., Seferdjeli, L., & Poizat, G. (2019). Formation basée sur la perturbation : Preuve de concept par la conception et le test d'un environnement numérique de formation en radiologie médicale. *Activités, 16*(2), 1–25.
Shapiro, L. (2014). *The Routledge handbook of embodied cognition*. Routledge.
Suchman, L. (1987). *Plans and situated actions : The problem of human-machine communication*. Cambridge University Press.
Suchman, L. (1993). Response to Vera and Simon's situated action : A symbolic interpretation. *Cognitive Science, 17*, 71–75.
Theureau, J. (2004a). *Le cours d'action : Méthode élémentaire*. Octarès.
Theureau, J. (2004b). L'hypothèse de la cognition (ou action) située et la tradition d'analyse du travail de l'ergonomie de langue française. *Activités*. https://doi.org/10.4000/activites.1219
Theureau, J. (2006). *Le cours d'action : Méthode développée*. Octarès.
Theureau, J. (2019). *Cognition distribuée et Cours d'action, Activités [online], 17*(2). https://doi.org/10.4000/activites.5308
Varela, F., Rosch, E., & Thompson, E. (1991). *The embodied mind*. MIT PRESS.
Varela, F. J., Thompson, E., & Rosch, E. (1999). *L'inscription corporelle de l'esprit*. Seuil.
Von Uexküll, J. (1965). *Mondes animaux et mondes humains*. Gonthier.
Walsh, K., & Jaye, P. (2012). The relationship between fidelity and cost in simulation. *Medical Education, 46*(12), 1227.
Yucel, C., Hawley, G., Terzioglu, F., & Bogossian, F. (2020). The effectiveness of simulation-based team training in obstetrics emergencies for improving technical skills. *Simulation in Healthcare: Journal of the Society for Simulation in Healthcare, 15*(2), 98–105.

The Psychological Validity of Training Simulations: Analysis of a Simulation with Role-Playing Games to Experiment the Gesture of "Relational Touch"

Christine Vidal-Gomel

Abstract This chapter proposes an analysis of a role-playing game simulation designed to train caregivers to the "gesture of relational touch"—i.e. a sequence of gestures practiced during the care supposed to give the patient a moment of relaxation and well-being. More than just a simple technique, the gesture of relational touch is a real personalised act of care and a multidimensional activity. We integrate these characteristics into the training design, particularly in a role-playing game simulation. Data were collected during four different training sessions. They were entirely recorded and transcribed. The different dimensions of relational touch that the trainees experimented with in the simulation situation are presented (e.g., the importance of continuity of contact with the patient). Some trainees found also resources to rediscover the meaning and value they attribute to their work. These results offer an opportunity to discuss the psychological validity of simulations, taking into account the opportunities for mediation they offer. It stresses that this simulation mobilizes the trainees' collective meaning of their trade and the shared resource that is "transpersonal history," which can be used in the design of simulations, thus providing "transpersonal mediations." It thus opens perspectives to place the profession at the heart of simulations for vocational training.

Keywords Role-playing-game simulation · Professional gesture · Mediation · Scheme · Transpersonal mediation

Due to the need to train caregivers without putting patients in a risky or uncomfortable situation, and in a context of important technological developments, simulation has become an essential tool in healthcare training. At the same time, these technological developments mask other forms of simulation such as role-playing games,

---

C. Vidal-Gomel (✉)
Centre de Recherches en Education de Nantes, University of Nantes,
Nantes, France
e-mail: christine.vidal-gomel@univ-nantes.fr

S. Flandin et al. (eds.), *Simulation Training through the Lens of Experience and Activity Analysis*, Professional and Practice-based Learning 30,
https://doi.org/10.1007/978-3-030-89567-9_5

which are essential when the training goal is to learn how to interact with a patient. Role-playing games are an old and inexpensive way of designing simulated situations for training (Demaurex & Vu, 2013). In this case, the scenario is played by one (or more) actor(s). Most often, the trainees themselves play these roles. They contribute to the "design in action" of a situation in which one (or more) trainee(s) will have to act a part for learning purposes. Currently, the healthcare world is trying to acquire a higher level of control of these situations through the use of simulated patients (patients who participate in a simulation exercise based on their own experience and appropriate training), standardized patients (healthy people trained to simulate a story and symptoms that are predefined in a script), the development of procedures, and the standardization of simulations (Barrows, 1993; Howley, 2013). This range of tools has an interest in itself: It allows the trainer to control the characteristics of the situations presented to the trainees. But what do these tools really allow us to learn about the work situations that are a priori targeted by these training courses, but can be very far from these standards and in which, most often, quality and reliability depend on adaptive behaviors rather than on the reproduction of learned processes (Hollnagel, 2013; Braithwaite et al., 2015)? What should we keep in mind regarding these work situations so as to make sure that they allow for professional development? Full-scale simulations answer these questions by reproducing some dimensions of the work situations as faithfully as possible in simulation exercises designed for training. And yet, several authors have underlined that this is not systematically the most relevant solution for professional training (Bainbridge & Ruiz Quintanilla, 1989; Samurçay & Rogalksi, 1998; Béguin & Pastré, 2002; Dahlstrom et al., 2009; Vidal-Gomel & Fauquet-Alekine, 2016). In this chapter, we aim at developing the reflection of Baker and Marshall (1989), who propose that we take into account the "psychological validity" of the simulation. We will analyze it from the perspective of the mediation—as defined by Vygotski (1978)—between the designed simulated situation and the category of situations that is supposed to be mastered by the end of the training course. We will base our reflection on the design and analysis of a simulation exercise for the training of health professionals in the gesture of relational touch. To begin with, we will define more precisely what we mean by experimenting and learning when we talk about professional training. Then, we will discuss what it means to analyze the validity of simulations from a perspective of mediation, and present the axes we selected in order to design a training course based on the use of a simulation exercise related to the gesture of relational touch. Four sessions of this training course have been analyzed. We will explain the methodology used and present our main results, notably some unexpected ones: The designed simulation gives nurses the opportunity to rediscover the meaning of their work. This will lead us to discuss the psychological validity of simulations.

1 Experimenting and Learning in a Simulated Situation

Experimenting and learning are closely tied together, sometimes even mixed up. And yet, their relationship is neither simple nor unequivocal. Indeed, although experience is necessary for acquiring professional skills, it is not sufficient, as everyone does not take advantage of a situation in the same way (Vidal-Gomel, 2007). Moreover, learning "on the job," from the situation, also has its limits. Controlling some work situations can require theoretical knowledge that cannot be acquired by oneself and/or at work. Furthermore, even in the case of more directly operational aspects of one's professional skills, everything cannot be learned in a work situation because of the risks it entails, or the rarity of some events, for instance.

Simulated situations are a way to compensate for these difficulties, while also offering learning opportunities. They are comprised of three phases that enable trainees to learn things before, during, and after the exercise (Vidal-Gomel & Fauquet-Alekhine, 2016):

- Before: The briefing phase can be used to acquire the necessary knowledge to perform the action required in the simulated situation in the next phase.
- During: Learning through performing the action is required in the simulated situation, possibly under the guidance of the trainer—i.e., the simulation itself. This phase allows trainees to feel and acquire new sensations, and have experiences related to the action and the situations presented to them.
- After: During the debriefing phase, it is necessary to give trainees the opportunity to conduct an in-depth analysis of what has been done (Samurçay & Rogalski, 1998). This leads to paying particular attention to the difference between the performance of the action and its results (success or failure), and the understanding of what has caused them. In other words, it is important to differentiate "success" and "understanding" (Piaget, 1974). During the debriefing phase, the analysis must allow for awareness, which is essential to conceptualization (Piaget, 1974; Samurçay & Rogalski, 1998). This point of view differs from what is usually said of debriefing in the healthcare sector in France. Indeed, according to the Granry and Moll report (2012)—which is considered as a reference on this topic—this phase of the simulation "must allow each participant to identify their strengths and weaknesses" (p. 62). This identification, on the condition that it is not exclusively normative, is only the first step in the realization process, where the detailed analysis of one's own activity or that of another person through auto- or allo-confrontation helps deepen the analysis (Pastré, 1999; Mollo & Falzon, 2004; Mollo & Nascimento, 2014).

Another advantage of simulated situations in training is that they allow trainees to apprehend risky situations without having to face the consequences, train in order to master rare procedures (Baker & Marshall, 1989), and experience the limits of a technological system or their own skills, which can contribute to improving the management of risky situations (Amalberti, 1996). They also enable trainers to select, reshape, or chunk some characteristics of work situations in order to facilitate learning processes and control their progress (Samurçay & Rogalski, 1998).

It is within this framework that we suggest apprehending the design and analysis of a simulation exercise for the training of health professionals in the gesture of relational touch.

2 Psychological Validity and Mediation in the Design of Training Simulations

To design a simulated situation for training, it is necessary to step aside and look at the work situations we want trainees to learn how to control: Indeed, a relevant training course does not systematically rely on the figurative representation of reality, but on its psychological validity. Therefore, it is necessary to understand "in what respects the simulation duplicates psychological features of real operation, including task complexity, perceptual skills, decision-making and stress" (Baker & Marshall, 1989, p. 295). From this perspective, the simulation becomes a means of mediation, supporting the development of the trainees' skills to ensure they can face a range of situations—those that are supposed to be mastered by the end of the training course. We examine here the relationship between the simulated situation and the targeted work situations, using the concept of mediation. This concept does not apprehend training course design from the perspective of reproduction; instead, it analyzes mediations as defined by Vygotski (1978), and thus allows us to apprehend the relationships between the simulated situations and the targeted work situation based on the professionals' activity in these training situations, and the meaning they give to these relationships.

Vygotski defined the notion of mediation as an "intermediate link" between the stimulus and the response that transforms the activity: "*The intermediate link in this formula is not simply a method for improving the previously existing operation, nor is a mere additional link in an S-R chain. Because this auxiliary stimulus possesses the specific function of reverse action, it transfers the psychological operation to higher and qualitatively new forms and permits humans, with the aid of extrinsic stimuli, to control their behavior from the outside. The use of signs leads humans to a specific structure of behavior that breaks away from biological development and creates new forms of a culturally-based psychological process*" (Vygotski, 1978, pp. 39–40). We take over this point of view to analyze the various mediations that training situations can offer and which promote development.

Several types of non-mutually exclusive mediations can be distinguished:[1]

[1] An analysis focusing on the trainer's activity would feature other types of mediations, for example, in the designing phase (Rabardel & Samurçay, op. cit.) or at the moment the simulation exercise is performed: In some cases, the trainer plays different kinds of roles and adjusts the variables of the simulated situation to the trainees' skills (Samurçay & Rogalski, op. cit.; Vidal-Gomel & Fauquet-Alekhine, 2016). We will not analyze those aspects of the simulation here.

- Pragmatic mediations oriented toward the goal of the action, its transformation, its management, etc., that concern the phase where the trainees perform the action (Rabardel & Samurçay, 2001; Béguin & Pastré, op. cit.). In a simulated situation, the goal is to do "something," to provide a product or a service, be it real or fictitious: performing a surgical procedure on a dummy or measuring the blood pressure of a peer in training, for instance.
- Epistemic mediations oriented toward acquiring knowledge regarding the object and its properties (Rabardel & Samurçay, op. cit.; Béguin & Pastré, op. cit.), which are crucial, when the goal is to have trainees perform a simulated surgical procedure, for example, in order to give them the means to acquire knowledge about it.
- Heuristic mediations that concern the relationships the subject develops with themselves through the use of the tool. Dubey (1997) looks into the reasons why pilots are so invested in flight simulation exercises. He demonstrates that the simulated situations enable them to manage their worries regarding the risks inherent to piloting an aircraft. Such simulations become a tool of psychological self-management.
- The simulated situations that lead to the development of skills needed for teamwork offer collaborative mediations (Samurçay & Rabardel, op. cit.). For example, cross-training, which consists in making each member of a team occupy the position of one of their colleagues during the simulation, allows them to acquire knowledge on the constraints and difficulties of other functions, thus fostering cooperation and mutual assistance and improving the team's efficiency (Salas & Cannon-Bowers, 2001).
- Finally, exercises based on simulated situations can be performed by trainees with the help of the trainer (Samurçay & Rogalski, 1998; Rabardel & Samurçay, op. cit.). The guidance they provide in the situation is a priori considered as a formative mediation.

3 Analyzing the Gesture of Relational Touch

The practice of relational touch, also called "massage therapy," has numerous benefits for patients dealing with pain (Ferrel-Torry, 1993) or anxiety (Oh, 2004), and in several medical specializations such as geriatrics (Harris, 2010), pediatrics (Pasturel, 2007), or cardiology (Anderson, 2007). In France, the practice of "massage" is the exclusive prerogative of masseur–physiotherapists since 1946. In this context that was not very favorable to the development of relational touch, efforts were made first of all to demonstrate the advantages of this practice for patients. In 2006, a health professional was able to have this skill officially recognized in the establishment she worked at. Since then, relational touch training courses have been developing[2] (Simon, 2012). To design such courses, it is necessary to understand what a professional gesture is.

When the activity is characterized by an observable involvement of the body in the action, as is the case with relational touch, the concept of professional gesture is often used to illustrate the required skills: The notion of gesture *"expresses the part played by the body in the activity"* (Leplat, 2013, p. 10).[3] Analyzing a gesture leads us to immediately consider that there is no such thing as the "right gesture," identical for everyone, that could be reproduced whatever the characteristics of the situation may be. The gesture and its quality depend on the way in which individuals have been able to take advantage of the constraints and resources of their own body, their environment, and the task they had to perform according to the objectives they had set for themselves (Brill, 2012).

The gesture cannot be reduced to its observable part. It includes biomechanical, psychological, social, and cognitive dimensions (Lémonie & Chassaing, 2014). The relational touch gesture mobilizes haptic sensations that simultaneously integrate cutaneous, proprioceptive, and motor information linked to the movements involved in cutaneous exploration (Gentaz, 2000). It also involves the whole body: Indeed, the movement of a one segment of the body when performing an action has repercussions on the rest of the body, which responds to it by, for example, maintaining balance. The pressure exerted with the weight of the body engages postural muscles and supports (Gaudez & Aptel, 2008).

Like any other activity, the professional gesture depends on the coupling of the subject's characteristics with those of the situation (Leplat, 1997). Thus, the work organization, the available spaces, etc., are determining factors. As is the case with any other activity, the gesture produces a result that can be assessed by the subject himself, another person or the professional organization. In return, the subject is transformed: Performing the gesture in the work situation contributes to the development of their health (in a lasting or transitory way, in the short, medium, or long term) and their skills. The professional gesture integrates principles that can be collectively elaborated (Tomàs et al., 2009).

We can explain professional gestures through the notion of "scheme" (Vergnaud, 2011). It is an invariant organization of the activity for a category of situations, an active organization of experience. It is important to note that it is not the activity in itself that never varies but its organization, its structure, in a manner of speaking. A scheme is composed of (Vergnaud, 2009):

[2] However, in France, the data related to relational touch are rare and the practice itself is not widely developed. The Joël Savatofski Institute, a training institute specializing in this field, estimates that in 2015, around 4000 people had been trained. According to the Minister of Health, that same year, there were 638,248 nursing staff.

[3] We focus here on the conscious, voluntary gesture of relational touch.

- a set of goals and sub-goals relevant to a certain category of situations;
- a set of rules of action or conditional reasoning processes (if... then...statements such as, for instance "if the situation is X, then I'd better do Y...") used to diagnose, predict, and make choices in a given situation;
- a set of operational invariants ("invariants opératoires") comprised of 1) concept designating situational characteristics that must be identified, modified, and/or controlled because they are of primary importance in the work process; and 2) propositions believed to be true that constitute the laws governing work processes and activities, according to the worker. Both concepts and theorems foster conditional reasoning and inferences in a situation;
- possibilities of dynamic inferences based on situational factors taken into account when in action (Tourmen et al., 2017, p. 348).

The notion of scheme allows us to take into account the multidimensional nature of professional gestures. Indeed, the scheme is "integrative": It comprises cognitive, biological, motivational, affective, and collective dimensions (Récopé et al., 2013). It is influenced by the characteristics of the situations in which it has been elaborated and evolves through assimilation and accommodation.

Schemes have both a private and a social dimension. We consider that every dimension of the scheme can be at least partially identified[4] and debated collectively, thus contributing to the construction of its social dimension that can be appropriated by individuals. Indeed, debating over experiences and being given the possibility to discuss the action in all its details, with appropriate methods, enable trainees to work on the link between their experience of the situation and the incarnated nature of the activity. According to Vygotski's works (1978), language is not merely an expression of the activity. It does not exhaust it nor can it translate it completely. However, using words to evoke the activity transforms it. Summing up some works in the field of neurosciences, Davezies (2012) contributes the following details: "*Evoking the action means simulating it inwardly [...]. The exchange of words does not only put one concept in relation with another, it circulates sensory-motor configurations between the interlocutors. It thus transmits, in the same movement, ideas and corporal dispositions to taking action. At the next opportunity, the activity will start again without needing to wait for reflection, but drawing from a database of dispositions to taking action enriched by discussion*" (op. cit., p. 10). The simulation we designed to train caregivers in relational touch is based on these considerations.

[4] The methods implemented, such as self-confrontation and allo-confrontation interviews (Mollo & Falzon, 2004), do not allow for a complete and systematic exploration of the implicit or embedded aspects of the activity.

4 Designing and Analyzing a Training Course in Relational Touch

We differentiate "the simulated situation" and the "simulation situation" (Vidal-Gomel & Fauquet-Alekhine, 2016). The simulated situation is the situation as it was designed and planned by the designers. It differs from the simulation situation, i.e., the simulation as it occurs according to the participants' actions (trainees and trainers), and the difficulties they face. The gap between the simulated situations and the simulation situations is the one that exists between what is planned and what is real, or between "work as imagined" and "work as done" (Wisner, 1995; Hollnagel, 2013; Hollnagel, 2017).

A number of choices must be made: What is the reference situation—i.e., the one that represents the category of situations which trainees should be able to manage at the end of the training course? What are the aspects of the reference situation that should be transposed into the simulated situation—i.e., what are the mediations provided to the trainees? What are the trainers' didactic choices?

Before accounting for the choices that were made for the simulation we are going to analyze, we will specify what kind of training course it was integrated into.

4.1 Training Course in the Gesture of Relational Touch

This training course in relational touch for health professionals was co-designed with the trainer. It takes two days, spaced a month apart. During the first day of training, the participants are invited to initiate a global reflection process on the importance of touch in the relationship between the caregiver and the patient, notably in the daily care gestures such as mobility-related help, nursing, or more technical medical care. They are then initiated to relational touch gestures that, after that first day, they will be able to use in their daily care routine, or even as a care gesture in itself after having identified a situation that calls for it (anxiety, pain, etc.). The second day of training takes place one month later, so as to give the participants some time to implement relational touch at their workplace. The beginning of the second training session is dedicated to the problems they may have encountered in their endeavors to use relational touch in a work situation. A discussion takes place to elaborate potential solutions with them. After that, the role-playing training sequence starts.

4.2 Choices Made for the Design of the Simulated Situation

For the reference situation, the choice was made to propose a relational touch intervention that could easily take place during the caregivers' daily work routine whatever their specialization (pediatrics, general medicine, etc.), that would not require specific equipment, and that would not take too long, since time constraints are often significant in hospitals.

The first transposition choice was made as early on as the selection of the reference situation. By choosing a reference situation that could easily take place during the caregivers' daily work routine, the designers integrate the constraints of day-to-day work into the simulation. Caregivers do not have much time to do their job (Estryn-Behar, 2013). In line with constructive ergonomics, the idea is to not reproduce idealized work situations during training, without making the trainees adapt to the characteristics of their position, but to aim at fostering individual development (Delgoulet & Vidal-Gomel, 2015). Furthermore, it was decided not to use "standardized patients" but to have trainees play the role of the patients.

Using role-playing games between trainees gives them the opportunity to learn without causing any inconvenience to the patient. Trainees work in pairs, one providing the massage and one receiving it. The "patient" is sitting on a chair; the "masseur" is standing up. The person receiving the massage can give feedback in real time, which provides valuable information for the learner (Leplat, 1970), notably on how to avoid eliciting unpleasant sensations in a future real patient. This simulation gives the learner the opportunity to experiment, try things, make mistakes, and learn without making a real patient uncomfortable. The massage is applied to the upper limbs, back, and nape of the neck, head, and face. This relational touch gesture is performed through the clothes.

Pragmatic mediations (performing a massage on a subject) aim at helping the learner acquire knowledge about the object (the massage and its effect on the subject receiving it should provide epistemic mediations) but also about the masseurs and the way they get involved in the action: heuristic mediations, for example, what strength should be exerted? What is the best posture to exert it correctly? How should the masseurs use the surface of their hands and fingers?

The didactic choices concern the organization and contents of the different phases of the simulation: briefing, performing the simulation, and debriefing. The briefing phase is short: All trainees are invited to carry out a quick relational touch technique—around 5–7 min long—that can be used in all care circumstances. Performing the simulation, the trainer's plan is to guide the performance of the massage by reminding the trainees of the various steps and conducting a precise scaffolding activity, not guiding one masseur in particular but addressing the whole group. This phase of the training course is less about explaining and correcting than allowing for debate and for the collective analysis, during the debriefing phase, of what has been acquired in the previous training phases and implemented during the simulation. The whole simulation situation is filmed. The debriefing phase is organized so as to allow for individual and collective in-depth analysis. During debriefing, the film is used as an aid to conduct an allo-confrontation interview (Mollo & Falzon, 2004) that can be schematically defined as a collective commentary on the traces of the activity (accessible via the filmed material), guided by a facilitator (here, the trainer), and requiring of all the actors that they adopt an understanding, judgment-free point of view. This interview is conducted mainly with the two volunteer actors who were filmed throughout the role-playing game, in the presence of all the other trainees, who can also watch the film. The interview is facilitated by the trainer who encourages the actors to comment on the images of their massage. She guides them and gets the trainee who plays the role of the masseur to talk about the experience (what they wanted to do, how they did it, what they felt), as well as the one who plays the role of the patient receiving the massage (questioned mainly on what they felt). Every participant is invited to take part in the debate at any time, without judgment.

The objective of the allo-confrontation is to create the conditions of a collective reflexive analysis. Debating, expressing divergent points of view, and conducting a collective analysis can indeed allow everyone to re-examine their own operating modes, discover others, identify their respective interests and limits, highlight difficulties, share them, and collectively find solutions. The various participants must be able to contribute without fear of being singled out or judged. The trainer makes sure that the established framework is respected (Mollo & Nascimento, 2014).

4.3 Data Collection and Analysis

All trainees were enrolled on a voluntary basis in the relational touch training course offered by their institution. They were all nurses and caregivers in activity. Four training sessions took place, each with about ten people. Every time, we filmed the role-playing game, focusing on a pair of volunteer trainees. The allo-confrontation interviews were also filmed with the consent of all attendees.

All filmed sessions were entirely transcribed. The analysis focuses on the exchanges that took place during the debriefing phase. They at least partially indicate what the trainees have the opportunity to learn through this simulation. The data analysis relies on the notion of "scheme" (op. cit.). We aim at identifying the components of the schemes that are verbalized: goals and sub-goals, processes, rules, inferences, and operational invariants.

For example:

- Goal: "I am trying to maintain contact,"
- Sub-goal: "If I want to maintain contact, I have to move my hands down,"
- Process: "I start with the shoulders, then I go down the arms, and then the hands,"
- Inferences: "her arm is supple, it is not rigid,"
- Operational invariants: "The pressure exerted with the whole weight of the body behind it is much better" is considered as a "property that is thought to be true regarding reality."

In this analysis, it is not so much the specific scheme implemented by an individual or the differences between individuals that interest us than the multiple dimensions it comprises, which can be experienced and learned by trainees.

5 Simulation Situation: What Have Trainees Been Able to Feel and Learn During Relational Touch Training?

Many dimensions of the relational touch gesture are expressed in the interactions that take place during the allo-confrontations; notably, one common goal emerges: getting the patient to relax. It is present in all the simulations. To reach it, it is necessary to massage the various body areas in a certain order: upper limbs, back, and nape of the neck, head, and face. Regularly and throughout the exercise, movements the participants say are meant to create "connection" that is performed on the whole body in order to give a more global physical sensation to the patient. This organized process is guided by the trainer (Vidal-Gomel et al., 2018). Additionally, the allo-confrontations highlight the importance of transitional phases between the different sub-goals: **A continuity of contact** has to be maintained. For example:

> *Trainer (T): Here, I see that when you reach the fingertips during the lissage* (NB: preliminary phase of the massage), *you put one hand directly back on the top of the head, why is that?*
> *Masseur (Me): Well, it's to* ***maintain contact****, so she won't feel "abandoned" since she's starting to relax...it's to create a connection, in fact, a* ***continuity****, because the fingertips and the head are distant from each other, so it's to* ***avoid surprising her*** *if all of a sudden once we've reached the fingertips, I touch the top of her head again. (allo-conf. extract, simulation 2)*

The notion of contact is central to the organization of the activity. It is an operational invariant that guides every phase of the massage: establishing contact and maintaining contact throughout the operation, until it is time to "break contact," in the words of one of the masseurs:

> *T: How do you feel the massage at that moment?*
> *Me: Well, not sure I'm doing it right! I'm trying to be coherent, to have a* ***continuity of contact*** *until the end! Anticipating the end, it means maintaining* ***a continuity of pressure. Until the moment you break contact****. (allo-conf. extract, simulation 1)*

The quality of the contact depends on the pressure exerted by the masseur. It must evolve according to the massaged areas: The pressure should not be the same when you massage the back, a shoulder blade, or the face. Here too, the trainer provides guidance regarding the modalities of the massage (Vidal-Gomel et al., op cit.): "So, the shoulder, light pressure, putty, hand, fingers"; for the back: "You remember, the bear paws!" However, the way the massage is performed and the patient is made to relax is also influenced by the sensations of the participants, which can be shared (see the two following extracts), and by physiological knowledge. For instance, one of the masseurs explains the choices she made while stretching her "patient's" arm: "It's for her body, to respect her anatomy, in fact." The following extracts concern the sensations felt by the participants:

T: Why do you focus on this area of the back?
Me: I'm trying to find something. When you want a massage, it's often this area that **calls for it.**
Person receiving the massage (Ms): Yes, ***that's how everyone feels****. It seemed logical to me, too. (allo-conf. extract, simulation 1)*

The way the masseurs position themselves in relation to the person receiving the massage and the way they distribute their body weight are essential conditions for exerting the desired pressure:

T: You seem to be shifting from one foot to the other?
Me: At that moment, yes, I was. You can't see it on the images, but **I was putting my weight on her back**. This way, **I don't overexert myself**: **I don't put too much strain on my back. It's more agreeable and more gradual at that moment**, because there is no strength in the wrong sense of the word; **it's not just the strength of the arms.**
Collective commentary of the group (CC): Yes, it's incredible this ***pressure with all the weight behind it, it's true that it prevents the masseur from overexerting herself, but it feels much better too, it is much more enveloping, soft and gradual at the same time*** *and* ***the pressure is good****, too! (allo-conf. extract, simulation 3)*

Other extracts also account for the involvement of the body in the action:

My body *follows the movement. Well, I mean with my hands! But my body as well!* Commenting on the fact that she is visibly shifting from one foot to the other, a masseur explains: *Actually, I'm trying to find what feels* ***the most comfortable for me, but for her as well.***

Various indicators are taken into account by the masseurs and help them control their actions: e.g., the "patient" facial expressions, or the tensions they can feel in their muscles:

At that moment, actually, I think I'm looking at her face: it's a nurse's reflex! It's to ***see whether she's relaxed, or tense****, in fact I'm checking if everything is alright. Her eyes are closed, so I guess it is... [...] if I move her arm gently, it's going to go lax, I guess, I mean here her arm is like* ***a ragdoll****, so that means she's relaxed [...] Well it's very* ***supple****, it's* ***not rigid****, you* ***can't feel any resistance****. You can't see it, but I can* ***feel it when I'm touching her****, when I'm handling her arm (allo-conf. extract, simulation 4).*

Several dimensions of the relational touch scheme were expressed during the allo-confrontations. The scheme is composed of the following elements: goal (getting the patient to relax), sub-goals (the various body areas, the different phases of the massage, the transitions), operational invariants that the massage relies on (contact, pressure, body weight; properties thought to be true regarding reality, identified from shared experiences or knowledge of human physiology), and lastly, indicators allowing the masseurs to control the action (facial expressions, feelings of tension or resistance of the muscles). The analyses we conducted thus led us to highlight the scheme of relational touch. It is important to note that it is not the same as the individual relational touch patterns developed by the trainees. To analyze those, it would have been necessary to conduct more in-depth interviews with each participant, and identify how their previous patterns had been mobilized and transformed during the training session, which was impossible due to the constraints of data collection. The dimensions of the scheme that have been identified are social dimensions common to everyone.

Additionally, the trainees playing the part of the patients had the opportunity to experience the sensations provided by the massage. They were able to share them during the debriefing phase and debate over them. The simulated situation created through the role-playing game allowed them to have a specific experience: that of a patient in an unusual situation: They benefited from a massage performed with a technique they were supposed to learn. They were put in a position where they could feel the effects of this massage. By trying to put this experience into words and sharing it with the collective, the trainees receiving the massage were able to inform their own experience and their understanding of the gesture of relational touch.

6 Relational Touch: Subjective Involvement, Relationship with Oneself and One's Profession

Performing the relational touch gesture is not merely a technical act. For instance, establishing contact with a patient requires preparation. You need to focus on yourself and your own sensations, as evidenced by this interaction between the masseur (Ms) and the person receiving the massage (Me):

> *Me: That part of the massage was great! I could feel this warm sensation on my back, it felt so nice and comfy!*
> *Ms: Well, it's good to hear that, err...thank you! (laughter). But in fact, as I was saying, I think I was getting into it, and yet I was slow on the uptake. But once I got into it, it's true that I really pampered you! I'm joking, but I was* ***attentive****, what I wanted above all was to* ***give you a good massage****, we've seen that.* ***It's like with every type of medical care****, in fact, if you're annoyed and you don't want to do it or you're in a bad mood, or you don't click with a patient, they'll feel it straight away. We're human, you know!* ***You need to be in the right state of mind*** *to give someone a massage, otherwise, err, well I guess it's less agreeable...****I think you can't force yourself to do that, anyway.***

A successful massage requires a real involvement; it is not possible to pretend. Two aspects should thus be considered: the involvement of the body and the subjective involvement in the ongoing action: It is necessary to be in "the right state of mind." This opinion, which seems to be shared by all the actors present during the four simulations, is reminiscent of the concept of "active presence" identified by Récopé et al. (2013) when observing volleyball players: a particular form of self-involvement in the action. During the game, some players adopt a "watchful attitude" (they are "on the lookout," with their knees half-bent). They are ready to intervene even when the ball is not thrown in their direction. These results emphasize a form of "*presence to the world*" within the action performed. Of course, in the relational touch gesture, the attention is not focused on the same object (the game) and does not have the same goal (winning the match): Here, the focus is on a patient and the goal is to build a relationship with someone in a caregiving situation. It touches the very core of the profession. We could call it the "caregiver's active presence."

This active presence required by the role-playing game and the participation in the collective debate are not neutral for the actors. As soon as the allo-confrontation is over, as soon as the camera is off, their profession resurfaces in another way: Working conditions are evoked, notably the impossibility of doing a quality job and taking care of the patients enough. This is symptomatic of the psychosocial risks largely documented in the literature (Gollac & Bodier, 2011; Van Belleghem et al., 2014), the healthcare sector being particularly vulnerable to these risks in France (Estryn-Behar, 2013). The trainer uses a powerful expression to describe this kind of situation, which she has had to face several times during her training sessions and that she dreads: "It is the Tears Office!"

These difficulties are not present in these new relational touch simulations. The professionals no longer simply focus on the impossibility of doing a quality job. By allowing caregivers to exchange with their peers, the relational touch training course and its allo-confrontations also contribute to providing them with resources, as evidenced in the notes taken by the trainer[5] about a particularly striking moment of collective expression:

> *Once the camera is turned off, one of the caregivers starts crying and smiling. I ask her if everything is alright. She tells us what this exercise means for her. She understands now that* ***the core of her profession still exists****: taking care of others with empathy, making them feel better. She says that she feels like she is* ***surrounded by wonderful people****, she feels like a* ***caregiver among caregivers****, and that* ***lifts her spirits****. Four or six other caregivers present have tears in their eyes and agree. They are grateful to have been able to participate in this* ***training course that lifts their spirits****, they say, and contributes to* ***rekindling their desire to do their job well****, a job they chose for the* ***human values*** *attached to it,* ***which they do not find much anymore*** *in their daily work routine. They say that, at the end of the day,* ***even for a short while, they can still establish contact with a patient and make them feel better, take care of them, even if it is not as often as it used to be****. They say that* ***there are still things they can do****, and they want to develop that in their respective hospital units. They add that these exchanges during the collective confrontation interview are* ***essential, that they lift the spirits*** *and* ***help progress****, and enable them to* ***reflect*** *on their caregiving routine to move forward.*

7 Discussion

In this training course in relational touch that includes a simulation, the briefing phase consists of an initiation to the gesture; the simulation in itself is based on a role-playing game and the debriefing phase is conducted like an allo-confrontation. These last two phases allow for partly different mediations that are necessary to the learning process.

During the simulation phase, the simulated situation mainly provides pragmatic and formative mediations: The objective is to massage a peer under the trainer's guidance. It also provides epistemic and heuristic mediations: epistemic ones, with

[5] At our request, the trainer keeps a logbook, notably to write down everything that cannot be filmed.

the discovery of the properties of the massage, alone or through interactions with the person receiving the massage; heuristic ones, with the understanding of how to get one's body involved in the action or involve oneself psychologically, for instance. However, these aspects have mostly been highlighted based on the allo-confrontations, which fulfill two functions: that of a means of expression and understanding of what relational touch is, in order to better master it, and that of a moment of exchange between professionals.

As a means of expression and understanding, allo-confrontations rely on collaborative and formative mediations. The provision of feedback on the two volunteers' feelings and sensations, the masseur's goals, the ways in which she performed the massage, etc., was facilitated by the trainer. These various contributions were completed and enriched by all the participants present, which brought to light different dimensions of the gesture of relational touch, which we analyzed and identified as being part of a scheme. The epistemic and heuristic mediations of this phase of the simulation are explicit.

The allo-confrontations reveal the social dimensions of the relational touch scheme. They are a database from which anyone can draw inspiration to elaborate their own way of doing things (Clot & Faïta, 2000; Kloetzer et al., 2015), and thus contribute to the evolution of professional gestures (Tomás et al., 2009).

Those are not the only functions of the allo-confrontation in these training courses: The exchanges enable the participants to rethink their profession (*the core of the profession still exists, taking care of others with empathy, making them feel better*) and to find ways to give themselves some leeway in order to do their job better in a less-than-favorable context, through exchanges with their peers (*a caregiver among caregivers*), and by putting their professional caregiver identity (*taking care of others with empathy, making them feel better*) at the center of the picture. The allo-confrontations are a moment of at least partial re-empowerment of the participants, which depends on the possibility for them to debate and think about the reality of their work (Daniellou, 1998). They allow for a reactivation of the "professional genre," i.e., the "*social history of or presuppositions regarding the ongoing activity, an impersonal and collective memory that influences the professional's attitude when performing the activity in situation: the way they hold themselves, the way they address others, the way they start and end an activity, and the way they ensure that it reaches its goal efficiently. These ways of taking things and considering people in a given work environment constitute a database of appropriate or misplaced behaviors recorded in this work environment's history. This history sets the expectations of the genre that allow professionals to bear—in every sense of the word—with the unexpected that comes with reality. Mobilizing the genre of a profession also means 'becoming attuned' to it. It means being able to 'stick to it' in every way*" (Clot & Faita, 2000, pp. 12–13). From this perspective, this phase of the simulation allows for "transpersonal mediations," considering that the transpersonal history of the profession is precisely the one that constitutes the professional genre and evolves collectively (Kloetzer et al., 2015).

Finally, in this simulation situation, we chose to use the data that were produced for the training course (the filmed massages and collective debriefing sessions, focusing on the volunteers) and to rely on the notes taken by the trainer in her logbook. Thus, we were able to analyze what had been collectively worked on, and we were able to identify what the trainees had had the possibility to learn during training, but we cannot say for sure what has actually been learned by each of them. To assess that, it would have been necessary to implement a completely different type of data collection process, based on the possibility to meet the participants before the start of the training course, in order to build up a trusting relationship and to get all trainees to agree with the idea of being filmed. This type of training course (a one-off course in which the participants enroll on short notice) is not well suited for such an approach. Furthermore, seeing as our research project deals with implicit and embedded aspects of skills, more classical methods like face-to-face interviews or questionnaires are not really relevant.

8 Conclusion

When it comes to training caregivers in how to perform a relational touch gesture, a massage that is supposed to give the patient a moment of relaxation and well-being, the interaction with the patient revolves around care. The training situations based on role-playing games thus remain essential (Demaurex & Vu, 2013). Contrary to the current trends that tend toward the standardization of these interactions, the simulated situation that we analyzed in this chapter relies, on the one hand, on the performance of the action in situation and, on the other hand, on the collective analysis of what has been achieved. The debriefing phase is conducted like an allo-confrontation interview, which allows for an in-depth analysis, not from the perspective of strengths and weaknesses as is the prescribed norm in France (Granry & Moll, op. cit.), but taking into account what has been done, how it has been done, examining in details the "how" and "why" it has been done, and done that way. The aim is to comprehend the effects of one's action on another human being (getting the person to relax and making sure that this state of relaxation has actually been reached) and understand how these effects are obtained (how to use one's body weight to perform the massage, for example). To paraphrase Piaget's words (1974), this is not only a matter of success (or failure), but a matter of understanding the reasons behind this success (or this failure). This requires to keep reliable traces of the activity (here, the filmed footage) and to rely on the trainer to conduct and guide the analysis; otherwise, the focus would stay task-oriented instead of becoming activity-oriented (Teiger & Laville, 1991). Here, the analysis is sharpened and shared with a group of colleagues, allowing individuals to benefit from collective input (Mollo & Nascimento, 2014). The notion of scheme (Vergnaud, 2011; Tourmen et al., 2017) makes it is possible to specify all dimensions of the professional gesture, which can thus be precisely analyzed and shared by all participants.

Several dimensions of psychological validity are at stake in this simulation. According to Baker and Marshall's (1989) initial definition, the concept of psychological validity focuses on the cognitive dimensions of the activity (task complexity, perceptual skills, decision-making) and integrates stress. Seeing as it includes a simulation and uses allo-confrontation to conduct the debriefing phase, this relational touch training course does not just contribute professionally relevant knowledge and operating procedures; it implies a subjective involvement that questions the participants' relationship with themselves and their profession. The simulation enables the actors to rediscover subjective involvement at work and the values they feel are theirs, along with the history of the profession they share. The simulation, and in particular the debriefing phase, also provides opportunities for mediation: It mobilizes the trainees' collective spirit and the common factor that is transpersonal history, thus providing "transpersonal mediations." So, psychological validity takes on an additional meaning by reactivating subjective involvement and the sense the subject gives it. Those are key dimensions when it comes to facing deteriorating working conditions that pose psychosocial risks (Gollac & Bodier, 2011; Van Belleghem et al., 2014), and work situations in which others (their well-being, their development) are at the very core of the job. Psychological validity is thus a key element to consider when designing simulated situations for professional training in the healthcare sector. When reflecting on the design of simulations, the debate shifts from the characteristics of the simulated situations to the simulation situation, i.e., the coupling between the characteristics of the subject and those of the situations, and the effects of this coupling (Leplat, 1997) on the development of the actors, with regard to both their skills and their health. Indeed, the psychosocial risks shed light on the importance of psychological involvement for preserving health at work and during training. This shift from simulated situations to simulation situations is analyzed here from the perspective of mediations, from those that were thought out by the designers to those that were appropriated by the trainees. With this approach, the training course does not only integrate the task (what must be done) but also include the activity (Teiger & Laville, 1991), and its relationship with the profession and its values (Clot & Faïta, 2000; Kloetzer et al., 2015), in other words, aspects of "what the training course puts in motion" beyond the expected behavior, and that, from our point of view, relate to the professionals' skills.

References

Amalberti, R. (1996). *La conduite des systèmes à risque*. PUF.

Anderson, P. (2007). Massage therapy: A comfort intervention for cardiac surgery patients. *Clinical Nurse Specialist, 21*(3), 161–165.

Bainbridge, L., & Ruiz Quintanilla, S. A. (Eds.). (1989). *Developing skills with information technology*. Wiley.

Baker, S., & Marshall, E. (1989). Simulators for training and the evaluation of operator performance. In D. L. Bainbridge & S. A. Ruiz Quintanilla (Eds.), *Developing skills with information technology* (pp. 293–312). Wiley.

Barrows, H. S. (1993). An overview of the uses of standardized patients for teaching and evaluating clinical skills. *AAMC Academic Medicine, 68*(6), 443–451.

Béguin, P., & Pastré, P. (2002). Working, learning and designing through simulation. In S. Bagnara, S. Pozzi, A. Rizzo, & P. Wright (Eds.), *Proceedings of the 11th European Conference on Cognitive Ergonomics (ECCE'11): « Cognition, culture and design »* (pp. 5–13). CNR, Istituto di Scienze e technologie della cognizione.

Braithwaite, J., Wears, R. L., & Hollnagel, E. (2015). Resilient health care: Turning patient safety on its head. *International Journal for Quality in Health Care, 27*(5), 418–420. https://doi.org/10.1093/intqhc/mzv063

Bril, B. (2012). Apprendre des gestes techniques. In E. Bourgeois & M. Durand (Eds.), *Apprendre au travail* (pp. 141–151). PUF.

Clot, Y., & Faïta, D. (2000). Genres et styles en analyse du travail: Concepts et méthodes. *Travailler, 4*, 7–42.

Dahlstrom, N., Dekker, S., van Winsen, R., & Nyce, J. (2009). Fidelity and validity of simulator training. *Theoretical Issues in Ergonomics Science, 10*(4), 305–314.

Daniellou, F. (1998). Une contribution nécessaire au recensement des « Repères pour affronter les TMS. In F. Bourgeois (Ed.), *TMS et évolution des conditions de travail. Les actes du séminaire Paris 98* (pp. 35–46). Éditions ANACT. https://www.anact.fr/tms-et-evolution-des-conditions-de-travail-seminaire-paris-1998. March 2020.

Davezies, P. (2012). Enjeux, difficultés et modalités de l'expression sur le travail : point de vue de la clinique médicale du travail. *Pistes, 14*(2). http://pistes.revues.org/2566

Delgoulet, C., & Vidal-Gomel, C. (2015). The development of skills: A condition for the construction of health and performance at work. In P. Falzon (Ed.), *Constructive ergonomics* (pp. 3–18). CRC Press.

Demaurex, F., & Vu, N. (2013). Séance de simulation avec patient standardisé. In S. Boet, J.-C. Granry & G. Savoldelli (Eds.), *La simulation en santé. De la théorie à la pratique* (pp. 51–62). Springer.

Dubey, G. (1997). Faire "comme si" n'est pas faire. In P. Béguin & A. Weill-Fassina (Eds.), *La simulation en ergonomie: connaître, agir, interagir* (pp. 39–53). Octarès.

Estryn-Behar, M. (2013). *Agir sur les risques psychosociaux des professionnels de santé*. Groupe Pasteur Mutualité.

Ferrel-Torry, J. (1993). L'utilisation du toucher-massage thérapeutique comme une intervention en soins infirmiers pour modifier l'anxiété et la perception de la douleur cancéreuse. *Cancer Nursing, 16*, 93–101.

Gaudez, C., & Aptel, M. (2008). Les mécanismes neurophysiologiques du mouvement, base pour la compréhension du geste. *Le travail humain, 71*(4), 385–404. https://doi.org/10.3917/th.714.0385

Gentaz, E. (2000). Caractéristiques générales de l'organisation anatomofonctionnelle de la perception cutanée et haptique. In Y. Hatwell, A. Streri, & E. Gentaz (Eds.), *Toucher pour connaître. Psychologie cognitive de la perception tactile manuelle* (pp. 19–34). PUF.

Gollac, M., & Bodier, M. (Eds.) (2011). *Mesurer les facteurs psychosociaux de risque au travail pour les maîtriser*. DARES, Ministère du travail et de l'emploi. http://travail-emploi.gouv.fr/IMG/pdf/rapport_SRPST_definitif_rectifie_11_05_10.pdf. March 2021.

Granry, J.-C., & Moll, M.-C. (2012, March). *État de l'art (national et international) en matière de pratiques de simulation dans le domaine de la santé. Dans le cadre du développement professionnel continu (DPC) et de la prévention des risques associés aux soins*. Rapport de mission. Haute autorité en santé. https://www.has-sante.fr/upload/docs/application/pdf/2012-01/simulation_en_sante_-_rapport.pdf. March 2021.

Harris, M. (2010). The physiological and psychological effects of slow-stroke back massage and hand massage on relaxation in older people. *Journal of Clinical Nursing, 19*, 17–26.

Hollnagel, E. (2013). A tale of two safeties. *Nuclear Safety and Simulation, 4*(1), 1–9.

Hollnagel, E. (2017). Can we ever imagine how work is done? *Hindsight 25*, 10–13 (Summer 2017). https://www.eurocontrol.int/sites/default/files/publication/files/hindsight25.pdf

Howley, D. L. (2013). Standardized patients. In A. I. Levine, S. DeMaria Jr., & A. D Schwartz (Eds.), *The comprehensive textbook of healthcare simulation* (pp. 173–190). Springer. https://doi.org/10.1007/978-1-4614-5993-4_13

Kloetzer, L., Clot, Y., & Quillerou-Grivot, E. (2015). Stimulating dialogue at work: The activity. Clinic approach to learning and development. In L. Filliettaz & S. Billett (Eds.), *Francophone perspectives of learning through work conceptions, traditions and practices* (pp. 49–70). Springer.

Lémonie, Y., & Chassaing, K. (2014). From the adaptation of movement to the development of gesture. In P. Falzon (Ed.), *Constructive ergonomics* (pp. 82–97). CRC Press.

Leplat, J. (1970). La connaissance des résultats. In J. Leplat, C. Enard, & A. Weill-Fassina (Eds.), *La formation par l'apprentissage* (pp. 157–198). PUF.
Leplat, J. (1997). *Regards sur l'activité en situation de travail : contribution à la psychologie ergonomique*. PUF.
Leplat, J. (2013). Les gestes dans l'activité en situation de travail. Aperçu de quelques problèmes d'analyse. *Pistes, 15*(1). http://journals.openedition.org/pistes/2951
Mollo, V., & Falzon, P. (2004). Auto-and allo-confrontation as tools for reflective activities. *Applied Ergonomics, 35*(6), 531–540.
Mollo, V., & Nascimento, A. (2014). Reflective practices and the development of individuals, collectives and organisations. In P. Falzon (Ed.), *Constructive ergonomics* (pp. 223–238). CRC Press.
Oh, H. (2004). Effects of hand massage and hand holding on the anxiety in patients with local infiltration anesthesia. *Taehan Kanho Hakhoe Chi, 34*, 24–33.
Pastré, P. (1999). Comprendre après coup grâce à la simulation. *Education Permanente, 139*, 90–115.
Pasturel, A. (2007). Toucher-massage : mieux soigner et soulager l'enfant. *Cahiers de la puéricultrice, 205*, 29–31.
Piaget, J. (1974). *Réussir et comprendre*. PUF.
Rabardel, P., & Samurçay R. (2001). Artifact mediation in learning. Invited conférence in *New challenges to research on learning*. International symposium organized by the Center for Activity Theory and Developmental Work Research. University of Helsinki (Finland): March 21–23, https://www.rabardel.fr/%C3%A9crits-scientifiques/. Nov 2021.
Récopé, M., Boyer, S., Rix-Lièvre, G., & Coutarel, F. (2013). Une modélisation de l'activité est-elle nécessaire ? Est-elle envisageable ? *Ergologia, 9*, 45–74.
Salas, E., & Cannon-Bowers, J. A. (2001). The science of training: A decade of progress. *Annual Review of Psychology, 52*, 471–499.
Samurçay, R., & Roglaki, J. (1998). Exploitation didactique des situations de simulation. *Le travail humain, 61*(4), 333–359.
Simon, A. (2012). Se réapproprier son corps grâce au toucher-massage. *La revue de l'infirmière, 61*(181), 40–41.
Teiger, C., & Laville, A. (1991). L'apprentissage de l'analyse ergonomique du travail, outil d'une formation pour l'action. *Travail et emploi, 47*, 53–62.
Tomás, J.-L., Simonet, P., Clot, Y., & Fernandez, G. (2009). Le corps: L'œuvre du collectif de travail. *Corps, 1*(6), 23–30.
Tourmen, C., Holgado, O., Métral, J., Mayen, P., & Olry, P. (2017). The Piagetian scheme: A framework to study professional learning through conceptualization. *Vocations and Learning, 10*, 343–364. https://doi.org/10.1007/s12186-017-9174-y
Van Belleghem, L., De Gasparro, S., & Gaillard, I. (2014). The development of the psychosocial dimension of work. In P. Falzon (Ed.), *Constructive ergonomics* (pp. 64–79). CRC Press.
Vergnad, G. (2009). The theory of conceptual fields. *Human Development, 52*, 83–94. https://doi.org/10.1159/000202727
Vergnaud, G. (2011). La pensée est un geste. Comment analyser la forme opératoire de la connaissance. *Enfance, 1*, 37–48. https://doi.org/10.4074/S0013754511001042
Vidal-Gomel, C. (2007). Compétences pour gérer des risques professionnels: un exemple dans le domaine de la maintenance des systèmes électriques. *Le Travail humain, 70*(2), 153–194.
Vidal-Gomel, C., & Fauquet-Alekhine, P. (2016). Reflections and theoretical contributions regarding trainers' practice and simulation. In P. Fauquet-Alekhine & N. Pehuet (Eds.), *Simulation training: Fundamentals and applications* (pp. 1–29). Springer. https://doi.org/10.1007/978-3-319-19914-6_1
Vidal-Gomel, C., Simon, A., & Nizard, J. (2018). De l'analyse de l'activité de l'expert à celle des acteurs de la formation pour caractériser le geste professionnel de toucher-relationnel. *TransFormation*, 18. https://pulp.univ-lille1.fr/index.php/TF/article/viewFile/236/200
Vygotsky, L. S. (1978). *Mind in society: The development of higher psychological processes*. Harvard University Press.
Wisner, A. (1995). *Réflexions sur l'ergonomie (1962–1995)*. Octares.

Design Process for a Virtual Simulation Environment for Training Healthcare Professionals in Geriatrics

Raquel Becerril-Ortega, Hélène Vanderstichel, Lucie Petit, Maria José Urbiolagallegos, Joanne Schoch, Sébastien Dacunha, Amine Benamara, Brian Ravenet, Jean Zagdoun, and Laurence Chaby

Abstract This research covers the design of a digital simulation tool, from identification of training needs to analysis of the simulation produced by testers from a demonstration scenario. It is based on the development of a simulation tool for training caregivers in geriatrics in France, as part of a multidisciplinary research and development project known as VirtuAlz and supported by the French National Research Agency. Training needs were identified from a study of the current challenges of communicating with patients with Alzheimer's disease or other related forms of dementia. There are two parts to the process of designing the simulation

---

R. Becerril-Ortega (✉)
CIREL - Centre Interuniversitaire de Recherche en Éducation de Lille, F-59000, Univ. Lille, ULR 4354, Lille, France

Inria [French National Institute for Research in Digital Science and Technology], Paris, France
e-mail: raquel.becerril-ortega@univ-lille.fr

H. Vanderstichel · L. Petit
CIREL – Centre Interuniversitaire de Recherche en Éducation de Lille, University of Lille, Lille, France
e-mail: Helene.vanderstichel@univ-lille.fr; Lucie.petit@univ-lille.fr

M. J. Urbiolagallegos · J. Schoch · S. Dacunha
Broca Living Lab, Université Paris Descartes, Paris, France

A. Benamara · B. Ravenet
LIMSI-CNRS [French National Centre for Scientific Research Computer Science Laboratory for Mechanics and Engineering Sciences], Orsay, France
e-mail: brian.ravenet@limsi.fr

J. Zagdoun · L. Chaby
ISIR [Institute for Intelligent Systems and Robotics], Sorbonne Université, CNRS UMR, Paris, France
e-mail: jean.zagdoun@isir.upmc.fr; laurence.chaby@parisdescartes.fr

S. Flandin et al. (eds.), *Simulation Training through the Lens of Experience and Activity Analysis*, Professional and Practice-based Learning 30,
https://doi.org/10.1007/978-3-030-89567-9_6

environment. First, the design of the simulation scenario builds on what caregivers actually do (from observations and interviews). Second, the design process continues through the analysis of the figurations produced during the simulation by a group of experienced and inexperienced testers. This work offers the potential of promising avenues for the design, which is being produced jointly by simulation specialists and experts from the field of simulation environments for training purposes.

Keywords Simulation · Training design · Alzheimer's disease · Professionals healthcare · Nonverbal communication

1 Introduction

With the increase in life expectancy of France's (De Plazaola & Rignols, 2018)[1] and European's population, the number of elderly people likely to develop Alzheimer's disease or related forms of dementia is increasing year on year (Carcaillon Bentata et al., 2017).[2] If the overriding theme is a treatment that would cure, slow down or halt this type of pathology, there is also a significant issue for the care assistants and nursing staff involved in the care of these patients.

Caring for people with Alzheimer's disease or a related dementia would require specific knowledge and skills from caregivers to communicate effectively with them and to ensure each other safety and dignity. What is the best way to train them to conduct themselves and communicate appropriately at each stage of the disease? What training should be introduced to help them overcome the day-to-day challenges of interacting with these patients?

The VirtuAlz[3] research project reflects these concerns. It involves a consortium of researchers in the fields of geriatrics, robotics, computing, educational and training science and a business specialised in digital simulation for the healthcare sector. It involves the design of a simulation tool (virtual patient) for training healthcare professionals (nursing staff and care assistants) working with patients with Alzheimer's disease or other related forms of dementia. The importance of training is rooted in a common scientific and technological lever for all four research teams: the development or redevelopment of communication skills in a care setting.

---

[1] In 2017, life expectancy in France was 85.3 years for women and 79.5 years for men. In 2018, 19.6% of the population was aged 65 years or over, compared with 18.8% in 2016. One in 10 inhabitants was aged 75 years or over. In 2040, one in four will be aged at least 65 years (p. 26).

[2] In 2010, 996,000 people (9.8% of the over-65s) had Alzheimer's disease or a related form of dementia; the forecast figure for 2030 is more than 1.5 million.

[3] Research project funded by the French National Research Agency (ANR).

The first part of this article begins with a review of the literature which addresses some important aspects of caregiver-patient communication, which is central to the therapeutic approach; it identifies the main difficulties, especially when interacting with elderly patients with Alzheimer's disease or related forms of dementia. We have noted there is no consensus on best practice for effective communication between caregivers and these types of patients. The focus then turns to the importance of teaching communication in the initial training of nursing and care staff in France. This first part ends with an analysis of training needs, as the cornerstone of this project to design a simulation-based training course.

The second part sets out the various stages in the development of a simulation tool, including work analysis and design of a proof of concept (PoC) test scenario. Firstly, to make up for the absence of an actual specification, an analysis of caregivers' work helped to identify the skills and strategies used. We then describe the development of the simulation scenario based on a typical communication situation, namely, the patient's refusal to take medication.

The third part describes the first test with the prototype simulation tool featuring the scenario of administering medication. The analyses conducted with the two groups of experienced and novice testers' show: a preference for a patient relationship-focussed communication strategy; differences in strategy depending on the testers' experience and improvements between two consecutive test sessions.

Based on the findings, this work concludes by highlighting the relevance of designing a simulation that hinges on analysis of training needs as seen in the difficulties experienced by professionals, and the joint creation of simulations with professionals. One promising avenue for design lies in analysing the simulation sessions based on the figurations produced by the testers involved in the simulation.

2 Communicating with Patients with Alzheimer's Disease or Related Forms of Dementia

2.1 Communication as a Central Focus of Caregivers' Work

Patient communication is central to caregivers' work, as illustrated by the substantial scientific literature in specialist nursing care journals (Morse et al., 1992; Dean et al., 1982; Gastmans, 1998; Hansebo & Kihlgren, 2002; Jones, 2003; Tuckette, 2005; Williams et al., 2005; Riviere et al., 2019; Van Manen et al., 2021). This communication can be defined as an interpersonal process that extends throughout the duration of the care given, which is often very limited. In addition, it is subject to the constraints imposed by a dynamic and often unpredictable clinical environment. Hagerty and Patusky (2003) favour the theory of human relatedness in their understanding of the process, whilst other authors bemoan the lack of a unified theory or call for consideration of communication with greater focus on the patient's point of view (McCabe, 2004; Halldorsdottir, 2008).

The systematic review proposed by Rivière et al. (2019) focusses on the essential aspects of the interpersonal care relationship between caregivers and elderly patients with no cognitive deficiency, during their inpatient stay. This study identifies three defining categories for relationship quality in care settings: factors related to the caregiver, factors related to the elderly patient and those related to the context. With due consideration for the importance of how work is organised, this study stresses the training of nursing staff as a lever for changes in their behaviour, attitudes and communication to meet the needs of older patients. Communication between caregivers and elderly patients is considered more sensitive, since it may be frustrated to differing degrees depending on the pathology. In this case, there are a number of obstacles to effective communication: caregiver-elderly patient relationships; any visual or hearing impairment in patients; their levels of stress and anxiety; the confusion and disturbed behaviour of some elderly people (Moore & Proffitt, 1993).

In Alzheimer's disease or related forms of dementia, the symptoms of psycho-behavioural deficit (apathy; withdrawal; hypersomnia and muteness) or disturbance (objection; aggression; agitation; aberrant motor behaviour such as wandering; disinhibition; delusions; hallucinations and sleep disorders) that are characteristic of this kind of disease[4] make the difficulties of communicating with patients even more acute. According to Van Manen et al. (2021), the communication theories adopted are not specific to dementia sufferers, while neurocognitive decline affects communication functions such as finding words, and understanding and holding a conversation, through to total loss of language in the final stages of the disease. Lastly, according to Harwood et al. (2018), the 26 studies published in the scientific literature between 2010 and 2017 offer no means of identifying clear communication strategies that can be used to train healthcare professionals in overcoming the obstacles to communication with dementia patients in hospital for short-term care.

2.2 *Communication Training for Nursing Staff in France*

There have been many changes since the first nursing qualification[5] was awarded in France which laid down the length, content and organisation of training. The state diploma programme has only considered the relationship between caregiver and

[4] The existing tools for evaluating the different psychological aspects of Alzheimer's disease or related forms of dementia are known as behavioural scales, which may come in the form of different artefacts that measure patients' psychological and emotional state. The proposed indicators provide the principal observable evidence for patient identification and classification. One of the best known in France is the Neuropsychiatric Inventory (NPI).

[5] Decree of 27 June 1992 introducing the certificate of competence for professional nurses, and Order of 24 June 1924 (French Official Journal of 14 September 1924) on the content of the curriculum for French state nursing schools.

patient since 1972, when nursing studies were revised.[6] The current skills matrix for the state nursing diploma and the training requirements[7] feature learning about communication between caregivers and patients – the basis for the therapeutic relationship – as one of the basic strands of training for nurses and care assistants.

Nursing training comprises six semesters of 20 weeks each. This makes a total of 4200 h, split equally between theoretical learning and clinical training in various placement settings. Of the 10 skills identified as necessary and evidenced by the award of the state diploma, skill no. 6, "Communicating and managing relationships in a care environment" relates to communication between caregiver and patient. The skills matrix provides indicators (observable signs for implementation of communication) for meeting the criteria for evaluating the relevance of the interpersonal situation analysis and adapting to the specific needs of patients with mental disorders.

Skill no. 6, to be linked with other, more technical skills,[8] is broken down into five Teaching Units delivered across four of the six semesters of initial nursing training, and covering psychology, sociology, anthropology (125 h of teaching in semesters 1 and 2) and interpersonal care (100 h of teaching in semesters 2, 3 and 5). Interpersonal care is focussed on communication and is as much a part of caring for patients as technical care (Formarier, 2007; Rothier-Bautzer, 2016; Gaborit, 2017). It is defined as "verbal or non-verbal interventions intended to establish communication for the purpose of providing care for a person or a group." Interpersonal care teaching covers seven items[9] and addresses the right professional distance, non-verbal communication (gaze, posture, facial expression, gestures, types of touch, etc.), the categories of conversation that nursing staff may hold and different levels in the caregiver-patient relationship. It is assessed in placement settings by experienced professionals.

---

[6] Decree 72 818 of 5 September 1972 on preparatory studies and state nursing diploma exams, and Order of 5 September 1972 on the teaching programme and organisation of placements for the state nursing diploma.

[7] Order of 31 July 2009 on the state nursing diploma, and annexes II (skills matrix) and III (training requirements) published in the French Official Bulletin for Health, social protection and solidarity, no. 2009/7 of 15 August 2009.

[8] Such as competency no. 1, "Evaluate a clinical situation and establish a nursing diagnosis", competency no. 2, "Design and conduct a nursing care project", and competency no. 4, "Implement actions for diagnostic and therapeutic purposes", described in the skills matrix for the state diploma.

[9] Define, establish and create the conditions and guidelines for communication favourable to care procedures, taking account of the individual's level of understanding; welcome and listen to individuals requesting health or personal care, taking into account their life history and their background; initiate and maintain verbal and non-verbal communication with individuals, taking account of impairments in communication; pursue and establish a climate of trust with the person being cared for and their relatives, with a view to a therapeutic partnership; provide an individual with information about care, seeking their consent; identify the specific interpersonal and communication needs in the following situations: distress, end of life, grief, denial, refusal, conflict and aggression; adopt an appropriate approach to communication for individuals and their relatives depending on the situations identified.

As with the nursing profession, care assistants are regulated by decrees, orders, circulars and regulations. Care assistants report to nursing staff[10] and often work as part of a multidisciplinary team. Their role involves delivering "personal and everyday care designed to make up in full or in part for a lack of or a reduction in the independence of an individual or a group of individuals".[11] Training for the state care assistant diploma is delivered by dedicated training institutes and takes 41 weeks (1435 h), alternating theory (595 h of teaching over eight modules corresponding to the eight competencies for the job role) and clinical placements (840 h). Module no. 5, "Communication relationship" devotes 70 h of theoretical learning to the interpersonal aspects of communication, including in the context of end of life, but in the event of an attack or violence. These lessons are supplemented by a 4-week placement to ensure that future professionals are able to communicate in a way that is appropriate for the individual and their situation, and for their relatives.

Analysis of two documents specifying the initial training for nursing staff and care assistants highlights that communication between caregiver and patient is designed for the delivery of care. Communication training is cross-functional and is seldom attached to specific situations such as, for example, communication situations in geriatric care. Lessons on Alzheimer's disease and related dementia are delivered as part of initial training, but future practitioners are only given the opportunity for contact with patients with this type of disorder in at least one of the placements on their course. Healthcare personnel learn in the first time on the job, and also, to a lesser degree, during their initial training.

2.3 An Emerging Need for Communication Training

Firstly, analysis of the literature highlights the absence of any unified theory or formal practices as regards the challenges of communication between nursing staff and patients with Alzheimer's disease or related dementia. The studies reviewed also indicate a lack of formal strategies that would help overcome the difficulties to ensure appropriate communication. They show that conquering communication barriers requires caregivers to put into practice a varied skill set such as, for example, their experience with other patients with dementia or verbal and non-verbal communication disorders. Furthermore, the different strategies may vary in response to the situation and are also dependent on the purpose of the interaction.

Secondly, analysis of the specifications documents for initial and ongoing training of nursing staff in France highlights a shortfall in the area of communication. In the absence of formal documentation and skills transfer to manage interactions with patients with Alzheimer's disease or related forms of dementia, caregivers learn to

---

[10] R.4311-3 to R.4311-5 of the French Public Health Code.

[11] Annex I to the training requirements for the professional care assistant diploma, in the Order of 22 October 2005 on training leading to the state care assistant diploma.

deal with these situations in the workplace. Some may be offered continuous professional development on, for example, the characteristics of the major neurocognitive disorders linked to Alzheimer's disease or related forms of dementia before they join a special unit for acute patients. Most of them learn on the job, however. They, therefore, develop a body of knowledge for themselves based on their initial, continuous training and work experiences, and this provides an initial resource that can be tapped into for developing communication strategies.

In short, the VirtuAlz project is endeavouring to meet this need for training on communication issues. The aim is to develop a simulation tool to provide training in verbal and non-verbal communication for healthcare professionals working with people with Alzheimer's disease or related dementia. Its primary audience is students, nursing staff and healthcare assistants who are newcomers to geriatrics, with no experience and/or little knowledge of how major neurocognitive disorders are managed in the elderly. It will form part of a training module on communication and interpersonal care intended to develop students' skills before they go into the workplace (preparation for taking up a role in geriatrics or for the geriatrics placement during initial training, etc.).

3 Developing a Simulation Tool for Training Healthcare Professionals

In France, simulation has become an invaluable teaching aid (Boet et al., 2013; Granry & Moll, 2012) for training caregivers, while managing risks. It is referred to in the field of healthcare training as Simulation-Based Education (SBE), a field of research and practice that uses learning and development theories such as cognitive load, reflective cycle, informal learning, Stanislavski's system and cultural historical activity theory (Nestel & Bearman, 2015).

Our vision is based on simulation as a basis for developing and examining experience. It relies on simulation scenarios devised using work-related situations encountered by caregivers (Prissette & Dupuy-Maribas, 2016). In line with work that establishes a constructivist approach to learning (Piaget, 1947a, b), simulation helps to train caregivers for situations requiring interaction with individuals with Alzheimer's disease or related forms of dementia.

VirtuAlz is being designed by a multidisciplinary research team (Petit et al., 2021), using a proof of concept (PoC) approach. The PoC aims to demonstrate the project's feasibility by designing, building and testing a basic prototype. The prototype is being developed as the project progresses, via an iterative process of interaction between members of the consortium and with end users. The first stage of the design process took place in 2018 and involved analysing the work-related situations in which caregivers communicated with patients with Alzheimer's disease or related forms of dementia. The investigations identified verbal and non-verbal interactions that were considered to be ordinary and/or critical situations, as well as some strategies for managing these situations. The second stage took place in 2019 and consisted of developing simulation scenarios based on work-related situations. The third, in 2020, concerns the test and evaluation phase of the prototype simulator.

3.1 Approach of Caregivers' Work

Analysis of caregivers' work in the hospital setting when interacting with Alzheimer's patients is based on a protocol that features interviews (12 semi-guided interviews conducted in 2018, of which eight were used for this study) and observations (more than 30 h of observation using the shadowing technique [McDonald, 2005]).[12]

Our focus is the activities of daily living (ADLs), including help with dressing, meals, use of toilets, bathing and daily hygienic care in the hospital setting. It is true that patients with severe language disorders are more likely to refuse care (Belzil & Vézina, 2015). Given the lack of specific requirements, we sought to identify those communication practices that caregivers consider to be effective and relevant. In considering and observing interactions in their usual context, this study does not focus solely on "dysfunctional behaviours" but also takes into account "successful situations" (*ibid.*).

There are two distinguishing characteristics of non-verbal communication between caregiver and patient: firstly, it compensates for barriers to communication specific to Alzheimer's disease and other dementia; secondly, the particular communication strategy to be adopted must be appropriate to each patient (Becerril-Ortega et al., 2019). Other studies confirm this. Belzil and Vézina (2015), for example, show a lack of cooperation and refusal to receive care. This seems to be critical because restlessness, resistance or aggression, which result in various situations probably have different trigger factors, different functions and ultimately, require different management strategies. The ultimate goal in VirtuAlz project is to make caregivers aware of the role of verbal and non-verbal communication in managing care situations, as well as how to adapt communication strategies to the context and to the behaviours resulting from the illness.

Processing of the data collected in this first stage identified 20 critical situations based on the patient's condition. These situations are linked to the progression of the disease and its characteristics: moments of lucidity; difficulty accepting the disease; wandering around from morning till night; logorrhoea; cognitive impairment at night-time (night terrors, fear of not waking up) or on waking (disconnection from reality); falling out of bed during the night; temporal (especially during the night) and/or spatial disorientation; attempting to escape; resistance, restlessness or aggression, sometimes with care refusal.

[12] The results were published in Becerril-Ortega & Petit (2017), Becerril-Ortega et al. (2019).

3.2 *Identifying a Critical and Challenging Situation: Administering Medication*

Management of a resistant patient who is refusing care is a frequent situation for caregivers and it was, therefore, selected for the design of the first simulation scenario. More specifically, it concerns resistance to administration of medication. This situation is a common occurrence for both nursing staff and care assistants and can also be critical, in particular when the patient's refusal takes the form of aggression in their expression and behaviour.

There are three types of factor that influence communication between healthcare professionals and patients with Alzheimer's disease or related forms of dementia: factors related to the practitioners, especially their verbal and non-verbal communication; factors related to the beneficiaries of care, in particular if they have severe language disorders; factors related to the context, including how care is organised and the time available for it (Van Manen et al., 2021; Belzil & Vézina, 2015). Research tends to demonstrate that in dealing with these kinds of situations, the more patient-focussed the communication, the greater the probability of cooperation during care (Savundranayagam et al., 2016). However, although the different caregiver behaviours may, to a certain extent, be likely to incite resistance or cooperation, the condition of the care beneficiary is a bigger determinant of their response (Belzil & Vézina, 2015).

Our research nonetheless points to the following strategies adopted by nursing staff and care assistants to address this. To characterise the emotional state of patients whose expressiveness is limited, whatever the means used, caregivers develop a systematic observation strategy as a priority. The observables collected on the patients' emotions and states contribute to the strategies developed to manage recurrent situations that have already occurred in the past. Therefore, observing to understand the emotional state (anger, joy, sadness, anxiety and fear) of people Alzheimer's disease is a major challenge for caregivers.

The observations were completed by semi-directive interviews with 12 health professionals. More specifically, we questioned them about:

- Work situations and their difficulties, illustrated by examples of interaction situations experienced with patients.[13]
- Elements of communication – verbal, paraverbal and non-verbal – taken into account in interactions with patients: "How do you recognise when a patient is sad? Do you look at their face? their gestures? their tone of voice? changes in behaviour?"
- Strategies, the way they adapt based on (i) their knowledge of the disease; (ii) their knowledge of the patients, their life history and (iii) the resources available in the work environment.

[13] We also noted that it was common practice to mix crushed medicines into food, when this approach was agreed in the institutional protocol and the family had given their consent. However, this strategy is a matter of debate, for ethical reasons and the risk it may represent: if the patient notices, there is a risk that they will refuse to eat.

Based on current knowledge and the practices observed, the following recommendations can be made:

- Approaching the patient is a crucial point, providing the opportunity to assess their physical and emotional state via questioning and careful observation. Consequently, **knowledge of the patient**, the severity of their language disorders and any previous resistance to care is decisive.
- Should they show resistance, **stressing** the necessity of the care helps to manage the situation, for example, by reminding the patient of the benefits of treatment, and using authoritative arguments.
- Based on the evidence, the caregiver may also attempt to influence the patient's emotional state by adapting their verbal and non-verbal communication: by diverting their attention; by adopting non-verbal communication that encourages cheerfulness and relaxation (chatter, smiles, intonation); by drawing on their life history or their interests to alter their state of mind.
- In case of repeated refusal, the strategy considered most effective nonetheless appears to be to adopt an **understanding attitude** and **postpone care**, in particular to turn the patient's memory disorders to the caregiver's advantage.
- It is important that the caregiver does not take resistance to care personally. Since this attitude has more to do with the prior condition of the patient, nursing staff need to be able to call on a colleague or doctor if necessary.

These recommendations could change in future, as knowledge of the disease and how to communicate with these patients develop. Nevertheless, they provided a basis for writing the first simulation scenario.

3.3 Developing a Simulation Scenario

The VirtuAlz project relies on digital simulation with a virtual patient – a 3D avatar with a dynamic behaviour scheduler – and automatic, real-time interpretation of the learner's behaviour based on social signals. The aim of the training is to explore the specific characteristics of communication with patients with Alzheimer's disease, and question and analyse practice to prevent critical situations from developing as a result of the deterioration of interactions in a care setting.

Looking at a tall vertical screen (55″ high) to simulate actual size, the test participant can interact with the virtual patient, who then reacts to the words and to the behaviours and expressions of their conversation partner. The participant uses a controller to select options and consult the patient record. They can get closer to or move further away from the patient, within the bounds of a predefined area.

In this initial version, which uses the Wizard of Oz technique[14] (Benamara et al., 2020), the virtual patient is controlled by a human experimenter, or wizard. The patient's verbal and non-verbal responses can be determined in real time (direction of gaze, orientation of the head, eyes, eyebrows, etc.). The patient's gestures and bodily animation are predefined, along with the background (the scene takes place in the hospital room, with a patient sitting in her armchair).

Situations that are candidates for creating scenarios must meet particular educational and learning requirements common to two professions (nurses and care assistants); they involve close interaction – both verbal and non-verbal; and deterioration should be possible, turning an ordinary situation into a critical one. Technical limitations, especially as regards signal capture and animation of the virtual agent, should also be considered.

The proposed pilot scenario therefore involves the situation of a patient refusing to take medication. The different elements of the simulation scenario – setting, persona, verbal and non-verbal interactions, and the available choices of action – are derived by synthesising the data gathered during the first stage and cross-referencing it with the technical requirements for creating the software and animation.

3.3.1 Instructional Preparation of the Scenario Associated with Refusal to Take Medication

The background depicts the room of Mrs Francesca Dupont, a former singer and long-term patient. It is midday or late morning. She is awake and sitting in an armchair next to her bed.

The caregiver has two aims: to ensure the patient takes her medicine and to stimulate her. The patient can express herself verbally and can eat and drink independently. The situation may deteriorate, and the patient is likely to resist taking her medicine (thinks she has already taken it; is afraid she might be poisoned; refuses care more generally). She may show signs of aggression and memory loss during the interaction.

There are three points in the scenario: approaching the patient, the procedure (succeeding in administering the medication) and leaving. Despite the linearity imposed by technical demands, it is possible to go back and forth, start over and introduce obstacles, while maintaining the (temporal and spatial) chronological continuity of the reference situation.

[14] Wizard of Oz or WOZ is an experimental technique in which the user interacts with a system that is actually partly controlled by a concealed human experimenter referred to as a "magician" or "wizard". This procedure is used to gather interactions with target users prior to building the fully autonomous system. These interactions are used to observe the user's behaviour and analyse the wizard's choices and from there, to establish the foundations for the model that will later automatically generate the non-verbal behaviour of the virtual patient, depending on the situation and the user behaviours detected.

3.3.2 Example Sequence: Approaching the Patient

"The caregiver" Example of action selection:

[They knock on the door and go into the room with the equipment. They are relaxed, have an open posture, and look at the patient and may smile. At the same time, they speak, pleasantly and warmly. Or they may not...] What do they say?

(a) I've come to give you your medicine (with the intention of carrying out the procedure promptly).
(b) Hello, Mrs Dupont. I'm your nurse/care assistant. I've come to give you your medicine. How have you been since this morning? (to gather information).
(c) Hello, Mrs Dupont. I've come to give you your medicine. What a lovely day it is! Have you seen the sunshine? (to stimulate).

Patient. Examples of responses from the VP:

(a) Oh no you don't! I don't want your filthy medicine! Leave me alone! (anger).
(b) Well, I was fine until just now. I've already had my medicine, though. That's not my medicine. You're getting mixed up. (annoyance).
(c) Hello! Yes, it's a lovely day. I hadn't noticed! (cheerful)"

4 Test Simulation Administration of Medication

For the test with the initial prototype, data were gathered using volunteers from the Broca Living Lab[15] in Broca Hospital. It involved testing an initial scenario with computer tool development specialists in the field of geriatrics.

4.1 Overview of the Protocol

The test was performed by two categories of test operators who were divided up according to their scientific and professional knowledge of Alzheimer's disease and its consequences for patients. The first group, the experts, is composed of staff providing bedside care for patients and/or psychologists working with patients. The second group, the novices, is composed of nursing staff at the start of their career

[15] The result of a partnership with AP-HP (Paris teaching hospitals), the Broca Living Lab has three teams developing technological research and innovation for healthcare and independent living: the healthcare professionals at Broca hospital; the EA 4468 research team "Alzheimer's disease: diagnosis, procedures and technologies" and LUSAGE Lab, its gerontology technology laboratory; CEN Stimco, the French national centre of expertise in cognitive stimulation.

and with less than 2 years of experience, or specialists in the design of computer tools. Twelve tests were performed, of which eight proved useful.

The tests included in our analysis followed these steps:

- Step 1: overview of the test
- Step 2: prebriefing, introduction to the virtual patient and the context of care
- Step 3: guided simulation (with options)
- Step 4: non-guided simulation (sandbox type)

The virtual patient's responses to the participant's actions are controlled by the wizard, following the script for the scenario of taking medication and using the software developed. In the guided version, the participant selects an action or dialogue option, confirms their choice and then interacts with the virtual patient. A "microphone" icon is displayed while they are speaking. The virtual patient responds, then, depending on the wizard's selection, the participant moves to the following sequence. Despite the linearity imposed by technical demands, it is possible to go back and forth, start over and introduce obstacles. For example, the Wizard can step in to keep the patient in a specific state – neutral, sad, annoyed, etc. – or change their behaviour abruptly. To supplement the data, different types of interactions and possible developments were tested. In the non-guided version, the participant can interact directly with the patient, although other options are available: "Continue doing that", "Try something else" or "End the discussion".

The simulations were filmed using a video camera. Each film allows for observation of the participant, the actions taken via a command and the results of the actions (cf. annex table).

4.2 *Instructional Preparation of the Simulation Based on Three Specific Cases*

There are two points of instructional preparation in the simulation, or development of a learning scenario from three cases inspired by a work-related situation. The first point corresponds to modelling based on the issues in the situation as identified from analysis of the work (Figs. 1, 2 and 3). The second point refers to the simulation, strictly speaking, and involves analysis of the sequence of testers' work. Analysis of the simulation is supported by an available corpus of videos processed using a deductive approach, via observation, detailed description, coding and analysis (Derry et al., 2010). Analysis of the work involving the participant and the wizard/virtual patient led to the adoption of a multimodal (verbal and non-verbal) approach to the interactions (Pham Quang, 2015). The events relating to the interactions were counted and characterised.

We identified: moments of thinking out loud (questions to the wizard or to self; narration, etc.); actions on the application (display of options, selection, etc.); verbal responses; behavioural discontinuities (changes in expressiveness, tone, direction of

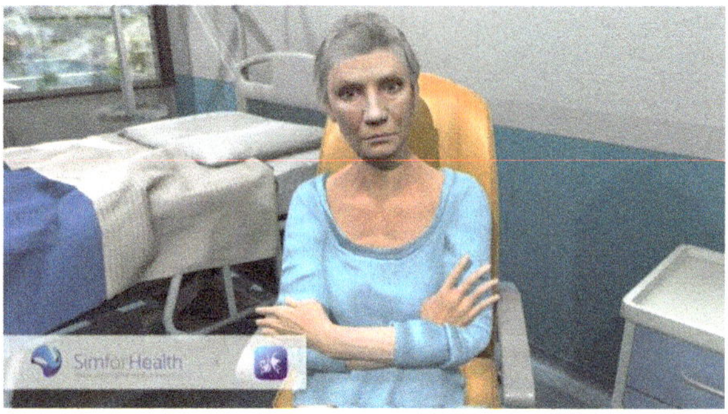

Fig. 1 Screenshot of Mrs. Dupont, who has Alzheimer's disease

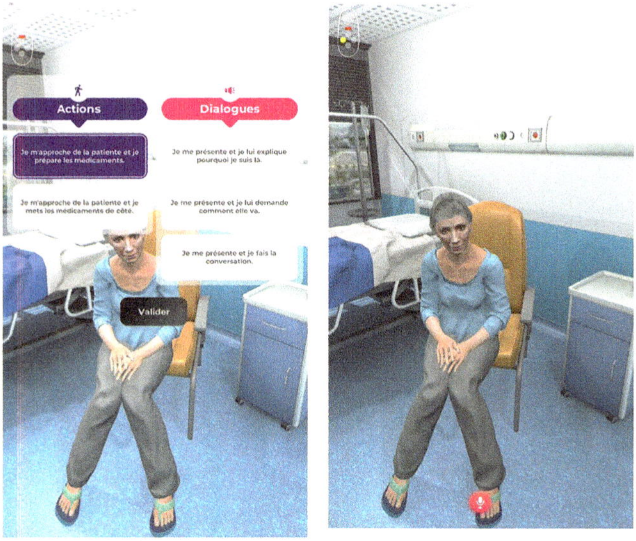

Fig. 2 Screenshot of the scenario

gaze, etc.) and changes of pace during work (pausing, slowing down). The data were then interpreted in light of the volunteers' prior knowledge and experience of communicating with sufferers of Alzheimer's disease or related dementia.

Since work is a continuous process, we decided to examine it independently from the order in which operations were done for administering medication, namely, entering the room, the technical act of administering medication and leaving the room. The total of 46 different interactions examined relate to each of these steps, without distinction. By contrast, instructional analysis of the simulation reveals three use cases which are explained below. Within these use cases, we analyse the figurations produced by the testers in using the simulation.

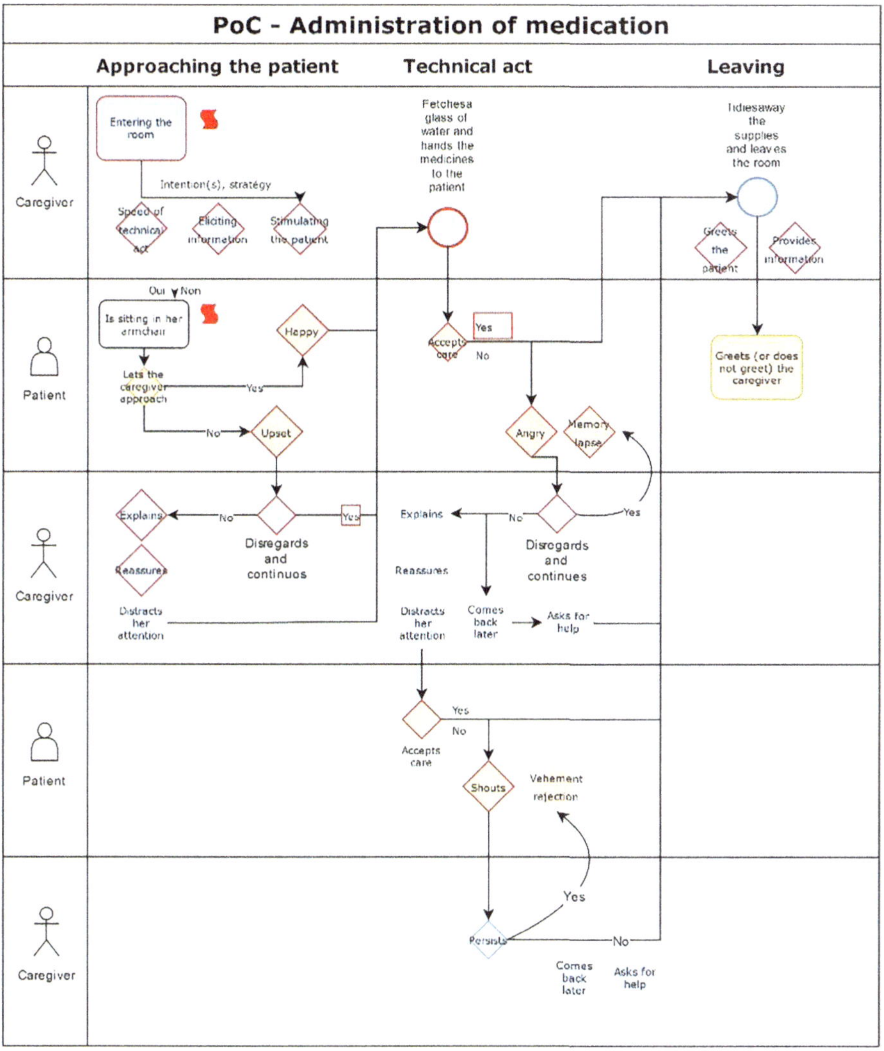

Fig. 3 Interaction diagram for the situation of taking medicine

4.2.1 Use Case 1: Task Completion-Focussed Communication Strategy

The first use case involves a **task completion-focussed communication strategy** prioritising speed of execution, informing the patient and giving explanations. Of the events observed, the following are relevant: selection of options such as "I explain to the patient what I'm doing" or "I persist"; verbal responses intended to inform or explain, or that emphasise speed of execution; lack of any changes in expressiveness or tone, or any adjustment of pace while the action is taking place.

This is a *representative excerpt* from Enwin's guided simulation:

- VP. Hello.
- VP. Hello (upset).
- E. I've brought you your medicine.
- VP. I don't want it. (…) I'm in pain (looks at the caregiver, more upset).
- E. Well, that's exactly why I've come to give you your medicine, to help you feel better (looks at the patient).
- VP. I don't want to (looks away, then looks at the caregiver again, upset).
- E. (displays the options, selects "I explain to her what I'm doing") Yes, you do, you'll see. I gave it to you yesterday (...).
- VP. All right (non-committal).
- E. (displays the options, selects explain "I her what I'm doing") Good, I'll give it to you. Come on, you'll see, it'll soon be over with.

4.2.2 Use Case 2: Patient Relationship-Focussed Communication Strategy

The second use case refers to a **relationship-focussed communication strategy**, based on consideration of the patient's state, ability to express themselves and adaptation to their particularities. Of the events observed, the following are relevant: the selection of options such as "I start a conversation", "I put the medicines to one side" and "I accept her refusal"; interrogative verbal responses used to obtain information about the patient and feedback ensuring the patient's state, ability to express themselves and adaptation to their particularities are taken into account; non-verbal responses conveying an understanding attitude.

This is a *representative excerpt* from Emilene's guided simulation:

- E. Hello, I'm your nurse, Emilene. (leans forward slightly) How are you today? (smiles)
- VP. Hello, I'm not feeling well (upset).
- E. What's wrong? Why aren't you feeling well?
- VP. I'm not feeling well (upset).
- E. (looks at the script and the patient in turn) Didn't you sleep well?
- VP. What are you doing here? What do you want? Leave me alone!
- E. I've come to give you your medicine.
- VP. I don't want it (frowns).
- E. Why don't you want it?

4.2.3 Use Case 3: Patient-Focussed Communication Strategy

The third use case is a **patient-focussed communication strategy** that considers the situation in its entirety and the patient's life history and background. Of the events observed, the following are relevant: the selection of options such as "I make conversation"; verbal responses referring to the patient's family, their activities and interests; non-verbal responses conveying a positive attitude (reassurance, stimulation).

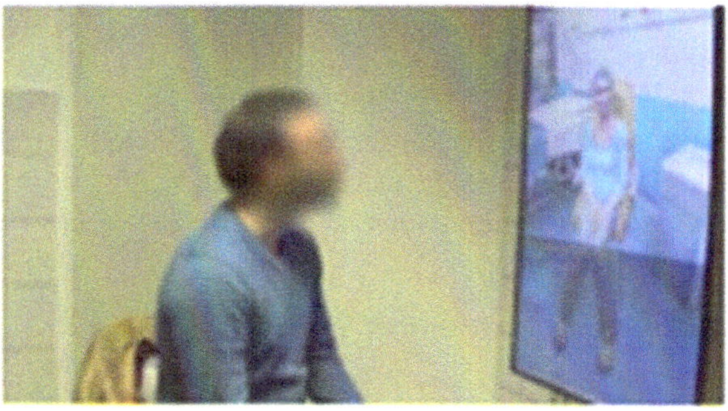

This is a *representative excerpt* from Benjamin's guided simulation:

- B. (looking at the patient) Hello, Mrs Dupont!
- VP. Hello.
- B. I'm Benoit. I'm a doctor and I've brought you your medicine (pulls up a chair to get closer to the patient). How are you feeling?
- VP. I'm not feeling well.
- B. [...] I know (nods). I talked to your husband about it. [...] (Smiles and looks at J., then looks at the patient again) Jérôme, your husband, will be coming to see you later and he told me he might also bring you something to listen to music on.
- VP. Oh! (smiles)
- B. I seem to remember that you're a singer?

4.3 Analysis of Communication Strategies: Testers' Figurations in the PoC

Turning to the methodological protocol, we first point to the improvement in the data-gathering process that results from the presence of the Wizard. The Wizard encourages talking which is essential for eliciting the different forms of figuration. This produces numerous explanations from the testers. There is a distinction between the guided simulation (v1), involving the Wizard, and the non-guided simulation (v2). Given that, we cannot measure how the training provided by the guided simulation impacts the non-guided simulation, but it can be seen that participants find it easier to use the simulator. It should be remembered that the aim of this POC test is to validate the approach to designing simulation situations for training on communication strategies, as well as to provide technical enhancements.

In the first simulation (v1), the testers got to know the system and explored what was possible with the simulator. Some participants asked the wizard lots of questions during the simulation. For example, with Emilene: "- *E. (displays the options and reads them in a whisper) Can I do two things? – J. Yes, you can select the action and then display it again to select the dialogue. – E. Can I talk to her yet? – J. Yes, you can talk to her now; you can do it in whichever order you like. – E. Okay.* ". And with Barberine: "*B. So, it records live, does it? (points back and forth to the PC near the screen) – J. Erm, well, as it's a Wizard of Oz, I can see you for the moment and I'm controlling the patient's responses. – B. Okay.* ". A difference in the testers' behaviour and expressiveness was observed between the first and second simulations. More hesitation was seen in the guided version (v1) and fewer than half interacted directly with the virtual patient by addressing her and adapting their non-verbal communication. In the non-guided version (v2), all interacted directly with the virtual patient and adapted their intonation. They were therefore more comfortable with the simulator, even if one of the testers reported finding it difficult to "talk to the telly" and focussed his attention on what the scriptwriter may have intended.

4.3.1 Communication Strategies Largely Focussed on the Relationship with the Virtual Patient

It was noted that the number of events for each participant remained stable in both simulations, v1 and v2, and that duration could have an impact on the number of events (the longer the tester lingered, the more events there were).

Figure 4 below shows the number of figurations identified for all testers and all simulations, with their events (thought spoken out loud, option choice, verbal and non-verbal response) enabling their reproduction according to the three cases.

For all testers, whether experienced or not, and for all simulations, the strategies are mostly patient relationship focussed. Of the total of 46 cases, ten strategies were identified as being task-oriented, 31 as relationship-oriented and six as patient-oriented.

The predominant, relationship-oriented strategy characteristically considers the patient's clinical and psychological state, how they express themselves and adaptation to their particularities. In this first excerpt, Benjamin accepts **the patient's refusal to cooperate** and refers back to an earlier conversation (that never took place):

"B. How are you feeling? VP. I'm not feeling well. B. Can you tell me a little bit more about that? VP. I don't want to (turns her head and looks away) B. No? Well, you don't have to. Erm...Are you still experiencing the pain you told me about last time? ". In this second excerpt, Benjamin focusses on the **patient's clinical state**: "B. Hello, Mrs Dupont. Hello. VP. (looks at the caregiver). B. Hello. Have I woken you up? VP. Yes. B. How are you? Are you feeling tired? VP. Yes, I'm tired. B. (nods his head briefly) I'm Benjamin (pulls his chair towards the patient, places his hand in the centre of his chest). VP. Oh (appears upset). B. Do you remember who I am? VP. No. B. I'm the doctor looking after you at the hospital. "

In another excerpt, Emilene **asks the patient questions to gain a better understanding of her state and start a conversation**: "E. How are you today? (smiling slightly); VP. Hello, I don't feel well (upset); E. What's wrong? Why aren't you

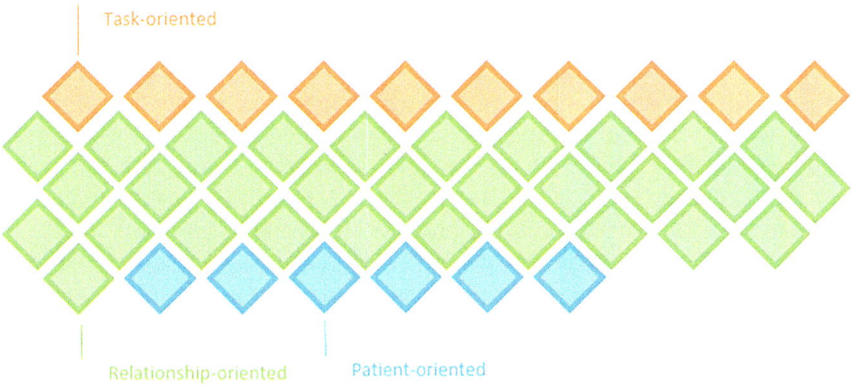

Fig. 4 Distribution of the 46 cases by communication strategy

feeling well?; VP. I don't feel well (upset); E. (looks at the script and the patient in turn) Didn't you sleep well?; VP. What are you doing here? What do you want? Leave me alone! E. I've come to give you your medicine; VP. I don't want it (frowns); E. Why don't you want it? ".

Lastly, in this final excerpt, Alesander **echoes the patient's responses and asks her questions** to find out more: "A. (selects 'I go into the room', mimes opening the door). Hello, Mrs Dupont. Are you well? – VP. No. – A. Why not? What's wrong? – VP. I'm in pain. I'm bored. I'm tired. - A. All right (slight smile). You're in pain, you're bored and you're tired. And what have you been doing this morning? VP. I don't know. "

All testers, regardless of experience, used the relationship-oriented strategy no matter what the virtual patient's prior state was or their resistance to care. This tends to show that participants took account of the priority focus. There are in fact some elements in line with the recommendations included in the description of the issues of refusal to take medication, such as evaluation of the patient's physical and emotional state, and acceptance of their refusal.

4.3.2 Differences in Communication Strategies Between the Experienced and Inexperienced Testers

Those testers with professional experience of patients with Alzheimer's disease or related forms of dementia made use of strategies from the third case, i.e. with patient-focussed communication. For example, Benjamin attempts to influence the patient's emotional state, while providing her with stimulus. "*- B. So, what were you thinking about when I came in? – VP. I'm tired. [...] I'm bored. – B. You're bored? Okay. Did you know that there are activities here at the hospital every day? You can play games, chat to other people who are also in hospital... -VP. Yes, I'll go and join in this afternoon. – B. Oh, that's great news!* ". Rachida attempts to cheer the patient up by suggesting an activity she might like: "*- R. Erm...Have you had any visitors today? – VP. No (smiles) – R. Are you expecting anyone? – VP. No (sad) – R. Maybe you'd like to join in with the workshops, then? – VP. Sure. – R. Today, there's a painting workshop and a gentle fitness class. Do you prefer painting or gentle fitness?* ". We identified a total of six cases that could fit into a patient-oriented strategy. They relate to the recommendations in response to the challenges identified in the situation of refusal to take medication. These strategies consider the situation in its entirety and the patient's life history and background.

In the less experienced testers, the tests initially shed light on communication strategies focussed on the success of the task (left-hand chart). Between the first (v1) and second (v2) simulations, the testers developed their strategies and moved more towards the relationship and the patient, in particular in the phase of approaching the patient. Figure 5 shows the breakdown of the cases, with a few examples illustrated subsequently.

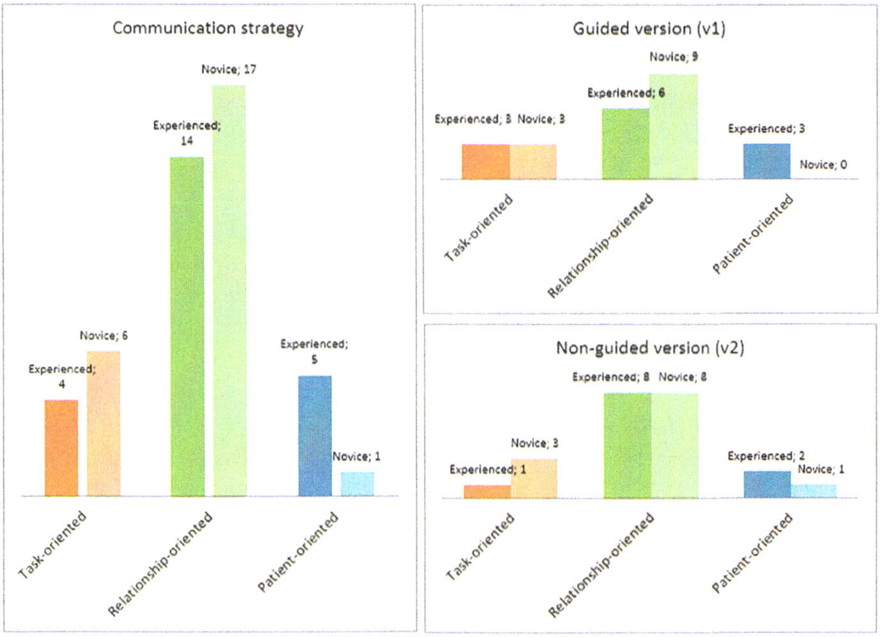

Fig. 5 Distribution of the 46 use cases by communication strategy (left); distribution in the guided simulation (top right); distribution in the non-guided simulation (bottom right)

4.3.3 Changes of Strategy Between the Guided (v1) and Non-guided (v2) Simulation Based on the Testers' Experience

The **experienced testers** attempted to vary the strategies used between the two simulations, to flesh out the scenario, AI learning and the cases derived from the work. For example, in the guided version (v1), Benjamin starts with a relationship-centred and then a patient-centred approach; in the non-guided version (v2), he alternates these approaches twice (relationship, patient, relationship, patient), varying the question types and using references to the patient's life history in a different way (to distract her in v1, to provide stimulus and encourage her to take part in activities in v2).

In the guided version (v1), Emilene adopts an approach that is relationship-, patient- and then relationship-focussed again. In the non-guided version (v2), Emilene adopts an approach that is relationship-, task- and then relationship-focussed. In opting for task-centred communication, she provides further clarification of the knowledge and technical skills associated with the work by introducing explanations on the medicinal treatment, matters of a clinical nature (on bowel function, for example) and miming getting the medicines ready. Lastly, in the non-guided version (v2), Souad develops the relationship-focussed approach and provides commentary for the wizard: *"In this case, we're working solely on refusal of care, and therefore on refusal to take medication. When patients are restless, they move around a lot. In my view, the first step is to catch the patient's eye, but here you've automatically put her right in front of me, so I already have her gaze and her attention. And that's what caregivers are missing, catching the patient's eye, capturing their attention. That's what's missing in the clinical setting, that's what they forget to do. Personally, I would offer a choice of patient position: a patient right in front of you, to the side, looking in completely the opposite direction."*

The **learning design testers, who were less experienced in interactions with patients,** but were skilled in application design, were more helpful in evaluating the ergonomics of the application and the extent to which the patient was realistic (graphic design, expression, etc.) In terms of communication, Enwin's initial focus (v1) was on the aim of the task – giving medicines – despite the patient's annoyance: "*E. (selects I explain what I'm doing and reassure her, then moves closer to the screen and leans towards the patient) Hello. – VP. Hello (slightly annoyed) – E. I've brought you your medicine.*" In the second simulation (v2), the strategy for approaching the patient encourages cheerfulness through chatter: " *– E. (displays the options, selects I start a conversation) Hello (moves a step closer). [...] How are you this morning? – VP. Very well, thank you. How are you? – E. Very well. Did you sleep well?* ".

In this second example, between the guided (v1) and non-guided (v2) simulations, Alesander moves from a strategy focussed on informing and explaining the merits of his actions to a communication strategy involving distraction of the patient to avoid her focussing on the medication.

Alesander v1: "- I knock on the door and open it (miming). Hello, Mrs Dupont, I'm your nurse. – VP. Hello. Come in. (annoyed) [...] – A. (moves closer to the screen, mimes placing the medicines on the bedside table). There we are. – VP. (looks at the caregiver angrily). Why are you doing that? – A. Erm, I'm moving towards the patient, I'm putting the medicines on the side (motions towards the bedside table). I've come to give you your medicine, Mrs Dupont (looks at the position indicators at the top of the screen). – VP. I don't want it. No way, I've already taken your filthy medicine! That's not my medicine. Leave me alone! – A. Yes, it is your medicine. [...] Do you know what this medicine is for? You'll feel better if you take it."

Alesander v2: "- A. (mimes opening the door). Hello, Mrs Dupont. Are you well? – VP. No. – A. Why not? What's wrong? – VP. I'm in pain. I'm bored. I'm tired. – A. All right (slight smile). You're in pain, you're bored and you're tired. And what have you been doing this morning? – VP. I don't know. [...] – A. Okay then. What would like to do to stop you feeling bored? – VP. I don't know. "

We think this result is important, as it indicates that training with the use of the simulation could, in time, help to make a better choice of communication strategy, with an emphasis on the figurations based on the three cases available in the VirtuAlz tool. While promising, a larger number of tests are needed to confirm these results, as there were a total of three cases where testers' strategies were translated or changed to more effective cases in terms of communication strategies. These were the result of an improvement between the two points v1 and v2. Two involved experienced testers and one involved a beginner.

5 Conclusion

This research addresses the design of a simulation tool using a PoC scenario, from identification of training needs to analysis of the simulation produced by experienced and novice testers.

The first part provides the context for this work. We point out the challenges of communicating with patients with Alzheimer's disease or other dementia (2.1) and report on training in communication for nursing staff in France (2.2). Lastly, we identify an emerging need for communication training (2.3).

The second part introduces the three stages of scenario development. Faced with a gap in the requirements of caregivers' work in interactions with patients with Alzheimer's disease or related dementia, caregivers' work (3.1) is analysed to identify ordinary situations and the ways in which they may deteriorate, effective strategies for action, etc. Once the issues of refusal to take medication have been identified (3.2), an instructional preparation phase models the situation, taking account of the technical constraints identified, such as linearity or limitation of interactions (3.3).

The third part focusses on analysis of the simulation to test the PoC scenario. First, we present the protocol used to collect data (4.1). The first phase of testing takes place with a Wizard and entails both a guided simulation (v1) and a non-guided simulation (v2). Eleven participants with different experiences in interacting with patients with Alzheimer's disease or related forms of dementia took part in the prototype testing phases.

Since work is a continuous process, we decided to examine it independently order of operations in the scenario of administering medication, namely, entering the room, the technical act of administering medication and leaving the room. The interactions examined relate to each of these steps, without distinction.[16] By contrast, instructional analysis of the simulation reveals the three cases: task-oriented, relationship-oriented and patient-oriented communication strategies (4.2). Within these cases, we analysed the figurations produced by the testers while using the simulation. We identified communication strategies that were mainly relationship-focussed (4.2.1); in the case of the experienced testers, they were patient-oriented. We also noted changes between simulations v1 and v2, resulting in diversification of strategies for the experienced testers, and in translation to relationship-oriented and patient-oriented strategies for the novice testers (4.2.2).

Based on these promising results, two perspectives are already contributing to the design of the VirtuAlz training:

- The first few tests were used to evaluate the prototype and further our knowledge of the wizards' and caregivers' strategies, in particular for design of the AI and feedback. Their contributions helped to improve the technical basis, adapt the scenario and refine the WOZ control for the purpose of testing with expert healthcare personnel from Broca Hospital. In particular, we developed a tutorial to clarify the guidelines and operating instructions for the simulator. We also harmonised the events produced by the wizard, so we can evaluate and compare the simulations of future prototypes better.
- Around 30 expert healthcare personnel will take part in the second phase of testing for the VirtuAlz project, in order to clarify the figurations for testers and the options for translation during the simulation. Their participation will help us to gather the data needed to develop the AI that will replace the wizard, to evaluate the proposed situation and to formulate criteria for formative assessment in conjunction with automatic real-time interpretation of the non-verbal behaviour of the learner/caregiver and to guarantee the ecological validity of the situations offered to the simulation.

In conclusion, this work is intended to contribute to the design of simulation environments for skills training. This design was produced jointly by simulation specialists and practitioners in the field using a methodology based on analysis of training needs and the simulations produced.Funding Information This project, called VirtuAlz, is funded by the French National Research Agency (ANR-17-CE19-0028; 2017-2021).

[16] This is one of the limitations of this work, relating to the ecological validity of the observations. This question was the subject of a later specific work.

Annex Table

First name	Guided version	Duration	Non-guided version	Duration	Age	Job role	Experience in the medical or paramedical field	Experience with the elderly and/or with patients with Alzheimer's disease or related forms of dementia
Alesander	1	26:56	1	22:45	18–24 years	Cognitive psychology student	Yes – Psychologist (6 months)	Yes – Cognitive and behavioural assessments
Amal	1	03:40	1	02:25	18–24 years	Occupational therapist	Yes – Occupational therapist (1 year)	Yes – Placement in an elderly care association
Balthasar	1	10:20	1	05:00	25–34 years	Doctoral neuropsychology student	Yes – Neuropsychologist (2 years)	Yes – Memory evaluation
Benjamin	1	13:44	1	08:10	35–44 years	Researcher in cognitive psychology and development	No	Yes – 5 years of research on different projects (from cognitive stimulation to psychosocial procedures)
Barberine	1	09:40	1	03:42	18–24 years	Student in VR Computer Engineering	No	Yes – User tests with elderly people
Cécile	0		1	03:15	25–34 years	Graphic design student retraining	No	No available data
Emilene	1	07:25	1	04:00	35–44 years	Healthcare executive	Yes – IFSI (French Institute of Nursing Training) Trainer (10 years)	Yes – In a care department
Enwin	1	04:05	1	02:30	25–34 years	Researcher	No	No
Julia	1	07:15	0		35–44 years	Graphic Designer Communications Officer	No	Yes – User testing
Max	1	03:30	0		25–34 years	Student in Cognitive psychology and ergonomics	Yes – Less than 1 year	No
Rachida	1	21:35	1	08:50	35–44 years	Clinical psychologist Doctoral instructor	Yes	Yes

References

Becerril-Ortega, R., & Petit, L. (2017). Approcher les professionnel·le·s de santé en situation d'interaction avec des patient·e·s atteint·e·s de MAAD. Enjeux méthodologiques. *Actes du 4e colloque international de l'association RPDP*, Juin 2017, Lille.

Becerril-Ortega, R., Petit, L., & Vanderstichel, H. (2019). Élaboration d'un outil de simulation pour la formation de soignant.e.s en gériatrie. Expérimenter pour apprendre ou questionner ses pratiques. *5° colloque international de la didactique professionnelle*, Oct. 2019. Montréal, Canada.

Belzil, G., & Vézina, J. (2015). Impact of caregivers' behaviors on resistiveness to care and collaboration in persons with dementia in the context of hygienic care: An interactional perspective. *International Psychogeriatrics, 27*(11), 1861–1873. https://doi.org/10.1017/S104161021500099X

Benamara, A., Ravenet, B., Prigent, E., Chaby, L., & Martin, J.-C. (2020). Patient virtuel Alzheimer : vers une modélisation informatique des pathologies émotionnelles et expressives. *Workshop sur les Affects, Compagnons artificiels et Interactions, CNRS, Université Toulouse Jean Jaurès, Université de Bordeaux*, Juin 2020. Saint Pierre d'Oléron, France. hal-02933484.

Boet, S., Granry, J.-C., & Savoldelli, G. (2013). *La simulation en santé : De la théorie à la pratique*. Librairie Eyrolles.

Carcaillon Bentata, L., Thuret, A., Beltzer, N., Trifatene, K., & Robert, P. (2017). *La Banque nationale Alzheimer, un outil pour la surveillance épidémiologique des démences en France?* Santé publique France. [Public health France.]

De Plazaola J.-P., & Rignols, E. (coord.) (2018). *Tableaux de l'économie française* [French economic tables], edition 2018. Insee [French National Institute of Statistics and Economic Studies].

Dean, M., Misra, P., Kakkar, D. N., & Kaur, J. (1982). Hospital interactions: Communication by nursing personnel. *The Nursing Journal of India, 73*(10), 254–258.

Derry, S. J., Pea, R. D., Barron, B., Engle, R. A., Erickson, F., Goldman, R., & Sherin, B. L. (2010). Conducting video research in the learning sciences: Guidance on selection, analysis, technology, and ethics. *The Journal of the Learning Sciences, 19*(1), 3–53.

Formarier, M. (2007). La relation de soin, concepts et finalités. *Recherche en soins infirmiers, 89*(2), 33–42.

Gaborit, D. (2017). Éléments pour une pratique du soin relationnel en accueil de jour gériatrique. *Empan, 106*(2), 116–121. https://doi.org/10.3917/empa.106.0116

Gastmans, C. (1998). Interpersonal relations in nursing: A philosophical-ethical analysis of the work of Hildegard E. *Peplau. Journal of Advanced Nursing, 28*(6), 1312–1319.

Granry, J.-C., & Moll M.-C. (2012). *État de l'art (national et international) en matière de pratiques de simulation dans le domaine de la santé*. Dans le cadre du développement professionnel continu (DPC) et de la prévention des risques associés aux soins. HAS. https://www.has-sante.fr/upload/docs/application/pdf/2012-01/simulation_en_sante_-_rapport.pdf

Hagerty, B., & Patusky, K. (2003). Reconceptualizing the nurse-patient relationship. *Journal of Nursing Scholarship, 35*(2), 145–150.

Halldorsdottir, S. (2008). The dynamics of the nurse–patient relationship: Introduction of a synthesized theory from the patient's perspective. *Scandinavian Journal of Caring Sciences, 22*(4), 643–652.

Hansebo, J., & Kihlgren, M. (2002). Carers' interactions with patients suffering from severa dementia: A difficult balance to facilitate mutual togetherness. *Journal of Clinical Nursing, 11*(2), 225–236.

Harwood, R.-H., O'Brien, R., Goldberg, S.-E., Allwood, R., Pilnick, A., Beeke, S., Thomson, L., Murray, M., Parry, R., Kearney, F., Baxendale, B., Sartain, K., & Schneider, J. (2018). *A staff training intervention to improve communication between people living with dementia and health-care professionals in hospital: The VOICE mixed-methods development and evaluation study*. NIHR Journals Library.

Jones, A. (2003). Nurses talking to patients: Exploring conversation analysis as a means of researching nurse-patient communication. *International Journal of Nursing Studies, 40*(6), 609–618.

Mc Donald, S. (2005). Studying actions in context: A qualitative shadowing method for organizational research. *Qualitive Research, 5*(4), 455–473.

McCabe, C. (2004). Nurse–patient communication: An exploration of patients' experiences. *Journal of Clinical Nursing, 13*(1), 41–49.

Moore, L. W., & Proffitt, C. (1993). Communicating effectively with elderly surgical patients. *AORN Journal, 58*(2), 345–350.

Morse, J., Bottorff, J., Anderson, G., O'Brien, B., & Solberg, S. (1992). Beyond empathy: Expanding expressions of caring. *Journal of Advanced Nursing, 17*(7), 809–821.

Nestel, D., & Bearman, M. (2015). *Simulated patient methodology: Theory, evidence, and practice*. Wiley Blackwell.

Petit, L., Vanderstichel, H., Urbiolagallegos, M. J., Benamara, A., Zagdoun, J., Chaby, L., & Becerril Ortega, R. (2021). Recherche, interdisciplinarité et conception de formations : Le projet comme analyseur de l'interdisciplinarité au sein d'une activité collective. *Actes du 55ème Congrès de la SELF, L'activité et ses frontières. Penser et agir sur les transformations de nos sociétés*. 12 et 13 janvier 2021.

Pham Quang, L. (2015). *Émotions et apprentissage en situation tutorale au travail: le cas d'agents de soin mortuaire*. CNAM.

Piaget, J. (1947a). *Psychologie de l'intelligence*. Armand Colin.

Piaget, J. (1947b). *La représentation du monde chez l'enfant*. Puf.

Prissette, S., & Dupuy-Maribas, C. (2016). *Formation par la simulation et soins infirmiers : méthodes, organisations, applications pratiques*. Éditions Lamarre.

Riviere, M., Dufoort, H., Van Hecke, A., Vandecasteele, T., Beeckman, D., & Verhaeghe, S. (2019). Core elements of the interpersonal care relationship between nurses and older patients without cognitive impairment during their stay at the hospital: A mixed-methods systematic review. *International Journal of Nursing Studies, 92*, 154–172.

Rothier Bautzer, É. (2016). Chapitre 2. Une approche sociologique du soin comme travail relationnel. *Journal international de bioéthique et d'éthique des sciences, 27*(1), 41–57. https://doi.org/10.3917/jib.271.0041

Savundranayagam, M. Y., Sibalija, J., & Scotchmer, E. (2016). Resident reactions to person-centered communication by long-term care staff. *American Journal of Alzheimer's Disease & Other Dementias, 31*(6), 530–537.

Tuckette, A. G. (2005). The care encounter: Pondering caring, honest communication and control. *International Journal of Nursing Practice, 11*(2), 77–84.

Van Manen, A., Aarts, S., Metzelthin, S., Verbeek, H., Hamers, J., & Zwakhaken, S. (2021). A communication model for nursing staff working in dementia care: Results of a scoping review. *International Journal of Nursing Studies, 113*, 103776.

Williams, K. N., Ilten, T. B., & Boer, H. (2005). Meeting communication needs: Topics of talk in the nursing home. *Journal of Psychosocial Nursing Mental Health Services, 43*(7), 38–45.

Ergo-Scripting in Activity-Based Training Design: An Illustration from the Design of a Virtual Environment

Vincent Boccara, Renaud Delmas, and Françoise Darses

Abstract This chapter presents our ongoing work on an 'ergo-scripting' approach. The method has been developed and implemented over the past few years in the context of several research projects. Ergo-scripting is based on the argument that the design of learning scenarios must be supported by ergonomic and didactic analyses of work. The process is divided into three steps. The first consists in developing the design project for the simulation tool to be used for training. The aim is to identify the design objectives of the new tool in collaboration with all actors (sponsors, designers, users). The second step consists in analysing the work that trainees are expected to undertake and examine the foundations and implementation of existing training courses from the point of view of trainers and trainees. This step aims to identify baseline production and training situations. The third step consists of scripting training situations. The aim is to develop scenarios that will be used to simulate workplace situations in order to enable the trainee to develop vocational skills. This step seeks to delimit the content of the scenario(s) as a function of the simulated workplace situations and the vocational skills to be developed. We illustrate one use of this method in the context of the VICTEAM project. The aim of the project was to design a virtual training environment that could be used to train medical leaders in the non-technical skills they require to cope with a mass casualty event (attack, external operation, etc.).

V. Boccara (✉)
CNRS, Laboratoire Interdisciplinaire des Sciences du Numérique, Université Paris Saclay, Orsay, France
e-mail: vincent.boccara@universite-paris-saclay.fr

R. Delmas
CNRS, Laboratoire Interdisciplinaire des Sciences du Numérique, Université Paris Saclay, Orsay, France

Institut de recherche biomédicale des armées, Brétigny sur Orge, France
e-mail: delmas@limsi.fr

F. Darses
Institut de recherche biomédicale des armées, Brétigny sur Orge, France
e-mail: francoise.darses@intradef.gouv.fr

S. Flandin et al. (eds.), *Simulation Training through the Lens of Experience and Activity Analysis*, Professional and Practice-based Learning 30,
https://doi.org/10.1007/978-3-030-89567-9_7

Keywords Training design · Scenario · Scripting · Vocational training · Ergonomics

1 Introduction

This chapter presents our ongoing work on an "ergo-scripting" approach. The method has been developed and implemented over the past few years in the context of several research projects (Boccara & Delgoulet, 2015; Couix et al., 2015). Ergo-scripting is based on the argument that the design of learning scenarios must be supported by ergonomic (Falzon, 2014) and didactic (Mayen, 2015) analyses of work. We illustrate one use of this method in the context of the VICTEAM project. The aim of the project was to design a virtual training environment that could be used to train medical leaders in the nontechnical skills they require to cope with a mass casualty event (attack, external operation, etc.).

2 The Ergo-Scripting Approach

The ergo-scripting approach draws upon concepts and methods from ergonomics (Falzon, 2014) and vocational didactics (Mayen, 2015). In ergonomics, it finds its origins in work that has been ongoing for a little over 30 years, which uses workplace analyses to support design projects and anticipate the operational leeway that should be built in from the start of the project (Daniellou, 2004; Béguin & Cerf, 2004; Barcellini et al., 2014). It also draws upon contributions from vocational didactics; on the one hand, in the design of training based on the analysis of workplace situations and, on the other hand, conceptualization in action as a dimension that is organized by, and organizes human activities (Pastré, 1999; Mayen, 2015; Tourmen et al., 2017; Samurçay & Rogalski, 1998). Finally, it takes inspiration from research in psychoergonomics. The latter proposes a very different approach to professional skills which are considered as resources for human activity (Samurçay & Rabardel, 2004; Boreham et al., 2002), and to the design of vocational training situations (Samurçay & Rogalsky, 1998).

The process is divided into three steps. The first consists of developing the design project for the simulation tool to be used for training (§ 2.1). The aim is to identify the design objectives of the new tool in collaboration with all actors (sponsors, designers, users). The second step (§ 2.2) consists in analyzing the work that trainees are expected to undertake, and examine the foundations and implementation of existing training courses from the point of view of trainers and trainees. This step aims to identify baseline production and training situations. The third step (§ 2.3) consists of scripting training situations. Here, the aim is to develop scenarios that will be used to simulate workplace situations in order to enable the trainee to develop vocational skills. This step seeks to delimit the content of the scenario(s) as a function of the simulated workplace situations and the vocational skills to be developed.

In this chapter, we propose that the ergo-scripting method can help to overcome four, well-known pitfalls found in design projects (Daniellou, 2004; Martin, 2005):

1. Poor oversight by the contracting authority that results in the over-specification of the project's objectives by the project manager.
2. Late consideration of the characteristics and constraints of actual work, the importance of which only becomes apparent at the time of an evaluation.
3. A lack of perspective regarding the work to be carried out, limited to instructions.
4. Exclusive reliance on expert opinion, no *in situ* analysis of the actual work of operators.

2.1 Step 1: Developing the Design Project for the Simulation Tool to Be Used for Training

Classically found in ergonomics (Guerin et al., 1991), this step consists in examining the intentions of the company or institution that is running the project. The goal is to ensure that the transformation of the existing situation does meet the training objectives and respond to operational challenges. The aim is twofold: to improve the system's performance and maintain, or even improve, the health of all the actors involved (sponsors, designers, and users). To achieve this, it is necessary to analyze the limits of existing tools and training situations; it is also necessary to specify the needs of trainers and trainees, along with any conditions for access to real-work situations. Finally, the goals and conditions of the training must be unambiguously identified. For example, the decision to design a virtual training environment presupposes that there is a clear understanding of the extent to which this tool is able to bridge the gap between an inadequate, existing training situation and the desired one.

This step must involve all of the actors who will be working in this future situation with the proposed system (or, at the very least, representatives of trainers and trainees) together with their social partners (Daniellou, 2004; Barcellini et al., 2014). The partnership must be *participative*, in the true sense of the term. It is important that future users are not only involved at the evaluation and usability testing phases—they must be included right from the beginning—during needs analysis and drawing up the functional specification (Darses, 2004; Darses & Reuzeau, 2004). This approach establishes the conditions that support the participation of the various actors throughout the project and enables them to collectively identify the challenges inherent in the design of the new training situation with respect to didactic objectives, content, tools, and, more broadly, working conditions.

2.2 *Step 2: Ergonomic and Didactic Analyses*

2.2.1 One Work Analysis: Two Inseparable Approaches

The first element in this step is to analyze the real-life workplace situations that are the focus of training. It is relatively well understood by the designers of training or simulation tools. Nevertheless, it is often limited to an analysis of the prescribed task. Although it is clear that ergonomic analysis examines the prescribed task, above all, it aims to gain an in-depth understanding of how workers carry out this task in everyday situations given their different personal characteristics, such as age, experience, gender, skills, etc. Figure 1 shows this axis as Pole A.

However, the ergonomic analysis must be complemented by an analysis of work in training situations, represented by Pole B in Fig. 1. Following Boccara and Delgoulet (2015), we argue that it is necessary to consider the training situation as a workplace situation in its own right. This axis is often given little thought, or even ignored, in training design projects, and its value is overlooked. However, we know the extent to which the introduction of a new training system can transform learning conditions for trainees, and working conditions for trainers.[1] The ergonomic analysis of these workplace situations becomes a key resource that guides and feeds into the construction of future training situations in the same way as in technical-organizational change projects.

The analysis of work carried out in these two areas is part of a "*global approach, in which the analysis of the activity* [of workers] *becomes part of an analysis of the economic, technical and social factors the operator must face, and an analysis of the impacts of how the firm operates on the population concerned and economic performance*" (Daniellou, 1996, p. 185). The analysis of work cannot, therefore, be

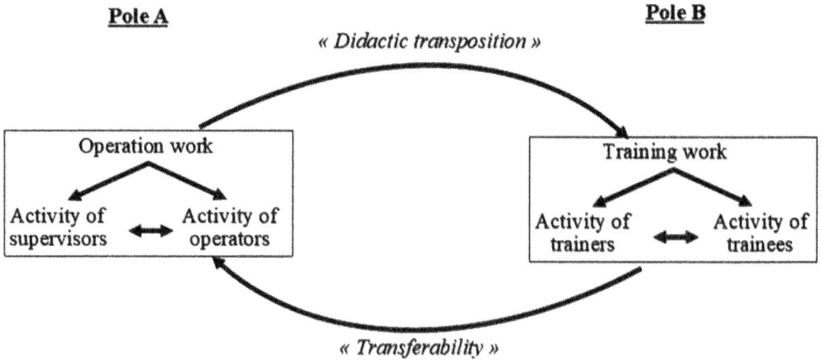

Fig. 1 Generic schema of the objects of the analysis of work. (Adapted from Boccara and Delgoulet 2015)

[1] We do not elaborate on this point here. We invite the reader to consult Boccara and Delgoulet (2015) who provide a detailed argument.

reduced to an analysis of prescribed tasks. It must encompass all of the levels that shape operational and training situations, in particular, organizational and institutional levels.

We use classical ergonomic methods for our analysis. Typically, we begin by carrying out a documentary analysis, collecting training documentation, and workplace instructions. These are supplemented by observations of real-life situations (Guérin et al., 1991) and initial exploratory interviews, followed by more sophisticated tools, such as confrontation interviews (Mollo & Falzon, 2004) that provide more detailed information on the areas of interest as a function of the scenarios to be designed. This type of interview provides a detailed understanding of the cognitive processes and conceptualizations that organize workers' operating modes and self-regulation strategies.

This ergonomic analysis of workplace situations also includes a didactic dimension that is structured along three axes. The first aims to characterize baseline professional knowledge. Samurçay and Rogalski (1998, p. 345) define this as "*categories of objects and processing found in effective practices that make it possible to move from here-and-now situations that are experienced to concepts and methods that make it possible to represent them and foresee potential others*". The second axis describes vocational skills from a dual point of view: those required by the task and those used by operators. In this context, we draw upon the COMPETY model. This theoretical framework includes skills that are compatible with an approach focused on situated human activities (Samurçay & Rabardel, 2004). The third axis aims to account for the didactic transpositions that occur in current training situations with respect to baseline vocational situations from two perspectives: (1) those that occur during the design of training systems, which can be traced through system documentation; and (2) those that occur in real training sessions (Samurçay & Rogalski, 1998; Becerril Ortega et al., 2018).

2.3 Step 3: From Analysis to the Design of Training Scenarios

2.3.1 Using Situations That Highlight Tensions Between What Is Desirable and What Is Possible as a Way in

Ergonomic and didactic analyses of workplace situations are another ways to build a library of situations that could be usefully integrated into training situations. Here, we revisit the work of Mayen et al. (2010), which puts aside the notion of skills when designing training, instead focusing on the workplace situations that professionals must master. This avoids an approach focused on skills, which can become difficult to depart from when working with other training design actors. The underlying logic is consistent with ideas found in vocational didactics (Mayen 2015) and some of the ergonomics literature related to training design (cf. Vidal-Gomel, 2021 for a review). Mayen proposes that the design process should focus on vocational situations that allow the trainee to develop relevant skills (Mayen, 1999), since the ultimate goal of training is that professionals will be able to "*manage, cope, get by, and sometimes even master*" these situations ((Mayen et al., 2010, p. 64). In the end, the trainee is not expected to have acquired an encyclopedic knowledge of procedures and rules. Generally, the company—or the institution—expects them to be able to use procedures and rules as one of several instruments that demonstrate "*task intelligence*" (Montmollin, 1988); trainees use; and build upon their new-found knowledge to deal with all of the different situations they encounter in the workplace.

If we extend this line of reasoning, the challenge of scripting a training situation is therefore not to develop a "situated" procedure, but rather to learn how to manage a workplace situation. The challenge is to script rich workplace situations, in which procedures and rules are only one of many performance components that support their management. In this context, the COMPETY model can be used to identify a set of components found in embedded competencies, which can be used to manage workplace situations: (1) representations; knowledge; and concepts; (2) instrument systems that combine artifacts and use patterns; (3) activities that organize action (patterns, rules, procedures, etc.); and (4) categories of situations.

2.3.2 Develop a Library of Baseline and Characteristic Action Situations

Ergonomic and didactic analyses of workplace situations offer a way to develop a library of *reference situations* (Daniellou, 2004), rather than a library of *procedures, rules or tasks to be carried out*. In other words, real-life workplace situations (observed and/or narrated) are identified that are significant with respect to the training objectives. They include normal workplace situations, degraded situations, incident or accident situations, etc. They can be routine, rare, a source of concern, etc. They may also be situations that are significant for the operators who must manage them. Although they do not constitute a model of what should be achieved, they are a suitable entry point to guide the scripting of training situations.

Starting with these reference situations, it is then necessary to identify *characteristic action situations* (CAS) as a function of four dimensions: (1) the objectives to be achieved and those being pursued; (2) criteria for success; (3) vocational categories; and (4) factors likely to influence the internal state of the people involved (Daniellou, 2004). Mayen et al. (2010) propose a conceptualization that is similar to the CAS based on vocational didactics that use the notion of the *generic situation*, which they analyze as a function of six dimensions: (1) goals and conditions (material, social, technical, and natural); (2) complexity; (3) variables that play a role in the situation from the point of view of the actors involved; (4) indicators related to the state of the variables; (5) actions carried out by the actors involved (mental and linguistic gestures); and (6) the resources needed to carry out tasks. Based on these two approaches, we use eight dimensions to describe CAS, adopting an ergo-scripting approach: (1) goals and conditions (material, social, technical, and natural); (2) the criteria for success, from the point of view of both what is required, and that of those who carry out the task; (3) variables that characterize the complexity of the situation from the point of view of those who must manage it; (4) the actors involved (directly and indirectly); (5) variables that influence the situation from the point of view of the actors involved; (6) indices and indicators related to the state of variables; (7) operating modes and self-regulation strategies implemented by the actors involved; and (8) the material and social resources needed to carry out the task.

The challenge is then to build a repository of vocational situations made up of reference situations and CAS. These elements become an intermediate object in the design process with the aim of highlighting tensions between two orientations, what is desirable and what is possible (Daniellou, 2004), by encouraging project actors to adopt the point of view of usage (Folcher, 2015). More specifically, Folcher distinguishes between the usage manager, the contracting party, and the project manager. According to the latter author, the ergonomist does not help the contracting party (who expresses what they want the future to look like) or the project manager (who is responsible for technical feasibility). Nor do they function as an interface. Instead, he or she is a third-party who is responsible for a different aspect: usage. Here, we should understand usage in the broad sense of all of the human activities that will be a direct part of the future training situation. It also refers to the analysis of human activities which are seen as a resource for producing reference points and making design choices, which are the responsibility of the different actors in the design process (sponsors, designers, and users).

Moreover, usage does not end when the design project ends; on the contrary, it often begins: "*Whether it is a question of technical and organizational systems, standards or rules, real frameworks or digital environments, what is designed will be appropriated, transformed, and shaped by users to serve purposes that are part of the complex and unpredictable interplay of the constraints and possibilities of their situated activities*" (*op. cit.* p. 41). This implies, for example, anticipating—from the design stage—not only the activities of users such as trainers and trainees, but also the maintenance of the technical systems that are deployed in the training situation. Thus, the training design project must integrate mechanisms and timeframes related to the process of appropriation of the technologies that will be implemented by users once the good or service has been put into use (Béguin & Cerf, 2004).

In our experience, this workplace analysis produces a very rich library of situations, among which only a few are technically feasible given the characteristics of the training project: available technologies, human and financial resources, training challenges, etc. The repository becomes a tool that can feed into and guide the complex compromises that arise in training design projects. It goes beyond a tool for the design of training scenarios, and becomes one that can be used to (re)examine work and how it is carried out in production and training situations, from two perspectives: improving both occupational health and performance.

2.3.3 Develop Scenarios Based on Reference Situations

Before starting to build a scenario, it is best to begin by defining the object to be designed. Whether in the scientific ergonomics literature or in the field of training, the notion of the scenario is poorly defined and polysemic (Boccara & Perez-Toralla, 2021). We can identify at least four ways. In the field of training, the scenario is designed by instructors who need to meet didactic objectives (e.g., Peeters et al., 2014). It represents a procedure, a guide that should be followed to carry out a task, or a situation that learners are trained in. The scenario can either refer to an everyday, normal situation, or a rare, complex emergency. In the field of ergonomic design, the scenario is a tool that makes it possible to represent (existing or future) usage, which supports the design of an artifact, a workplace situation, or even how work is organized (e.g., Daniellou, 2004; Vincent & Blandford, 2015; Nelson et al., 2014). Scenario design is generally based on the contribution of designers and users with varied profiles. In the field of decision-making, a scenario is a dynamic interactive model, composed of variables that must be manipulated to identify possible responses to a complex situation (e.g., Turoff et al., 2016). In the field of safety, it refers more to a standard model that is constructed from real, historical data that represent an accident, an incident or a typical situation in which the former occur (Duguay et al., 2001; Distefano & Leonardi, 2018).

Although there are many ways to build scenarios in training situations (e.g., Stacy & Freeman, 2016), in our experience, they are often based on extracting information from prescriptive documents supplemented by so-called expert opinion. The resulting scenarios are then structured as follows: beginning with *procedure X* that must be taught, we associate a *scenario X′* (which reproduces the procedure as faithfully as possible), which is implemented by *script X′*. We can add levels of difficulty to these scripts: beginners versus experts, with or without assistance, with or without time constraints, etc. These levels of difficulty do not, however, represent variation in the implementation of the procedure with regard to the characteristics of the situation. The scenario remains structured by a prescribed procedure; deviations from this procedure are recorded. From this perspective, the architecture of the script is structured around a library of prescribed procedures rather than situations.

From our point of view, a training situation scenario must make it possible to simulate all or part of a workplace situation for learning purposes. In other words, we can draw upon Mayen's (2012) proposal, which establishes the boundaries of training design as the design of *potential development situations* for trainees. This does not, however, tell us much about what is learned and the actual progress made by trainees during and after their training. Development goes beyond training situations (Boccara et al., accepted). It refers to transformations in the subject that require, notably, time for them to become established. Its dynamics combine the short, medium, and long term, they are nonlinear and past, present, and future are intertwined. It is therefore nonhomogeneous: it is made up of growth spurts, periods of stability, and regression, either transitional or more sustained. It is also conditional: it can be said to be a potential that may or may not be realized as a function of the support provided by the environment.

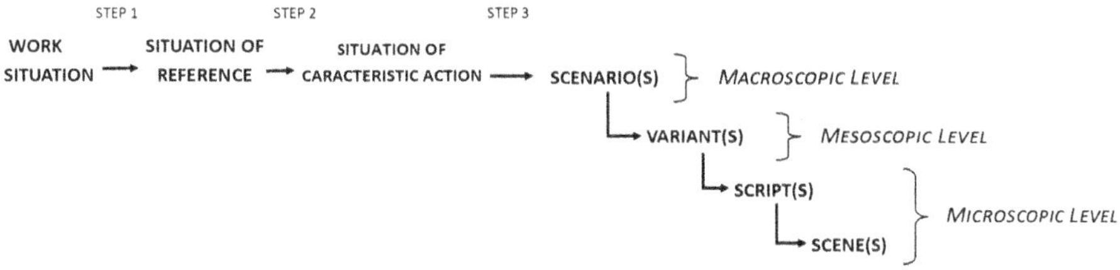

Fig. 2 Schematic illustration of the three levels describing a scenario

With this background, we argue that a scenario corresponds to a sequence of events within an (material and social) environment. The latter corresponds to the transposition of a CAS that integrates learning and development potentialities, for those who will have to manage them in training. This definition calls for a structure that is flexible and can be adapted to a training situation scenario. We therefore propose a scenario that is divided into three levels: *macroscopic*, *mesoscopic,* and *microscopic*. At each of these levels, *reference situations* and *CAS* feed into the gradual construction of the scenario(s). These three levels do not constitute formalism or a language. They simply provide a descriptive framework that makes it possible to propose "intermediate objects" (Jeantet, 1998; Jeantet et al., 1996) upon which design actors can collaborate during the scripting process and progressively integrate the reasoning needed for the design of the training situation (Fig. 2).

The Macroscopic Level The macroscopic level delimits the scenario, its objects, its phases, and its timeframes, from the point of view of the processes and activities of operators. This makes it possible to identify what will not be included in the scenario, but will need to be introduced as a preamble to facilitate the trainee's understanding of the situation. By analogy, this level corresponds to a synopsis of the training situation that the trainee will have to manage. The description can take the form of a relatively short narrative that helps to understand the initial state, the events that occur, any unexpected turns, and possible outcomes of the situation. However, it remains a skeleton that can later be presented differently depending on design constraints (technical, material, human, financial, time, etc.) and learning and training challenges. It relies upon the outputs of work analyses in order to develop an organized structure that can be discussed within the design group with respect to "what" and "how" trainees will be trained (Olry & Vidal-Gomel, 2011).

A starting point in the development of the macroscopic representation of the scenario is an in-depth analysis of the work process and the tasks that compose it. This description aims to formalize "who", "must do what", "when", "where", "with what resources", and according to "what criteria" (quality, production, cost, etc.). It also requires identifying gaps between prescribed, expected, redefined, and actual tasks, in order to begin to identify the different reasoning, success criteria, and initial elements related to the variables that operate in the work situations in question.

This first level of description makes it possible to discuss and debate the perimeter of the scenario to be built and to situate it within the broader work process that it is part of. The principal focus of this level is the library of reference situations. Characteristic action situations are often too fine-grained, although they can also be used. They are more often a resource for working at the mesoscopic and microscopic levels.

The Mesoscopic Level This level corresponds to "variants" that provide a more refined description of the scenario. They include a description of tasks, subtasks, actors, professional dilemmas, locations, available resources, success criteria, and the objectives pursued. They make it possible to specify the situations that the trainee could be asked to manage in the training system. The aim is to specify skills that are likely to be acquired by comparing these simulated situations with the didactic objectives linked to the scenario. The latter are related to instantiations of the reference situation that support the development of these skills in the trainee. Characteristic action situations are typically used to envisage possible or desirable variants of a scenario. The preliminary work analysis phase can incorporate a description of them. They are a valuable resource when identifying operational invariants and sources of variability that should be taken into account in order to maximize the learning potential of situations proposed in the training system. As at the previous level, the selection must be done collectively within the project to gradually integrate the options, limits, and constraints of the various project stakeholders (designers, decision-makers, end-users, etc.).

The Microscopic Level This level refers to the concrete operationalization of a scenario in such a way that it can be "played out" in a future training situation. Scenes are constituent elements of scripts that can be used to "stage" the CAS that are the focus of training. The aim here is to reflect the environment, actions, and interactions, along with any relevant changes in the environment that will help the trainee to learn to confront, manage, or cope with one or more situations. In other words, so that they live the experience.

At this level, analyses of activities, and work carried out upstream are a key resource when identifying the forms of action and interaction, the deployment of operating modes and strategies related to standard professional knowledge, together with the form and content of communication with virtual characters in simulated situations. Like the two other levels, this activity must involve all project members, and must highlight tensions between what is desirable from the point of view of vocational learning and what is possible from a physical, technical, organizational, and social point of view. This level provides the most fine-grained insight into didactic transpositions in the design process. Two criteria can be helpful in judging these transpositions: (1) internal relevance during training; and (2) external relevance between training and work (Delgoulet, 2015). Internal relevance during training refers to the appropriateness of the training system with respect to the characteristics of trainees and trainers, material, financial, organizational, and human resources, and the targeted learning and development challenges. External relevance refers to the coherence of the training situation with regard to the content of work, learning objectives, and the reciprocal coherence between working conditions in production and those during training. The notion is related to the question of the faithfulness and validity of the simulation, whether this relates to the psychological, physical, social dimension, etc.

This level of description also makes it possible to clearly refine "to what" and "how" trainees should be trained (Olry & Vidal-Gomel, 2011). The latter can feed into a set of specifications for the training system (tools, simulators, number and qualifications of trainers, number of trainees, prerequisites, content, time, etc.). Here, we draw upon the ergonomics literature on intervention design, which anchors the intervention in verbal simulation methods on mockups by comparing prescriptive and action scenarios in a participative manner (Barcellini et al., 2014; Van Belleghem, 2018). In our case, one tool that has proved to be effective in several projects for groups of designers is a table that describes, step-by-step, "who does", "what", "where", and "how". The table is complemented by a flowchart that provides a graphical representation of possible paths. This type of tool can easily become an intermediate design object that can be enriched by various members of the project group (e.g., regulators, managers, engineers, trainers, and users). It can be used in two ways: (1) to build a clear sequence of experiences for the trainee; or (2) as a sequence of prototypical scenes that are considered to be a sort of envelope of possibilities. In both cases, the challenge is to define the place and the role(s) of actors in the training system—trainer(s) and trainee(s)—in a simulation situation and a simulated situation given the physical, technical, and organizational constraints. This approach is particularly useful as it supports discussion, beginning in the upstream phases, of two ongoing unknowns in vocational training design projects: the experience of trainers and the experience of trainees.

3 Illustration of the Ergo-Scripting Method Taken from the VICTEAMS Project

3.1 Step 1: Developing the Design Project for the Simulation Tool to Be Used for Training

3.1.1 The Requirement

The design and implementation of training in how to manage a mass casualty influx are particularly difficult. Starting with design, these programs train teams in various medical roles, and achieve different objectives depending on their function (caregiver, leader, etc.). The first objective is to learn technical skills (e.g., for a caregiver, how to correctly apply a tourniquet) or technical knowledge (e.g., for the leader, how to supervise triage). The second is to learn so-called nontechnical skills. These cognitive, psychosocial, and emotional skills are widely described in the literature (Flin et al., 2008). For example, a medical leader must acknowledge the opinions of members of the healthcare team, but still provide leadership; a caregiver must be able to communicate with others and know when to ask for help from the leader. The third is to train tactical and medical teams to work together so that constraints related to effective victim management do not conflict with the optimal execution of the mission.

While technical objectives, notably learning manual skills and caregiving can be easily achieved using unsophisticated scenarios, the same cannot be said for nontechnical skills, such as those related to medical leadership. The latter are found in complex situations, both in terms of interactions (diverse personalities, with diverse initial knowledge, under intense stress, etc.) and in terms of the sequence of operational constraints (change in the patient's condition, more-or-less serious injuries, available resources, multiple tasks, high degree of scalability, etc.). Currently, only full-scale simulations that run over several days allow the implementation of, and training in nontechnical skills. In this respect, the benefits of *in vivo* training are undisputed: trainees, who are fully absorbed by the dynamics and the realism of the simulated situation, can be supervised by experienced trainers. These full-scale simulations go beyond the simple application of procedures and behaviors. They provide case studies that trainees can draw upon during operations, and they can be regularly updated using feedback from operational theatres. Some can be used to simulate operations that run over several days, notably to simulate the effects of fatigue.

However, such training programs are very expensive, both with respect to human resources and logistics, which limit their implementation. This observation has led to the development of technological tools—serious games or immersive virtual environments—that could, if not replace, at least complement *in vivo* training programs. Such tools have the potential to support learning with respect to certain aspects of the management of a mass influx of victims—through repetition, a focus on specific learning objects, postevent review during debriefing, stopping, and resuming the simulation, or even accelerating or slowing down time. In this context, the pluridisciplinary research project *Virtual Individual Characters for Team Training: Emotional, Adaptive, Motivated, and Social* (VICTEAMS, 2015–2019) aimed to design a prototype virtual training environment. The virtual environment consists of scenarios that simulate complex, dynamic situations and supports training in nontechnical skills for medical leaders. These objectives require: (1) giving the learner significant freedom to act during the simulation; (2) dynamic control of scenarios to maximize learning and maintain coherence between them, from both internal (within the virtual world) and external (in relation to real situations) points of view; and (3) the ability to explain events, the actions taken by the different characters, and the virtual situations.

3.1.2 The Challenge of Scripting the Virtual Environment

Designing such a virtual environment poses several technological challenges: computer models, computing capacities, graphic rendering, etc. But they also raise other challenges that relate to how to design simulated situation scenarios. While technological progress means that it is possible to build ever-more-efficient virtual environments for vocational training, designing scenarios that accurately reflect complex and rapidly changing work situations remains a challenge (Barot, 2014). As noted above, scenarios in virtual environments are typically designed in cooperation with experts working in the profession, who tell designers the procedures and rules that trainees must learn and follow. Scenarios feature one (or more) learning "pathways" that the trainee must follow in order to acquire knowledge of procedures and rules, a strategy that overcomes the problem of the diversity and variability found in real-world work situations. Such scenarios are inflexible and cannot be adapted to the actions that are actually undertaken by the learner during the simulation (Barot, 2014). Moreover, this approach assumes that there is a repository of instructions regarding the work that has to be carried out and the skills that have to be trained. However, when a project begins, these elements have to be determined: on the one hand, many years of work must be dedicated to formalizing and constructing a doctrine and, on the other hand, the construction and implementation of full-scale training courses rely on the knowledge of a small community of experienced professionals. One of the many challenges is, therefore, to develop a work analysis method that can contribute to the design of training scenarios in the virtual environment.

3.1.3 Structuring the Project and Its Actors

A pluridisciplinary consortium was formed that brought together computer scientists, automation specialists, designers, physicians, psychologists, and ergonomists. The fire fighter of Paris (BSPP) and the medical officer training school (EVDG) represented end-users (both trainers and trainees) as these two structures have dedicated training managers and trainers. The first two years of the project were an opportunity to build a shared vision of the objectives, which lie at the crossroads of research challenges specific to each partner, challenges related to system usage, and commercial challenges. Eventually, a consensus developed regarding the specifications presented below. The role of the virtual environment is to help train medical leaders in the nontechnical skills that they need to care for casualties during a mass influx of victims. We therefore decided that the trainee would wear a head-mounted helmet (HTC Vive) that would immerse him or her in a virtual environment, populated by autonomous characters with whom he or she could interact. In this environment, the person would be able to assume the role of medical leader during a mass influx of victims. Ultimately, it is expected to complement existing professional training systems, in two respects. The first is that it should be a learning tool for trainees (interns, experienced military doctors, OPEX preparation, and BSPP doctors). The second is that it will be a complementary instrument for trainers. From this perspective, we envisage that it will be used either in the presence or the absence of a trainer, in order to satisfy the wide range of training situations found within the armed forces medical service (SSA) and the BSPP.

3.1.4 Step 2: Ergonomic and Didactic Analyses

Our analysis of work began with a review of required documentation (job descriptions, training programs, trainers' documents, etc.) and 15 days of observation of full-scale training situations. We then conducted 16 in-depth interviews with managers and trainers (designers and facilitators) of these training courses (six semidirective interviews each lasting three hours, followed by ten confrontation interviews). It should be noted that the exceptional nature of events involving the management of a mass influx of victims did not allow us to conduct observations in real operational situations. We were only able to access these situations through interviews. Additional data collection could have been based on feedback from external operations, but that was beyond the scope of this project.

This data collection exercise allowed us to run a series of analyses concerning the work of medical leaders during a mass influx of victims, together with the work of trainers and trainees in training situations. To avoid redundancy and respect space limitations, here we do not present each of these analyses in detail. Readers who wish to know more will find in-depth analyses in the thesis of Renaud Delmas (2019).[2] On the other hand, the following sections present some of the results of these analyses, which were then used as intermediate design objects in the ergo-scripting approach.

3.1.5 Step 3: From Analysis to the Design of Training Scenarios

In this section, we present several intermediate objects that were used at the three levels of the ergo-scripting approach presented in Sect. 2.3.3 above: macroscopic, mesoscopic, and microscopic.

The Macroscopic Level At this level, we constructed a graphic representation of the process of managing a mass influx of victims. Here, the aim was to highlight the complexity of the work process as a function of several dimensions, and make it clear to all of the actors involved in the design of the virtual environment (Fig. 3). This schematization of the work process represents, in the horizontal plane: (1) time scales, (2) the main steps in the process, and (3) the events that characterize these steps. The vertical plane represents: (4) groups of actors who participate in the process either on-site or remotely; which then (5) makes it possible to specify the tasks and the sub-tasks that each person is responsible for, along with the timeframe and any dependencies using logical descriptors. This graphical representation also makes it possible to highlight the needs of actors in terms of: (6) spatio-temporal and temporo-operational coordination.

The representation described above allowed all actors involved in the design to gradually delimit the scenario given the framework of the project (Fig. 3, dotted

[2] https://tel.archives-ouvertes.fr/tel-02107648

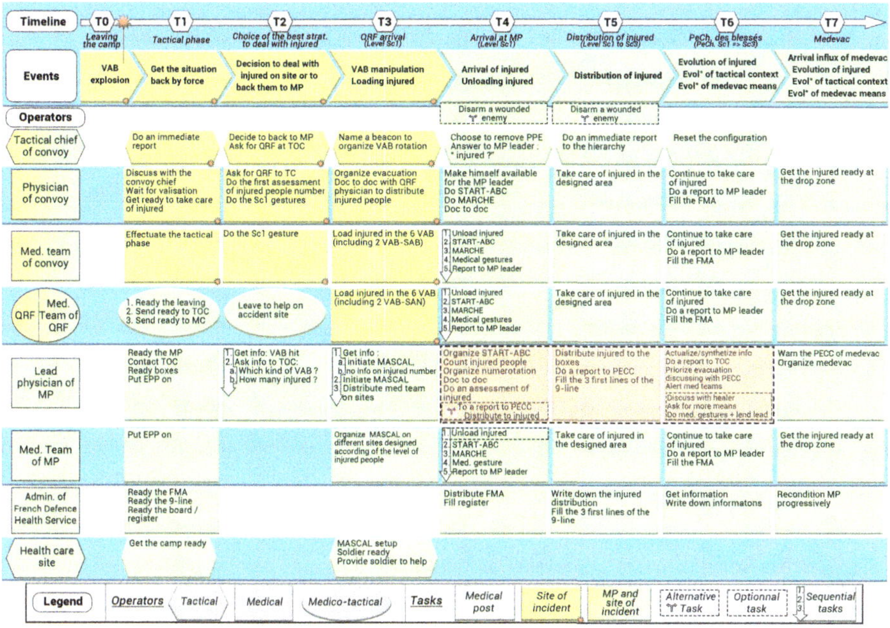

Fig. 3 Schematic illustration of the work process in relation to a mass influx of victims

square). Times T4 to T6 represent the process of handling a mass influx of victims, which is contextualized within a complex, overall process. This perimeter was the outcome of extensive discussions regarding the current training needs of medical leaders with respect to nontechnical skills, complementarities with existing training systems, and technical feasibility (in terms of a virtual environment that could be developed given the project's resources and the skills of the consortium's actors). At another level, this graphical representation, supplemented by analyses of workplace situations, also highlighted and facilitated a discussion of the components that were required to be present in simulated situations in the virtual environment. The tool played a key role in the definition of the specifications of the components that were required to ensure the relevance and coherence of the virtual scenes compared to the real-world work process. These components included the set of virtual characters and their functions, the environment, vehicles, physical objects, time dynamics, the duration of scenes, etc. On the one hand, all of these factors potentially impacted the complexity of the situations to be simulated and, on the other hand, acted as variables that should be taken into account in order to build rich simulated situations that would optimize learning, and contribute to the overall goal of developing the nontechnical skills of medical leaders.

The Mesoscopic Level (Fig. 4) The objective at this level was to propose intermediate objects that could feed into the collective design of rich simulated situations. We focused on two intermediate objects that would provide input to the design of the

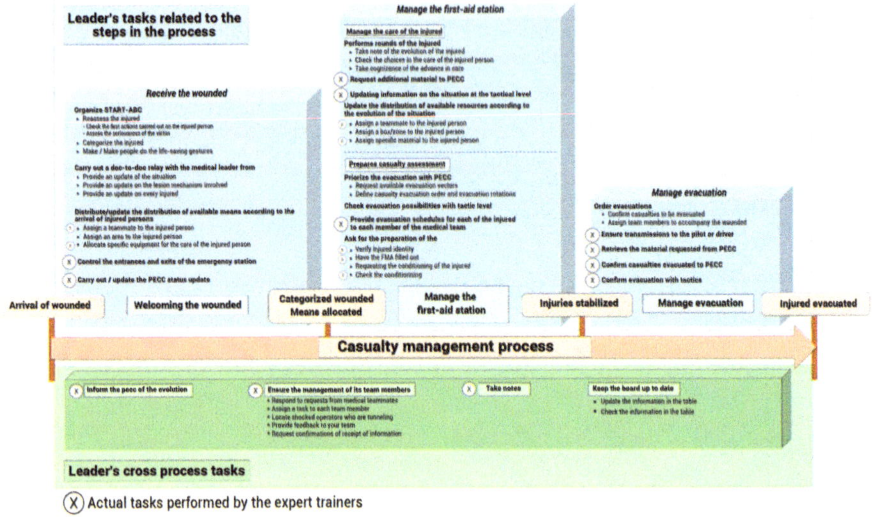

Fig. 4 Schematic illustration of the tasks of a medical leader

scenario and potential variants: (1) a detailed model of the medical leader's tasks between T4 and T6 (Fig. 4); and (2) a list of nontechnical skills that medical leaders should be trained in (Fig. 5).

The first step was to gain a better understanding of the tasks of the medical leader during a mass casualty event. The objective here was to produce a detailed model of the task in question, that was considered to be representative of the activities of medical leaders (Hoc & Leplat, 1995). This model could then be the focus of a discussion within the design team and would feed into the scenario and the virtual scenes that computer models were expected to produce. The idea behind the task analysis is that it should provide an entry point to understanding the goals that medical leaders do pursue (manpower/what is possible), must pursue (requirements) or should pursue (what is desirable) during a mass influx of victims. By comparing these three points of view, we were able to debate them when designing and developing training situations in the virtual environment: should medical leaders be trained to meet the goals that they actually pursue in real life? Should they be trained in best practice in managing a mass influx of victims? Or should they be trained in a range of ways to manage a mass influx of victims that take account of the characteristics of the situation?

The collected data was used to develop an initial model of the medical leader's tasks from T4 to T6. This model was then submitted to trainers who enriched and supplemented it, with the aim of identifying the hierarchical and temporal structure of these tasks (Fig. 4). The analysis led to the development of three blocks of subtasks corresponding to the work process between T4 and T6, along with a transversal group of subtasks that could be interspersed and included as a function of circumstances. Like the model of the work process, we identified the logical

		Leadership		Communication		Teamwork		Situation awareness		Decision making		Managing stress		Managing fatigue		Other	
		MED	CRM	MED	CRM	MED	CRM	MED	CRM	MED	CRM	MED	CRM	MED	CRM	MED	CRM
Skill 1	Adapts his communication style to the situation		S	S	S				S						Ø	Ø	Ø
Skill 2	Assumes responsability for decisions, does no show signs of hesitation	S	S								S				Ø	Ø	
Skill 3	Ensures and adapts his leadership role even if he is not the most ranked	S	S						S	S				Ø	Ø		Ø
Skill 4	Ensures his or her role as a proactive boss	S	S							S	S					Ø	
Skill 5	Request / retrieve an acknowledgement of receipt from each team member		S	S	S		S						Ø		Ø	Ø	Ø
Skill 6	Ask for the silence to make a point to everybody	S	S	S	S	S										Ø	Ø
Skill 7	Listens to the proposals of its team members		S	S	S	S	S					Ø		Ø		Ø	Ø
Skill 8	Avoids having to reorganize the entire system with each new piece of info	S	S	Ø	Ø			S	S	S	S			Ø		Ø	
Skill 9	Avoids being too much in contact with the wounded, positions itself behind the wounded	S		Ø	Ø	S		S	S	S	S		S		Ø		
Skill 10	Reliable transmission of information by synchronizing the gaze with the listener	S	S		S	S		Ø								Ø	Ø
Skill 11	Manages the physical distance with his teammates	X		X		X		X		X		X		X		X	
Skill 12	Manages the noise level of its environment		X		X	S	X		X		X	S	X		X	Ø	X
Skill 13	Manages the stress of his team members		X		X		X		X	Ø	X		X	S	X	Ø	X
Skill 14	Manages fatigue			Ø								S			S	Ø	
Skill 15	Manages stress	S		S									S			Ø	Ø

Legend:

- X: The ability for which participants' responses follow a random distribution
- S: Salient attribution between NT-ONLY skills / NTS-ORIGINAL categories
- Empty boxes: Non salient attribution between NT-ONLY skills / NTS-ORIGINAL categories
- Ø: Total absence of attribution between NT-ONLY skills / NTS-ORIGINAL categories *(NB: also non salient)*

Fig. 5 Examples of nontechnical skills of medical leaders as a function of the categories of nontechnical skills proposed by Flin et al. (2008)

structures that link these tasks in terms of temporo-operational scheduling. At another level, this schematic representation highlighted the complexity of the work of medical leaders working for all the project's partners. This intermediate object was, therefore, a way to collectively debate the goals and strategies of professionals, explore other ways to carry out tasks, and, in particular, highlighted the dilemmas that this group encounters in certain situations. It was very clear that it was an effective starting point in helping the design group to understand the complex job of medical leaders.

As a complement to the task analysis, we built an experimental corpus of nontechnical skills for medical leaders (Delmas, 2019).[3] This was motivated by the observation that there was no standard list of nontechnical skills within the Army Health Service when the project started, despite the fact that these skills are targeted in combat rescue training, particularly Medichos courses. We began by conducting confrontation interviews with ten trainers, all experts in their field, based on the performance of two military doctors who played the role of medical leaders in a full-scale training exercise with comparable scenarios. We identified 230 skills, 30 of which were considered to be nontechnical by the ten trainers. We then related each skill to one or more of the seven categories of nontechnical skills defined in the scientific literature[4] regarding two populations: (1) military physicians; and (2) military personnel trained in crew resource management (Fig. 5). This rigorous, time-consuming scientific method was used to extract embedded know-how from working professionals, and it resulted in a structured set of nontechnical skills used by medical leaders when managing a mass influx of victims. The corpus was a

[3] It is not possible to provide full details of the methodology here. We refer the interested reader to R. Delmas (2019) who provides an extensive explanation.

[4] For a review, we refer the reader to Flin et al. (2008).

crucial resource when developing specifications related to the characteristics of situations to be simulated and the didactic transpositions that must occur for the virtual environment to be a way for medical leaders to develop their nontechnical skills.

The Microscopic Level (Fig. 2) In the context of the VICTEAMS project, we did not develop a graphical representation or tools that would be useful to present in this chapter. Our analyses resulted in written reports that constituted input data to various working groups with project actors. Medical leaders must carry out certain actions in the virtual environment, such as answering radio communications, writing on a white board, writing on a notepad, filling out documents, performing a medical procedure, etc. These actions also needed to be possible in the virtual environment. Decisions relating to the transposition of these actions to simulated situations mainly focused on the feasibility of technological choices related to the virtual environment's hardware and software. On the other hand, communication between the medical leader and autonomous virtual characters was a particular concern, as it was one of the core competences required by partners, in particular, working with other team members and team organization that relies heavily on verbal and nonverbal communication. In other words, communication was at the heart of the corpus of nontechnical skills (Fig. 5).

The next step was to define desirable forms of exchange from the point of view of the targeted learning between the leader and his or her team members (played in the virtual world by autonomous virtual characters). To achieve this, we selected all of the video sequences corresponding to the time between T4 and T6 in the scenario. These sequences were transcribed in full and analyzed using the ArgInDSM (Argumentation in Dynamic Situation Management) model (Merand & Darses, 2017). The latter model combines the theoretical framework of argumentation (Perelman & Olbrechts-Tyteca, 1958/2008; Toulmin, 1958/2003) and the Dynamic Situation Management architecture (Hoc & Amalberti, 1995). It characterizes the interactional position that interlocutors adopt in problem-solving from the perspective of four argumentative aims: Feeding (level 1 of the DSM model), Building (level 2), Critiquing a position regarding the problem and Approving/Disapproving the interlocutor's position (level 3). Each of these aims is supported by an argumentative function that expresses a position, such as Identify, Propose, Evaluate or Validate. This analysis can identify most of the communication modes that are useful as nontechnical skills for medical leaders. These analyses contributed to the specification of the communications that should be "playable" in the virtual environment, notably between the trainee medical leader—who takes the role of "player"—and his or her teammates who are simulated by autonomous virtual characters, and who are equipped with verbal and nonverbal communication functions.

4 Future Work

Our methodological approach has been under development for several years. To date, we have only been able to partially implement it in the context of the various research projects that we have contributed to, notably in connection with the design or evaluation of training that aims to place trainees in simulations using various tools (virtual environments, full-scale case studies, digital microworlds, etc.).

A first goal of our future work is to successfully implement the overall method in a training design project. A second goal is to enhance technical aspects of the method so that training design actors can use it without being a specialist in any of the underlying disciplines. The idea is to be able to offer a kind of toolbox that will enable designers to be better equipped. On the one hand, these tools must be sufficiently simple and flexible to become intermediate design objects rather than another prescriptive tool that makes the process more rigid. On the other hand, the aim is that it should be possible for a user to deploy the method in a project that runs for a period ranging from a few weeks to a few months, a timeframe that is relatively short for this type of tool.

References

Barcellini, F., Van Belleghem, L., & Daniellou, F. (2014). Design project as opportunities for the development of activities. In P. Falzon (Ed.), *Constructive ergonomics* (pp. 150–163).

Barot, C. (2014). *Scénarisation d'environnements virtuels. Vers un équilibre entre contrôle, cohérence et adaptabilité*. Université de Technologie de Compiègne.

Becerril Ortega, R., Flandin, S., & Vidal-Gomel, C. (2018). Faire émerger le réel du travail pour concevoir la formation: Autour des enjeux méthodologiques de l'analyse de l'activité des adultes pour la formation. *TransFormations, 18*.

Béguin, P., & Cerf, M. (2004). Formes et enjeux de l'analyse de l'activité pour la conception des systèmes de travail. *Activités, 1*(1), 54–71.

Boccara, V., & Delgoulet, C. (2015). L'analyse des travails pour la conception en formation. Contribution de l'ergonomie à l'orientation de la conception amont d'un environnement virtuel pour la formation. *Activités, 12*(2). http://www.activites.org/v12n2/V12n2.pdf

Boccara, V., & Perez-Toralla, M. S. (2021). What is a good scenario in vocational training design? Considerations based on a literature review. *21th World Congress Ergonomics*, 13–18 june. Vancouver, Canada.

Boreham, N., Samurçay, R., & Fischer, M. (2002). *Work process knowledge*. Taylor and Francis. 244 p.

Couix, S., Boccara, V., & Fucks, I. (2015). Training design for a not yet existing activity: The case of Remote Monitoring System for Risk Prevention (RMSRP) operator in French Nuclear Power Plants. *19th World Congress Ergonomics*, 9–14 Août. Melbourne, Australia.

Daniellou, F. (1996). *L'ergonomie en quête de ses principes*. Toulouse: Octarès Éditions.

Daniellou, F. (2004). L'ergonomie dans la conduite de projets de conception de systèmes de travail. In P. Falzon (Ed.), *Ergonomie* (pp. 359–373). PUF.

Darses, F. (2004). La conception participative : vers une théorie de la conception centrée sur l'établissement d'une intelligibilité mutuelle. In J. Caelen & P. Mallein (Eds.), *Le consommateur au cœur de l'innovation : la conception participative* (pp. 25–41). Editions du CNRS.

Darses, F. & Reuzeau, F. (2004). La participation des utilisateurs à la conception des systèmes et dispositifs de travail. In P. Falzon (Ed.), *Ergonomie* (pp. 405–420). PUF.
Delgoulet, C. (2015). *L'expérience à l'épreuve des apprentissages professionnels : conflit ou harmonie ? : Construire la pertinence interne et externe des dispositifs d'apprentissage pour le développement des femmes et des hommes au travail*. Manuscrit d'habilitation à dirigé des recherches. Université de Bordeaux. https://halshs.archives-ouvertes.fr/tel-01226828
Delmas, R. (2019). *Nature des compétences non techniques du leader médical à la prise en charge d'afflux massif de victimes : une étude à partir du point de vue des formateurs*. Thèse de doctorat, Université Paris Saclay, https://tel.archives-ouvertes.fr/tel-02107648
Distefano, N., & Leonardi, S. (2018). A list of accident scenarios for three legs skewed intersections. *IATSS Research, 42*(3), 97–104.
Duguay, P., Cloutier, E., Levy, M., & Massicotte, P. (2001). Profil statistique des affections vertébrales avec indemnités dans l'industrie de la construction au Québec. *Le travail humain, 64*(4), 321–342.
Falzon, P. (2014). *Constructive ergonomics*. CRC Press.
Flin, R., O'Connor, P., & Crichton, M. (2008). *Safety at the sharp end: A guide to non-technical skills*. Ashgate Publishing Company.
Folcher, V. (2015). Conception pour et dans l'usage, la maitrise d'usage en conduite de projet. *Revue des interactions humaines médiatisées, 16*(1).
Guérin, F., Laville, A., Daniellou, F., Duraffourg, J., & Kerguelen, A. (1991). *Comprendre le travail pour le transformer*. Éditions ANACT.
Hoc, J.-M., & Amalberti, R. (1995). Diagnosis: Some theoretical questions raised by applied research. *Cahiers de Psychologie Cognitive, 14*(1), 73–101.
Jeantet, A. (1998). Les objets intermédiaires dans la conception. Eléments pour une sociologie des processus de conception. *Sociologie du Travail, 3*, 291–316.
Jeantet, A., Tiger, H., & Vinck, D. (1996). La coordination par les objets dans les équipes intégrées de conception de produit. In G. Terssac & E. Friedberg (Eds.), *Coopération et conception* (pp. 87–100). Octarès.
Martin, C. (2005). *Maîtrise d'ouvrage / Maîtrise d'œuvre—Construire un vrai dialogue—La contribution de l'ergonome à la conduite de projet architectural*. Octarès.
Mayen, P. (1999). Des situations potentielles de développement. *Education Permanente, 139*(2), 65–86.
Mayen, P. (2012). Professional situations: A professional didactics point of view. *Phronesis, 1*(1), 59–67.
Mayen, P. (2015). *Vocational didactics: Work, learning, and conceptualization*. In L. Filliettaz & S. Billett (Eds.), *Francophone perspectives of learning through work: Conceptions, traditions and practices*. Springer.
Mayen, P., Métral, J.-F., & Tourmen, C. (2010). Les référentiels en formation : enjeux, légitimité, contenu et usage. *Recherche et formation, 64*, 31–46.
Mérand, J., & Darses, F. (2017). ARGUinDSM—A model of argumentation in team problem-solving situation: An application to nuclear control room teams. *Presented at the 13th international conference on naturalistic decision making*, Bath, UK.
Mollo, V., & Falzon, P. (2004). Auto-and allo-confrontation as tools for reflective activities. *Applied Ergonomics, 35*(6), 531–540.
MontMollin (de), M. (1988). *L'intelligence de la tâche*. Paris : P. Lang.
Nelson, J., Buisine, S., Aoussat, A., & Gazo, C. (2014). Generating prospective scenarios of use in innovation projects. *Le travail humain, 77*(1), 21–38.
Olry, P., & Vidal-Gomel, C. (2011). Conception de formation professionnelle continue: tensions croisées et apports de l'ergonomie, de la didactique professionnelle et des pratiques d'ingénierie. *Activités, 8*(2), 115–149. http://www.activites.org/v8n2/v8n2.pd
Pastré, P. (1999). La conceptualisation dans l'action : bilan et nouvelles perspectives. *Education permanente, 139*, 13–37.
Peeters, M., van den Bosch, K., Meyer, J. J. C., & Neerincx, M. A. (2014). The design and effect of automated directions during scenario-based training. *Computers & Education, 70*, 173–183.

Perelman, C., & Olbrechts-Tyteca, L. (1958/2008). *Traité de l'argumentation. La nouvelle rhétorique. 6ème édition* (6th ed.). Editions de l'Université de Bruxelles.
Samurçay, R., & Rabardel, P. (2004). Modèles pour l'analyse de l'activité et des compétences, propositions. In R. Samurçay & P. Pastré (Eds.), *Recherche en didactique professionnelle* (pp. 163–180). Octarès.
Samurçay, R., & Rogalski, J. (1998). Exploitation didactique des situations de simulation. *Le Travail Humain, 61*(4), 333–359.
Stacy, W., & Freeman, J. (2016). Training objective packages: Enhancing the effectiveness of experiential training. *Theoretical issues in ergonomics science, 17*(2), 149–168.
Toulmin, S. E. (1958/2003). *The uses of argument* (2nd ed.). Cambridge University Press.
Tourmen, C., Holgado, O., Métral, J., et al. (2017). The Piagetian *Schème*: A framework to study professional learning through conceptualisation. *Vocations and Learning, 10*(3), 343–364.
Turoff, M., Bañuls, V. A., Plotnick, L., Hiltz, S. R., & de la Huerga, M. R. (2016). A collaborative dynamic scenario model for the interaction of critical infrastructures. *Futures, 84*, 23–42.
Van Belleghem, L. (2018). Activity simulation in design: Achievements and perspectives. *Activités, 15*(1), https://journals.openedition.org/activites/pdf/3129
Vidal-Gomel, C. (2021). *Formation et prévention des risques professionnels. Vers des formations capacitantes*. Dijon: Raison et passions.
Vincent, C. J., & Blandford, A. (2015). Usability standards meet scenario-based design: Challenges and opportunities. *Journal of biomedical informatics, 53*, 243–250.

Part II
Empirical Lessons from Experience and Activity-Based Approaches to Simulation Training

This part gathers empirical accounts examining activity and experience of professionals through the study of work-as-done in simulation training programs. It informs the field of simulation by original and acute findings on professional engagement and performance in simulation training and the derivation of relevant guidelines for simulation design.

Chapters 8, 9 and 10 of this part account for activity studies of professionals' actions, decisions, communications, interactions, and configurations while dealing with urgent and/or critical events (firemen and policemen).

Chapters 11, 12 and 13 account for fine-grained explorations of individuals' lived experience, concerns, sensemaking and situational dispositions of policemen, soldiers, and healthcare workers facing complex and potentially – physically and mentally – intense simulated occupational configurations.

Simulation to Experiment and Develop Risk Management in Exceptional Crisis Situations: The Case of the Casualty Extraction Teams

Laurie-Anna Dubois, Sylvie Vandestrate, and Agnès Van Daele

Abstract This chapter focuses on simulation as a tool for experimentation and development of risk management activity among first responders in exceptional crisis situations. To do so, we rely on a study on simulation training for specialized firefighter teams: Casualty Extraction Teams (CET). These teams are responsible for rescuing victims, particularly during post-attack crises. We are first interested in the characteristics of crisis situations. These are related to the adaptation requirements that the risk management activity of the responders must meet to be effective. Simulation training is important to develop this activity, under certain conditions. We then approach crisis management as a borderline case of dynamic situation management. This allows us to focus both on invariants in terms of cognitive mechanisms, underlying the effective risk management activity in this class of situations, and on a necessary variability related to the adaptation processes required according to the type of situation. We report the results of a study analyzing the design and implementation of simulation training for CETs. Finally, based on the results of this study, we propose several avenues to increase the relevance of this training and, more broadly, consider simulation training aimed at developing risk management activities in exceptional crisis situations.

Keywords Simulation · Training · Exceptional crisis situations · Risk management activity · Firefighter

1 Crisis Management for Firefighters: Adaptation and Preparation Through Simulation

A crisis cannot be reduced to a triggering event. Rather, it refers to a process marked by ruptures, uncertainty, and destabilization. As Rogalski (2004) points out, in the firefighters' system of activity, a crisis is marked by a switching from

L.-A. Dubois (✉) · S. Vandestrate · A. Van Daele
Work Psychology Unit, University of Mons (UMONS), Mons, Belgium
e-mail: laurie-anna.dubois@umons.ac.be

S. Flandin et al. (eds.), *Simulation Training through the Lens of Experience and Activity Analysis*, Professional and Practice-based Learning 30,
https://doi.org/10.1007/978-3-030-89567-9_8

routine to non-routine, following the occurrence of an unexpected event that generates significant risks and exceeds pre-existing resources in terms of action procedures and actors. It is not only characterized by a high level of uncertainties and risks but also by the need for coordination between multiple actors. Moreover, when the number of victims is high, its management requires that responders modify their system of criteria or even values. Thus, in disaster medicine, priority is no longer given to the victims whose lives are most at risk, but to those who can most likely be saved by the intervention. In fact, the shift into crisis requires adaptation. Routine local organization of rescue, based on pre-established procedures, is no longer appropriate.

In civil security, confrontation with the crisis is not uncommon. Thus, experienced firefighters are relatively accustomed to managing crises, such as large-scale disasters (industrial accidents, road or rail disasters, etc.). In these situations, they know how to act safely, including in the event of unforeseen circumstances. Safety rules in the broadest sense (plans, procedures, etc.) guide their interventions. However, to keep control of the situation, given its changing and uncertain nature, they are led to continually adapt these rules to the context (Cardin, 2016). In these situations, safety cannot be based solely on the avoidance of dreaded events through compliance with the prescribed rules. It also depends on the risk management activity[1] put in place by the responders to deal with unforeseen situations. This activity is part of what is called safety in action (De Terssac & Gaillard, 2009). It combines regulated and managed safety (Morel et al., 2008; Nascimento et al., 2015; Rocha et al., 2015; Vidal-Gomel, 2017). However, not all crisis situations that firefighters may face are characterized by the same adaptation requirements. Some crises, such as the post-attack crises discussed here, which can be qualified as exceptional[2] crises, refer to adaptation requirements that cannot all be met in the same way as in the management of routine interventions or large-scale disasters. In fact, these crises have characteristics that can hinder the development of safety in action on the job. This means that there is not a certain similarity in the risk management activity in the different types of situations. Indeed, the different types of situations refer to dynamic situations that share common cognitive requirements. Furthermore, the unexpected events that may occur in all these situations are often related to foreseeable or even probable events. Unpredictability mainly concerns the timing of these events. As Rogalski (2004) points out, in the firefighters' activity system, doctrinal knowledge in operational management and command integrates logics (operational, organizational, and means) that remain valid

[1] It is important to note that the activity of risk management in crisis situations can be considered according to two main characteristics: its dynamic character (in relation to the requirements of adaptation for the individual) and its collective character (in relation to the requirements of cooperation for the teams). In this chapter, we focus mainly on the first of these characteristics.

[2] A crisis is generally referred to as exceptional or "non-conventional" because it is a rare occurrence, and, as a result, most of the responders who must manage it are in a situation they have never faced before in the field. This type of crisis is also not (or hardly) predictable. Responders are not (or hardly) aware of the possibilities for effective action to manage it.

in all types of situations. In a research on the determinants of the effectiveness of firefighting teams, Jouanne (2016) shows that there are similarities in the determinants (including adaptation) in the management of routine interventions, disasters, and crises. Nevertheless, the results also highlight a certain specificity of crisis management. Indeed, it is not the same adaptation processes that have a positive effect on the effectiveness of teams in the three types of situations. In other words, in exceptional crises, specific adaptation problems, often difficult to solve in real time, arise for responders in their risk management activity. This limits the transposition of the experience acquired in other situations (routine interventions or disasters). Failure to resolve these adaptation problems can lead to a loss of control and serious consequences, including for the responders themselves, who may be at risk of death.

Given these findings and the underlying issues, it is easy to see why simulation-based training is important in this area. It can allow responders to experiment and develop the effectiveness of their risk management in a simulated crisis. However, to achieve this objective, the training design must consider all the adaptation requirements that risk management in exceptional crisis situations entails for these professionals. Nevertheless, such consideration is still not widespread in the field. Indeed, crisis exercises are still often organized according to the same simple and well-defined logic: to check that a system can respond as planned to accident situations. It is a question of verifying in simulation that the participants comply with pre-existing safety rules. Although this logic – which could be described as a "compliance test" – is useful at all levels of the organization, it is not sufficient when it comes to preparing responders for the management of an exceptional crisis. In the field, the security managers are still reluctant to encourage the development of adaptation processes to deal with the unexpected. They remain focused on the transmission and acquisition of pre-existing safety rules. Here, we find the idea that safety is based on compliance with the prescribed rules (Flandin et al., 2018). However, to manage risks in a crisis, compliance with the prescribed rules has many limitations. As LaPorte (2007a, b) points out, the objective of training cannot just be reduced to the use of plans to counteract surprise, but also to prepare the responders to be surprised. Similarly, the goal of training cannot be limited to enforcing pre-set rules, but also to learning how to adjust those rules and build new ones to deal with uncertainty. The ambition to train in exceptional crisis management requires, on the one hand, to define the risk management activity that is effective in this type of situation and the development of which must be targeted in training and, on the other hand, to design simulation training systems that can guarantee such development.

2 Adaptation Requirements Related to Risk Management in Exceptional Crisis Situations

As Rogalski (2004) proposes, crisis management is a borderline case of dynamic situation management, that is, a situation characterized by its own evolution. Because of uncertainty, managing such a situation puts professionals, victims, the environment, etc. at risk. In this context, the risk of losing control of the situation is at the center of professionals' concerns. This risk has two sides: the external risk of losing control because of the situation's own evolution (especially the unexpected) and the internal risk through cognitive saturation (Chauvin, 2003). To avoid loss of control, risk management can be seen, from a cognitive perspective, as the search for a compromise between the safety and performance requirements of the task and the need to preserve cognitive resources (Amalberti, 2001, 2013; Hoc & Amalberti, 2003, 2007). This compromise is expressed in decision-making by the adoption of different types of strategies to manage risks among responders: anticipatory and reactive strategies (Cuvelier, 2016; Hoc et al., 2004). The former allows, above all, to prepare to act in the face of risks by considering available resources. They are linked to the high planning requirements that the activity must meet to avoid a loss of control. The latter is implemented to manage risks that are not anticipated, immediate, and to which one must react. It is essentially a matter of understanding what is happening and being able to act to keep control of the situation. Understanding what is happening means developing a representation to give coherence to new, unexpected events. This is based on an activity of sensemaking (Weick, 1993, 1995; Weick et al., 2005). This activity also takes on a collective dimension when risk management is based on distributed decision-making. In this case, this activity must reveal a "credible future" in which the actors agree to engage (Weick, 1995). Several studies have shown that trust, especially interpersonal trust, is a key factor in this activity (Colquitt et al., 2006; Karsenty, 2010). In general, the cognitive characteristics of dynamic situations (proximity of control, scope of supervision, speed of the process) require the implementation of appropriate adaptation processes in which cognitive control plays a major role. Indeed, the latter must permanently allow a sufficient level of performance at an acceptable cost (physical, cognitive, emotional) (Hoc, 2004). Responders adapt in order to maintain control of the situation, that is, to maintain its evolution in a domain where they can satisfy acceptable task requirements, by allocating cognitive resources in a bearable quantity (Hoc et al., 2004).

Viewing crisis management as a borderline case of dynamic situation management highlights the importance, whatever the situation, of risk management activity among responders. Moreover, to be effective, this activity relies on the same cognitive mechanisms. However, beyond these invariants, it is also important to point out the necessary variability of adaptation processes to meet requirements that are more specific to crisis situations. These are essentially related to uncertainty, which is particularly marked in exceptional crises and can take different forms: unexpectedness, unpredictability, inconceivability, etc. To account for this necessary variability in adaptation processes, we rely on a model proposed by Wybo (2012). This model distinguishes three complementary levels: the level of structures, the level of relationships, and the level of sense. The first level, that of structures, corresponds to what is planned to respond to known events. It mainly concerns emergency situations covered by pre-existing rescue plans and resources. The second level relates to the adaptation of structures by responders to the actual context of the situation, particularly during crises. Faced with the unexpected, responders adapt plans, strategies, and the use of resources to limit damage. At this level, it can be argued that the system resists deteriorated situations not envisaged at the time of its design. This capacity for resilience is largely based on the experience of the responders[3] which is built, at least in part, in the field when the situations concerned are not rare. In these situations, the unforeseen events that experienced responders manage to deal with are generally of two types: known events whose timing is unpredictable and unpredictable events because the full consequences cannot be predicted in advance. To deal with these unforeseen events, responders implement both anticipatory and reactive strategies. For example, they develop alternative plans based on the anticipation of likely events. When this anticipation is not easy because of the unpredictability of the situation, this leads them to adopt fewer compromising strategies to preserve sufficient flexibility in the plan or carry out real time replanning (Hoc, 2004). When uncertainty is high, anticipation does not avoid all risks. To maintain control of the situation, responders also implement reactive control. This involves analyzing the current situation and, more broadly, understanding what is happening to be able to act. To reduce uncertainty, this sensemaking activity essentially aims to place the current situation in a framework corresponding to a type of situation that is already known and associate an already known procedure with it (Klein, 1997). It is therefore based on knowledge, including meta-knowledge, already acquired by the responders. The third level, that of sense, is set up when the first two prove to be insufficient. It is a more particular feature of exceptional crises where unforeseen events related to unknown or even inconceivable threatening events whose occurrence cannot be thought of in advance may occur. In this context, the plans drawn up in advance do not exist, and the action plans in progress prove to be unsuitable. Therefore, this level refers to an ability to "remake sense" to the deteriorating situation and define priorities for action. This translates into the appearance of new ways of acting, outside of routine. It involves improvising appropriate responses by relying on additional resources, both external (e.g., team reinforcement) and internal (e.g., increased cognitive control). Faced with the unforeseen aspects of an exceptional crisis, the knowledge that each participant has of his or her own functioning, especially his or her own misunderstandings, also plays a crucial role in the trade-offs between "understanding the situation as well as possible" and "acting at the right time" (Cuvelier, 2016).

If in the management of an exceptional crisis, the activity of "remaking sense" is crucial, it must also be stressed that it is difficult to develop because it depends

[3] It is also based on the quality of interactions between responders.

on many conditions, including the frequency of confrontation with the unexpected and the time available for reflection. In addition, several obstacles can hinder it. Thus, at the individual level, Karsenty and Quillaud (2011) identify the following obstacles: the absence of detection of an abnormal fact; the impossibility of taking a step back and the resulting lack of attentional availability; the maintenance of a sense of understanding despite uncertain, inconsistent, or ambiguous information; and the confident selection of immediate interpretations or the lack of rigor in the analysis of the situation. These obstacles are interrelated. They often lead responders to remain fixated on the first interpretation of the situation, which they consider acceptable, but which turns out to be wrong. On a collective level, the same authors highlight two main obstacles: inadequate levels of interpersonal trust and the absence of contradictory debate within the team. These obstacles are also interrelated. For example, an excess of mutual trust can become a factor of complacency, with no control over what others do or say. It can also lead responders to become more comfortable with the (mis)interpretations of others and reduce constructive confrontation. However, often, the crisis leads to a deterioration of trust relationships in teams. In any case, this hinders the collective activity of "remaking sense" in a crisis.

Based on the above, it can be argued that the effectiveness of risk management in a crisis cannot be dissociated from the adaptation processes needed to deal with the unexpected. However, to do so, there is limited scope for transposing the experience gained to other, more familiar situations. This requires an activity of "remaking sense" and the improvisation of new and adapted responses to keep control of the situation. Many factors, both internal and external to the responders, hinder the development of this activity in the field. However, under certain conditions, simulation training can remove these obstacles and promote the development of this activity. This is what we wanted to verify through a case study, of which we will present the main results.

3 Simulation-Based Training in Risk Management in Exceptional Crisis Situations: The Case of CETs

In this section, we report the results of a study analyzing the design and implementation of simulation-based training for CET. CETs are specialized teams of firefighters whose mission is essentially to intervene during an exceptional crisis, such as a post-attack crisis, in a potentially dangerous area known as the "red zone" to save as many casualties as possible. To do this, CETs wear special equipment and intervene under the protection of police officers. This enables them to access casualties more quickly than other rescue services and thus increase their chances of survival. The aim is to evacuate casualties from the red zone as quickly as possible to a more secure area where the chain of rescue will continue, after providing some of them with extreme emergency first aid.

3.1 Context

3.1.1 "CET" Training

In Belgium, the "CET" training courses were set up based on the recommendations of the parliamentary commission of inquiry established after the terrorist attacks of 2016. The first "CET" training was given in 2017. Our research focuses on this training. It lasted a total of 7 days and included both theoretical and practical courses. These courses were mainly based on two frameworks: the "Terror Awareness" and the "Tactical Emergency Casualty Care" (TECC). The first framework focuses on the specific context of safety and rescue services' interventions after a terrorist attack. Through this training content, different types of knowledge are transmitted to firefighters: knowledge about the sequence of a terrorist attack, the types of weapons and improvised explosive devices likely to be found at the scene, the way an explosion takes place, the possibilities of escaping from it, etc. It is also a question of introducing firefighters to the crucial elements to be considered during an intervention in the red zone. Several rules to be respected to ensure one's own safety during an intervention in the red zone are transmitted, such as "never turn your back on the threat." The second framework, the TECC, is based on feedback from the military. It concerns more specifically the first aid to be given to casualties in the event of war injuries. The subjects covered include the causes of preventable deaths. Most of this training content consists of the transmission of methods and techniques. The methods, mainly the MARCH and MIST methods,[4] make it possible to organize the first actions and initiate the chain of rescue.

During the training, methods and techniques were described. The trainers also demonstrated how to carry out first aid procedures to bring emergency first aid to casualties and how to use techniques to extract them from the red zone. The CETs then carried out "drill" exercises aimed at putting these gestures and techniques into practice on themselves or on their colleagues. Finally, from the end of the second day of training, role-playing exercises were organized. These are usually led by two trainers. These exercises constitute the simulation training system that we are interested in. A total of 11 role-play scenarios were organized. Their total duration is 4 hours and 20 minutes. They typically take place in three phases: briefing, simulation session, and debriefing. In each scenario, some firefighters play their own role (that of CET), while others play fictitious roles, such as casualties.

[4] MARCH for "Massive bleeding, Airflow, Respiration, Circulation, Hypothermia" and MIST for "Mechanism, Injury, Sign, Treatment." With the MARCH method, the aim is to identify the casualties whose early death due to, for example, hemorrhage or asphyxia, could be prevented by extreme emergency care. It also involves performing technical procedures, such as the application of an arterial tourniquet or the use of emergency compression dressings to provide this care. Simultaneously, the application of MIST consists of providing casualties with a map indicating the causes of their injuries, the injuries found, their symptoms, and any treatment already carried out. This allows better communication with the actors who take over after the casualties have been extracted.

3.1.2 Composition, Tasks, and Risk Management of CETs

A CET team usually consists of seven people: a leader called "team leader," an assistant, and five stretcher-bearers. The stretcher-bearers usually work in pairs. The team leader assigns missions to the pairs of stretcher-bearers and liaises with the police, especially when a threat is discovered or when casualties are ready to be evacuated. The assistant, designated by the team leader, is responsible for equipment and casualties. He informs the team leader of the number of casualties to be extracted and when they are ready to be evacuated.

In Belgium, during post-attack crises involving numerous casualties, including serious injuries and deaths, a specific zoning system is set up by the police. A "black zone" is demarcated. This is the zone of effective (or direct) threat, where only officers of the special intervention forces of the federal police can enter. The "red zone," in the immediate vicinity of the black zone, is a potential threat zone where only Specialized Assistance Units of the local police (SAU) and the CETs can intervene. The task of the SAU is to ensure the protection of the CETs. The CETs are responsible for carrying out casualties identification to locate and enumerate casualties. Through this identification, it is also possible for CETs to carry out extreme emergency rescue actions on those casualties for whom this is most beneficial in the immediate term. These are casualties whose early death is preventable and who are most likely to be saved by the intervention. This identification is also accompanied by an identification of the state of the casualties, the injuries noted, the treatment already given, etc., which facilitates communication with the other actors in the rescue chain. It is then necessary to gather the casualties, who can be rescued, in a sheltered area, called a "victims nest." The dead are left in place. In the "victims nest," the CETs focus on possible further emergency rescue actions and on lifting, strapping, and stretching the casualties to a more secure area, called the "orange zone," from which the rescue chain continues. In a post-attack crisis, the dreaded event, the attack, can no longer be avoided since it has already taken place. The important dimension of the risk to be considered is the seriousness of the consequences, particularly from the point of view of the survival of the casualties. However, these consequences are often difficult to predict because the evolution of the situation is open to uncontrolled factors, such as the uncertain evolution of the casualties' condition, about which the responders do not always have reliable information. To this uncertainty is added the possible occurrence of other threats that could result in a risk for the responders themselves: risk of over-attack, risk of destruction of first responders, or even risk of destabilization of the entire rescue organization. This type of crisis confronts not only the responders with high risks to the casualties but also themselves because there are strong possibilities of attacks on their physical or psychological integrity. The preservation of resources (material, human, procedural) – to continue in order to act despite the uncertainty – is a priority.

Risk management consists essentially of intervening to limit the consequences of the attack and maintaining control of the situation despite the unforeseen events. To limit the consequences of the attack, it is a matter of managing the risks to the casualties. The aim of such management is to save as many casualties as possible, considering the resources available. This requires prioritization. Priority is given to the seriously injured who have the greatest chance of survival. In other words, the aim is to prevent avoidable early deaths. Even if the CETs, as experienced firefighters, are used to managing risks to casualties, at least two elements differ in the post-attack crisis. The first is the pathologies suffered by some casualties, which can be likened to war injuries. These are not, or only rarely, encountered in firefighting practice. The second element is the criteria for making choices as to which casualties should be given priority in terms of the number of wounded, the seriousness of their condition, and the fact that the available resources have been exceeded (at least temporarily). In a post-attack crisis, it is not the casualties whose lives are most at risk who are given absolute priority, but those most likely to be saved by the intervention. Another characteristic feature of CET risk management in a post-attack crisis is the importance of risk management for oneself and one's colleagues. Indeed, given the potential threats in the red zone, one must ensure one's own safety and that of other responders. The preservation of operational means is a prerequisite for the care of casualties. Several means are put in place to ensure this safety: wearing safety equipment and protection provided by police officers. In addition, there are safety rules (e.g., "never turn your back on the threat") that CETs must respect. However, given the uncertainty of the situation, these means and rules have limitations. To deal with all threatening events that may occur and, particularly, unknown events, CETs must implement an activity of "remaking sense" to the deteriorated situation. They must be able to improvise appropriate responses to keep the situation under control.

3.2 Questions and Methodology

The main question that guided our study was "How does the simulation training studied contribute to the experimentation and development of effective risk management activity in CET?". In other words, given the adaptation requirements of the reference activity, what can be said about the relevance of this training? And if need be, how can this training be redesigned to increase its relevance? To answer these questions, we relied on an activity analysis of trainers and CET in simulation. A total of 6 trainers and 28 firefighters (all male) were involved in the training. Among the firefighters, there were 18 French-speaking and 10 Dutch-speaking. We focus here more particularly on the French-speaking ones. They were supervised in simulation by trainers F1, F2, and F3. They all had their first-aid-ambulance diploma (prerequisite for the training) and had between 4 and 10 years of professional seniority as firefighters. The method consists of the observation, from an audio-video recording, of 11 simulations (which took place during the 2017 CET training) lasting between 5 and 48 minutes. The data collected are traces (verbal and non-verbal) of trainer and CET activity during the three phases of the simulations.

3.3 Results

3.3.1 Activity of Trainers

3.3.1.1 Scenario Design Based on Typical Situations

The scenarios for the simulations, designed by the trainers, refer to typical situations defined according to whether the CET interventions are to be carried out outdoors (open environment) or indoors (closed environment). Other characteristics that determine the scenarios are the presence or absence of imminent danger and casualties-related characteristics. Imminent danger refers to threatening events that are known to occur in the red zone. These are therefore known events the uncertainty of which is mainly about the moment of occurrence. The presence of grenades in the vicinity of casualties is an example. When they occur, these events threaten the safety of CETs and may therefore hinder the continuity of rescue operations for casualties. However, the risks to CETs associated with these known events can be avoided by respecting safety rules that are taught prior to the simulations in the theory sessions. The characteristics of the casualties concern their number, which may vary from 5 to 13, the nature of their injuries, and their type (civilian or CET). These characteristics refer mainly to the management of risks for the casualties. They condition the methods, techniques, and gestures that must be applied. These prescriptions were also presented at the beginning of the training, during theoretical sessions, and were the subject of prior "drill" exercises. According to the trainers, the combination of these characteristics makes it possible to develop difficult scenarios. For example, according to this logic, it is more difficult for CETs to extract large numbers of casualties in an open environment with imminent danger. In the scenario development process, it is planned to confront CETs first with the easiest scenarios and then with the more difficult ones. Compared to the reference situation, there are several deviations in both the design and implementation of the simulated situations. For example, in simulation, all casualties can be rescued. The scenarios as designed do not encourage CETs to prioritize casualties and possibly "drop" some, given their condition on the one hand and the resources available on the other. Processes for projecting casualties' vital prognoses are not solicited. Furthermore, only the CETs are involved in simulation during the first 4 days of the training. It is only at the end of the training, during the last 2 days, that police officers in charge of protecting CETs are also involved. Furthermore, the role of the "team leader" is not always assigned to a CET during the sessions. This role is then played by a trainer. Finally, there is a lack of simulation equipment, such as the lack of cards necessary for the application of MIST.

3.3.1.2 Interventions Aimed at Reproducing the Prescriptions in Simulation

During the briefings, which are generally of short duration, the trainers transmit to the CETs the information necessary for the scenario to unfold: roles played by the various participants, location of casualties, etc. Through these prescriptions, the trainers insist above all on what is expected from the CETs, that is, to reproduce the prescriptions previously transmitted in terms of methods, techniques, gestures, or safety rules. During the simulation sessions, the trainers observe the CETs and intervene from time to time to remind the participants of the prescriptions to be applied. No events are introduced by the trainers that are intended to disrupt the activity of the CETs by calling into question the applicability of the prescriptions. Finally, during the debriefings, the trainers are in control of the conduct of this phase. They take stock of what has happened, point out errors in the CETs in terms of discrepancies from the prescriptions, and clarify the prescriptions again.

3.3.2 CET Activity

The activity analysis of CETs reveals a significant number of prescriptions that are not, or only partially, fulfilled in all typical situations (see Table 1).

Table 1 Number and frequency of prescriptions not or partially fulfilled by CETs in simulation sessions

Typical situations				Number of prescriptions to be applied	Number of unfulfilled or partially fulfilled prescriptions
Simulation in an open environment	With imminent danger	With casualties	Simulation 6	39 (100%)	23 (59.0%)
			Simulation 7	28 (100%)	10 (35.7%)
			Simulation 10	19 (100%)	7 (36.8%)
		Without casualties	–	–	–
	No imminent danger	With casualties	Simulation 2	24 (100%)	11 (45.8%)
			Simulation 8	7 (100%)	3 (42.9%)
			Simulation 11	17 (100%)	5 (29.4%)
		Without casualties	–	–	–
Simulation in a closed environment	With imminent danger	With casualties	Simulation 3	36 (100%)	18 (50.0%)
			Simulation 5	27 (100%)	15 (55.6%)
			Simulation 9	20 (100%)	6 (30.0%)
		Without casualties	Simulation 1	8 (100%)	5 (62.5%)
	No imminent danger	With casualties	Simulation 4	28 (100%)	20 (71.4%)
		Without casualties	–	–	–

Further analysis of the data shows that the observed discrepancies are characterized by omissions, which can be described as unintentional, on the one hand, and by voluntary discrepancies, on the other.

3.3.2.1 Omissions

Most of the discrepancies identified are omissions related to the acquisition of prescriptions still in progress at the CETs. Most of these prescriptions are specific to the post-attack crisis and are therefore different from those usually found in firefighters. They refer to risk management for the casualties. An example of such an omission observed is the following: immediately covering a casualty with a survival blanket without prior verification of the presence of massive hemorrhage. The prescriptions also include rules that CETs must follow to avoid events that may threaten their own safety. Therefore, it is a question of risk management for oneself or colleagues. However, in simulations, it can be observed that CETs frequently fail to apply these rules, which leads to interventions by trainers to recall them. Finally, omissions are also linked to shortcomings in the design of simulated situations compared to the reference situation. In most of the situations studied, police officers were not involved, and a CET was not assigned the role of "team leader." These omissions also concern a lack of resources in simulation. For example, it can be observed that due to a lack of equipment, weapons found in the red zone are never marked with a glowstick, even though this marking enables police officers to identify and take charge of them. Similarly, no MIST card, although essential to the rescue chain, is tied around the neck of the casualties. We also note that casualties are almost never marked with a striped ribbon that indicates the presence or absence of signs of life. These omissions create difficulties in communication and coordination among actors.

3.3.2.2 Other Types of Discrepancies

Other types of discrepancies were also noted. These were voluntary discrepancies that result in additions or deletions of actions from the prescriptions. These discrepancies are to be linked to inappropriate prioritization of risks by the CETs. In general, CETs tend to prioritize the management of risks to casualties at the expense of the management of risks to themselves or their colleagues, irrespective of the simulated typical situation (with or without imminent danger). The additions of actions to the prescriptions mainly concern the management of risks to casualties. This is because CETs tend to take more emergency rescue action on casualties than is necessary. For example, they not only apply a tourniquet to stop visually identified bleeding (which is prescribed) but also apply a pressure bandage to wounds that cannot be treated with a tourniquet. However, according to the procedure, this bandage must be placed elsewhere than in the red zone, to avoid staying too long in this potentially dangerous area. This often leads trainers to question CETs in the following way: "What are we doing in the red zone?" and "Don't stay too long in this zone!" The deletions of actions are mostly related to managing risks for oneself or colleagues. If a colleague is injured, the prescription stipulates that all CETs must evacuate him or her as quickly as possible and stop taking care of the casualties. However, in many situations, the CETs do not deal exclusively with their injured colleague. This is called into question by the trainers during debriefings, as the following verbatim report shows: "... within 30 seconds, the colleague must be conditioned and evacuated. Only then is the conditioning of the casualties resumed. But colleagues first! We're not here to be shot ..." For the trainers, when a CET member is injured, the rescue chain is broken, and the collective extraction of the injured colleague makes it possible to rethink the rest of the intervention together, with a reduced number of staff. It is also a question of preserving the psychological integrity of the CETs during the intervention because everyone has contributed to "saving" the injured colleague and everyone knows that the injured colleague now has access to adequate care.

3.4 Discussion and Some Avenues for Rethinking CET Training

Based on all the results of the study, it is quite clear that the trainers aim to have the CETs reproduce in simulation the prescriptions previously taught. The scenarios are designed according to typical situations related to the prescriptions to be respected. For the trainers, it is the strict application of methods, techniques, rules, and gestures that must allow the risks to be managed. The training design does not sufficiently consider all the adaptation problems that risk management in a post-attack crisis can pose to CETs, thus limiting the relevance of the training. In particular, the requirement to keep control of the situation despite the occurrence of unforeseen events is given little consideration. Although some of the prescriptions include the possible occurrence of unexpected events, these are only events related to known threatening events. No threatening events, which are not considered in the prescriptions, are introduced by trainers during simulations. For trainers, CETs shall not deviate from the prescriptions. The prescriptions are not questioned by the occurrence of threatening events unknown to the CETs, which are not simulated. The risk management activity that CETs are encouraged to implement is aimed at mastering the prescriptions and not, more broadly, at mastering the situation despite uncertainty. Furthermore, in the training studied, it seems that trainers do not pay enough attention to the previous experience of CETs as firefighters. While most of the discrepancies between the prescribed and simulated CET activity are due to ongoing acquisition, some of these discrepancies are due to other difficulties. These result in inappropriate risk management prioritization. Indeed, CETs tend to prioritize risk management for casualties to the detriment of risk management for themselves or their colleagues. In addition to a "simulation effect," which is always possible and reduces the perception of threats, these difficulties may be thought to result from the transposition of experience acquired in more familiar situations, without sufficient questioning in the post-attack crisis. Finally, what also limits the relevance of the training studied is the absence of typical components of the reference activity in a simulation for which CETs are to be trained. Thus, most simulations do not involve police officers, the role of a "team leader" is not systematically assigned to a CET, and several material resources, necessary for the application of the prescriptions, are not available.

Taking these results into account, we would now like to propose some interesting avenues for rethinking training. First, it should be remembered that in the type of training we are interested in here, the trainees are experienced professionals. Therefore, it seems important to us to consider this previous experience. In general, we believe that simulation should allow trainees to re-elaborate their previous experience in risk management to meet all the adaptation requirements related to exceptional crises. Re-elaboration of previous risk management experience cannot come solely from the acquisition of new prescriptions, as seems to be assumed by the trainers in the study under review. It requires a questioning of the activity, which may result from confronting the trainees with simulated situations that hinder the effectiveness of their usual risk management activity. To do this, one possible approach could be for the trainers to insert perturbations into the scenarios during their design or during simulation sessions depending on the activity of the trainees. In a sense like that proposed by Schot et al. (2019), perturbation here is defined as any event that confuses the trainees and encourages them to improvise new responses adapted to keep control of the situation. Regarding risk management in exceptional crisis situations, contrary to what happens in the training studied, it is important that the perturbations inserted do not only concern the occurrence of known threats whose avoidance can be integrated into the prescriptions. They must also correspond to the occurrence of unknown, surprising, and generally very stressful threats. To learn how to keep control of the situation despite uncertainty, trainees must be able to simulate the need for a change in their activity, even if it is framed by prescriptions. As already mentioned by other authors (Durand & Salini, 2016; Schot et al., 2019), the choice of perturbations and their dosage during their insertion in simulation are decisive elements to be considered. Indeed, the aim is to provoke sufficiently disturbed situations for the transformation of the risk management activity to be necessary. However, it is also a question of provoking these situations in a controlled manner to avoid certain counter-productive effects, such as the sideration of the trainees and their immediate disqualification in simulation.

Experimenting in simulation the need for a transformation of the risk management activity is even more important because in exceptional crisis situations, compared to other situations, there are changes in the criteria to be considered in decision-making. However, as was found in the study, trainers focus mainly on the new prescriptions to be acquired and do not discuss much with the CETs about what is different from their usual practice as firefighters. For the trainers, compliance with new prescriptions in simulation seems to be sufficient to learn how to manage risks effectively. However, the results show that it is not as simple, especially when it comes to prioritization for effective implementation of the prescriptions.[5] There are two types of prioritization that raise questions. The first is the prioritization of casualties. CETs are not faced with the simulation requirement of having to choose which casualties to rescue. Indeed, in all scenarios, except for deceased victims, all other casualties are to be dealt with by CETs. No scenario foresees that certain casualties should not be rescued due to, for example, an unavoidable early death. The absence of this requirement in simulation, although essential to meet in natural situations, does not allow trainees to question their previous experience in terms of managing risks to casualties. From our point of view, this is a major shortcoming in the design of the training scenarios studied. The second type of prioritization that raises questions concerns the management of risks to oneself or colleagues. In the training studied, CETs have difficulties because they tend to prioritize the management of risks to casualties to the detriment of their own safety. It may be thought that they tend to transpose unsuitable routines into simulation. In the face of these observations, it is obviously important to think about what should be considered in the design of training to "allow trainees to change what they cannot keep" (Flandin et al., 2017, p.250). At this level, in addition to the perturbations insertion approach already mentioned, another approach is related to the transmission of "unavoidable" safety rules to be respected in the exceptional crisis in question. In the training studied, some of the prescriptions concern this type of rule. They are expressed by major prohibitions, such as "never turn your back on the threat." Given the rarity of exceptional crises, everything that is transmitted in simulation in the form of prescriptions has little chance of being retained. Therefore, it seems appropriate to orient the training toward the transmission of a limited number of new rules that cannot be ignored in the situation concerned and must be retained. Training can always be supplemented by other means, less costly than simulation, such as exercises for training in technical gestures.

Even if it is addressed less in the training studied, the collective dimension of risk management in exceptional crisis situations is also important to consider. For CETs, this dimension refers to synchronous cooperation with peers, including the "team leader," and police officers responsible for protecting them. This cooperation is specific to the post-attack crisis. It must be established within and between teams that are not stable since their members do not usually work together. The results of the study showed that only a limited number of simulations are characterized by the designation of a team leader among the CETs and the simultaneous presence of police officers. However, to learn how to manage risks collectively, it is necessary that the police officers are also involved in the same simulated situation. More fundamentally, other conditions linked to the interactions between the actors must also be met. Without aiming at exhaustiveness, we can mention the interest, when the trainees do not know each other, to generate interactions in simulation to teach them how to manage the interferences between their respective activities. This is indeed essential to cooperate effectively by coordinating actions and developing a shared

[5] Linked to the choice of their timing or order of completion.

representation of the situation (Hoc, 2001, 2004). In the case of exceptional crisis situations, it also seems relevant to encourage interactions between actors in simulation that can contribute to their mutual understanding, sharing of their knowledge, the collective activity of "remaking sense" in the deteriorated situation, and, ultimately, effectiveness of improvisations to be implemented to keep control of the situation despite uncertainty (Adrot & Garreau, 2010). Moreover, it can be recalled that in crisis situations, the actors are interdependent and that risk management therefore relies heavily on the management of these interdependencies. At this level, a good adjustment of interpersonal trust according to the characteristics of situations and actors is essential (Carli & Telion, 2018; Karsenty, 2010). Thus, CETs must have sufficient confidence in police officers to place themselves under their protection, but they must also be able to develop a certain amount of mistrust to think that police officers are not infallible. We think that the simulation should be used more to teach trainees how to regulate their interpersonal trust in exceptional crisis situations.

Finally, the post-simulation debriefing is a crucial phase to enable trainees to transform their risk management activity. Thus, debriefings should not be reduced, as is the case of the training studied, to feedback from trainers on the discrepancies between what was achieved by the simulation trainees and what was expected and, finally, to a reminder of the prescriptions to be met. In doing so, the trainers mainly guide the trainees toward the observation that their activity is "incorrect" but do not guide them toward the transformation of this activity. When the simulations are filmed, which is not the case in the training studied, the trainers can use these recordings to allow the trainees not only to recall the sequence of events and the activity deployed in simulation but also to carry out a reflective analysis on this activity. This analysis can allow trainees to reconsider past activity, especially when it proves ineffective, to understand the reasons for inappropriate actions and imagine new ones. Risk management in exceptional crisis situations escapes, at least in part, from the rules, which they refer to prescriptions or rules of action linked to the previous experience of participants in more familiar situations. Therefore, it would be interesting if, during debriefings, trainers could go back over the sequences of simulated situations where risk management is not covered by the rules. At this level, a collective reflective analysis, involving all the trainees concerned, could allow the sharing of experience, not only in terms of the experience lived in simulation but also of previous experience lived at work, as well as opening the space for possible responses to keep control of the situation. Following the example of what is already being done in the field in certain risk situations, it would be less of a question of guiding the professionals toward a single solution but more of leading them to build a common vision of what is acceptable or not in terms of deviations from the rules, allowing them to develop a common reference frame for safety arbitration (Daniellou, 2012; Nascimento et al., 2015).

4 Conclusion

This chapter aimed to show the importance of simulation training to experiment and develop risk management activity in exceptional crisis situations. We argue that when, in the given field of activity, the trainees are experienced professionals, simulation should allow them to re-elaborate their previous experience to meet all the adaptation requirements related to risk management in exceptional crisis situations. These requirements refer to the need to maintain control of the situation despite uncertainty. In this context, because of the unforeseen events, risk management is at least partially outside the rules, whether these rules are related to prescriptions or rules of action derived from the previous experience of participants in more familiar situations. To be effective, risk management requires "remaking sense" of the deteriorated situation to improvise appropriate responses.

We were interested in simulation training for experienced firefighters who need to be ready to respond to quickly evacuating casualties in a post-attack crisis. The analysis focused on the design of situational scenarios and their implementation in simulation by trainers. The results show that this training is primarily part of a normative approach to safety based on the principle that the transmission and strict respect of prescriptions allow effective risk management. However, this approach has significant limitations when it comes to managing risks in exceptional crisis situations. Based on the limitations identified in the study, we have also proposed in this chapter several avenues for designing simulation-based training for the development of risk management in exceptional crisis situations. These suggestions are far from being exhaustive. They have been formulated based on the results of this study. An empirical verification of their relevance and a reflection on their possible generalization to other areas of activity and other exceptional crisis situations have yet to be carried out.

References

Adrot, A., & Garreau, L. (2010). Interagir pour improviser en situation de crise. Le cas de la canicule de 2003. *Revue Française de Gestion, 203*, 119–131.

Amalberti, R. (2001). La maîtrise des situations dynamiques. *Psychologie Française, 46*(2), 105–117.

Amalberti, R. (2013). *Piloter la sécurité: Théories et pratiques sur les compromis et arbitrages nécessaires*. Springer.

Cardin, Y. (2016). *L'analyse de l'activité comme préalable à la conception d'un environnement virtuel de formation : le cas d'une formation à la gestion d'incendies en milieu urbain chez les sapeurs-pompiers*. Thèse de doctorat, Université de Bretagne Occidentale, Brest, France. https://hal.archives-ouvertes.fr/tel-01278346.

Carli, P., & Telion, C. (2018). Paris City disaster: Response to the recent terror attacks and lessons learned. *Current Trauma Report, 4*(2), 96–102. https://doi.org/10.1007/s40719-018-0119-1

Chauvin, C. (2003). Gestion des risques lors de la prise de décision en situation d'interaction dynamique : approches systémique et cognitive. In J. M. C. Bastien (Ed.), *Actes des 2e Journées d'étude en Psychologie Ergonomique (EPIQUE'2003)* (pp. 123–134). Inria.

Colquitt, J. A., LePine, J. A., Zapata, C. P., & Wild, R. E. (2006). Trust in typical and high-reliability contexts: Building and reacting to trust among firefighters. *Academy of Management Journal, 54*(5), 999–1015.

Cuvelier, L. (2016). *Agir face aux risques, regard de l'ergonomie*. FonCSI.

Daniellou, F. (2012). *Facteurs humains et organisationnels de la sécurité industrielle. Des questions pour progresser*. FonCSI.

De Terssac, G., & Gaillard, I. (2009). Règle et sécurité : partir des pratiques pour définir les règles. In G. De Terssac, I. Boissières, & I. Gaillard (Eds.), *La sécurité en action* (pp. 13–34). Octarès Editions.

Durand, M., & Salini, D. (2016). Éducation à la résilience : une démarche événementielle. In J.-P. Assal, M. Durand, & O. Horn (Eds.), *Le Théâtre du Vécu - Art, Soin, Éducation* (pp. 303–315). Raison et passions.

Flandin, S., Poizat, G., & Durand, M. (2017). Développer la résilience en renouvelant la formation à et pour la sécurité : une recherche en cours. In B. Barthe, O. Gonon, & C. Brun (Eds.), *Présent et futur de l'ergonomie : actes du 52ème de la Société d'Ergonomie de Langue Française (SELF)* (pp. 247–251). Resact.

Flandin, S., Poizat, G., & Durand, M. (2018). Improving resilience in high-risk organizations: Principles for the design of innovative training situations. *Development and Learning in Organizations, 32*(2), 9–12. https://doi.org/10.1108/DLO-03-2017-0027

Hoc, J.-M. (2001). Towards a cognitive approach to human-machine cooperation in dynamic situations. *International Journal of Human-Computer Studies, 54*(4), 509–540. https://doi.org/10.1006/ijhc.2000.0454

Hoc, J.-M. (2004). La gestion de situation dynamique. In P. Falzon (Ed.), *Ergonomie* (pp. 517–530). Presses universitaires de France.

Hoc, J.-M., & Amalberti, R. (2003). Adaptation et contrôle cognitif : supervision de situations dynamiques complexes. In J. M. C. Bastien (Ed.), *Actes des Deuxièmes Journées d'Étude en Psychologie Ergonomique (EPIQUE'2003)* (pp. 135–147). Inria.

Hoc, J.-M., & Amalberti, R. (2007). Cognitive control dynamics for reaching a satisficing performance in complex dynamic situation. *Journal of Cognitive Engineering and Decision Making, 1*(1), 22–55.

Hoc, J.-M., Amalberti, R., Cellier, J.-M., & Grosjean, V. (2004). Adaptation et gestion des risques en situation dynamique. In J.-M. Hoc & F. Darses (Eds.), *Psychologie ergonomique : tendances actuelles* (pp. 15–48). PUF.

Jouanne, E. (2016). *Gestion de crise chez les Sapeurs-Pompier : déterminants socio-cognitifs de l'efficacité des équipes*. Thèse de doctorat en psychologie, Université de Bretagne Sud, Bretagne. https://tel.archives-ouvertes.fr/tel-01425954.

Karsenty, L. (2010). Comment faire confiance dans les situations à risque ? In A.-S. Nyssen, P. Mairiaux, A. Van Daele, A. Piette, & F. Laigle (Eds.), *Fiabilité, Résilience et Adaptation, Actes du 45ème Congrès de la SELF* (pp. 205–212). SELF.

Karsenty, L., & Quillaud, A. (2011). Gestion de l'imprévu et construction collective du sens de la situation : Quelques leçons tirées de l'analyse d'incidents. In A. Garrigou & F. Jeffroy (Eds.), *L'ergonomie à la croisée des risques, Actes du 46ème Congrès de la SELF* (pp. 261–265). SELF.

Klein, G. (1997). The Recognition-Primed Decision (RPD) model: Looking back, looking forward. In C. E. Zsambok & G. A. Klein (Eds.), *Naturalistic decision making* (pp. 285–292). Lawrence Erlbaum Associates.

LaPorte, T. R. (2007a). Critical infrastructure in the face of a predatory future: Preparing for untoward surprise. *Journal of Contingencies and Crisis Management, 15*(1), 60–64.

LaPorte, T. R. (2007b). Anticipating rude surprises: Reflections on "crisis management" without end. In L. R. Jones & C. Roberts (Eds.), *Communicable crises: Prevention, management and resolution in the global arena* (pp. 27–46). Information Age Publishing.

Morel, G., Amalberti, R., & Chauvin, C. (2008). Articulating the differences between safety and resilience: The decision-making process of professional sea-fishing skippers. *Human Factors, 50*(1), 1–16.

Nascimento, A., Cuvelier, L., Mollo, V., Dicioccio, A., & Falzon, P. (2015). Constructing safety: From the normative to the adaptive view. In P. Falzon (Ed.), *Constructive ergonomics* (pp. 95–109). CRC Press.

Rocha, R., Mollo, V., & Daniellou, F. (2015). Work debate spaces: A tool for developing a participatory safety management. *Applied Ergonomics, 46*, 107–114.

Rogalski, J. (2004). La gestion des crises. In P. Falzon (Éd.), *Ergonomie* (pp. 531–544). PUF.

Schot, S., Flandin, S., Goudeaux, A., Seferdjeli, L., & Poizat, G. (2019). Formation basée sur la perturbation : preuve de concept par la conception et le test d'un environnement numérique de formation en radiologie médicale. *Activités, 16*(2), 1–25.

Vidal-Gomel, C. (2017). Training to safety rules use: Some reflections on a case study. *Safety Science, 93*, 134–142.

Weick, K. E. (1993). The collapse of sensemaking in organizations: The Mann Gulch disaster. *Administrative Science Quarterly, 3*, 628–652.

Weick, K. E. (1995). *Sensemaking in organizations*. Sage Publications.

Weick, K. E., Sutcliffe, K. M., & Obstfeld, D. (2005). Organizing and the interim of sensemaking. *Organization Science, 16*(4), 409–451.

Wybo, J.-L. (2012). *Maîtrise des risques et prévention des crises : Anticipation, construction de sens, vigilance, gestion des urgences et apprentissage*. Lavoisier.

Analyzing the Collective Activity of Firefighters During Urban Fire Simulation

Cyril Bossard, Magali Prost, Yohann Cardin, and Gilles Kermarrec

Abstract This chapter proposes the study of the collective activity of a team of firemen in a simulation situation. In reference to the data/frame theoretical model, this study analyzed team sense-making through the articulation of individual activities. The methodology was inspired by the principles of in situ analysis developed within the NDM framework. Observation and communication data were recorded from 11 firefighters in training situations and completed by verbalization data collected during subjective re-situ interviews. Data analysis was based on the use of multi-score format. The results highlight the (im)possibilities of inter-individual interaction that are created throughout a training situation. The "Sense-making Articulation of Global Activity" (SAGA) mode of representation makes the articulation of individual sense-making visible. This study highlights the influence of the functional (mission of each agent) and spatial (position of each agent) configurations of the team on team sense-making during a maneuver. Within the team, two levels of understanding of the situation (macroscopic and microscopic) coexist with local and typical forms of coordination involving all or part of the team. As a result, the team sense-making appears as an enchainment of cycles of local sense-making in which the team leader is the coordinator. All of these results allow us to suggest ways to improve the design of simulations for firefighting team training.

Keywords Team sense-making · Semi-open space · Simulation · Firefighters

---

C. Bossard (✉) · M. Prost · Y. Cardin · G. Kermarrec
Université de Brest, EA 3875, CREAD, Centre de Recherche en Éducation, Apprentissage et Didactique, Brest, France
e-mail: cyril.bossard@univ-brest.fr

S. Flandin et al. (eds.), *Simulation Training through the Lens of Experience and Activity Analysis*, Professional and Practice-based Learning 30,
https://doi.org/10.1007/978-3-030-89567-9_9

1 Introduction

This chapter presents an analysis of the activity of firefighters' teams in practical training situations designed for firefighters. More specifically, the objective is to analyze the team sense-making during a simulation in order to propose ways to improve it.

1.1 Simulation for Training Purposes

The use of simulation in a pedagogical perspective is a practice particularly exploited in domains considered as risky such as the military domain (Grau et al., 1998; Jensen, 2009), aviation (Rankin et al., 2016), or virtual teams (Rafaeli et al., 2009). The main interest lies in the fact that simulation allows, without risk for the learner, to promote the acquisition of skills when performing specific tasks that are difficult to reproduce in reality. Its use allows the manipulation of problematic variables, such as the consequences of actions in risky situations, the complexity of technical and organizational systems, or the temporality of the processes involved (Samurçay & Rogalski, 1998).

Within this framework, the simulator is defined as an "artifact that simulates (partially or totally) the functioning or behavior of a technical system, an installation, or a natural phenomenon" (Vidal-Gomel et al., 2011, p. 117). The latter is generally the result of modeling work on the real activity. It can be material (with interfaces for the trainees and possibly for the trainers) or purely symbolic (and not be a technological object per se). In the case of the training of firefighters that we have studied, the simulator is not a specific technological object but a global operational device defining the status and roles of each member of the team within a figurative environment (Béguin & Pastré, 2002).

Although the studies carried out on work situations in the field of ergonomics psychology have largely studied the individual dimension, they point to the need to analyze collective activity (Leplat, 1991; Hoc, 2003). At the same time, it appeared important for researchers (as well as for managers) to understand processes inherent to these situations leading, or not, to the passage of the skills of each individual to a collectively efficient team. This concern for the collective dimension was therefore logically integrated into the design of the training systems. The firefighting profession is characterized by the fact that it is not practiced in isolation but almost exclusively within a team based on a precise and perfectly established organizational system (Lipshitz et al., 2007). Collaboration between members of the firefighting team is essential in view of the plurality of risks, the evolving and uncontrollable nature of situations, and the time pressure (Samurçay & Rogalski, 1993; Klein et al., 2010). In order for there to be collective efficiency in the field of work, the necessity for individuals is that they be able to share the same task, i.e., the same goal and the same working conditions (Leplat, 1993). In the case of the firefighting teams we studied, this common goal is to stop an incident and rescue victims.

1.2 The Team Sense-Making Model (Klein et al., 2010)

In order to understand how a team functions, valuing sense-making by a collective in a situation remains an avenue of research to explore. By adapting their individual data/frame model to the collective, Klein et al. (2010) attempt an approach aimed at specifically understanding "the process by which a team manages and coordinates its efforts to explain the current situation and anticipate future situations, particularly under uncertain and ambiguous conditions." In this perspective, the authors take up the different activities that make up the original cyclical model and elevate them to their collective dimension (Fig. 1).

Klein et al. (2010) extract from this team sense-making model various strategies that contribute to the collective construction of a cognitive framework appropriate to the relevant data of the situation. All these strategies are listed and detailed in Table 1.

To the best of our knowledge, this theoretical model has only been applied within a study on air traffic control (Malakis and Kontogiannis, 2014). The authors specifically studied team sense-making processes performed by the air traffic management collective in very low visibility conditions. These collectives involve controllers

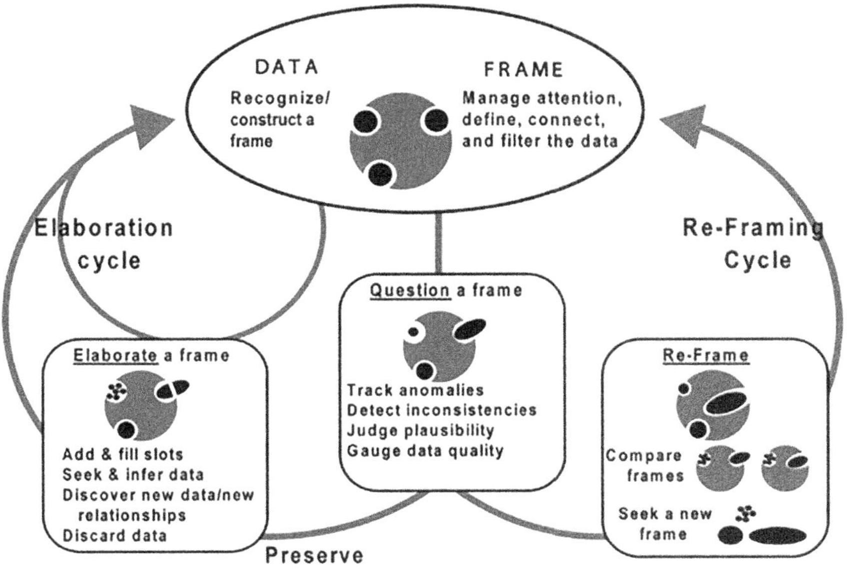

Fig. 1 Expanded data/frame diagram to team sense-making taken from Klein et al. (2010)

Table 1 Team sense-making strategies adapted from Klein et al. (2010)

Team sense-making	Emerging strategies
Recognize a frame	The team formulates criteria or rules used to identify the frame A team member announces what the frame is The team collaborates to identify the frame
Question a frame	Designate a team member to play the role of "devil's advocate," and raise doubts about the relevance of a frame The team creates rules or identifies triggers to alert that the frame may be irrelevant Team members speak up and discuss what could go wrong with using the frame
Re-frame (compare)	The team compares the frame and votes for one of them Team builds consensus on the most appropriate frame Leader announces which frame is most appropriate
Re-frame (seek)	The individual suggests a frame that is adopted, modified, or rejected by the team after comparing frames Team speculates on data and suggests causal views: Leader or team member combines views within a frame The team collaborates to synthesize competing frame
Elaborate a frame	The team discusses and dismisses anomalous data as transient or otherwise insignificant signals Data synthesizing team members lead data "collector" activities to seek new data to verify the frame Synthesizing and collecting team members collaborate to discover new relationships that preserve or extend the frame

located in the control tower and on the tarmac as well as possibly a team leader. An interesting point lies in the modulable character (in numerical terms and consequently of attribution of functions) of the collective according to the density of the traffic which, independently of the conditions inherent to the studied situations, implies a fortiori different coordination processes according to the moments when these situations take place. Using the critical decision analysis method, Malakis and Kontogiannis (2014) verified the operability of the model in the real conditions of a risky activity. In this way, they highlighted the sense-making processes developed collaboratively within these collectives as well as the strategies put in place specifically for the domain. These results allowed the development of efficient technological devices adapted to the real activity of air traffic controllers in difficult conditions (e.g., in low visibility situations).

This study is of real interest in the context of our work insofar as the group studied, although in continuous audio contact, is highly spatially dispersed. As a result, the accessibility to information is not the same for all the team members (especially in terms of visual information) and requires them to communicate more in order to share the same information. This element is also underlined by the authors, in the perspective of designing technological management devices, by taking into account the aircraft's piloting team. Although pilots were not interviewed in the study, Malakis and Kontogiannis (2014) point out the lack of shared situational awareness between them and the control team in that the weather information specifically provided to them is not entirely identical. As a result, this informational gap can lead to certain dysfunctions in the collective construction of meaning of a situation, especially if it takes place under difficult conditions.

2 Objective and Theoretical Rationale

1. The main objective of this chapter is to report on the collective activity of the firefighting team in a practical training situation. To this end, we conducted an empirical study based on two assumptions. The fire department teams, in our case in an urban environment, are led to evolve in compartmentalized spaces partially preventing communication (verbal or visual) between the members. In order to determine the processes of team sense-making in a "fragmented" team (Grosjean and Lacoste, 1999), we start from the presupposition that this object can be understood from the articulation of individual sense-making.
2. Taking into account the subjective and individual character of the agent in a collective requires an understanding of the experience of each member during the action and of their articulation. Therefore, our work is part of a naturalistic approach intended to account for the meanings that the team members construct through their permanent interaction with the simulation situation. We postulate the coexistence within the collective of different levels of understanding of the situation. This plurality of forms of understanding would be both the result of the different functions allocated to each member and of the (im)possibilities of interaction brought about by the context. The understanding of the situation could be organized according to a relation to a "framework" of sense-making at the individual level and possibly shared at a collective level (team sense-making model; Klein et al., 2010).

3 Methodology

The presuppositions presented above require the development of a specific methodology capable of accounting for the collective's agency in relation to environmental constraints. Thus, the method of multi-score transcription seems suitable in that it is a prerequisite for identifying the dynamics of team sense-making (Guibourdenche et al., 2017). We bet that this method could allow to highlight (im)possibilities of interaction constrained by the environment and to associate the latter with team sense-making.

3.1 Context and Participants

The study was carried out in the context of training sessions on urban fire management for fire managers organized by a French departmental fire service. The training sessions take the form of a full-scale simulation on a technical platform. During an emergency, the fire chief is the first officer to arrive on the scene with his team. His responsibility is to quickly take charge of the first emergency measures. The team leader is in charge of a response truck with five team members: the driver, the supply pair (BAL), and the attack pair (BAT). The driver's role is to drive the truck to the scene of the incident and possibly manage the water supply to the fire hoses for the team members attacking the fire. The BAL is in charge of supplying water to the fire hoses and possibly supporting the team members attacking the fire. The BAT's mission is to explore the scene of the incident and to attack the fire with the hoses. These functions, although perfectly defined, are likely to be modified during a maneuver according to the real needs of the field.

The study was conducted in collaboration with 11 volunteer firefighters participating in the fire chief training organized by a departmental fire service in France. At the time of data collection, their average age was 36 years (standard deviation, 7.62). At the time of the study, their experience as a firefighter was 12 years on average (SD 3.58). Participants were named using a code corresponding to the maneuver (between 1 and 3) followed by their position name (chief, BAL-1, BAL-2, BAT-1, BAT-2): for example, code 3 BAT-1 corresponds to the leader of the attack pair (BAT) in maneuver 3.

3.2 Data Collection

In this work, we were interested in three maneuvers performed during the training in full-scale simulation on a technical platform. These maneuvers will be numbered from 1 to 3 according to their chronological order during the training. Maneuver 1 corresponds to a fire response in a city's technical services. Maneuver 2 involves a fire in an apartment adjacent to a home for the elderly and involving a victim. Maneuver 3 involved a fire in a street with a heavy truck (with one victim). These maneuvers had a duration of 12′43″, 18′10″, and 10′17″, respectively.

During these three maneuvers, the data collection procedure was applied each time to the entire intervention team except for the driver (played by a professional not involved in the training process). In this way, on each intervention, five trainees were involved, playing the roles of squad leader, BAT leader, BAT team member, BAL leader, and BAL team member, respectively.

The data collection procedure was based on in situ analysis methods. Three types of data were collected:

- Observational data on the activity of the trainees during the scenarios. These observational data were collected through the audiovisual recording of the

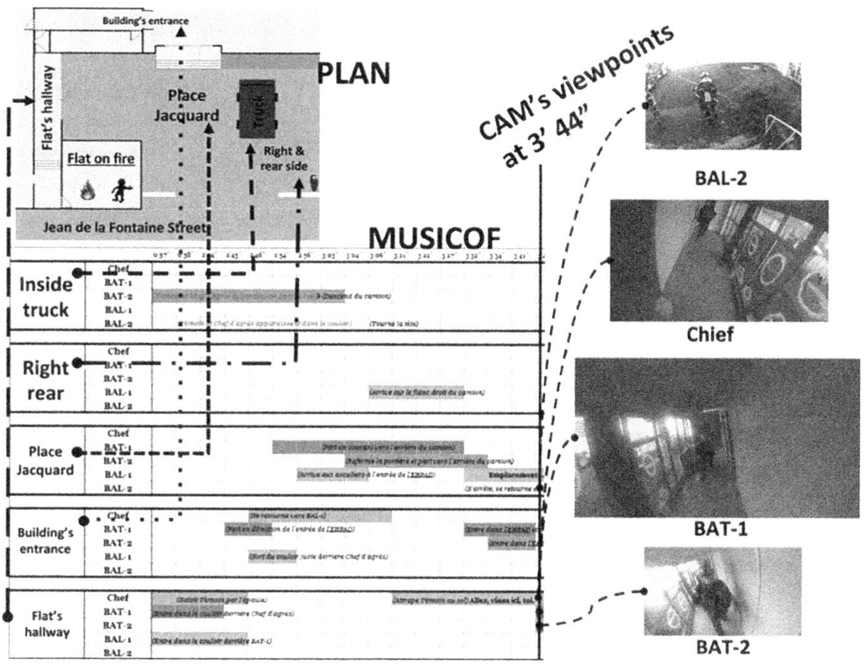

Fig. 2 Relationships between the reference spaces (represented by the floor plan on the upper left and the photos on the right) and the MUSICOF transcription

behaviors during the maneuver. The situations were filmed from two points of view, both providing extrinsic data, using two types of digital video cameras. On the one hand, the use of a shoulder-mounted camera made it possible to record the team's activity from an external point of view (movement in space, gestures, postures). On the other hand, the use of a head-mounted camera on the helmet of each trainee (see Fig. 2) made it possible to report on their activity from the actor's own field of vision (participant's point of view in the course of the action).

- Communication data involving the trainees during the simulations. These data are mainly recovered from the recording of the head-mounted camera.
- Verbalizations obtained during individual interviews in subjective re-situ (Rix & Biache, 2004; Rix-Lièvre, 2010) directly following the execution of the maneuver on site. This form of interview, which gives access to intrinsic data, consists of confronting an actor with audiovisual traces of a period of his activity taken from his own point of view (in our case, via the cameras mounted on the helmets).

3.3 Data Analysis

The analysis consisted in reconstructing the chronicle of the situations (temporal unfolding) by synchronizing the extrinsic data (behaviors and communications) and the intrinsic data (verbatim) collected for each participant. To do this, the analysis was based on the following six steps: (1) multi-score transcription; (2) sequencing of the maneuvers; (3) identification of individual sense-making; (4) categorization of the level of individual sense-making; (5) representation of the team sense-making; and (6) validity of the analysis.

Initially, this work exploited the MUltI-SCOre Format (MUSICOF), which allows the analysis of collective activity in semi-open space (Guibourdenche et al., 2017). We performed a multi-score transcription using the video films, from all the cameras used simultaneously during the study situations. All of the participants' behaviors were reported and were supplemented with verbalizations from individual interviews with each participant. All these data were gathered together using MUSICOF for each maneuver. These tables are constructed along two axes: a horizontal axis to respect the temporal course of the situation and a vertical axis to respect the spatial configuration of the intervention sites. Figure 2 shows an example of the MUSICOF format used in this study.

For each maneuver, the overall intervention environment was divided into different spaces that could reflect the (im)possibilities of interaction for the collective. For each of these predefined spaces, each member of the team is represented in the multi-span chart by two lines: the upper line for his or her behaviors and communications and the lower line for placing opposite his or her corresponding verbalizations collected during the interview.

The second step consisted in sequencing the maneuvers by detecting "moments of rupture" within the collective activity (45 in total). These moments of rupture correspond to changes in the collective in terms of spatial configuration (separation and gathering of team members during the maneuver) or functional configuration (orders and missions given to each member by the team leader). These different configurations will be presented in the "Results" section.

In the third step, we identified the individual sense-making activities corresponding to behavioral markers such as communications and behaviors noted during the situation and/or verbalizations collected during interviews.

The fourth step consisted in categorizing individual sense-making according to the level of individual understanding (377 individual activities in the whole study).

The fifth step is related to the graphical representation of the team sense-making. For this purpose, we designed a representation mode called "Sense-making Articulation of Global Activity" (SAGA) which consists in illustrating, for each sequence identified during the situation, the articulation of team members sense-making (according to the data/frame model) according to the spatial and functional configurations of the team. Figure 3 illustrates the spatial partitioning of a team in a semi-divided functional configuration of firemen with SAGA.

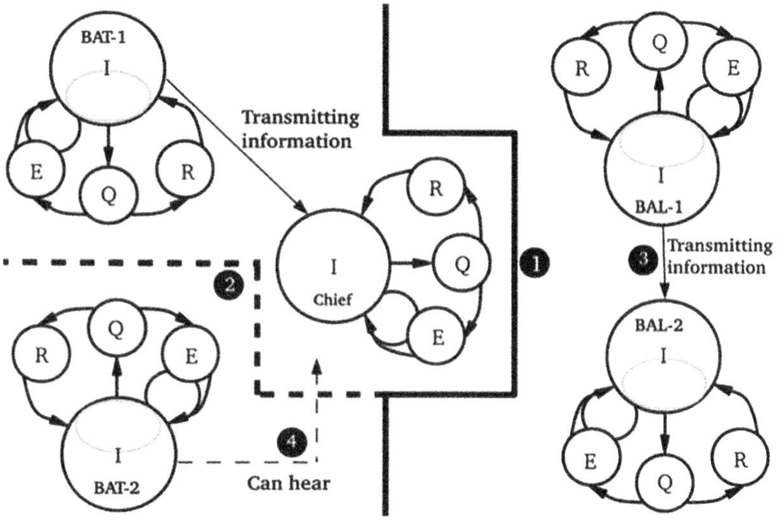

Fig. 3 An illustration of the Sense-making Articulation of Global Activity (SAGA). Letter E elaborate a frame; letter Q question a frame; letter R re-frame; bold line radical impossibility for interaction; discontinuous line limited possibility of interaction

Finally, we ensured the validity of the analysis by relying on the three principles of Corbin and Strauss (2008): completeness, exclusivity, and fidelity (sequencing, coding, inter-coder agreement calculations).

4 Results

4.1 Individual Sense-Making

The sequencing procedure extracted 45 sequences from the three maneuvers studied. Maneuver 1 has 15 sequences, maneuver 2 has 19 sequences, and maneuver 3 has 11 sequences.

The step of identifying individual sense-making following the data/frame theoretical model allowed us to distinguish 377 individual sense-making over the whole study. The distribution of these individual sense-making for each member during the three maneuvers is summarized in Tables 2, 3 and 4.

The number of occurrences of individual sense-making following the data/frame model (Klein et al., 2010) shows that two processes are particularly favored by firefighters. The recognition of the frame and the elaboration of the frame are the most mobilized by the firefighters whatever the role (leader/team member) or the maneuver involved.

From the 377 individual sense-making, a second analysis allowed us to distinguish two levels of individual sense-making: microscopic and macroscopic. The

Table 2 Distribution of individual sense-making of each member of firefighters team in maneuver 1

Maneuver 1	Recognize a frame	Elaborate a frame	Question a frame	Re-frame (seek)	Re-frame (compare)
Chief	2	20	2	1	0
BAT-1	4	19	2	2	0
BAT-2	4	16	3	1	0
BAL-1	5	13	3	1	2
BAL-2	3	11	1	0	0

Table 3 Distribution of individual sense-making of each member of firefighters team in maneuver 2

Maneuver 2	Recognize a frame	Elaborate a frame	Question a frame	Re-frame (seek)	Re-frame (compare)
Chief	3	17	4	2	0
BAT-1	6	23	6	2	1
BAT-2	6	23	6	3	1
BAL-1	6	12	1	0	0
BAL-2	7	14	1	1	0

Table 4 Distribution of individual sense-making of each member of firefighters team in maneuver 3

Maneuver 3	Recognize a frame	Elaborate a frame	Question a frame	Re-frame (seek)	Re-frame (compare)
Chief	2	14	1	1	0
BAT-1	7	16	2	2	0
BAT-2	6	14	2	2	0
BAL-1	3	22	1	0	0
BAL-2	3	18	1	1	0

macroscopic level corresponds to the situation as a whole (type of incident, presence of victims, potential dangers, configuration of the site) and the type of maneuver applied to it (missions of each pair or partner, task planning). The microscopic level refers to the contextual elements (e.g., hydrant location, fire behavior, victim's health status, required equipment) and actions or procedures (e.g., fire attack, victim assistance, feeding) related to the execution of a specific mission. Over the course of the study, 182 individual sense-making were associated with a macroscopic level, and 195 of these were associated with a microscopic level.

4.2 Highlighting of Six Typical Structures of Team Sense-Making

The 45 collective activity sequences identified from the 3 maneuvers were represented using SAGA for each of them. This step allowed the extraction of local structures of firefighting team sense-making. Specifically, these results highlight six typical structures of team sense-making: alertness, binomial development process, negotiation, team sense-making standby, mission reassignment, and team sense-making adjustment.

4.2.1 Alertness

The first structure of team sense-making corresponds to the first sequence of each maneuver. This takes place in the truck when the fire chief receives the departure message from the call center. During this sequence, the team is in a "grouped configuration" in the truck, which gives all members the opportunity to interact. The departure message from the call center gives the fire chief the address where the team will have to intervene and can then be more or less detailed on the characteristics of the incident. The fire chief then passes on to his team members the information he has gathered from the call center concerning the situation. This is illustrated in Fig. 4. He also gives them all the safety rules relative to the type of incident to be managed as well as certain information concerning the application of the future maneuver (e.g., location of fire hydrants). To compensate for a possible lack of

Fig. 4 SAGA: alertness

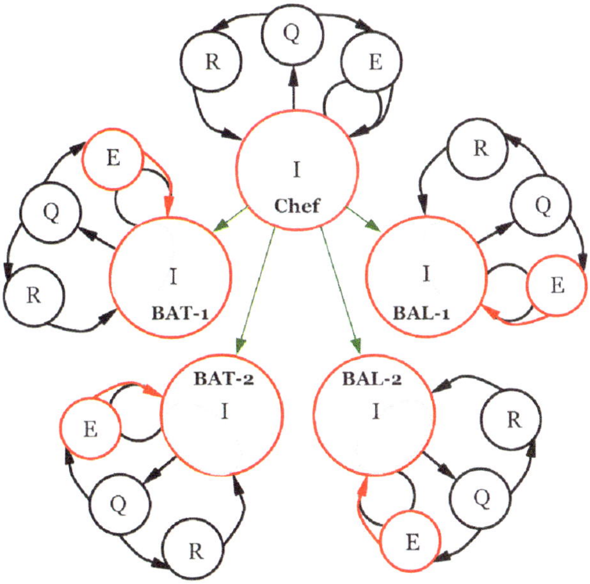

information, this moment can also be used by the fire chief to transmit to his team his possible assumptions about the situation (e.g., "We don't have the notion of a victim but I imagine that the truck must have a driver").

4.2.2 Binomial Development Process

The second structure concerns a binomial elaboration process (it appears six times in our data set). It corresponds to a transmission of information between the two members of the same binomial so that each of them can elaborate their respective microscopic framework. The transmission of information can be unidirectional in the case where only one of the two partners has access to the information and transmits it to the other. This case appears, for example, in maneuver 3, when the BAL attacks the fire. The BAL leader carries the lance but is unable to update his understanding of the situation because the headwind prevents him from seeing what is going on. It is the BAL team member behind him who shifts a little to see what is going on and gives him information as he goes along (e.g., "Maybe put yourself a little stronger." "We'll move. We're going to get closer." "That's okay, fire out apparently. I'll pass it on.").

This transmission of information can also be bidirectional in the case where each of the partners gives the other the information that it considers relevant. This is the case during maneuver 1 when the TAO enters a smoky room in order to cut the electric meter and to extinguish the fireplace. The two partners exchange information on what they, respectively, consider relevant in their situation. This exchange then allows both parties to elaborate and align their respective microscopic frameworks. The structure of this team sense-making can be illustrated in Fig. 5.

4.2.3 Negotiation

This structure (which appears 9 times) concerns moments of questioning by a member of the pair and presents three variants illustrated in Fig. 6.

Globally, a member of the pair, by initiating a questioning of his microscopic framework, informs his partner who will also proceed to a questioning of his microscopic framework. An exchange of information between partners follows, which can be compared to moments of negotiation, and leads to one or other of the variants presented. Thus, this process of questioning can have a symmetrical structure insofar as the two partners will conclude either by preserving their microscopic framework (variant a) or by re-framing it (variant b). These cases appear, for example, during a situation where the BAT is lost in the apartment where they have to rescue a victim and regularly question their microscopic frameworks in order to know if they have taken the right path in relation to what the team leader is asking. This questioning leads either to the preservation of their respective frames (considering that they have taken the right path and that they are close to finding the victim) or to

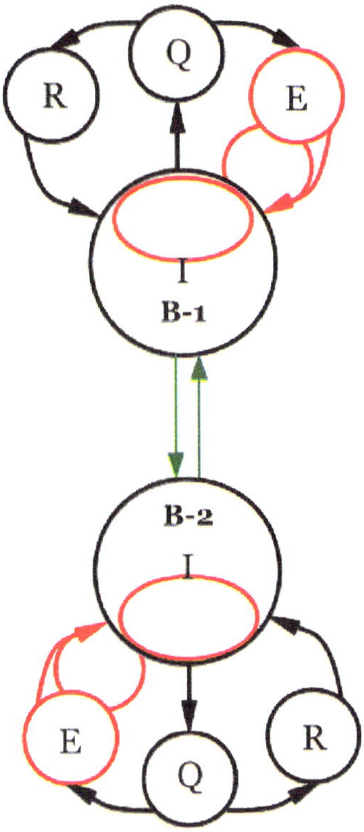

Fig. 5 SAGA: binomial development process

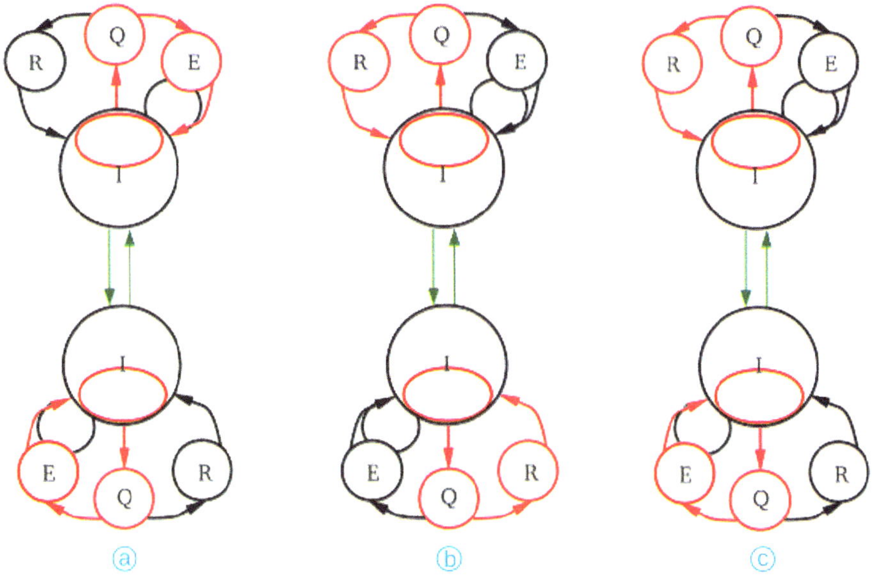

Fig. 6 SAGA: negotiation

the search for a new frame (considering finally that they have taken the wrong path and that they must find another one).

This questioning can also present an asymmetrical structure (variant c) when, following a negotiation, one member of the pair preserves his microscopic frame while the other creates a new frame (re-framing). This situation arises, for example, during maneuver 1 when the BAL team member informs the BAL leader of his skepticism regarding the location of the supply division in relation to the location of the fire. The BAL chief then reconsiders his action and moves the division in accordance with his teammate's remarks. The BAL leader therefore proceeds to refocus, while the BAL team member preserves his initial microscopic frame.

4.2.4 Mission Reassignment

The fourth structure of team sense-making relates to moments of transition where a pair reports the result of its mission and/or its availability to the team leader (Fig. 7). The team leader takes advantage of these moments to elaborate his macroscopic framework by taking into account information on the state of progress of the maneuver that he is implementing. Following this process of updating, he further clarifies the mission to the teammate or transmits a new mission to him. This structure, illustrated by Fig. 7, appears six times in our data. For example, during maneuver 1, the fire chief finds the BAT when he leaves the smoke-filled building. The latter gives him an account of what they have done and also of the significant elements that they

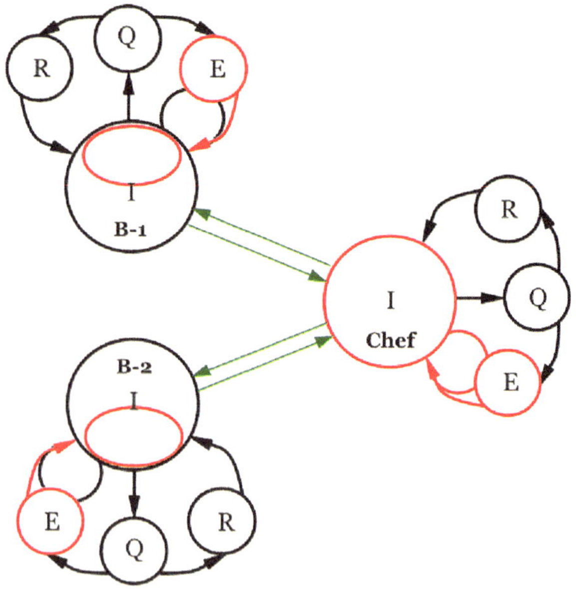

Fig. 7 SAGA: mission reassignment

have noted. The fire chief then explains their mission, insisting on the ventilation of the building in order to evacuate the smoke.

4.2.5 Team Sense-Making Stand-By

This structure (present 12 times in the data) concerns moments of waiting for a pair (or a single agent) when the latter has finished his mission and is available. These moments without any specific function allow the agents to elaborate their macroscopic framework by taking into account the activity of the fire chief and/or the other team members in order to update their understanding of the situation. This sense-making is directly dependent on the spatial configuration of the team and the possibilities of interaction that it offers to the inactive agents. This is illustrated by maneuver 2, during which the BAL is left without an assigned mission for a long time. During the first four sequences, the two partners constituting the BAL proceed to an elaboration of their respective macroscopic framework by taking into account mainly information concerning the activity of the team leader to which they have regular access. However, this possibility of interaction is abruptly interrupted when the fire chief enters the truck to pass the ambient message. This interruption then prevents the BAL from any elaboration of its macroscopic framework. This process of elaboration on the part of the BAL resumes immediately the next sequence when the fireman gets out of the truck. This structure of team sense-making is illustrated by Fig. 8.

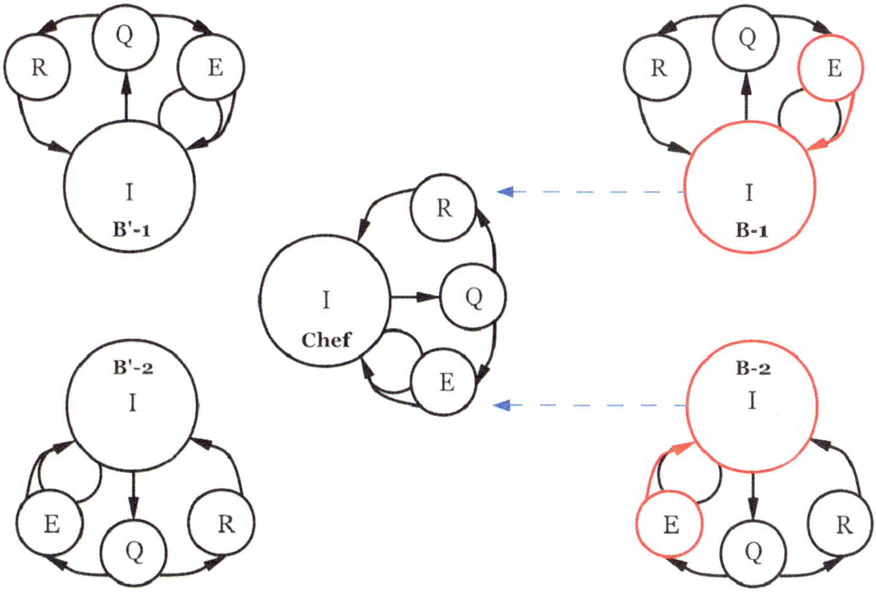

Fig. 8 SAGA: team sense-making stand-by

4.2.6 Team Sense-Making Adjustment

The last structure of team sense-making (which appears only once) concerns a particular moment of questioning of the microscopic framework within a pair leading the partners to a process of re-framing by comparing their microscopic and macroscopic frameworks (Fig. 9).

Although this structure cannot be considered as typical of firefighters sense-making, it can constitute a significant element of the collective activity that can be directly linked to a risk of collective underperformance. Indeed, the assignment of a mission to a pair (or to a single agent) means that the latter will mainly focus on the construction of its microscopic framework related to its objective. However, during the execution of this mission, the detection of certain information relative to the global situation (thus entering into their macroscopic framework) is likely to no longer fit into their microscopic framework. This disturbance may provoke a questioning of the framework, leading to a re-framing process by comparing the microscopic and macroscopic frameworks. This is what happens during maneuver 2 when the BAT returns with his equipment to the corridor leading to the apartment where the fire is located. At this point, the BAT's mission is to set up all the necessary equipment at the entrance to the apartment to attack the fire and rescue the victim inside. However, when he enters the corridor, he comes across the fire chief who is rescuing the witness who has been intoxicated by smoke. Taking into account this information, which is not related to their mission (microscopic) but to the situation as a whole (macroscopic), will create a disagreement in their understanding process. Indeed, the BAT leader and his teammate will stop all action (BAT teammate: "So there, we see that the fire chief, he takes out the witness he had [...] Now we ask ourselves, should we give the fire chief a hand? Should we abandon our mission? So we didn't really know what was going on. That's why we're watching a little bit.").

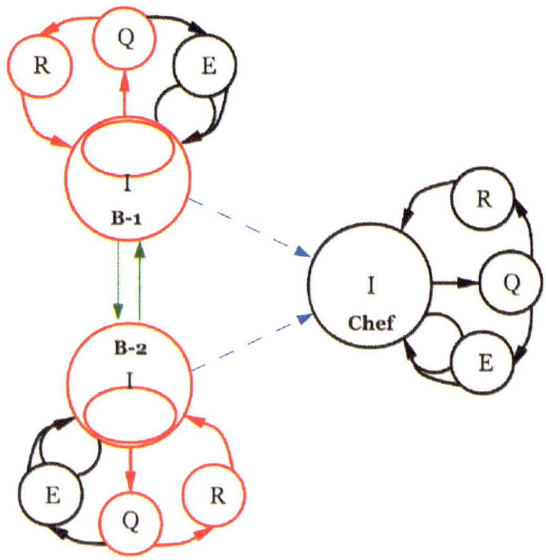

Fig. 9 SAGA: team sense-making adjustment

The BAT will only resume its activity after the intervention of the trainers who will consider, within the framework of the simulation, that the witness has been rescued and that the fire chief can consequently give the executory mission to the BAT.

5 Discussion

The main objective of this study was to report on the collective activity of the firefighting team in a practical training situation. This analysis was concretized by the implementation of a representation mode (SAGA) intended to put in visibility the articulation of the individual activities according to the functional and spatial configurations of the collective. The results of our study will be discussed according to three axes: (1) the articulation of the two levels of comprehension of the situation to be trained; (2) change of role and function to enrich sense-making at individual and team levels; and (3) typical structures of team sense-making to be taken into account to design new simulations.

5.1 The Articulation of the Two Levels of Comprehension of the Situation to Be Trained

The functional diversity that characterizes the team results in each member understanding the situation according to his or her own objective, his or her own point of view. Indeed, by looking at the way in which each individual understands the situation and develops sense-making, we were able to highlight the coexistence of two levels of understanding within the collective: macroscopic and microscopic. Our results show that the team leader focuses exclusively on a macroscopic understanding of the situation. This aspect corresponds to his function, insofar as it requires him to understand the problem he is dealing with (recognition of the situation) and to deduce from it the missions he must entrust to his team members. In this way, from a personal point of view, he is rarely led to act directly on the situation, except on an ad hoc basis. Thus, his analytical work remains global with respect to the situation (type of incident, presence of victims, potential dangers, spatial context) and does not require an extremely "fine" understanding of the situation. Even if the specific and precise understanding of the elements of the situation characterizes more the activity of the crew members (BAT and BAL), our results show that all of them adopt both levels of understanding during a maneuver (macro and micro). The team members adopt a macroscopic level of meaning-making with respect to the situation until the team leader assigns them a specific mission. From then on, they turn to a microscopic meaning-making process specific to the situation (e.g., rescuing a victim, extinguishing a fire) and partial understanding of the overall situation. It seems relevant to support the team leaders in their ability to orient the activity of each team member according to their function and the level of understanding that this function requires (macroscopic or microscopic). For example, a trainer could guide the activity of the officer in charge of entering an apartment with the lance in order to find a victim. In the case of such a mission, the agent enters into a microscopic sense-making process related to a specific objective to be reached. This help could thus concern precise elements such as the safety measures to be put in place before entering a closed room and then the clues to be taken into account in the smoky environment in order to understand the configuration of the place. Simulation has a particular interest here again by proposing realistic and credible situations, training the agents to identify and share significant information specific to the situation in order to build a macroscopic understanding when it is necessary for the team. Thus, in firefighting teams, the sense-making of the situation is done in action, mixing an individual activity focused on the mission to be achieved and a social activity focused on the understanding of the situation from the team's point of view. Finally, the training could be improved by asking the trainers to insist on the back and forth between these two levels of understanding of the situation for each member of the team. The training would then allow for modulated learning alternating between personalization and homogenization.

5.2 *Change of Role and Function to Enrich Sense-Making at Individual and Team Levels*

The consideration of team sense-making as an articulation of individual sense-making allowed us to note its heterogeneous character. Our results show a disparity of individual sense-making within the firefighting team as well as levels of understanding of the situation. This heterogeneity results from the influence of individual functions because a firefighting team is characterized by the diversity of roles allocated to each of its members. Although these roles have a strong influence, they do not entirely substitute for the functions actually performed in the field. The case of the fire chief is different because role and function overlap insofar as his responsibility is to direct his team members in order to resolve the incident in progress, which is relatively generic to be transposable from one situation to another. However, as far as his team members are concerned, the function of each one depends on the mission entrusted to him by the fire chief. It is not uncommon, for example, for the BAT, theoretically intended to extinguish the fire, to be called upon to manage the water supply instead of the BAL (example in maneuver 3 of our present study). In this way, depending on the missions dictated by the fire chief, the intervention team can take on different functional configurations during a maneuver, thus influencing the understanding of the situation of each individual. This opens up an opportunity for training firefighting teams, since it is not only a matter of training them to take on the role specific to their function, but also of teaching them to change roles during an intervention according to the needs of the situation. The representations

SAGA show here all their relevance because they help to build pedagogical scenarios in which the actors can train these adaptability skills through team sense-making. Simulations offer interesting possibilities thanks to replay and individual and/or collective viewing (with the possibility of changing the point of view) to build a shared frame during debriefing sessions. Simulation allows learning by doing, being part of active pedagogies, where different relationships to the frame can be deployed. Thus, from a pedagogical point of view, it seems important that the trainers accompany the trainee fireman to pilot and manage the activity of his team throughout the situation. This aspect is already the object of interest in the training but in an informal way and always after the simulation activity (during the debriefing). Our study shows the importance of this team sense-making skill, which allows us to recommend to simulation designers to fully integrate it into the scenarios and to make it a pedagogical activity in its own right.

5.3 Typical Structures of Team Sense-Making to Be Taken into Account to Design New Simulations

The heterogeneous nature of the collective construction of meaning also lies in the (im)possibilities of interaction in the environment. Alterations in the possibilities of communication (verbal or visual) constrain the members of the team because of the compartmentalized environments in which the teams have to evolve. According to the movements of each one during the maneuver, the team is led to present varied spatial configurations acting on the mechanisms of collective construction of meaning. It appears from then on "local" and "typical" structures of team sense-making. The configuration of the places, associated with the absence of remote communication devices (e.g., microphones), leads the members of the team to be able to communicate only with the people in the vicinity. We then observe "very localized" structures of team sense-making which take different forms according to the movements and the activity of each one. This phenomenon can be observed at different levels of the collective, either on a part of the team (e.g., a pair readjusting its understanding during its mission) or on its totality (the team leader who transmits information to the rest of the team gathered in the truck). Our results show regularities in the modes of coordination between team members leading us to identify six typical structures of team sense-making.

The team sense-making take a multitude of forms in the course of the missions entrusted to each pair (or team member) and of their movements within the environment continuously modifying the (im)possibilities of interaction between each individual. The set of typical structures of team sense-making that could be extracted contributes to constitute cycles of local coordination corresponding mainly to the activity of the two pairs and intermingling to constitute the global activity of the team during a maneuver.

From a pedagogical point of view and in the perspective of progressive learning, these environmental constraints could be overcome by equipping the team members with microphones. This would allow them to exchange important information at any time, overcoming the need to be in close proximity to communicate. This system would facilitate the collective activity of the team and could be a step before training situations without the possibility of exchanges other than in immediate proximity. From there, a certain progressiveness could be established by leaving all communications between the trainee team leader and his team members free and then by reducing them as the training progresses (e.g., limiting the number of communications during a situation or only authorizing calls initiated by the trainee team leader and prohibiting calls from team members). These pedagogical situations would allow to train team sense-making, an "embedded" phenomenon where the agents need to share very precise and specific information about the situation (e.g., "headwind" in the results). Locating this relevant information in the situation, which is similar to affordances, requires specific training that must be taken care of by the training of teams.

In conclusion, the model of team sense-making used in this work appears useful for describing and understanding the back and forth between action, its effects, and the frame for acting in a dynamic situation. The consequences for training are interesting because it implies to favor an intuitive functioning in simulation enriched with affordances and a reflexive or rational functioning in the case of debriefing by exploiting the changes of point of view or the replay, for example.

References

Béguin, P., & Pastré, P. (2002). Working, learning, interacting through simulation. In S. Bagnara, S. Pozzi, A. Rizzo, & P. Wright (Eds.), *11th European conference on cognitive ergonomics: Cognition, culture and design* (130p). Consiglio Nazionale delle Ricerche.

Corbin, J., & Strauss, A. (2008). Strategies for qualitative data analysis. Basics of Qualitative Research. *Techniques and procedures for developing grounded theory*, 3.

Grau, J.-Y., Doireau, P., & Poisson, R. (1998). Conception et utilisation de la simulation pour la formation: pratiques actuelles dans le domaine militaire. *Le Travail Humain, 61*(4), 361–385.

Grosjean, M., & Lacoste, M. (1999). *Communication et intelligence collective: le travail à l'hôpital*. PUF.

Guibourdenche, J., Bossard, C., & Cardin, Y. (2017). Situating the "music of" households and firemen in semi-open spaces: contribution to the analysis of collective activity's spatio-temporal dynamics. *Cognition, Technology & Work, 19*(1), 191–206.

Hoc, J.-M. (2003). Coopération humaine et systèmes coopératifs. In G. Boy (Editeur), *Ingénierie cognitive: IHM et Cognition*. Hermès Science publications.

Jensen, E. (2009). Sensemaking in military planning: A methodological study of command teams. *Cognition, Technology & Work, 11*(2), 103–118.

Klein, G. A., Wiggins, S., & Dominguez, C. O. (2010). Team sensemaking. *Theoretical Issues in Ergonomics Science, 11*(4), 304–320.

Leplat, J. (1991). Activités collectives et nouvelles technologies. *Revue Internationale de Psychologie Sociale, 4*, 335–356.

Leplat, J. (1993). Ergonomie et activités collectives. In F. Six, et X. Vaxevanoglou (Éditeurs), *Les aspects collectifs du travail*. Octarès.
Lipshitz, R., Omodei, M. M., McLennan, J., & Wearing, A. J. (2007). What's burning? The RAWFS heuristic on the _re ground. In R. R. Hoffman (Editeur), Expertise out of context: *Proceedings of the sixth internationale conference of naturalistic decision making* (pp. 97–112). Lawrence Erlbaum Associates.
Malakis, S., & Kontogiannis, T. (2014). Exploring team sensemaking in air traffic control (ATC): Insights from a field study in low visibility operations. *Cognition, Technology & Work, 16*(2), 211–227.
Rafaeli, A., Ravid, S., & Cheshin, A. (2009). Sensemaking in virtual teams: The impact of emotions and support tools on team mental models and team performance. *International Review of Industrial and Organizational Psychology, 24*, 151–182.
Rankin, A., Woltjer, R., & Field, J. (2016). Sensemaking following surprise in the cockpit—A reframing problem. *Cognition, Technology & Work, 18*(4), 623–642.
Rix, G., & Biache, M.-J. (2004). Enregistrement en perspective subjective située et entretien en re situ subjectif: une méthodologie de constitution de l'expérience. *Intellectica, 38*(1), 363–396.
Rix-Lièvre, G. (2010). Différents modes de confrontation à des traces de sa propre activité. *Revue d'anthropologie des connaissances, 4*(2), 358–379.
Samurçay, R., & Rogalski, J. (1993). Cooperative work and decision making in emergency management. *Le Travail Humain, 56*(1), 53–77.
Samurçay, R., & Rogalski, J. (1998). Exploitation didactique des situations de simulation. *Le Travail Humain, 61*(4), 333–359.
Vidal-Gomel, C., Fauquet-Alekhine, P., & Guibert, S. (2011). Réflexions et apports théoriques sur la pratique des formateurs et de la simulation. In P. Fauquet-Alekhine, & N. Pehuet (Editeurs), *Améliorer la pratique professionnelle par la simulation*. Octarès.

Subjective Evidence Based Ethnography: An Alternative to Debriefing for Large-Scale Simulation-Based Training?

Sophie Le Bellu, Saadi Lahlou, Joshua M. Phelps, and Jan Aandal

Abstract Debriefing methods are extensively used in vocational adult education after simulations, but guidelines and structured methods for conducting debriefings lag behind in the literature, even more when comes the necessity to implement them in mass. So, the problem is the following: in a context of simulation-based training, how might we conduct debriefings which enable effective reflection for learners and how to do this on a large scale? This chapter describes how we implemented SEBE (Subjective Evidence -Based Ethnography), a psychological research method based on observation and structured analysis of the learner's own experience through the prism of Activity Theory, within a police training camp at the Norwegian Police University College. As an alternative to the traditional debriefing provided by the police instructors upon completion of a realistic role-play, 32 police students, organized in pairs and belonging to the same cohort, voluntary participated in a SEBE intervention.

The research reported here was conducted in the framework of a European post-doctoral research project for which the first author was awarded an Intra-European Marie Curie fellowship (EC grant agreement n°330709).

S. Le Bellu (✉)
Renault SAS, Guyancourt, France

London School of Economics and Political Science, London, UK
e-mail: Sophie.Le-Bellu@Renault.com

S. Lahlou
London School of Economics and Political Science, London, UK
e-mail: S.Lahlou@lse.ac.uk

J. M. Phelps
Oslo New University College, Oslo, Norway

Norwegian Police University College, Oslo, Norway
e-mail: Joshua.Phelps@bhioslo.no

J. Aandal
Oslo Police Department, SWOT ECHO, Oslo, Norway

S. Flandin et al. (eds.), *Simulation Training through the Lens of Experience and Activity Analysis*, Professional and Practice-based Learning 30,
https://doi.org/10.1007/978-3-030-89567-9_10

Our findings indicate that the SEBE intervention has promising potential to enable professional educators to quickly train large cohorts during simulation exercises and to offer an alternative to traditional debriefing, thus providing a qualitatively different form of reflexivity to learners and new forms of educational material.

Keywords Debriefing · Professional Training · Police · Activity Theory · Subjective Evidence-Based Ethnography · Learning

1 Problematics, Limits of Current Approaches, and Research Questions

Professional training usually proceeds through a theoretical phase of instruction (in class, phase 1) (Bruner, 1968) followed by practice in more or less realistic exercises ("simulation"), with feedback by a professional trainer (phase 2), and finally training in the field, usually under the supervision of an experienced peer (phase 3). The first phase provides structured rules and information on good practice and their rationale, based on capitalization of extensive benchmarking, to feed reflexivity. The second phase enables learning by doing. The learner faces a problem where she/he must use existing resources and/or develop new ones to solve professional problems in action. The third phase is systematic improvement over the "natural" learning in a community of practice (Wenger, 2000), by legitimate peripheral participation (Lave & Wenger, 1991) where the learner observes more experienced peers and is gradually granted autonomy of practice under supervision (Paradise & Rogoff, 2009; Rogoff, 2003). Throughout each phase, a combination of supervision and reflexivity enables the learner to go beyond simple imitation or slavish reproduction to acquire an in-depth understanding of the concepts and practice, aiming an improvement of the performances (Argyris & Schon, 1974; Bobillier Chaumon et al., 2018; Conein, 1990; Kolb, 1984; Schön, 1983). From an activity point of view (in the ergonomics sense of the term), simulation-based training should allow the learner to develop a "constructive" dimension of her/his activity, that is to say to lead the learner to a transformation of her−/him-self by constructing new resources through the encounter of a problematic situation (Pastré, 2005). To enhance this construction, debriefing following a training activity is an important moment in the simulation phase: "we learn a lot by action, but we learn as much and even more by analysing our actions. And we should add that we don't not learn the same things" (Pastré, 2005).

Debriefings methods are extensively used in vocational adult education after exercises and simulations, notably in professional domains like nursing, healthcare, police, or emergency care professions (Lyons et al., 2015; Rossignol, 2017; Sawyer et al., 2016; Sjöberg & Karp, 2012; Söderström et al., 2016; Ulmer et al., 2018). This is essential to link practice and theory, pointing out what was done well or less well, what could be done better, but also to engage the learner in reflexivity on her/his own actions. "The concept of reflection on an event or activity and subsequent analysis is the cornerstone of the experiential learning experience" (Fanning & Gaba, 2007). Yet, while reflexivity in the simulation phase is recognized as an essential step of personal and professional development, tools and structured methods for conducting debriefings lag behind in the literature, even more when comes the necessity to implement them in mass. "There are surprisingly few papers in the peer-reviewed literature to illustrate how to debrief, how to teach or learn to debrief, what methods of debriefing exist and how effective they are at achieving learning objectives and goals" (Fanning & Gaba, 2007). Not only is it difficult to find generic guidelines for debriefing, but the fact reflexivity requires detailed, individualized analysis of practice means that it ideally must be adapted for each student and each performance. Often this is provided through individual feedback by an instructor, but this is time intensive and difficult to do on a large scale, for example, for a whole class of students. So, the problem is the following: in a context of simulation-based training, how might we more efficiently conduct debriefings which enable effective reflection for learners and how to do this on a large scale?

In this paper, we propose to implement a psychological research method called SEBE – Subjective Evidence Based Ethnography (Lahlou, 2011; Lahlou et al., 2015) – instead of the traditional debriefing within a simulation-based professional training and to investigate how appropriating it may lead to improvements to simulation training and reflexivity for professionals. The SEBE method is based on observation and structured analysis of the learner's own experience through the prism of activity theory. It combines a naturalistic capture of the actual sequences of actions (the subject's perspective), recording of the context, post-hoc "replay" interviews based on video tracks straight from the participant's perspective, and finally participants' own mediated memories of the recorded event. The specificity of the SEBE method for simulation training resides in the way researchers interview learners and in its theoretical background. In contrast to similar post-hoc self-confrontation techniques which are mostly non-directive, researchers conducting the SEBE replay interview often use, after a first phase where participants spontaneously comment upon their activity, a leading questioning where participants are encouraged to structure the comments of their activity based on the goals they pursue. In practice, at every moment of the tape where action changes (e.g. when the object of attention or action changes), subjects are asked to make explicit what are their goals at that moment. This includes positive and negative goals (what the subject wants to achieve, what the subject wants to avoid). Furthermore, participants are asked to point at what elements in the situation are contributing to their action: affordances of the context, embodied competences, and social regulation (e.g., local rules).

This goal-oriented technique taking its roots in the framework of Russian activity theory (Leontiev, 1978; Lomov, 1982; Nosulenko et al., 2005; Nosulenko & Samoylenko, 2009; Rubinstein, 1922a, b) allows an efficient and informative segmentation of the activity into short chunks with a subgoal, as well as identification of the relevant elements for decision and activity support. Each of these chunks of activity can then be analysed to understand how the situation given is processed by the subject to produce decision and action. This functional analysis of goal-oriented behaviour is especially interesting for redesigning the activity because it points at the components of the installation (Lahlou, 2017: the system supporting and channelling the action that helps or hinders the subject into reaching her/his subgoal). This can be used to redesign a better system (e.g. safer and fluid), but also to train participants (by making explicit what resources are needed and how they are mobilized) and identify the gaps in their embodied competences. In the latter case, in training, the first-person perspective films used by the SEBE method provide a very relevant and situated perspective into real action, including the distribution of attention; it literally provides the learners with vicariant experience of actual situations by "putting them in the shoes" of a real actor.

Previous studies have indicated that SEBE could have some potential for professional education, based upon studies within the nuclear industry involving maintenance work activities and developing training for material design purposes (Le Bellu, 2016; Le Bellu et al., 2010, 2016). The application of SEBE has been further refined for vocational training and other domains (Everri et al., 2020; Fauquet-Alekhine, 2016; Lahlou, 2011; Rieken, 2013). So far, applications of SEBE have been mostly in very technical contexts and on rather small groups. But SEBE as applied to simulation training for non-technical skills and on large scale is new. The research question investigated here is therefore: could the SEBE research instrument be an alternative to the classical debriefing approaches used in simulation-based training? Is it implementable and robust enough for application to sizeable of students' cohorts undertaking simulation-based training?

This book chapter describes how we applied SEBE within an operative police training camp at the Norwegian Police University College. Realistic simulation-based training has been a key component of operative training to prepare Norwegian police officers to make quick and apt decisions during critical incidents. During these simulations which are realistic role-play (actors or instructors are specially recruited for this purpose), students are quickly debriefed by an instructor upon completion of each scenario relatively to the educational objective of the case. These debriefings last generally a few minutes based on the notes taken by the instructor observing the case. As an alternative to this type of debriefing, we implemented SEBE upon 32 voluntary police students organized by pair and belonging to the same cohort. The technique is illustrated for a simulated case where each pair must handle difficult social interactions with the public and prioritize in their decision-making during a critical incident. This specific simulated situation where several actors perform falls within a learning area aiming at helping learners conceptualize a new situation (Pastré, 2005) and to develop and/or put in action the rules and knowledge learned before during theoretical class training or any other simulation or practical placement (Rasmussen, 1983).

In this section we presented the current state of the art and the research question.

In Sect. 2 we present the activity theory and the SEBE method.
Section 3 describes the experiment using SEBE in police training.

Section 4 presents the results of the qualitative and quantitative analysis of this experiment.
Section 5 discusses the findings and presents limitations and avenues for further research.

2 Subjective Evidence Based Ethnography (SEBE): Theoretical Background and Principles

2.1 The Russian Activity Theory

Before describing the SEBE method, it's necessary to provide an explanation of the theoretical background which founds the structuration we use in the analysis of the human activity.

In parallel to the French development of ergonomics centred on work activity (Leplat & Cuny, 1974; Ombredanne & Faverge, 1955), activity theories focused on the subject appeared in the USSR in the early twentieth century. Since then, many versions of activity theory have been developed worldwide (Bedny & Karwowski, 2004; Engeström, 2000; Nardi, 1996; Stetsenko, 2005; Von Cranach et al., 1982). Engeström's activity theory is particularly popular, having been developed to take into account organizational characteristics of the activity (such as the division of labour, tooling, and rules).

While theoretical work on activity theory is sophisticated, methodological approaches to its application in studying work activity lag behind. Our own research is based on the psychological structure of the activity developed by the Russian school of activity theory (Leontiev, 1978; Rubinstein, 1922a, b, 1940) but makes little use of its philosophical aspects linked to personality, conscience, or emotions.

Activity theory in the Russian tradition has been developed primarily by Leontiev (1978) and Rubinstein (Rubinstein, 1922a, b, 1940), who elaborated two somewhat similar versions of the structure of human activity. Generally, activity theory aims to render explicit the relationships between the different components of an activity, namely, motives, goals, tasks, actions, and operations.

In Leontiev's version, motives, interpreted not as a kind of experience of need but as a material or ideal object of need, determine the whole activity, which is carried out by means of actions directed by conscious goals. The expected result of activity, which is the goal, defines the actions necessary to reach it. However, actions are ultimately determined by the motive of activity. Indeed, one activity can be completed by means of different actions, and one action can be a component of different activities. Operations are concrete ways to realize an action and correspond to conditions of activity. Thus, in the Leontiev's theory, motives refer strictly to the whole activity, goals refer to actions, and operations refer to concrete situations.

Rubinstein's conception of activity structure is similar to the one proposed by Leontiev in the sense that the same activity components are outlined. However, according to Rubinstein, there is no strict correspondence between the motive and activity or between the goal and action. Activity-related motives and goals, unlike action-related motives and goals, usually have an integral nature, express a subject's general orientation and, thus, are called initial motives and final goals. At different stages of activity, activity-related motives and goals generate different specific motives and goals, which characterize actions.

Both activity theories provide an efficient conceptual framework for investigating "human and environment" interactions, while Rubinstein's version is focused on the philosophical and theoretical developments of an activity linked to concepts of conscience, personality, and the life of the subject.

Our previous research (Le Bellu et al., 2010) has stabilized and operationalized a version of activity theory developed in line with Lomov's engineering psychology at the Russian Academy of Sciences (Lomov, 1982; Nosulenko et al., 2005; Nosulenko & Samoylenko, 2009). In this version, activity theory considers activity as an oriented trajectory from a given state ("conditions given") to a consciously represented expected final state ("goal"), driven by internal motives (urge to reach some internal state of balance or satisfaction).

The trajectory of activity is thus considered as a succession of small problems to be solved ("tasks"), which can each be seen as reaching a local "subgoal" (intermediate stage in reaching the goal) in the conditions given by the environment (organization, tools…). Activity is subject-centric: performed from the perspective of the subject, in the context of layers of affordances that shape action pathways. To these should be added actions/operations (behaviour) components which can be observed and recorded, while others, such as motives or goals, are invisible. These invisible components can be revealed and characterized only by means of techniques developed to analyse and evaluate subjective representations of individuals. The modes of investigation that we used to trace and mediate relationships between externally observable parameters of activity (behaviour) and their internal components (thoughts and so on) are presented below through the SEBE technique.

2.2 *The SEBE Method*

Video ethnography is a naturalistic approach to collect and study the flow of activity during real-life practice in the field. Recently visual ethnographic methods and techniques have been expanding in the social sciences (sociology, anthropology, psychology, and ergonomics) to study human activity (Fleck & Fitzpatrick, 2009; Goldman et al., 2007; Heath et al., 2010; Lahlou, 1999; Mondada, 2003; Omodei et al., 2005). As activity is distributed, professionals use not only their embodied competence but also a series of physical tools and instruments to transform material objects (Rabardel, 1997) and mediating structures to perform cognitive operations. Indeed, Hutchins, after Pea (Pea & Kurland, 1984), calls "mediating structures" the artefacts used by humans as information processors:

> Language, cultural knowledge, mental models, arithmetic procedures, and rules of logic are all mediating structures too. So are traffic lights, supermarkets layouts, and the contexts we arrange for one another's behavior. Mediating structures can be embodied in artifacts, in ideas, in systems of social interactions [...] (Hutchins, 1995: 290–291)

Furthermore, action is situated and emerges in context (Lave, 1988; Suchman, 1987). Consequently, when we try to reconstruct the action and understand how professionals make decisions, we need to account for the contextual elements which contributed to the activity. These elements cannot be recovered easily from a participant's memory alone.

The SEBE method uses video recordings to bring the complete situation back to the participant at the time of recall, thus enabling the professionals to point to the relevant elements that supported their actions while they were happening. More specifically, SEBE (Lahlou, 2011) combines two video techniques: first-person perspective (FPP) video (Fig. 1) and replay interview (RIW). We use a first-person perspective capture to reconstruct the situation as it was seen by the participants at the moment of action, because, in complex situations, what was relevant for immediate action is usually what the participants paid attention to. They then watch their own footage and comment upon in it in a specially structured *replay interview (RIW)* that aims to reconstitute the activity, with its goals, subgoals, and more generally mental states and decision-making processes in connection with the elements present in context.

During SEBE, FPP video recording of an activity is first collected via subjective cameras (*subcams*, Fig. 1) which are miniature wide-angle video cameras with a stereo microphone (Lahlou, 1999), also referred to as "body cameras" in recent literature from within the police domain (Drover & Ariel, 2015; Lum et al., 2019; Voigt et al., 2017). Subcams are worn at eye level by a participant on a pair of glasses or other apparatus (e.g. helmet, hat, or pocket) adapted to the activity. If in the 1990s, researchers using (FPP) video were a few, since this time, body-worn video devices have been increasingly explored and adopted either by academic research in various domains (Drobnjak, 1997; Mackenzie & Kerr, 2012; Rix & Biache, 2004) or within professional settings.

Fig. 1 A police student wearing the subcam (left); first-person perspective from the perspective of an actor playing member of the public in a case (right)

Wearable recording devices facilitate data collection in a number of ways. Situated activities may be captured on film even while the participants are moving and provide access to their focus of attention. Data are collected without the contribution of any outside observer, and participants are free to organize their activity and movements. This combined with the relative unobtrusiveness of the body camera results in a very natural activity. It is important to note that participants tend to forget they are wearing the device, because they focus on their activity but also because a very stringent ethics protocol guarantees that they have full control over the data, not only during recording but afterwards also. So, they do not have to worry about the recording and can legitimately (in psychological terms) forget about it. Furthermore, there is not a researcher around carrying a video camera who would be a constant reminder of the recording.

In addition to the advantage of convenience, FPP footage provides memory cues and a more accurate representation (and soundscape) of the actual situation to participants. This representation is obtained in the second phase of SEBE, the replay interview (RIW). The RIW is a reflexivity exercise, which has interest per se for the professional or trainee as it makes explicit the implicit and raises awareness about actual practice (Fleck & Fitzpatrick, 2009; Gillespie, 2007; Schön, 1983; Suchman & Trigg, 1991). In the RIW the video recording is used to stimulate the participant's memory and to reconstruct the situation as it was experienced by the participants at the moment of action. The RIW technique is an adapted self-confrontation interview (Clot & Leplat, 2005; Ginsburg et al., 1985; Pinsky & Theureau, 1987; Theureau, 2003; von Cranach, 1982) whose specificity resides in the way researchers interview the participants and in its theoretical background (see section above on activity theory). As mentioned before, in contrast to similar post-hoc self-confrontation techniques which are mostly non-directive, researchers conducting the SEBE replay interview often use, after a first phase where participants spontaneously comment their activity, a leading questioning where participants are encouraged to structure the comments of their activity based on the goals they pursue. In practice, at every moment of the tape where action changes (e.g. when the object of attention or action changes), subjects are asked to make explicit what are their goals at that moment. This includes positive and negative goals (what the subject wants to achieve, what the subject wants to avoid). Furthermore, participants are asked to point at what elements in the situation are contributing to their action: affordances of the context, embodied competences, and social regulation (e.g. local rules).

RIWs aim to allow as accurate a reconstruction of the participant's activity as possible given his/her willingness and ability to verbalize, the specific skill set of the interviewer, and the level of trust during the interview. RIWs are also video recorded themselves for further analysis step.

Hence the FPP footage may empower participants to more precisely and accurately recall what they did, thought, and felt during an activity. Thus, a key advantage of SEBE involves its power for triggering recall of lived experience. Another advantage is that it provides researchers with material allowing a detailed step-by-step understanding of the constituents of activity: goals, subgoals, determinants of actions, decision-making processes, and so on (see our example of analysis and result in Sect. 4.1).

3 Material and Method: The SEBE Intervention in the Norwegian Police Education

3.1 Simulation-Based Operative Training in Norwegian Police Education

Before detailing the SEBE intervention, it is necessary to describe the operative training context in which we conducted our investigation. The present study was carried out within the operative training system developed by the Norwegian Police University College (PHS).[1] At the time of data collection, all third-year police students at PHS had to complete five modules of operative training throughout their final year of study to obtain a bachelor's degree in policing (Politihøgskolen, 2014). Our intervention focused on one of these modules, SERT, which was an intensive 3-week course designed and administered by police.

High-ranking instructors employed by PHS have responsibility for weapons and tactical training and administer a larger team of lower-ranked instructors recruited from the police districts for each 3-week course. Roughly 60 students participated at one of two camps for the 3-week duration of the course. Students received basic classroom and scenario-based instruction in weapons and police tactics during the first two weeks. The final week comprised mostly scenario-based training as students had to complete six live-action simulations without the assistance of instructors. Our intervention focused on one of these six simulations, the so-called *intoxicated man* scenario (Fig. 2).

In this case, police students must handle difficult social interactions with the public and to prioritize between two cases. The public (a drunken man and a parent)

Fig. 2 Picture of the *intoxicated man* scenario both from external (top row) and first-person (below row) perspectives

[1] Politihøgskolen (http://www.phs.no/en/).

are actors specifically recruited for this role-play, and the simulation takes place outdoor in the police camp, in a place looking like a park. Thus, the simulation environment is built so that a maximum of conditions is met to have the most realistic simulations and to enable a good projection and immersion of the police students in the lived situation.

More precisely, a student-pair receive a call from the Operation Central (OC) informing them to conduct a routine control-check on an intoxicated man who has created a public disturbance in a park. Midway through the case, a distressed parent unexpectedly approaches them to report a missing child. The patrol is expected to cope with the two cases at the same time and to quickly prioritize the missing child. The educational objective of the case is to thus examine whether student-pairs are able to identify the critical information, to understand its meaning, and to adapt their activities to the new situation by adjusting their initial goal. This is because, as future police officers, the police students are expected to be able to quickly adapt their responses to a changing situation. Thus, the task to be solved in this simulation raises to this educational question: *are the police students able to adapt to a changing situation and to make the decision to prioritize the most critical(urgent) case?*

The case is constructed so that the two police students become split up when the parent comes into the situation. Very often, as seen on Fig. 2, one of the police students keeps speaking with the intoxicated man, while the second police officer becomes engaged with the parent. The actor playing the parent is instructed by the police instructors to exhibit signs of stress and additionally demands immediate help from the police to locate the child. After a short time, the two police students begin to have a different situational awareness, as they are physically and mentally separated. Nevertheless, they must decide as a team: should they stick to their initial goal and remain focused on the first assigned mission (the intoxicated man), or should they reprioritize and try to save the child?

Throughout the case, one or two police instructors positioned near to the police students observe the simulation and take notes. The case is stopped by the instructors when they consider/understand that the students have made their decision for how to prioritize. Then, each student-pair receives a quick (approximately 3 min) verbal debriefing by an instructor upon completion of the scenario. Ideally, the content of this debriefing focuses on questions aiming to activate a reflection process with the police students: *did they have a common situation awareness among themselves, but also together with the OC? Did they share information with each other, and did they report back to OC on their actions? Were they aware of the individual goals they were pursuing throughout the case? Did they try to solve both tasks at the same time, and what were the consequences of that (splitting up, losing information, and doing a bad job in both cases)?*

The PHS instructors created this now well-established simulation to challenge students on principal decision-making during operative work. At first sight the case could be considered as "poor", as it might seem obvious to find a missing child is more important than handling a drunk man. However, instructors suggested that there was a degree of variability to student behaviour and there was additionally a clear hierarchy in terms of changing priorities. That's why we selected[2] this simulation in accordance with the instructors for implementing the SEBE method instead of the traditional short debriefing.

3.2 *Participants and Ethics*

The SEBE intervention was presented to a cohort of 60 final-year police students at the beginning of the final week of the SERT course. Thirty-two students agreed to participate in the study (M_{age} = 24.3, range 21–37 years old, 31% women, 69% male). Most had no professional experience before entering the police education system as few reported prior experiences in operative training in the military (N = 6) or criminal justice system (N = 1). All students had 1 year of practical placement in the police.

As our SEBE intervention involved capturing potentially sensitive[3] audio-video data (Everri et al., 2020), the research protocol was submitted and approved by two review boards: one research-ethics board within the two first author's institution and a second data-protection committee in Norway.[4]

3.3 *Data Collection Protocol*

The purpose of this stage was to collect data that would provide an approach to a subjective experience embodied in a cognitive activity of joint diagnostic and decision-making.

Based on the SEBE paradigm described above, each of the 32 police students participating in the SEBE protocol were equipped with a subcam right before starting the simulation (see Fig. 3, left picture). As they acted during the case, a first-person perspective of their visual scope, soundscape (including speech), and manipulations was recorded. As participants were organized in pairs during the simulation, this means that we collected two subcam footages per simulation, each one corresponding to the attentional perspective of each police student. In total, we collected 32 subcam footages for 16 simulations. The duration of the simulation

---

[2] We had to choose the most relevant simulation as a "pilot" use-case well in advance of the actual research, in order to adapt to the operative training in agreement with local police instructors. This required an in-depth reading and understanding of educational material and making choices without having observed cases prior to the actual research.

[3] Audio-video data collected can be sensitive either from a private perspective for the participant or from an institutional viewpoint, since this organization trains the future police officers of the country to specific techniques.

[4] Norwegian Centre for Research Data (https://nsd.no/nsd/english/index.html).

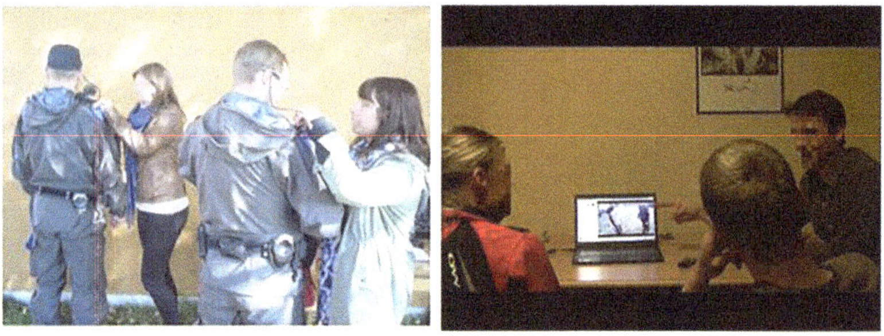

Fig. 3 Each volunteer police student of each pair is equipped with a subcam by the researchers (left picture) before starting the simulation (see Fig. 2) and then debriefed jointly by a researcher during a RIW session (right picture)

varied from 2 to 12 min (M length = 4 min) depending of the time student-pairs needed to make their decision.

Subcam footages were then used for conducting the replay interviews with each student-pair (see Fig. 3, right picture) to enable participants to get into reflexive mode and make them develop a joint understanding of how the patrol perceived the situation, made decisions, and communicated during the case. The 15 replay interviews (one pair of police students did not participate) took place during the students' free time, conducted in the evening after the simulation so as not to impede the schedule of students/instructors. Interviews were conducted at the training camp by four researchers in parallel and based on a semi-structured interview guide following the theoretical principles of activity theory (goals and plans to reach the goals). The student-pairs were also encouraged to comment upon their situational awareness, decision-making, perception of risk, and on communication between partners and with other protagonists of the scene.

Before starting, researchers provided the definitions of "goal" and "plan" to the participants: "For us, a goal is a representation of a desired state; that means what situation you want to reach. The plan is how you intend to get there". Participants reviewed their patrol's performance and practice by watching their FPP video recording. Practically, the interview started with the subcam footage of the police student who enters in contact with the intoxicated man first and then continued with the subcam footage of the second police student at the moment (s)he was contacted by the parent. It was also possible to switch from one subcam footage to another in case the police students would like to. The police students were asked to identify, articulate, and share the individual and/or common goals they pursued while they experienced the situation and to describe the way they reached their goals (plans). For structuring and articulating the comments upon the activity, the subcam footage was systematically paused at four critical time periods[5]: T0, mission assignment; T1, arrival in the park; T2, first encounter with the parent; and T3, decision-making

[5] These key times were identified during the research design phase, when reading the educational material.

(if this occurs). If the participant didn't spontaneously pause at these points, the researcher who conducted the interview did it. The length of the replay interviews lasted between 30 min and 1 h (M length = 42 min).

Finally, 20 days upon completion of the SERT module, an evaluation survey related to learning outcomes was distributed electronically to the participants in the SEBE intervention and a comparison group to examine potential effects of the SEBE intervention (Phelps et al., 2016). This evaluation survey was completed by 29 of the 32 original participants in the SEBE intervention and by 34 police students who were debriefed according to the classical PHS method (comparison group). Questions included items measuring background information, police identity, learning preferences (e.g. *I often reflect on my actions to see whether I could have improved on what I did*), attitudes toward operative training (e.g. *Competence about operative training makes the police's work easier)*, learning outcomes related to the course (e.g. *I have identified mistakes that I used to think were correct during the training camp*), and qualitative items related to learning outcomes during specific role play exercises (e.g. *List up to 10 things you learned on this case*).

3.4 Analysis of Qualitative Data (FPP Footages and RIWs)

Each RIW was transcribed. A systematic open coding scheme was then constructed by the first and second authors who independently coded each transcription and compiled a list of seven thematic categories: planification (goals and plans), risk perception, situation understanding, decision, communication, eye contact, and self-learning. We only coded a category as present when both raters agreed upon its presence; when they disagreed, the category was deleted. Those categories of verbatims were put in relations with the timeline/course(s) of action of the student-pairs visible in the subcam footages, according to the four key times identified during the research design phase (T0, mission assignment; T1, arrival in the park; T2, first encounter with the parent; T3, decision-making).

4 Results

4.1 Qualitative Results

While it might seem intuitive that the novice Police Students (PSs) choose the missing child over the intoxicated man, our findings indicated that they faced a number of challenges in the live-action simulation. Indeed, none of the pairs was able to reach the expected outcomes. Only half of the student-pairs (7 out of the 15) succeeded by clearly prioritizing the second unforeseen mission, as expected by the instructors. Moreover, four of the seven of these "successful" pairs used an extended period of time to implement the decision to leave the intoxicated man and join their partner. Six pairs "failed" by maintaining their attention on several goals at the same time by splitting their activities between the different priorities, while the two remaining patrols stayed physically and cognitively involved in the first mission and prioritized the intoxicated man (N = 2).

Combining FPP and RIWs for each pair allowed us to qualitatively analyse the cognitive paths underlying the joint activity of the PSs during all the situation. This activity analysis enabled us to investigate how the police students became projected in a novel learning setting involving ending up in a situation of multi-tasking. In an extremely short and challenging time frame, they passed from one unique and common goal to several individual goals and subgoals to be pursued in parallel (see example detailed below). This helps explain why the resulting reality was more nuanced and yielded diverse trajectories which diverged from the expectations of professional instructors regarding operational priorities.

We illustrate this finding by providing an extract of the analysis completed with the SEBE methodology. This extract highlights the situated and cognitive processes that occur when novice police officers must make joint decisions in such a case. We have used the labels PS1 (police student 1) and PS2 (police student 2) to represent the student-pairs who are jointly assigned by the OC (Operation Central) to control the intoxicated man in the park. PS1 is the student who engages with the intoxicated man, while PS2 encounters the parent.

At T0 (mission assignment to the police patrol by the OC) and T1 (encounter with the intoxicated man mission), all pairs reported to have shared common goal and subgoals.

More precisely, just after having received the instructions by the OC (their principal goal is to control an intoxicated man), all pairs but one reported to have quickly elaborated and decided upon a plan (subgoals and tasks sharing) on their way to meet their principal goal. When discussing their perceptions of risk during the RIW, most pairs reported that this kind of mission was low risk and that they were used to dealing with public disturbances involving intoxicated people. They explained they had based their decision-making strategies on standard procedures learned during their theoretical training and on similar cases they had already experienced in practical placement.

…that is a pretty ordinary mission so we made a plan that we had to hear what he had to say and get him away from the park so he won't disturb the others in the park anymore. RIW PS1, Pair 12

This is like a routine for us, so we know what to do. RIW PS2, Pair 14.

I felt that this was a mission that would be a low threat, because it's a mission that we've just been out working for one year in a practical period… RIW PS1, Pair 6.

It's so basic. It's almost the first thing we learn in the first year of school about the "Police Law" and what to do with intoxicated people and so on. RIW PS1, Pair 8.

… today it was a normal situation that we could come into every day and it's like something I've done in the past here when I was in practice … RIW PS1, Pair 11.

Each pair applied their initial plan (the same one for each pair) by assigning PS1 to first communicate with the man and to evaluate his level of dangerousness for adapting their actions and decisions depending upon his state: to tell him to leave and to drive him to home, hospital, or the police station (subgoals of PS1). In the meanwhile, PS2 remained in the background in charge of communicating with the OC by radio, having an overview of the setting, and thus maintaining security (subgoals of PS2).

However, at T2 (arrival of a new protagonist in the simulation), an unforeseen and sudden event occurs during the simulation. The introduction of the panicked parent and potential mission involves sudden changes in pace and goals dynamics. The underlying cognitive processes and strategies of the police patrol are led to change with the change of situation.

Interviewer: "So your goal is ..."
RIW PS1, Pair 1: "To focus on [the intoxicated man] and maintain contact and finish the goal we had earlier: make contact and get a solution".
Interviewer to PS2: "And I guess your goal has to change suddenly, correct?"
RIW PS2, Pair 1: "Yeah, it does. My main goal is first to calm this woman down and then to let her speak and find out why she is so upset. So my focus on [the intoxicated man] is taken away".
RIW PS1, Pair 1: A change of pace.
RIW PS2, Pair 1: "... and mix up between our goals. The main goal was first [the intoxicated man], and now it's changed to this woman for me so exactly at that point we didn't have a plan. First, I need to talk to this woman and find out why she's so upset. But ten seconds out I think we or at least I have a plan after speaking with her".

As soon as the PSs were interrupted by the distressed parent running in their direction, a second common goal involving orienting toward the new protagonist appeared. In the RIWs, PSs reported that having to deal with a second case in parallel to the first one was perceived as novel and highly challenging. In a short period of time, they had to reconstruct a new situational awareness "...as you can see in the video, it's a few seconds of chaos when she [the mum] is running almost at us and we're trying to figure out what's happening and if she's attacking us, or whatever" (RIW PS2, Pair 9); "I think only the drunk guy would have been routine...but when they [the instructors] add the woman, it's not routine anymore" (RIW PS1, Pair 9). Only two PSs reported to have previously experienced two cases in parallel. This means that from T2, most of the PSs were situated in a new learning area.

At this turning point of within the simulation, each student-pairs met a "cognitive collision" of their goals as they were clearly confronted with two distinct attentional courses to prioritize: "the intoxicated man" or "the parent". These two attentional courses (two principal and parallel goals) thus created the emergence of new individual subgoals for both PS1s and PS2s. PS1s stayed with the intoxicated man and suddenly went from pursuing one to three goals: communication with the man, keep an eye on his/her partner (safety goal), and develop an understanding of the new situation.

RIW PS1, Pair 6: "Try to look at her[my partner] in case the other woman [the mum], you never know, she may be sick, she may be violent, we never know, so I don't want to leave her alone with her if she's getting violent. At the same time, I try to talk to [the drunk man]".
Interviewer: "Yes, you do a lot of this [31 gazes from PS1 to PS2 have been calculated]".

As for PS2s, the parent added a new goal (to assess a new situation and make a decision) which competed with the first common one (controlling the intoxicated man). They had to understand and decide upon a course of action with the parent (T3), e.g. to collect further information, to report to the OC, to communicate with PS1, and/or to go in search of the child.

However, some PS2s met difficulties totally switching to the parent case. Our analyses indicated that some of them reported goals of keeping focusing on the intoxicated man or with their partner's safety (e.g. pair 9, 8, 15) in addition of the parent case. Indeed, ensuring partner safety was a tacit but omnipresent goal of all police students (either PS1 or PS2). This was especially apparent in our analysis of the subcam footages in which we observed that most student-pairs maintained eye contact with each other when they were separated. In fact, we measured 31 to 3 head movements in direction of the partner across each of the 15 simulations. In the RIWs, some participants, such as Pair 6, explained that they used positioning strategies in order to facilitate this eye contact (see extract above). The participants also reported that this tacit goal involving partner safety could come into conflict with other goals. Indeed, the PS2s who especially expressed the goal of their partner's safety also reported feelings of stress in the RIWs. These pairs faced communication difficulties either with their partner or with the parent. For example, see what Pair 4 reported.

RIW PS2, Pair 4: "*I didn't hear him saying I should concentrate on the woman because I still wanted to be there for my partner because I know for a fact that some people can switch like that so I want to have an eye on him as well*".
Interviewer: "*Right so one of your goals is safety for your partner?*"
RIW PS2, Pair 4: "*Safety for my partner and help her so I got many balls in the air*".

Our analyses also indicated that all the PSs who experienced this cognitive multitasking situation encountered difficulties in the simulation. This feeling was due to the fact that the PSs tried to maintain the different goals they were following at the same level of priority. In other words, they were not able to prioritize their goals. They were physically involved in the new mission, but they were cognitively dispersed, which resulted in a dilemma between body and mind. Moreover, participants reported that the cognitive cost of such cognitive dispersal was high.

From a student perspective, their participation in the SEBE intervention seemed to offer an opportunity to evaluate their own performances beyond the short feedback normally provided by instructors. Each pair had the chance to return and evaluate potential misunderstandings or develop a better understanding of their performance. For example, Pair 8 developed insights on how ineffective communication led to missing information. PS2 attempted to draw her partner's attention, but PS1 remained too focused on his own case. This discovery in the RIW led to the following exchange:

PS2, Pair 8: "Now there, when she looked at me, I was asking her if she is okay and if I can go and look around the corner".
PS1, Pair 8: "Oh, I didn't hear that. Yes, I see it now".
Furthermore, the PSs self-reported during the RIWs to have learned about their participation in the SEBE intervention:
PS1, Pair 8: "...thank you. I've learned from this [...]. I've never seen myself in a perspective like that".

PS1, Pair 1: "I really enjoy it. It gets us thinking more and I feel that looking at what I do afterwards at least doubles what I learn. I see new things now that I didn't think about earlier. [...] For example, [...] I didn't even think about that I was looking that much. I knew I was looking a bit, but I looked a lot more over to my partner. Or how you handle and communicate to the person as well".

4.2 *Quantitative Results (Survey Study Results)*

The survey study and its results are reported in details in a separate publication (Phelps et al., 2016). Therefore, this section focuses on the main findings. As mentioned above, we aimed to examine if our intervention may have led to different learning outcomes for the 29 students using SEBE by examining their responses on a course evaluation survey with a comparison group (N = 34) of students who participated in the standard simulation-based training (non SEBE intervention).

Results indicated that no differences in police identity or learning preferences were found between the intervention and comparison groups. However, main findings indicated that students in the SEBE intervention self-reported more learning outcomes related to decision-making and communication and could identify their own mistakes to a greater degree. They also articulated more learning outcomes in qualitative measures related to describing what they learned from the training exercise and what they could improve upon in comparison to group receiving the standard training (see Phelps et al., 2016, for more details).

These quantitative results add support to the qualitative findings that police students in the SEBE intervention mentioned to be concerned about self-learning at the end of the RIWs (see previous section) and provide promising signs that the SEBE method may enhance experiential learning for police students.

5 Discussion, Conclusion, and Research Avenues

The goal of this research was twofold. First, we investigated whether the SEBE research instrument could be an alternative to the classical debriefing approaches extensively used in professional training. Second, we examined whether SEBE would be implementable and robust enough for application to sizeable cohorts undertaking simulation-based training.

This chapter documents the first time in which SEBE was applied to a simulation case in operative training within Norwegian police education instead of a standard debriefing. On the basis of our analysis, findings (Sects. 4.1 and 4.2) indicate that the technique of goal-oriented RIW offers a different and more in-depth type of reflexivity for trainees, compared to a standard debriefing. Participants could review the results of their action in a secured and structured space of discussion, and others could confront them with what they expected and what they had learned during the instruction phase. Hence, students could detail their rationale by articulating their individual and common goals and understand the source of both success and failure in their own performance in a different manner. The survey study was conducted 20 days after the SEBE intervention aimed at quantitatively assessing the inputs of the method with a comparative group. Its findings also provide an indication that it created different outcomes than traditional debriefing. Students in the intervention group reported more and different learning outcomes related to what was discussed during the RIW, namely, decision-making, communication, better identification and explanation of mistakes, and a higher degree of description of what the students learned and could improve. Therefore, these qualitative and quantitative results, although exploratory, provide a further that the method could add support and value to the positive feelings of self-learning reported by the participants at the end of the RIWs and that this seems to move beyond what is to be expected by standard debriefing.

We suggest that future research considering SEBE as an alternative to classical debriefing should interestingly add a step of measurement/assessment, coming in complement or as an alternative to the survey assessment. This additionnal step would aim to compare the performance of both group of trainees (SEBE group and comparison group) confronted with an additional similar situation (simulated or real), after having participated to a SEBE intervention. It would allow to observe practically on the field, to which extent the police students improved their performance and conceptualized and appropriated new knowledge (cooperation, communication, handle multi-tasking, decision-making) – "operative genesis" process (Pastré, 2005; Rabardel, 2005).

Also, the in-depth and detailed example of qualitative analysis provided in Sect. 4.1 shows how the method enables researchers or instructors to finely cut and structure cognitive processes occurring during an activity involving non-technical skills. Particularly, the problem of decision-making presented in this simulation was analysed as a case of multitasking. From a theoretical perspective, the SEBE method could be further explored for research focusing on decision-making mechanisms and investigations of how to track the actual and time-stamped chain of actions and decisions while they occur.

It was also the first time we applied SEBE on a large scale to sizeable cohorts. According to a very strict organization (see Sect. 3), our team of 4 researchers was able to record the individual subjective perspectives of 32 trainees and to debrief them by conducting 15 qualitative joint replay interviews, all on the same day. To our knowledge, this is the first time a qualitative research method combining a high level of description of technical and/or cognitive processes and potential for professional learning has been deployed in a short time. This indicates that the SEBE intervention has the potential to enable professional educators to quickly train large cohorts during simulation exercises and offer an alternative to traditional debriefing, thus providing a qualitatively different form of reflexivity to learners.

Nevertheless, it is important to note that the preparation work dealing with the organization and information flow prior to the fieldwork is essential to create good conditions for a successful implementation. The current intervention did indeed face a number of challenges. First, merging both training and research schedules became important because we had to ensure that our intervention did not overly impede upon the original educational program. We also had to ensure that we had enough time to reliably collect data during the simulation and at the same time avoid disrupting the actual training schedule which had little room for deviation. Moreover, in spite of detailed preparation and organization, we also experienced several technological malfunctions (e.g. empty batteries, full memory cards, damaged cable, broken camera) during the data collection phase. These issues are however almost inevitable when collecting large amounts of digital data with few devices (here, only 7 subcams for 32 participants).

A second challenge was the selection of the simulation case for this research well in advance before the fieldwork. For example, a case which would entail police patrols larger than a dyad involves a dramatic increase in the number of possible trajectories a case could render. This greatly complicates the task of analysing and comparing performances due to the possible outcomes and differences in behaviour. In fact, we applied the SEBE intervention to two other simulations during the fieldwork and experienced this challenge during a simulation called "public stabbing" involving four police students. In this complex simulation, police students were asked by the instructors to search for and arrest an armed perpetrator in a mock city. Due to this increasing patrol size, the case resulted in a diversity of experiences and less control. Hence, we made the choice to narrow down this exploratory research to a case involving pairs, in which all patrols experienced more or less a similar situation involving clear-cut decision-making possibilities. Thus, potential behavioural trajectories were reduced, and analysis of situated and distributed processes between people and also the comparison of performances became more manageable. We thus reserve the question of how more complicated simulations may be investigated using SEBE for future research.

Our current findings show that SEBE has a promising potential to stimulate reflection and learning within simulation training. They also provide valuable knowledge regarding how to characterize the simulated situation in a perspective of SEBE application.

We would also like to add that at an organizational level, the head police instructors were receptive to the present method because it seemed to provide a new perspective on student learning in addition to a new arena to improve feedback. The operative modules are at key times adjusted at PHS to mirror current practical issues in the police and societal problems. For example, after the events of July 22, 2011 (the Utøya massacre), additional case-based training was added to the curriculum. The operative instructors were also in the process of designing new measures to improve evaluation of students. The openness to the present technique was thus also in line with increased focus on knowledge-based policing in Norway in which the police are under pressure to continue systematizing and learning from their own experiences (NOU, 2009) and designing innovative methods of education (Strategic plan, NOU, 2012, 2013). But, beyond the organizational and practical conditions discussed above, an organization or institution – whatever it is: training centre or industry – should reasonably raise the issue of the human resources and skills needed for implementing SEBE as a new educational tool. Because reflexivity is obtained through the individual or collective reviewing of the tape by participants, and because the questions used in the RIW are rather standard (what are the goals pursued, how they are achieved, which tools are used and specific themes related to the profession), we consider that, after a short training for becoming comfortable with the technique, the RIW does not need to be conducted by an expert of the activity. We consider it could be feasibly done by instructors, but it takes time to conduct such detailed individualized interviews and this time investment is not always possible or realistic in professional settings. Another option would be to make it by the students themselves, in turn, with each other (as an educational method of collective self-marking). The latter option would allow students to benefit of such detailed qualitative debriefings even for large size of cohorts, without not too much impeding on the instructors' time, and while keeping enhancing the learning of students.

Eventually, the subfilms produced by SEBE for conducting the replay interviews could be reused by the instructors for producing new educational material and imagining new exercises. For example, a compilation of this significant series of video recordings could provide a video base where we can see the same case completed in different ways. This base of first-person perspective video could then be used for making the students identify, annotate, and discuss on a series of good and less good practice, but also to concretely illustrate theory during class-training, or to review before going on the field. All these new uses could contribute to enhance an autonomous learning of the students by providing them an access to such a base for viewing as many times as needed.

References

Argyris, C., & Schon, D. A. (1974). *Theory in practice: Increasing professional effectiveness.* Jossey-Bas.

Bedny, G., & Karwowski, W. (2004). Activity theory as a basis for the study of work. *Ergonomics, 47*(2), 134–153.

Bobillier Chaumon, M.-É., Rouat, S., Laneyrie, E., & Cuvillier, B. (2018). De l'activité DE simulation à l'activité EN simulation: simuler pour stimuler. *Activites, 15*(1). https://doi.org/10.4000/activites.3136

Bruner, J. S. (1968). *Towards a theory of instruction (1st ed 1966).* Harvard University Press.

Clot, Y., & Leplat, J. (2005). La méthode clinique en ergonomie et en psychologie du travail. *Le Travail Humain, 68*, 289–316.

Conein, B. (1990). Cognition située et coordination de l'action, la cuisine dans tous ses états. *Réseaux, 8*(43), 99–110.

Cranach, M. Von (1982). *Goal-directed action.* Academic.

Cranach, M. Von, et al. (1982). Goal-directed action. In *European monographs in social psychology 30.* Academic Press in co-operation with European Association of Experimental Social Psychology.

Drobnjak, M. (1997, October 14–16). Using head mounted video camera to aid recall of events during military activities. In *39th Annual Conference of the International Military Testing Association.*

Drover, P., & Ariel, B. (2015). Leading an experiment in police body-worn video cameras. *Int Crim Justice Rev, 25*(1), 80–97. https://doi.org/10.1177/1057567715574374

Engeström, Y. (2000). Activity theory as a framework for analyzing and redesigning work. *Ergonomics, 43*(7), 960–974.

Everri, M., Heitmayer, M., Yamin-Slotkus, P., & Lahlou, S. (2020). Ethical challenges of using video for qualitative research and ethnography. In *Ethnography with a twist. Methodological and ethical challenges and solutions in contemporary research*. Routledge.

Fanning, R. M., & Gaba, D. M. (2007). The role of debriefing in simulation-based learning. *Simulation in Healthcare: The Journal of the Society for Simulation in Healthcare, 2*(2), 115–125. https://doi.org/10.1097/SIH.0b013e3180315539

Fauquet-Alekhine, P. (2016). Subjective ethnographic protocol for work activity analysis and occupational training improvement. *British Journal of Applied Science and Technology, 12*(5), 1-16-843.

Fleck, R., & Fitzpatrick, G. (2009). Teachers' and tutors' social reflection around SenseCam images. *International Journal of Human-Computer Studies, 67*(12), 1024–1036. https://doi.org/10.1016/j.ijhcs.2009.09.004

Gillespie, A. (2007). The social basis of self-reflection. In A. Rosa & J. Valsiner (Eds.), *The Cambridge handbook of sociocultural psychology*. Cambridge University Press.

Ginsburg, G. P., Brenner, M., von Cranach, M., Eiser, R., & Scherer, K. (1985). *Discovery strategies in the psychology of action*. Academic Press.

Goldman, R., Pea, R., Barron, B., & Derry, S. (2007). *Video research in the learning sciences*. Lawrence Erlbaum Associates.

Hutchins, E. L. (1995). *Cognition in the wild*. MIT Press.

Kolb, D. A. (1984). *Experiential learning: Experience as the source of learning and development*. Prentice-H.

Lahlou, S. (1999). Observing cognitive work in offices. In N. Streitz, J. Siegel, V. Hartkopf, & S. Konomi (Eds.), *Cooperative buildings. Integrating information, organizations and architecture* (Vol. 1670, pp. 150–163). Springer.

Lahlou, S. (2011). How can we capture the subject's perspective? An evidence-based approach for the social scientist. *Social Science Information, 50*(3), 607–655. https://doi.org/10.1177/0539018411411033

Lahlou, S. (2017). Installation theory: The societal construction and regulation of behaviour. In *Installation theory: The societal construction and regulation of behaviour*. https://doi.org/10.1017/9781316480922

Lahlou, S., Le Bellu, S., & Boesen-Mariani, S. (2015). Subjective evidence based ethnography: Method and applications. *Integrative Psychological & Behavioral Science, 49*(2), 216–238. https://doi.org/10.1007/s12124-014-9288-9

Lave, J. (1988). *Cognition in practice*. Cambridge University Press.

Lave, J., & Wenger, E. C. (1991). *Situated learning: Legitimate peripheral participation*. Cambridge University Press.

Le Bellu, S. (2016). Learning the secrets of the craft through the real-time experience of experts: Capturing and transferring professional expert tacit knowledge to novices. *Perspectives Interdisciplinaires Sur Le Travail et La Santé (PISTES), 18*(1). https://doi.org/10.4000/pistes.4685

Le Bellu, S., Lahlou, S., & Nosulenko, V. (2010). Capter et transférer le savoir incorporé dans un geste professionnel. *Social Science Information, 49*(3), 371–413. https://doi.org/10.1177/0539018410372582

Le Bellu, S., Lahlou, S., Nosulenko, V., & Samoylenko, E. (2016). Studying activity in manual work: A framework for analysis and training. *Le Travail Humain, 79*(1), 7–28. https://doi.org/10.3917/th.791.0007

Leontiev, A. N. (1978). *Activity, consciousness, and personality*. Prentice Hall.

Leplat, J., & Cuny, X. (1974). *Les accidents du travail*. PUF.

Lomov, B. F. (1982). The problem of activity in psychology. *Soviet Psychology, 21*, 55–91.

Lum, C., Stoltz, M., Koper, C. S., & Scherer, J. A. (2019). Research on body-worn cameras. *Criminology & Public Policy, 18*(1), 93–118. https://doi.org/10.1111/1745-9133.12412
Lyons, R., Lazzara, E. H., Benishek, L. E., Zajac, S., Gregory, M., Sonesh, S. C., & Salas, E. (2015). Enhancing the effectiveness of team debriefings in medical simulation: More best practices. *Joint Commission Journal on Quality and Patient Safety, 41*(3), 115–125. https://doi.org/10.1016/S1553-7250(15)41016-5
Mackenzie, S. H., & Kerr, J. H. (2012). Head-mounted cameras and stimulated recall in qualitative sport research. *Qual Res Sport Exerc Health, 4*(1), 51–61. https://doi.org/10.1080/2159676X.2011.653495
Nardi, B. (1996). *Context and consciousness: Activity theory and human computer interaction*. MIT Press.
Norges offentlige utredninger. (2009: 12). Et ansvarlig politi: Åpenhet, kontroll, og læring [A responsible police force: Openness, control, and learning].
Norges offentlige utredninger. (2012: 14). Rapport fra 22. juli kommisjon [Report from the July 22nd commision].
Norges offentlige utredninger. (2013: 9). Ett politi: rustet til å møte fremtidens utfordringer. Politianalysen. [One police: ready to meet future challenges. Analysis of the police].
Nosulenko, V., & Samoylenko, E. (2009). Psychological methods for the study of augmented environments. In S. Lahlou (Ed.), *Designing user friendly augmented work environments. From meeting rooms to digital collaborative spaces* (pp. 213–236). Springer.
Nosulenko, V. N., Barabanshikov, V. A., Brushlinsky, A. V., & Rabardel, P. (2005). Man–technology interaction: Some of the Russian approaches. *Theoretical Issues in Ergonomics Science, 6*(5), 359–383. https://doi.org/10.1080/14639220500070051
Ombredanne, A., & Faverge, J.-M. (1955). *L'analyse du travail. Facteur d'économie humaine et de productivité*. PUF.
Omodei, M. M., McLennan, J., & Wearing, A. J. (2005). How expertise is applied in real-world settings: Head mounted video and cued recall as a methodology for studying routines of decision making. In T. Betsch & S. Haberstrohe (Eds.), *The routines of decision making* (pp. 271–288). Lawrence Erlbaum and Associates.
Paradise, R., & Rogoff, B. (2009). Side by side: Learning by observing and pitching in cultural practices in support of learning. *Ethos, 37*(1), 102–138. https://doi.org/10.1111/j.1548-1352.2009.01033.x.LEARNING
Pastré, P. (2005). *Apprendre par la simulation. De l'analyse du travail aux apprentissages professionnels*. Octares Editions.
Pea, R. D., & Kurland, D. M. (1984). On the cognitive effects of learning computer programming. *New Ideas in Psychology, 2*(2), 137–168.
Phelps, J. M., Strype, J., Le Bellu, S., Lahlou, S., & Aandal, J. (2016). Experiential learning and simulation-based training in Norwegian police education: Examining body-worn video as a tool to encourage reflection. *Policing*, 1–15. https://doi.org/10.1093/police/paw014
Pinsky, L., & Theureau, J. (1987). Description of visual "action" in natural situations. In J. K. O'Regan & A. Levy-Schoen (Eds.), *Eye movements: From physiology to cognition, selected/edited proceedings of the 3rd European conference on eye movements. Dourdan, France*. Elsevier.
Politihøgskolen. (2014). Fagplan for bachelorstudiet BIII, (Curriculum for third-year bachelor's studies). http://www.phs.no/Documents/5_Studenter/Fagplaner/Fagplan%20B3%202014-2015.pdf
Rabardel, P. (1997). Des instruments et des hommes: propositions pour une conception centrée utilisateurs. *Int J Des and Innov Res, 10*, 7–20.
Rabardel, P. (2005). 13. Instrument, activité et développement du pouvoir d'agir. In *Entre connaissance et organisation: l'activité collective* (pp. 251–265). https://doi.org/10.3917/dec.lorin.2005.01.0251

Rasmussen, J. (1983). Skills, rules, and knowledge; signals, signs, and symbols, and other distinctions in human performance models. *IEEE Transactions on Systems, Man, and Cybernetics, SMC-13*(3), 257–266. https://doi.org/10.1109/TSMC.1983.6313160

Rieken, J. C. (2013). *Making situated police practice visible: A study examining professional activity for the maintenance of social control with video data from the field.* London School of Economics and Political Science.

Rix, G., & Biache, M.-J. (2004). *Enregistrement en perspective subjective située et entretien en re situ subjectif: une méthodologie de constitution de l'expérience*. Intellectica, 363–396.

Rogoff, B. (2003). *The cultural nature of human development*. Oxford University Press.

Rossignol, M. (2017). Effects of video-assisted debriefing compared with standard Oral debriefing. *Clinical Simulation in Nursing, 13*(4), 145–153. https://doi.org/10.1016/j.ecns.2016.12.001

Rubinstein, S. L. (1922a). Le principe de l'activité du sujet dans sa dimension créative. In P. Rabardel (Ed.), *Rubinstein aujourd'hui. Nouvelles figure de l'activité humaine* (pp. 129–140). Octarès/Maison des sciences de l'homme.

Rubinstein, S. L. (1922b). Le principe de l'activité du sujet dans sa dimension créative. In V. Nosulenko & P. Rabardel (Eds.), *Rubinstein aujourd'hui. Nouvelles figure de l'activité humaine* (pp. 129–140). Octarès/Maison des sciences de l'homme.

Rubinstein, S. L. (1940). Osnovy obshej psikhologii (Foundations of General Psychology). In *Génie logiciel et système expert*. Moscou: Edition "Utchpedgiz."

Sawyer, T., Eppich, W., Brett-Fleegler, M., Grant, V., & Cheng, A. (2016, June 1). More than one way to debrief: A critical review of healthcare simulation debriefing methods. *Simulation in Healthcare, 11*, 209–217. https://doi.org/10.1097/SIH.0000000000000148

Schön, D. (1983). *The reflexive practitioner. How professional think in action*. Basic Books.

Sjöberg, D., & Karp, S. (2012). Video–based debriefing enhances reflection, motivation and performance for Police students in realistic scenario training. *Procedia – Social and Behavioral Sciences, 46*, 2816–2824. https://doi.org/10.1016/j.sbspro.2012.05.570

Söderström, T., Karp, S., & Sjöberg, D. (2016). Developing police students' professional knowing through scenario training: The impact of preparation, implementation and debriefing. *EDULEARN16 Proceedings, 1*, 5930–5935. https://doi.org/10.21125/edulearn.2016.0258

Stetsenko, A. (2005). Activity as object-related: Resolving the dichotomy of individual and collective planes of activity. *Mind, Culture, and Activity, 12*(1), 70–88.

Suchman, L. (1987). *Plans and situated actions. The problem of human-machine communication*. Cambridge University Press.

Suchman, L., & Trigg, R. (1991). Understanding practice: Video as a medium for reflection and design. In J. Greenbaum & M. Kyng (Eds.), *Design at work: Cooperative design of computer systems* (pp. 65–89). Lawrence Erlbaum.

Theureau, J. (2003). Course-of-action-centered design. In E. Hollnagel (Ed.), *Handbook of cognitive task design* (pp. 55–81). CRC Press.

Ulmer, F. F., Sharara-Chami, R., Lakissian, Z., Stocker, M., Scott, E., & Dieckmann, P. (2018). Cultural prototypes and differences in simulation debriefing. *Simulation in Healthcare, 13*(4), 239–246. https://doi.org/10.1097/SIH.0000000000000320

Voigt, R., Camp, N. P., Prabhakaran, V., Hamilton, W. L., Hetey, R. C., Griffiths, C. M., ... Eberhardt, J. L. (2017). Language from police body camera footage shows racial disparities in officer respect. *Proc Natl Acad Sci U S A, 114*(25), 6521–6526. https://doi.org/10.1073/pnas.1702413114

Wenger, E. C. (2000). Communities of practice and social learning systems. *Organization, 7*(2), 225–246.

A Study of Police Cadets' Activity During Use-of-Force Simulation-Based Training: Empirical Lessons and Insights for Training Design

Rachel Boembeke, Laurane De Carvalho, and Germain Poizat

Abstract Many police around the world integrated simulation-based training into their programs, more particularly use-of-force simulation. The use-of-force is a core element characterizing law enforcement practices. It requires the acquisition of a wide set of knowledge, skills, and abilities (KSAs) and tactics. In this regard, simulation-based training is widely recognized as an effective approach. However, various questions have received little empirical attention, such as whether the simulation-based training helps trainees to make sense of early work experience (EWE) and how simulation-lived experience can resonate with real-work practices. Our study proposes a fine-grained analysis of police cadets' activity and lived experience during simulation-based exercises. It aimed at (a) identifying typical dimensions in the trainees' enacted activity and lived experience during simulated scenarios, (b) informing learning opportunities, and situated knowledge mobilized and built during simulated scenarios, (c) documenting how simulation-lived experience resonates with real-work practices or EWE, and (d) documenting the living and unfolding of the unexpected during simulated scenarios. It was conducted within the *course-of-action* theoretical and methodological framework, which proposes an enactive, phenomenological, and semiotic view of working/training practices. Practical implications for the design of use-of-force training and simulation-based training are formulated on the basis of this empirical study.

Keywords Use-of-force · Simulation · Enacted practice · Lived experience · Work analysis · Police training

R. Boembeke
University of Louvain-La-Neuve, Ottignies-Louvain-la-Neuve, Belgium
e-mail: rachelsteeman@hotmail.com

L. De Carvalho · G. Poizat (✉)
Faculty of Psychology and Educational Sciences, University of Geneva, Geneva, Switzerland
e-mail: laurane@kairos-dc.ch; germain.poizat@unige.ch

S. Flandin et al. (eds.), *Simulation Training through the Lens of Experience and Activity Analysis*, Professional and Practice-based Learning 30,
https://doi.org/10.1007/978-3-030-89567-9_11

Many police around the world incorporated simulation-based training into their programs and more particularly use-of-force simulation. The use-of-force is an element characterizing law enforcement practices (Bitner, 2003) and a substantial part of police training (Moreau de Bellaing, 2002; Moreau de Bellaing, 2006; Pichonnaz, 2011). It requires the acquisition of a wide set of knowledge, skills, and attitudes (KSAs) and tactics. More specifically, use-of-force training includes practical knowledge that involves fire training and techniques of the body which can be mobilized for physical coercion – whether or not it is associated with technical objects. These KSAs and tactics are used in daily practices, whether in the context of police checks, body searches, arrests, handcuffing, etc., in other words, in all situations involving the use-of-force (actual or potential).

The use-of-force training is sometimes limited to KSAs and tactics isolated instruction (with low ecological relevance) (e.g., Chappell, 2008). In this case, it can somehow be problematic because it fails to encounter the real-world situations and practices of police officers. In contrast, it is generally assumed that simulation-based training has different strengths in this particular context: (a) it provides more realistic instruction that covers a broader range of use-of-force options and enhances the resonance with real world; (b) it enables trainees to obtain experience enacting target KSAs within a safe environment, and it serves as a unique opportunity for facilitating learning, administering feedback, and promoting the transfer of training; (c) it supports experiential learning and encourages reflection on the effective of use-of-force (without being satisfied by acquisition and application of pre-established techniques); and (d) it makes it possible to develop expertise at individual and team level, to support the acquisition of both taskwork and teamwork competencies essential in law enforcement practices (Bennell et al., 2007; Dubois & Van Daele, 2018; Grossman et al., 2015; Sjöberg, 2014). Simulation-based training is being recognized as a highly effective approach to training, particularly when targeting complex KSAs as use-of-force, development of expert decision-making competencies in teams (at individual and team level), and development of team processes and emergent states. However, various questions have received little empirical attention such as whether the simulation-based training helps trainees to make sense of early work experience and how simulation lived experience can resonate with real-work practices; whether and how simulation-based training supports the transfer of training; whether and how simulation-based training could enhance connectivity between school and workplace learning or between formal and on-the-job training; or whether and how simulation-based training leads to experiment effective and unexpected use-of-force and test operational capabilities under intense conditions (especially through the use of non-lethal training ammunition (NLTA); Staller et al., 2019). Moreover, many articles in the field of training adopt a normative approach, describing what a simulation-based training should be and measuring performance (and outcomes), rather than descriptive and comprehensive approach – describing the "blackbox" of practice and lived experience in simulation-based training.

Several studies, using interactional and multimodal approaches to discourse or activity-oriented approaches, demonstrate the importance to study enacted, situated, and embodied practices in real work and in simulated exercises in order to document the benefits, the suitability, and the efficiency of use-of-force simulation-based training (Dubois & Van Daele, 2018; Phelps et al., 2018; Sjöberg, 2014; Stokoe, 2013). For example, Stokoe (2013) compared actual and role-played police investigative interviews in order to question how "authentic" simulation is. The results pointed that officers in real-world-related and simulation-related interviews opened interviews by formulating the same actions (e.g., identifying copresent parties), although during simulations, actions were more elaborated or exaggerated; that is, they were made interactionally visible and "assessable." Sjöberg (2014) investigated, through video analysis of actions and utterances, how simulations support learning of KSAs and how a student police patrol makes sense of a "simulated" critical incident, during the simulation itself. The results showed that the police patrol, and other role-players, had trouble negotiating the hybridity of the situation. The participants' actions did not fully mimic an authentic critical incident suggesting that they defined the situation as a passive educational situation. For this author, the results demonstrated that simulation-based training possibilities for supporting professional learning depend largely on role-playing and on the trainees' "simulation competency." Dubois and Van Daele (2018) analyzed police instructors' practices during simulation-based training using *work analysis* methods (e.g., Filliettaz et al., 2015). The results underlined that the instructors are constantly making compromises and are primarily concerned with making the scenario and the simulation-based training happen. Paradoxically, this leads them not to take advantage of all the learning opportunities (or learning affordances) offered by the simulation (another reason is that not all trainers are specialized in simulation-based training and do not have the associated skills).

The objective of our exploratory study was to complement these previous studies. It proposes a fine-grained analysis of police cadets' activity and lived experience during simulation-based exercises (TTI). It aimed at (a) identifying the invariant, typical, or critical dimensions in the trainees' enacted activity and lived experience during simulated scenarios (particularly typical concerns), (b) informing learning opportunities and situated knowledge mobilized and built during simulated scenarios, (c) documenting how simulation lived experience resonates with real-work practices or early work experience, and (d) documenting the living and unfolding of the unexpected during simulated scenarios.

1 Theoretical and Methodological Framework

This study was conducted within the *course-of-action* theoretical and methodological framework (Poizat & San Martin, 2020; Theureau, 2002, 2003, 2004). This framework proposes an enactive, phenomenological, and semiotic view of working/training practices. It is designed to provide a fine-grained analysis of actors' lived experience and makes it possible to document "in the wild" and "from within" working/training practices (Durand & Poizat, 2015; Poizat et al., 2016), as well as learning process in naturally occurring settings (Dieumegard et al., 2020; Drakos et al., 2021; Theureau, 2010a). This approach is relevant in our study because it gives privileged access to the subjective experience of the actors and allows us to understand activity from their point of view. This framework has already been used, for example, by Horcik et al. (2014), for studying the lived experience of seven learners during nurse anesthetist training sessions involving a full-sized patient simulator in a simulated operating room. This study pointed, through the analysis of participants' typical concerns, that trainees exhibit during simulation a specific mimetic experience and argued that double intentionality is promising for learning.

2 Method

This study was carried out at the Belgian Police Academy and covered seven simulation-based exercises on three topics: (a) the building control, in search of people who can be hidden inside of the building; (b) the pedestrian control, to intervene in the event of altercation, deterioration, or presence of suspicious persons in public space; and (c) the vehicle control, to verify that the vehicle and its occupants are in order or arrest fugitives. These controls are not without danger. The cadets must take into account hazard indicators such as the place, time and reasons of the control, as well as the people's behaviors. The management of the use-of-force must be pursued by cadets. Each simulation-based exercise is structured in three phases: (a) a briefing, (b) the simulation (3–15 min depending on the scenario and the degree of difficulty), and (c) a debriefing. The scenarios proposed are designed by the trainers on the basis of real-life police interventions and their own accumulated experience. Cadets who do not assume the role of police officers during the simulated-based exercise play the roles of assailants, accomplices, witnesses, victims, or onlookers.

2.1 Participants

Twelve police cadets volunteered to participate in this study. Their average age was 25 years. Our study was conducted with high standards of integrity and confidentiality, and their participation was made anonymous. At the time of the study, the aspirants had started training at the Police Academy 7 months ago. They hadn't practiced through simulation-based exercises yet.

2.2 Data Collection

Three types of data were gathered: (a) field notes and observations, (b) video recording of simulation-based exercises, and (c) micro-phenomenological self-confrontation data.

Field notes and observations. The first author was responsible for the field notes and observations. The field notes and observations supported a comprehensive understanding of simulation-based exercises' entire environment and provided documentation for micro-phenomenological self-confrontation.

Video recording of the cadets' behaviors and communications during the simulated scenarios and debriefing. The recordings of simulation-based exercises were made using a camera with a wide-angle lens. The recorded data served two purposes: (a) provide behavioral and contextual data (in particular on social, spatial, material, and temporal aspects) and (b) provide traces that stimulate a dynamic reenactment or re-situation in past activity during post-simulation interview.

Micro-phenomenological self-confrontation data. Micro-phenomenological self-confrontations were held within 2 or 3 months of the simulation-based exercise depending on the availability of participants. They lasted approximately between 5 and 10 min and were all recorded with a video camera. The video recording is used to check the correspondence between verbalizations and the recordings of behaviors and communications which were commented on. The micro-phenomenological self-confrontation is a precise research method (Dieumegard et al., 2020; Theureau, 2010b), which was used in our study to gain access to the cadets' lived experience, and it differs from debriefing (which was part of the training sessions and conducted by the instructors). The participants viewed the recording individually with the researcher, and they were asked to describe and comment on their activity step by step (and at the level that is meaningful for them). They were invited to express what they did, felt, thought, and perceived during the past activity as naturally as possible. The researcher used specific prompts to help the participant to "relive" and describe his or her activity as it was experienced, without a posteriori analysis, rationalization, or justification. These prompts were about sensations ("What sensations are you experiencing?"), perceptions ("What are you perceiving?"), areas of focus ("What has your attention?"), concerns ("What are you trying to do here?"), thoughts and interpretations ("What are you thinking about?"), as well as emotions ("What emotions are you experiencing?"). Behavioral indicators such as hesitations in the stream of language, unstructured sentences, or the inward-turned stare are used as indicators of reenactment or re-situation in past activity. An atmosphere of trust was established between the cadet participants and the researcher during the study. The non-evaluative purpose of this study was reiterated at the beginning of each micro-phenomenological self-confrontation.

Additional semi-structured interviews were also conducted with three instructors and four mentors to document the training needs and issues relating to the simulation-based exercises, as well as the evaluation of each scenario by expert police officers.

2.3 Data Analysis

The data were processed in five steps: (1) the construction of a two-level protocol, (2) the construction of each police cadet's *course of experience*, (3) the identification of the aspirants' typical concerns for each simulated scenario, (4) the identification of the mobilized knowledge and the one cadets are constructing during simulated scenarios, and (5) the identification of the level of surprise and of the unexpected dimension of the events induced during simulated scenarios.

Construction of a two-level protocol. This step consisted in reporting and putting in order the data related to the activity of each cadet in a two-column table. The first column consisted of brief descriptions of the actions and communications (verbal interactions) of the cadets during the simulated scenario. The second column consisted of the verbatim retranscription of the micro-phenomenological self-confrontation data.

Construction of the police cadets' course of experience. When an actor is invited to express his activity, he spontaneously slices its continuous flow in significant units of activity from his point of view. The first step consisted in informing the significant elementary units (USE) corresponding to the smallest significant unit of meaning for the actor. By hypothesis, these USE are the manifestation of a sign, called hexadic, insofar as it is made up of six components: the elementary unit of activity, the representamen, the involvement, the anticipation structure, the referential, and the interpretant. The second step consisted in the identification of the hexadic sign components based on a simultaneous analysis of the two-level protocol and of the video recordings and a specific questioning. The *elementary unit of activity* (U) is the fraction of the activity which is "shown, told or commented" by the actor. It can be a symbolic construction, an action (a practical action or a communication), a private speech, or a feeling. It has been identified by the following question: What is the cadet doing? What does he think? What does he feel? The *representamen* (R) correspond to those elements of the situation that are significant to the actor, "what makes sign" for the actor in the situation at the considered time t. It has been identified by the following questioning: What is the significant element in the situation for the cadet? Which element(s) of the situation does he consider? The *involvement* (E) expresses the significant concerns of the cadet at time t. The involvement has been identified by the following questioning: What are the cadet's significant concerns related to the element taken into account in the situation? The *anticipation structure* (A) is what is expected by the actor in the situation at time t, given his involvement. It has been identified by the following questioning: What are the cadet's expectations at time t resulting from his concern and from the considered element in the situation? What are his passive or active anticipations? The *referential* (S) corresponds to habits, types, rules of action, and situated knowledge (1) resulting from past course of experience and belonging to the actor's own culture and (2) effectively mobilized at time t. It has been identified by the following questioning: What is the mobilized knowledge by the cadet at time t? The *interpretant* (I) correspond to the validation, construction, and transformation of new habits, types, rules of action, and situated knowledge at time t. Defined as a construction of habits or types, this category reflects the fact that activity always goes hand with hand with learning or discoveries. It has been identified by the following question: What situated knowledge does the cadet (in)valid or build at time "t"? When the excerpt content of the two-level protocol and of the video recording related to an elementary unit of activity proved to be insufficient to document all the components of the sign, we implemented an inferences network taking into account the entire corpus.

The documentation of the signs components makes it possible to specify meaning-making process *in action* but also retention and pretention characteristics of the activity and experience. In our study, the main purpose of this description is to identify the cadets' typical concerns, the mobilized knowledge and situated knowledge that is built during the scenarios, and the level of surprise that characterize them.

Identification of the cadets' typical concerns. An analysis of the cadets' concerns has been conducted to gather all the concerns from a same theme in a category of higher level of generality (typical concerns). In general, the typical character of an experience, of a coupling to the situation, or of an experience component is determined by researchers through (a) a categorization on the basis of the occurrences observed in all the corpus and/or (b) the enunciation of a feeling of typicity by the actors themselves during the micro-phenomenological self-confrontations (Durand, 2014). During the data analysis, we relied on a categorization process to identify the cadets' typical concerns. We compared the involvements of each cadet's course of experience to gather the concerns of a same theme in a category of higher level of generality. The typical concerns have been gathered according to three criteria: (a) the relevance of the categories according to data, (b) a comparable level of generality between the categories, and (c) the use of designations that are discriminating enough to avoid overlap. The typical concern was named to reflect the similarity of concerns under this theme.

Identification of the mobilized and built situated knowledge of the cadets. This step consisted in documenting the different modalities of the construction of knowledge of the cadets on the basis of a comprehensive analysis of the course of experience and more specifically on an analysis of the transformation of the referential (S) and interpretant (I) contents.

Identification of the level of surprise and of the unforeseen nature of events. This last step consisted in analyzing the relationship R*A between the representamen and the anticipation structure in order to identify the level of surprise and the unforeseen nature of the situation experienced in simulation scenarios. The relationship between R*A is structured according to the same modality of relationship "appearance of a figure against a background of... " than the one R*E that takes place between the representamen and the involvement in the situation. The relationship R*E "apparition of R against the background of E" configures the order of relevance of a disturbance, while R*A configures the degree of possible disturbance or surprise gradient of those elements of the situation that are significant to the actor.

3 Results

Our results are presented in three parts. Firstly, we present the typical concerns of police cadets during building, pedestrian, and vehicle simulation scenarios. Secondly comes the knowledge constructed during simulation scenarios identified on the basis of a comprehensive analysis of the cadets' course of experience. Thirdly, we detail typical moments that question the level of surprise, involvement, load, and hostilities during scenarios (in relation to the unpredictable nature of the authentic situations and to the stressful nature of use-of-force situations).

3.1 Typical Concerns of Police Cadets During Simulation Scenarios

Typical concerns during "building control scenarios". The typical concerns identified during building control scenarios were (a) progress in the building/carry out door openings, (b) carry out angle openings, (c) be careful about the colleague's shooting lines, and (d) remove doubt in the rooms and secure these ones. As an example, the concern to progress through the building and to carry out door openings appears in the comments of some cadets when they mention they are heading toward danger and must open closed doors. Moreover, we see the concern to carry out angle openings in certain comments such as those made by Cadet 4: "Here, I'm carrying out my angle opening, getting out in the open as little as possible but just enough to be able to describe the room for the colleague." The micro-phenomenological self-confrontations also reveal the aspirants' concerns about the colleague's shooting lines as they carry out angle opening. Finally, as they advance into the building, there is a recurring concern to secure the rooms, as one of the cadets mentioned: "Here, we entered in criss-cross so we could enter by the side where we had the visual from the beginning. I check behind the couch to see if there is nobody (…) Here, quick view to be sure there is nobody in the corner either so we can go to the door."

Typical concerns during "pedestrian control scenarios". During the pedestrian control scenarios, the results pointed six typical concerns among the cadets. The first typical concern consists of the announcement of the arrival on the site. The participants know they have to inform the service of their presence on site and announce they are going to intervene. The second typical concern is about connecting with the people and immediately separate the individuals to take control of the situation, as illustrated in the following examples: "Here they're getting angry, we try to separate them directly. Now, I tell myself that I no longer have a visual of my colleague. We try to talk to them so that they can explain what's going on, to distract them to occupy their minds" (Cadet 10); "I push him away, I tell him to calm down, I try to talk to him and to always keep an eye on him in case he wants to start" (Cadet 5) – Researcher: "You keep them at a distance from each other?" – "Yes, especially since it's a family, the less they talk to each other, the better" (Cadet 5). The third typical concern refers to the adoption of an adequate position in regard to his/her partner. Indeed, at some point of the action, the cadets realize they might not see their colleague. They know it is incredibly important to be able to see what the partner is doing in order to proceed, which leads them to correct their position. In addition, the cadets try to draw the attention of the opponents during the control, which is their fourth typical concern. This is a way to maintain the situation under control and to avoid overreaction. This is linked to the fifth typical concern, evaluating the cooperation level of the person. That is to say, the nature of cooperation of the person influences the cadets' decisions. It allows them to release people and get to the end of the intervention faster if the person cooperates. Finally, the last typical concern of pedestrian control scenarios is to do a security body search. During the interviews, the cadets declare that doing the security body search is to be sure people don't have any object on them.

Typical concerns "vehicle control scenarios". Six typical concerns have been identified during the vehicle control scenarios. The first one is to wait for the partner's sign before progressing from behind. For instance, Cadet 3 says during micro-phenomenological self-confrontation: "so, now, I was an intervener, so he was the one providing the coverage. That's why he was the one who went to see her. I stood back and waited for him to call me"; or Cadet 9: "There, I was driving. I get out, I wait for my colleague to go to the vehicle. He has to call me logically. He is going to give me a sign when the person has rolled down the window. It takes a bit of time (...) then he gives me a sign, so I move forward. I follow the line to be in the blind spot of the rear-view mirror." The second typical concern is about making contact with the people watching out the positioning and the weak hand. Cadet 9 allows us to understand what this concern is all about: "He gives me the documents one by one. I hold them in the weak hand, therefore, not on the side of the gun." Furthermore, a comment of Cadet 1 during his micro-phenomenological self-confrontation shows the difficulty this can be, especially for left-handers: "I don't remember if I put them back in the weak hand because in fact, I have to put them back in the weak hand. Now I am better oriented with my strong hand. That's what I thought at the time, I guess. It's always this problem of a left-hander: weak hand, strong hand and orientation towards the car that is the opposite for a left-handed person after all." The third typical concern is to make contact with the person staying calm and measured in the response. Some situations make this concern particularly challenging – even when it's hard, the cadets experiment with the necessity to have self-control. Another typical concern is to check the documents maintaining the visual field. While they check if everything is in order, the participants position themselves to be able to keep an eye on the driver and the vehicle. Besides the exercises are opportunities to correct eventual mistakes as the cadets realize they might have turned their back on the driver, "thing you should never do" (Cadet 8). The next typical concern refers to the need of holding the radio with the weak hand. Sometimes it involves changing documents by hand. The last typical concern is to question the person if necessary.

The analysis of the course of experience shows that the cadets' experience during simulation is specific and complex far beyond the typical concerns. The concerns alternate between work-related concerns, concerns related to the practice and training of certain intervention techniques and tactics, as well as concerns related to the simulation scenario itself. These are barely visible in the examples presented above but are illustrated by the following excerpt with the Cadet 12 micro-phenomenological self-confrontation: "Afterwards, when I saw him leave... but the thing is, they [the practice instructors] say pretty quickly 'it's okay, we're stopping the exercise', so when he was gone, I thought he's going to say we're stopping the exercise, so I thought, there's no point in me continuing."

3.2 *Knowledge Mobilization and Construction During Simulation*

The results make it possible to describe the mobilized knowledge and the construction of new situated knowledge during simulation scenarios but also to bring out the elements that took part in this dynamics. Among the built situated knowledge, several are about the difficulty to implement procedures/rules in action and about the security and safety in a given situation. This difficulty might be linked to the stress or an attention directed to the wrong things. It is also apparent in some simulated interventions: "I should have been firmer from the beginning because I saw that he was playing with my feet" (Cadet 8); "Ah yes, there was L. as a witness too. I told her to stay nearby but afterwards, it's true that I completely forgot she was there" (Cadet 10); "I see that I hold it with my left hand but normally you have to hold the radio with your weak hand. Because if there's a problem, you have to let go of the radio, and you don't normally have to let go of the radio to pick up the gun" (Cadet 3). On top of that, the simulation-based exercises allow the participants to realize by themselves what they should have done differently, as the following example:

> And here the problem is that we are behind the wall and we have no way out. And we try to rotate to have an exit way. I thought we were going to get him out. And the problem is that we should have got him out of the room before we pushed him back. I wanted to search him in the room, but ideally, I should have got him out first before searching him. Because it's quite a small space. (Cadet 4 micro-phenomenological self-confrontation)

The cadets also mention several times situations of doubts or marked by an observation of ignorance. In these situations, the cadet learns he doesn't know yet and that he has no knowledge, habits, or types that can be "immediately" and "efficiently" mobilized in the given situation. It actually occurs in some interventions they have never encountered before. It is the case for the Cadet 6 who doesn't know if she's doing the right thing as they have never learned to manage several teams. A feeling of unease comes with a new experience. There is something the participants have never done, and they don't know where to stand, what to anticipate or what to do first:

> It was difficult to speak with the driver because the other lady was shouting, screaming all over the place. We were feeling really lost because we've never had a case like this one before. We didn't know who to get out of the vehicle first because usually we get the driver

> out first and my colleague chose to get the lady out. I tried to see with the driver what was happening and tried to have explanations about the situation while he was taking care of the lady. Yes, we were really lost." (Cadet 3 micro-phenomenological self-confrontation)

3.3 *Level of Surprise, Involvement, Load, and Hostilities During Simulation*

During simulation scenarios, the cadets experiment certain moments in a particularly intense way. We gathered here a few examples that illustrate the level of surprise experimented by the cadets during simulation and how they appropriate the unforeseen nature of the scenarios. However, the results point that the cadets expect the simulated intervention to be difficult, complex, degraded (or getting worse very rapidly), and with multiple traps which guide their expectation and preparation structure. The participants particularly expect to face weapons or to find hidden people. If this might often be the case, sometimes such expectations can be out of step with the scenario, as it is in the very revealing example given by a police cadet:

> I enter the room, turn on the lamp, my colleague meets me at the door. I open the lockers to make sure no one is there. I check between the lockers. No one is there. I report this to my colleague and go outside. I go back into the room again. I open all the lockers to be sure. I go back out. I report this to my colleague. And we leave. But it's true that we're more inclined to think that we're going to find someone. In fact, it was my colleague who said to me, "Go back", but it's true that the first room I said to myself, "Come on, it's not possible, there must be someone there" and then, finally, no, there was no one there. But it's true that we're no longer put in the idea that we're going to find someone (...) it's frustrating because we tell ourselves that maybe there is someone and we haven't found him. (Cadet 3 micro-phenomenological self-confrontation)

Moreover, even if the cadets encounter frequently hidden people or weapons in the scenarios, the cases are always different and therefore unknown. The participants never know what they will stumble upon and that comes with a certain amount of stress. On top of that, they can be really surprised by what happens, especially if it is something they didn't expect:

> We are asking ourselves the questions of "what is going to fall on us", at the level of the papers of what we are really going to have to control, we are asking ourselves all these questions at the same time as we make the call. And then, at that moment, there's the big guy coming out, so we don't know what to do. Do we have to finish our call, go for it? A little distraught. (Cadet 11 micro-phenomenological self-confrontation)

4 Discussion

This study provides a better understanding of the activity and experience of police cadets during simulation-based training. It completes previous analyses of trainers' practices (Dubois & Van Daele, 2018). It also confirms the results of previous work on simulation-based training lived experience and its transformative dimensions (Horcik et al., 2014; Horcik & Durand, 2015). The results will be discussed according to two lines: (a) an empirical focus – production of knowledge related to cadets' activity and lived experience during simulation-based training – and (b) a practical focus, concrete proposals related to the design of simulation-based training for police initial training. Further research is obviously necessary to make progress on each of the points below.

4.1 Contribution to the Knowledge of the Cadets' Activity and Lived Experience During Simulation-Based Training

First of all, our results show that cadets live a complex and non-homogeneous experience in simulation that differs from real work. They show that cadets experiment multiple typical concerns during simulation scenarios. Many of these typical concerns have to do with the response to the prescription, the application of doctrine and procedures, and their execution. Aspirants are focused on successful action and performance, as Dubois and Van Daele (2018) point out, and not on understanding the situation. However, during these simulation based-exercises, it is not the KSAs and tactics taught that are valued by the trainees, but rather a preparation for violence. Simulation does not say what awaits the trainees in the future but what affects them or can affect them in living situations. For them, it is not only a question of applying technical or tactical know-how, but of "doing what you can." The analysis of trainees' activity and lived experience highlights the difficulties they face in the implementation of procedures and rules in (simulated) action whether in terms of intervention and safety. Cadets build knowledge on this difficulty of procedure execution in action but also on "what they do not know (yet)." Indeed, the results seem to indicate that the "whirlwinds of doubt" or the "findings of ignorance" are in themselves a type of new knowledge. This experienced feeling of helplessness might seem problematic, but it is part of a learning of the body and affects, as well as the development of a form of humility and increased attention in practice. Moreover, the doubts felt by the cadets open up to possible investigations as well as a search for new types, new habits, and new rules of action.

The analysis of cadets' activity and lived experience also confirms that participants engaged in simulation-based training have a particular experience, qualified as mimetic, which cannot be reduced to real work (Drakos et al., 2021; Horcik et al., 2014; Horcik & Durand, 2015). The design of simulation-based training is more or less explicitly based on the assumption that a fictional and playful engagement on the part of the participants is necessary to establish a similarity-difference relationship with real work. Depending on the case, this is referred to a shared playful feigning or the suspension of disbelief. Cadets act "as if it were true," but this "as if" in turn refers "as its sine qua non, to a reality that is not of the order of false pretense" (Dubey, 1997, p. 49). The difference that separates reality from its simulation is at times denied and at other times recognized and even very widely reaffirmed. The notion of mimetic experience proposed by Horcik et al. (2014) clearly reflects this very particular engagement of participants in simulation-based training: a dual engagement "not linked to their work" (oriented toward simulation) and "not not-linked to their work" (oriented toward work). Experience in simulation implies a complexification of actors' concerns in comparison to real-work situations. Trainee's experience is not a mere artificial reproduction work but a more specific and ambiguous one resulting from a global engagement in the situation here-and-now in tension between two references ("to make contact with people"; "to give an image of a competent aspirant"; "to evaluate the degree of cooperation of the person"; "to identify the problems foreseen by the trainers"). Mimetic experience makes it possible to have a specific experience resembling another but not reducible to it: lived experience in simulation is "not work but not not work." This experience emerges from within and is inseparable from the dynamic of meaning-making specific to the actor. It cannot be directly influenced by the environment and the trainer. Participants are not engaged or immersed simply because the simulations are realistic or highly immersive, simulations are realistic or immersive because the actors invest it with their own experience (Dubey, 1997) – which is more "uncertain" with novice cadets in initial training. The dual intentionality related to mimetic experience is a founding characteristic of experience in simulation and learning in general. Like Horcik and Durand (2015), we consider that the effectiveness of simulation-based training depends more on the thickness of experience and meaning-making (and its recovery during debriefing) rather than on immersive features of the simulation.

Finally, the results show that the lived experience of the cadets is structured by the expectation and anticipation of problematic events prepared by the trainers. Cadets are "waiting for" and focused on the potential pitfalls and traps scripted by the trainers. In fact, it is not so much the event itself, but rather the moment when it occurs that can surprise in simulation. This is why, in simulation-based training, participants very often experience the unexpected-predictable or unknown-known but rarely the unexpected. The other characteristic in observed simulation-based exercises refers to the fact that cadets find themselves in a hurry, with no dead time, no real possibility to act or to be proactive, i.e., to foil the unexpected.

4.2 Design Issues for Simulation-Based Training for Police Cadets

In this last part, we outline some potential solutions for the design of simulation-based training for police cadets in initial training. We will not insist here on the importance of debriefing in simulation-based training and on the need to break with a conventional corrective approach confining them to an evaluation of the gap between prescribed and realized or to reminder of best practices, safety behaviors, or procedure follow-up, even if this remains an important object of attention.

Firstly, we believe it is important to incite a profound change in learning/training theories underlying simulation-based training and turn toward "developmental and empowering simulation-based training design." Simulation-based training for police cadets is actually focused on KSAs acquisition, performance measurement, and experiential learning theory. In a complementary manner, the developmental and empowering simulation-based training situations will be pursued as an objective, not the success of the action. Instead, simulation scenario should be designed with the objective of (a) opening up possibilities that were not seen before, (b) extending beyond what is already known, (c) revealing the invisible, (d) developing a becoming aware or mindful (not as a reflective act but as a receptivity to experience moving from "a looking for" to "a letting come"), (e) developing a becoming sentient and receptive to, or (f) developing a being to events. All these elements allow afterward, in other circumstances, to make sense in complex unforeseen situations.

Secondly, it seems fundamental to question the way in which design induces the unforeseen or the unthought, as well as the degree of perturbation "sought or desirable" in design-based training (Flandin et al., 2018, 2019, 2021, 2020; Schot et al., 2019). The efficiency of a non-curricular and non-instructional approach to simulation-based training relies essentially on the relevance and the dosage of the perturbations proposed by the scenario. At the same time, it seems particularly relevant to consider the challenge of time and temporalities in simulation-based training. This aspect, often neglected in design, is both a determining element of real-work situations (remaining focused and vigilant to time to avoid and prevent dangerous situations) and an essential driver in the design of simulation scenarios.

Thirdly, we argued that the thickness of the mimetic experience of the participants was a critical factor in simulation-based training. Addressing simulation-based training design from a description of actors' experience and meaning-making allows to redefine the relationship between real-work situations and simulated situations. Asking what makes sense for the actor in simulation must be a priority. For the trainer or the designer, it is above all the actions and behaviors of the actor that are significant. Things are different for the trainee. The identification of the meaning that a simulated situation takes on for the actor is an essential issue.

Fourthly, it would be interesting in initial training to conduct training experimentation including participatory design and in which trainees would be asked to design themselves the simulation scenarios (Malet et al., 2019a, b). In this case, the design of the simulation scenarios by the trainees becomes a part of simulation-based training. Scenarios used to be designed by the trainer. It was hypothesized here that designing scenarios would increase the opportunities for trainees to explore the constraints of the environment, to broaden the range of possibilities, and to question the "force" of some consensual modes of understanding and consensually coordinated actions. As Malet et al. (2019a, b) point out, the design of the simulation scenario by the learners leads them to check the plausibility of the scenario, its difficulty, its relevance for the training purposes, and its possible enrichment by past experiences. This participatory design method for simulation-based training, in which participants are asked to design the simulation scenarios themselves, appears to be very promising and relevant in initial training. Call upon trainees to design simulation scenarios avoids the design of unrealistic, irrelevant, too complex scenarios, but also leads them to a more deep understanding of the difficulties in "simulated or simulable" scenarios. Moreover, the imagination and invention deployed during the design of simulation scenarios fully contribute to the professional development and particularly enhance the "before" learning by significantly supplementing the traditional briefing. Malet et al. (2019a) consider that the participatory design of simulation scenarios, their implementation, and the ensuing collective debates contribute to critical learning and deep understanding of the field of possibilities and that the design of simulation scenarios is an "open-ended" space where the trainees could experiment beyond the prior prescriptions or procedures.

Finally, to conclude, we would like to emphasize that all this requires area and opportunity for experimentation in training, giving more time and material resources to the trainers, and strengthening the train-the-trainers programs. As pointed out by Dubois and Van Daele (2018), the form taken by simulation-based training in initial police training is due to the weak pedagogical, material, and temporal resources available to trainers. The trainers first and foremost strive to make simulation-based training exist – in other words, to make it take place physically in the training program and environment. Moreover, in the absence of training specific to simulation-based training, but also to other dimensions related to sciences of training, trainers rely primarily on professional knowledge to set up, manage, and evaluate simulation-based training situations.

References

Bennell, C., Jones, N., & Corey, S. (2007). Does use-of-force simulation training in Canadian police agencies incorporate principles of effective training? *Psychology, Public Policy, and Law, 13*, 35–58.

Chappell, A. (2008). Police academy training: Comparing across curricula. *Policing: An International Journal of Police Strategies & Management, 31*, 36–56.

Dieumegard, G., de Vries, E., & Perrin, N. (2020). The 'course-of-action' method in the study of lived experience of learners. *International Journal of Research & Method in Education, 44*, 67–81.

Drakos, A., Flandin, S., Filippi, G., Palaci, F., Veyrunes, P., & Poizat, G. (2021). From exploration to re-enactment: Instructional uses of a desktop virtual environment for training nuclear plant field operators. *Vocations & Learning*. https://doi.org/10.1007/s12186-020-09261-1

Dubey, G. (1997). Faire « comme si » n'est pas faire. In P. Beguin & A. Weill-Fassina (Eds.), *La simulation en ergonomie: connaître, agir, et interagir* (pp. 39–53). Octarès.

Dubois, L.-A., & Van Daele, A. (2018). Analyse de l'usage d'un dispositif de simulation pour la formation initiale de policiers à partir de l'activité de formateurs. *Education & Formation, e-308*, 83–94.

Durand, M. (2014). Activité humaine et éducation des adultes. In J. Friedrich & J. Pita (Eds.), *Recherches en formation des adultes: un dialogue entre concepts et réalité* (pp. 15–39). Editions Raison et Passions.

Durand, M., & Poizat, G. (2015). An activity-centred approach to work analysis and the design of vocational training situations. In L. Filliettaz & S. Billett (Eds.), *Francophone perspectives of learning through work: Conceptions, traditions and practices* (pp. 221–240). Springer.

Filliettaz, L., Billett, S., Bourgeois, E., Durand, M., & Poizat, G. (2015). Conceptualising and connecting Francophone perspectives on learning through and for work. In L. Filliettaz & S. Billett (Eds.), *Francophone perspectives of learning through work: Conceptions, traditions and practices* (pp. 19–48). Springer.

Flandin, S., Poizat, G., & Durand, M. (2018). Improving resilience in high-risk organizations: Principles for the design of innovative training situations. *Development and Learning in Organizations: An International Journal, 32*, 9–12.

Flandin, S., Poizat, G., & Perinet, R. (2019). *Contribuer à la sécurité industrielle «par le facteur humain»: Un regard pour aider à (re)penser la formation*. FonCSI.

Flandin, S., Salini, D., Drakos, A., & Poizat, G. (2020). Diseñar capacitaciones que faciliten la emergencia de nuevas significaciones frente a situaciones inéditas y críticas: curso de la expereincia y perturbaciones de la actividad. *Laboreal, 16*(2). https://doi.org/10.4000/laboreal.17042

Flandin, S., Poizat, G., & Perinet, R. (2021). *Proactivité et réactivité: deux orientations pour concevoir des dispositifs visant le développement de la sécurité industrielle par la formation – Les leçons du projet FOResilience*. FonCSI.

Grossman, R., Heyne, K., & Salas, E. (2015). Game- and simulation-based approaches to training. In K. Kraiger, J. Passmore, N. Rebelo dos Santos, & S. Malvezzi (Eds.), *The Wiley Blackwell handbook of the psychology of training, development, and performance improvement* (pp. 205–223). Wiley.

Horcik, Z., & Durand, M. (2015). L'expérience mimétique dans l'apprentissage adulte: le cas des formations par simulation. *Revue Suisse des Sciences de l'Éducation, 37*, 167–186.

Horcik, Z., Savoldelli, G., Poizat, G., & Durand, M. (2014). A phenomenological approach to novice nurse anesthetists' experience during simulation-based training sessions. *Simulation in Healthcare, 9*, 94–101.

Malet, D., Falzon, P., & Vidal-Gomel, C. (2019a). Developing patient handling competences through participatory design of simulation scenarios. In T. Cotrim, F. Serranheira, P. Sousa, S. Hignett, S. Albolino, & R. Tartaglia (Eds.), *Health and social Care Systems of the Future: Demographic changes, digital age and human factors – Proceedings of the healthcare ergonomics and patient safety* (pp. 357–364). Springer.

Malet, D., Falzon, P., & Vidal-Gomel, C. (2019b). *La conception participative en simulation: un moyen de développement du « soin de manutention raisonné »*. Communication au 5ème Colloque International de Didactique Professionnelle, Longueuil, Québec.

Moreau de Bellaing, C. (2002). Former, informer, conformer: Enseigner à l'École nationale de police de Paris. *Les Cahiers de la Sécurité Intérieure, 48*, 57–79.

Moreau de Bellaing, C. (2006). *La police dans l'État de droit. Les dispositifs de formation initiale et de contrôle interne de la police nationale dans la France contemporaine*. Thèse de doctorat en science politique, Institut d'études politiques, Paris.

Phelps, J., Strype, J., Le Bellu, S., Lahlou, S., & Aandal, J. (2018). Experiential learning and simulation-based training in Norwegian police education: Examining body-worn video as a tool to encourage reflection. *Policing: A Journal of Policy and Practice, 12*, 50–65.

Pichonnaz, D. (2011). Réformer les pratiques policières par la formation: Les obstacles à la transformation des relations entre les policiers et leurs publics. *Déviance et Société, 35*, 335–359.

Poizat, G., Durand, M., & Theureau, J. (2016). Challenges of activity analysis oriented towards professional training. *Le Travail Humain, 79*, 233–258.

Schot, S., Flandin, S., Goudeaux, A., Seferdjeli, L., & Poizat, G. (2019). Formation basée sur la perturbation: preuve de concept par la conception d'un environnement numérique de formation en radiologie médicale. *Activités, 16*(2). https://doi.org/10.4000/activites.4724

Sjöberg, D. (2014). Why don't they catch the baby? A study of a simulation of a critical incident in police education. *Journal of Vocational Education & Training, 66*, 212–231.

Staller, M., Cole, J., Zaiser, B., & Körner, S. (2019). Representative training with less risk: The effects of non-lethal training and conventional ammunition in police use of force training on heart rate variability. *Policing: A Journal of Policy and Practice, 13*, 411–425.

Stokoe, E. (2013). The (in)authenticity of simulated talk: Comparing role-played and actual interaction and the implications for communication training. *Research on Language and Social Interaction, 46*, 165–185.

Theureau, J. (2002). Dynamic, living, social and cultural complex systems: Principles of design-oriented analysis. *Revue d'Intelligence Artificielle, 16*, 485–516.

Theureau, J. (2003). Course-of-action analysis and course-of-action centered design. In E. Hollnagel (Ed.), *Handbook of cognitive task design* (pp. 55–81). Lawrence Erlbaum.

Theureau, J. (2004). *Le cours d'action: Méthode élémentaire*. Octarès.

Theureau, J. (2010a). La constitution des savoirs dans l'action. *Intellectica, 53*(54), 95–127.

Theureau, J. (2010b). Les entretiens d'auto-confrontation et de remise en situation par les traces matérielles et le programme de recherche « cours d'action ». *Revue d'Anthropologie des Connaissances, 4*, 287–322.

How Do Simulated High-Intensity Situations Train Leaders to Maintain Their Ability to Act in Unfamiliar, Unforeseen or Uncertain Environments?

Hervé De Bisschop and Serge Leblanc

Abstract In addition to being rooted in an enactive conception of the activity (Durand & Poizat, 2015; Theureau, 2003), one of the originalities of this research is to focus on the learning experienced by cadets while they are engaged in spaces of action that do not encourage their activity, but on the contrary hinder it: the hardening training course. The purpose of this training is to make these officer cadets experience simulated situations of physical, emotional and psychological over-stress, presenting similarities with their future professional life.

In order to better understand how, within such a simulation device, officer cadets experiment with their ability to maintain individuals' dispositions to act, we analysed the *engagement modes* of the trainees in their learnings to command among aversive environments.

The results show that alongside the well-known forms of executory and exploratory engagement, a "conservatory" mode of engagement appears, the aim of which is to preserve the conditions for perpetuating the action and capacities of each officer cadet.

This research leads to the formulation of principles for the design of trainings whose aim is to prepare professionals to deal with the unknown, the unexpected and even the unbearable.

Cases from crisis preparedness training at the *École Militaire Interarmes* (EMIA: Joint Military School).

H. De Bisschop (✉)
Agrosup Dijon, Formation et Apprentissages Professionnels- FoAP, Paris-Dijon, France
e-mail: herve.de-bisschop@agrosupdijon.fr

S. Leblanc
Université de Montpellier- LIRDEF, Montpellier, France
e-mail: serge.leblanc@umontpellier.fr

S. Flandin et al. (eds.), *Simulation Training through the Lens of Experience and Activity Analysis*, Professional and Practice-based Learning 30,
https://doi.org/10.1007/978-3-030-89567-9_12

Keywords High-intensity training · Command activity · Engagement modes

1 Introduction

The Research Objective, Object, Theoretical Framework and Setting
This research aimed to advance the design of simulations that prepare professionals to act effectively in particularly intense, indeterminate and difficult situations. As such situations can be overwhelming, the challenge for trainees is to maintain their capacities to act effectively, which might even be described as the singular experience of being prepared not to be prepared. The study thus focused on the trainees' lived experience by analysing the various ways they engaged in action. The approach was based on (i) theoretical postulates derived from the theory of action and (ii) the empirical study of an emblematic programme that appears to be promising, relevant and effective: training whose main purpose is to immerse learners in an uninterrupted succession of simulated situations that continuously impede their actions.

Studying the Modes of Engagement That Trainees Experience as They Are Trained to Lead
This chapter has five sections. First, we describe why the setting for this research and its specificities are relevant to our objective. Second, we present an explanation of why the enactive and semiotic conception of activity is well-suited to provide insight into how trainees experience different modes of engagement as they learn to lead in hostile environments. Third, we describe the key points of the study methodology. In the fourth section, we present the results, notably a unique mode of engagement developed by the trainees, and propose six principles propitious for designing training programmes dedicated to training professionals to act in risky, dynamic and unpredictable environments. Last, we conclude by presenting an opening onto a new perspective related to a second transformation experienced by the trainees: that of their attentional capacity.

2 Context and Challenges

Specificities and Relevance of the Study Setting
We begin by describing the main characteristics of preparedness training. We then specify how this simulation programme is relevant for studying how trainees live the experience of maintaining their capacities to act in uncertain and demanding environments.

2.1 Preparedness Training: A Programme of Continuous Simulations That Challenge Firefighters, Police Officers and Soldiers with Intense and Unusual Disturbances

Preparedness: Training by Dealing with Intense Physical, Psychological and Technical Difficulties

The training courses take place in French Guiana at the *Centre d'Entraînement en Forêt Équatoriale.*[1] It is designed for civil and military security professionals: firefighters, police officers and soldiers. The CEFE instructors have been certified by the most demanding 'jungle' schools[2] in the world. The course is based on the principle of preparedness, which 'is a set of procedures and individual and collective situations that contribute to improving the trainees' operational aptitude [...] by confronting them, under orders from their leaders, with the physical, psychological and technical difficulties that arise while executing their missions in unusual and hostile conditions and environments' (*État-major de l'armée de terre* 2010, p. 3).[3] Essentially, this means 'giving every soldier, within his formation, the "non-material" means to fulfil his mission' which entails dealing with the environment of right now; resisting over the long term; overcoming adversity; knowing sometimes how to endure the unendurable; being convinced of 'getting out of the trenches' whatever the risk and of not being alone to do so; showing situational intelligence and initiative; and being able to adapt to unusual or unforeseen circumstances and technological failures (Ibid., p. 4).

A Unique Simulation Programme

This professional training is based on lengthy, high-intensity simulations unfolding over 20 days. The trainees are immersed in a hostile environment: the equatorial forest, which 'can quickly become the first and the worst enemy for untrained or ill-prepared troops' (Walter, 2015, p. 214). The trainees thus must deal with adversity through exposure to simulated, unusual, unforeseen and even unbearable situations.

In practice, this course differs from simulations organized along the classic format of briefing/immersion/debriefing. Here, the simulation is organized around three main modalities: (i) intensive training comprising practical situations (e.g. crossing water, survival, obstacle courses, lighting fires, night orienteering, medical evacuation, round-the-clock life in the forest, etc.); (ii) ongoing instruction (e.g. on fauna, flora, hunting, hygiene rules, topography, construction of shelters and rafts, etc.) to ensure that the trainees acquire vital knowledge about dealing with survival situations and develop new modes of action in aversive environments; and (iii) the transmission of experience by senior peers (the instructors, seconded by the captain in charge of officer cadet training).

---

[1] CEFE: Equatorial Forest Training Centre.

[2] Brazil (CIGS of Manaus), Colombia (Lanceros) and Ecuador (Tigre).

[3] General Army Staff Note 727/DEF/EMAT/ES/B.EMP/OUT/33, April 2010.

In addition, preparedness training holds a specific place in the field of simulation training because, like simulators, it is based on a realistic reconstruction of the professional situations that future officers must be prepared for. Unlike simulators, however, it does not use technological devices to reproduce or simulate reality. Preparedness training is, in fact, situated in an in-between place, being both inside and outside the professional activity. Although the situations the trainees confront are simulated and the instructors play parts in them, all takes place in a real environment: the equatorial forest. This natural and hostile environment exposes the trainees to risks that will force them to learn to act effectively in response.

In summary, one of the originalities of this research is its focus on the trainees' experiences of learning while they engage in exercises that in no way facilitate their activity, but instead hinder or obstruct it. This training is therefore in contrast to the simulation programmes that favour the creation of educational spaces[4] that support and facilitate the trainees' activity.

2.2 *The Four Dimensions of a High-Intensity Simulation Programme*

A Rare Training Format: Immersion in Extreme Environments That Call for 'Extraordinary' Actions

Many studies have examined action in extreme environments: (i) rescue operations in hostile environments (Agresti, 2012; Gautier, 2010), (ii) hospital emergencies (Faraj & Xia, 2006), (iii) firefighting (Weick, 1993) and (iv) the flight manoeuvres of aerobatic crews (Godé & Lebraty, 2015). They have highlighted either the aversive characteristics of these environments (Hällgren et al., 2017; Hannah et al., 2009) or the need for 'extraordinary' practices, such as the constant need to avoid potentially fatal errors (Bigley & Roberts, 2001). Much of the research has been carried out in the military and police fields (Bechky & Okhuysen, 2011; Catino & Patriotta, 2013; Godé & Lebraty, 2015; Melkonian & Picq, 2010; Schakel et al., 2016) and has particularly underlined the extent to which action in these environments requires the capacity to preserve physical safety. However, little research has focused on training programmes based on the principle of immersion in hostile environments.

Training for Action in High-Risk Situations That Expose Trainees to Continuous Disruption

Preparedness training is based on an endogenous and positive conception of action in high-risk situations.[5] This differs from an exogenous and negative vision, both in terms of the purpose of the action and the nature of the targeted learning.

[4] See Sect. 2.2 below.

[5] With reference to the positive/negative distinction of risk management made by Johnston & Paton, 2001.

When the endogenous vision of risk is promoted, as is the case here, the goal of the action is less to reduce the occurrence of a feared danger or to remove the trainees from risk by instituting preventive measures and more to prepare them to be able to continue their leadership activities in the midst of disruptive or even dangerous environments.

From an exogenous and negative perspective on risk, the expected learning on how to maintain safety requires compliance with the rules (especially safety rules). This is part of a safety concept that Hollnagel called 'Safety 1' (2014), and, as Flandin et al. (2017) reminded us, it is focused on the anticipation of accidents and foreseeable crises, leading to 'the systematization of standards, rules and procedures and the minimization of the variability of operations' (Ibid., p. 3). However, from an endogenous and positive perspective on action in risky situations, safety depends on the trainees' ability to preserve their capacities to act. This has led to a focus on learning that favours the taking into account of the individual and group resources that are likely to preserve individual capacities. The question thus is how trainees can become accustomed to acting in ordinary ways in environments that are extraordinary because of their aversive nature.

Training That Breaks with the Training Programmes That Create Protected Environments

Preparedness training courses provide a contrast with the 'protected training environments' (Bourgeois & Nizet, 1997; Zeitler et al., 2017) that place emphasis on the quality of the environment and the relationship between trainees and trainers. The objective of preparedness simulations is to plunge the trainees into situations of incapacity embodied in experiences of inadequacy. This occurs by continuously confronting them with impossible situations arising from both the environment and the trainers' actions. The repeated obstacles gradually deprive them of their physical, psychological and mental resources.

Training Designed as a Series of Simulated Situations

Although simulation often takes the form of 'simulators' in the context of today's technological advances, it would be simplistic to limit it to the use of technological artefacts.[6] Indeed, in the fields of both psychology (Piaget, 1945; Wallon, 1941) and professional training, we are reminded that simulations can take various forms of 'acted-out situations' (Oget & Audran, 2016), whether or not they mobilize material and symbolic artefacts. This is the case with the preparedness course, which is based on activities situated in a real environment (the natural environment) and the uninterrupted succession for 20 days of simulated situations, as described by Vidal-Gomel et al. (2011, p. 116) based on Samurçay (2005, p. 224).

In summary, we propose to describe this hybrid object as a 'high-intensity simulation programme' that immerses trainees in real conditions and confronts them for several uninterrupted days with an unfolding series of simulated situations. These

[6]Without of course denying the many possibilities, such as observing the unobservable or reconstructing critical situations, or being exposed without risk to dangerous situations, etc.

simulations are not designed to protect the trainees from danger, nor to have them apply the prescribed norms. Instead, they are intended to train them to preserve their resources in brutal and hostile environments.

These characteristics give the training its unique character. They also offer a privileged view of what individuals experience as they learn to lead, even as they grapple with a risky environment that confronts them with the unknown, the unforeseen and the uncertain.

3 Theoretical Framework and Research Question

3.1 From an Enactive and Semiotic Conception of Activity

From the perspective of a socio-constructivist and phenomenological epistemology (Varela, 1979), the present research examines what trainees experience during preparedness training by analysing their activity within the theoretical framework of the course of action (Durand & Poizat, 2015). We assume, in line with Horcik et al. (2014), that 'training' can be understood using the methods of activity analysis. This analysis must therefore be conducted on the basis of a theory of activity that preserves the primacy of the learner's point of view (Dieumegard et al., 2019). We thus chose to situate this research within the theoretical and methodological framework of the course of action, which draws on an enactive and semiotic conception of activity (Theureau, 2003).

Doing so allowed us to include three useful notions: disruption, experience and the semiotic dimension of activity.

The first notion is disruption because, as we have seen, one of the main characteristics of high-intensity simulation programmes is the density and multiplicity of disruptive demands made on the trainees. These incessant disturbances continually interrupt the current activity of the officer cadets, throwing them into states of over-exertion of their physical, psychological or mental capacities. In the course of action, these disturbances hold a preponderant place in the sense that activity here is conceived as an asymmetric coupling between an actor and his/her environment. Coupling refers to an actor's moment by moment selection of what is likely to become a disruption so that an adequate response can be made (Theureau, 2006).

The second notion is experience because the best way to understand how disruption is lived by trainees is by accessing their experience. Course-of-action theory offers a methodological framework for accounting for what actors experience moment to moment. Within this framework, all activity is accompanied by lived experience that in part gives rise to conscious experience.[7] This latter can be described as the degree of familiarity that the actor has with him–/herself. Here, the

[7] This refers to what can be told, commented on and shown.

trainees' flow of lived experience can thus be described from an intrinsic point of view based on the analysis of their typical concerns.

In order to make explicit how an actor's experience can be understood from the analysis of his/her typical engagements, we turned to the semiotic dimension of activity. This dimension is rooted in the conviction of Theureau (2009), who was himself much influenced by Peirce (1931–1958), that humans think and act through signs. In this conception of cognition, mental representations—that is, what an individual has in mind from moment to moment—are the dynamics of bringing an object to mind through a sign that takes the place of the object in question. Cognition is conceptualized here, not as relations between thoughts and facts but as an interpretative movement emerging from the relations between the six components of the sign (called hexadic[8]). The semiotic framework of cognition thus postulates that access to the conscious part of an actor's lived experience can be acceptably described by the six components of the hexadic sign presented below.

The Key Role of Concerns in the Six Components of the Hexadic Sign

1. (E): *Engagement* describes the horizons of the actor's possibles at instant (t). These emerge from both the actor-environment coupling and the state of the actor's body and culture. **They are expressed in the actor's discourse by the concerns and intentions that pervade the individual at instant (t).**
2. (A): The *potential actuality* is the multiplicity of the actor's anticipations and expectations given his/her concerns at instant (t).
3. (S): The *referential* identifies the set of knowledge items that the actor can mobilize, given his/her concerns at instant (t).
4. (R): The *representment* is what disturbs the actor at a given instant, thus what effectively makes a sign for him/her. This may take the form of perceptions (sensory), proprioceptive sensations or what is recalled in memory at instant (t).
5. (U): The *unit of the course of experience* identifies what the actor does, says, thinks and feels at instant (t).
6. (I): The *interpretant*, as the operator of the actor's situated transformation of knowledge, contributes to the emergence and the validation or invalidation of the actor's knowledge.

In summary, the theoretical framework for the course of action and enaction provides insight into what trainees are experiencing from the analysis of their concerns, even when they are engaged in high-intensity simulated situations and are constantly being disturbed by incessant demands.

[8] These have been described in the empirical and technological course-of-action research programme (Theureau, 2003).

3.2 The Problem and the Research Objective: To Assess How Officer Cadets Experience Their Ability to Maintain the Resources of Individuals in a High-Intensity Simulated Training Situation

How Do You Learn to Persevere in Action When Everything Is Against It?
The studies that have analysed activity in dynamic and dangerous environments[9] (Hällgren et al., 2017; Hoc et al., 2004; Rogalski & Samurçay, 1993) have not only described these environments as generators of uncertainty, ambiguity, confusion and instability, but they have also shown the extent to which these environments pose a multitude of problems by impeding the participants' capacity to act. Among these problems are (i) difficulties in perception, understanding and drawing inferences, which complicate decision-making; (ii) the deterioration in modes of both cognitive and operational coordination, which makes cooperation less efficient; and (iii) the impact of the tensions created by the continuous re-evaluation of their preconceived expectations even as they find themselves facing contradictory demands. They thus need to be able to step back from regulatory activities while simultaneously engaging in the immediate and rapid execution of the actions required by an emergency. Last, it should be recalled that when danger becomes real with an injury, this breach of the individual's physical integrity decreases or even neutralizes their individual resources.

In short, in risky environments, individuals are immersed in an intensive experience that 'overtaxes' their physical, psychological or mental capacities. In these environments, they therefore face a double problem. First, even though they are immersed in an environment where everything distracts, interrupts and diverts them from what they have to do, they must still ensure that their overriding action remains focused on successfully completing their mission. Yet they must also find ways to preserve both the individual and group resources that are necessary for this.

How Do You Train for the Unforeseen, the Unexpected, the Uncertain—That Is, How Do You Prepare Someone Not to Be Ready?
Preparing future officers to lead in uncertain situations means having a curriculum designed to develop the capacity for discernment, decision-making and action in dynamic and dangerous environments that generate ambiguity, confusion, instability and stress. Yet these environments (i) make both cognitive and operational coordination difficult (Caroly & Barcellini, 2013); (ii) call into question preconceived anticipation strategies; (iii) force actors to continuously reassess their understanding of the situation; and (iv) create difficulties of perception, comprehension and inference (Melkonian & Picq, 2010; Rogalski & Samurçay, 1993).

Training professionals to know how to act in unknown, unforeseen, uncertain or even unsustainable environments is therefore a major challenge for the designers of

[9] Please recall that danger is defined as 'the intrinsic capacity of an activity, substance, technology or situation to harm the integrity of people, property or the environment' (Chauvin, 2014, p. 16).

these programmes: How do they prepare trainees for what cannot be imagined in advance, and what will always remain in part unimaginable (Dechy et al., 2016)?[10] The challenge here is to train them to think and act 'outside the box' as Samurçay and Rogalski (1998) have long emphasized. As learners, they first need to know how to recognize novel situations. However, as Flandin et al. (2018) have shown, this capacity to recognize novelty cannot be acquired only from the analytical and conceptual reasoning learned in sessions based on the appropriation of formalized knowledge.

In short, when training courses must prepare individuals to act in dynamic, risky and multi-outcome environments in which they have to handle often contradictory concerns and face situations as new as they are disturbing, it may be better to imagine design principles other than those traditionally used to prepare individuals for known, relatively stable and secure environments.

Dual-Purpose Research

In summary, the objective of this research was twofold: (i) to describe how officer cadets experience their ability to maintain the resources of individuals in a high-intensity simulated training situation and (ii) to propose principles that may guide the future design of such training programmes.

3.3 The Research Question: In a High-Intensity Simulated Training Situation, Around Which Typical Concerns Do Trainees Organize Their Engagement as They Learn to Lead?

To understand how officer cadets experience their ability to maintain the resources necessary for the action of those under their command, we mobilized the forms of engagement as the theoretical object because they describe the nature of the typical concerns driving the trainees as they learn.

According to course-of-action theory (Theureau, 2003), engagements emerge from the set of an actor's concerns and intentional states at instant (t). In the case of training, they reflect what the trainees are trying to do, not only moment to moment but also throughout the course of their experience. These engagements take a typical form, and they function as anchors for past, present and future situations. Two main forms of engagement are usually distinguished: an exploratory mode and an executory mode (Sève & Leblanc, 2003). When the engagement is exploratory, the actors focus on understanding the situation and seek relevant information. When it is executory, they focus on effectiveness and the modes of execution for what they are doing. In other words, they do 'what works' and avoid 'what does not work' (Durand

[10] Question in response to which the author invites us to investigate practices aimed at 'learning to act differently so as not to be surprised' (p. 8).

et al., 2006). But what happens in environments where activity is systematically impeded? Do we find these two modes operating here? Are they the only observable forms of engagement?

4 Methodology

4.1 The Field and the Population

Following this description of the characteristics of the CEFE preparedness training course for the EMIA[11] officer cadets, we now provide details on the trainees. The study population was made up of a brigade from the *École Militaire Interarmes de Saint-Cyr Coêtquidan*, comprising about a hundred students. These young professionals have had initial professional experience in regiments, police stations or fire stations. The brigade was made up mainly of men as women represent only 10% of the workforce in these professions.

4.2 Methodological Approach

4.2.1 Access to the Field: A Long Phase of Immersion and Acculturation

Data collection was preceded by an 18-month ethnographic immersion phase (De Sardan, 1995). The purpose was to become familiar with the professional environment and build the conditions for cooperation between the military students and the researcher, an essential requirement of the course-of-action observatory (Durand, 2008).

4.2.2 Data Collection and Processing: Identifying the Trainees' Typical Concerns

The second phase of observing the cadet training activity was divided between the *École de Saint-Cyr Coêtquidan* (2 weeks) and the CEFE (3 weeks). Data were collected in the form of video traces, activity traces and interviews. In the third phase, this material was processed by retrospective verbalization during 35 self-confrontation interviews (Theureau, 2010). The detailed construction of the data focused on six cases selected for their rich content, offering nearly 2 h of observation of trainees in action and 5 1/2 h of self-confrontation interviews.

[11] *L'École Militaire Interarmes.*

The processing was organized into three stages: (i) preparation of the data protocol using two-part tables comparing the trainees' behaviours and communications in action and their comments during the self-confrontation interviews; (ii) minute by minute decomposition of the conscious part of their lived experience through the six components (E, A, S, R, U, I),[12] which enabled a fine-grained documentation of their concerns as reflected by their engagements (E); and (iii) classification of the 36 typical concerns according to the mode of engagement.

5 Results and Generalizations

5.1 In Addition to the Traditional Exploratory and Executory Dimensions of Activity, a Third Dimension of Actor Engagement Emerges: Conservatory

The modes of engagement were examined by reclassifying the types of concern according to whether they were oriented towards seeking information (exploratory) or executing tasks, either in progress or upcoming (executory). We identified nearly 42% of the engagements that did not fit into either of these two categories and thus inductively derived a third type of engagement that we termed conservatory. Indeed, in situations in which it manifested, this type of engagement was less related to information-seeking or action as it was to preserving the conditions necessary for the exploratory or executory modes of activity.

From a quantitative point of view, it is interesting to note that among these three forms of engagement, two were equally and predominantly present: executory and conservatory, with each representing 41.7% of the typical concerns (Fig. 1).

A more detailed analysis (Fig. 2) of the intentions that structured the trainees' actions in these risky environments provided elements of response to our research question. Indeed, what concerned the officer cadets as they sought to preserve the conditions for immediate and future action was the need to conserve the physical and psychological, and both individual and collective, capacities of those under their command.

Last, by looking even more closely at this emblematic concern of conservatory engagement, namely, the typical concern to 'take care of your men', we observed more clearly how the officer cadets tried to maintain each individual under their command operating at full capacity. Figure 3 below shows that this consisted of (i) organizing work handovers, (ii) avoiding hyper-stress, (iii) organizing rotations on demanding 'posts' (iv) not leaving individuals alone, (v) ensuring enough recovery time, (vi) listening for signs of pain and stepping in to help, (vii) focusing energies on the main action, (viii) shortening the time spent coping with too many demands at once, and (ix) distributing out the missions.

[12] See the insert: the key role of concerns in the six components of the hexadic sign.

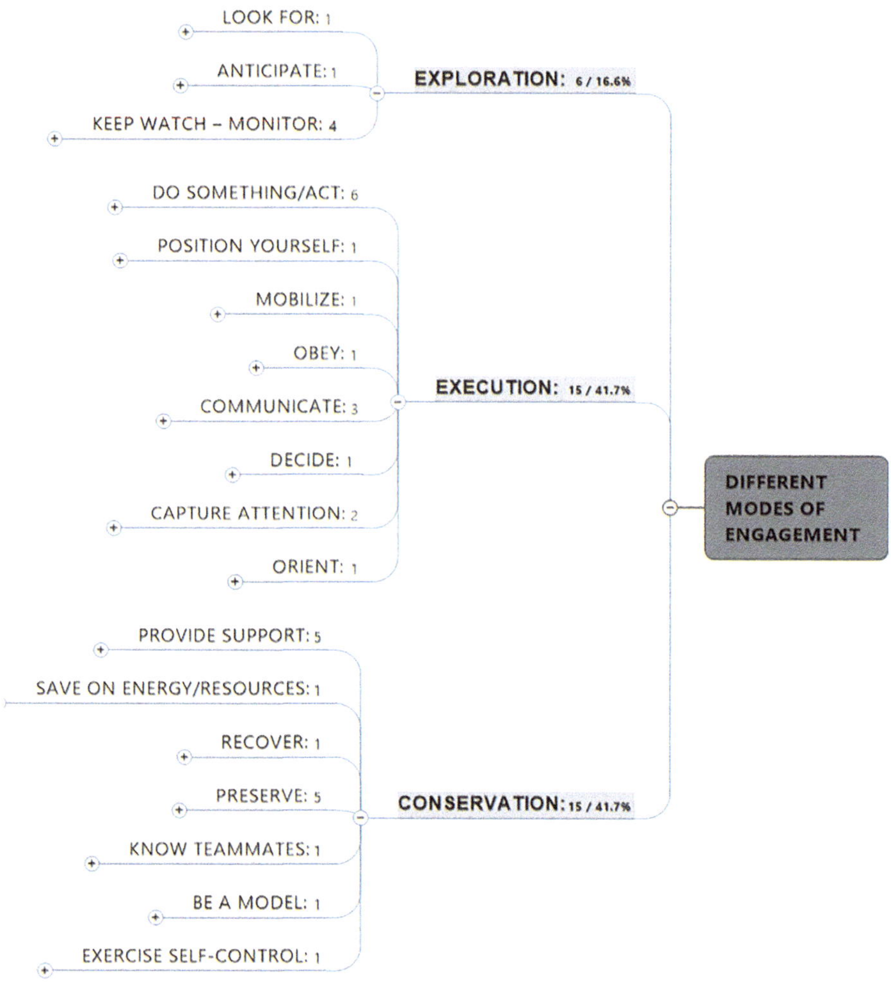

Fig. 1 The distribution in percentage of the three modes of engagement

Summary

These results show that during this immersion in a risky environment, the trainees discovered and learned that leading means to a great extent transforming the way they mobilize both their capacities and those of the individuals they are responsible for. Their immersive experience thus shifted from a mode primarily focused on doing what needed to be done to one primarily dedicated to maintaining and preserving the resources and capacities needed to continue doing what needed to be done. Thus, it appeared that an essential dimension of commanding required the deployment of intense conservatory activity.

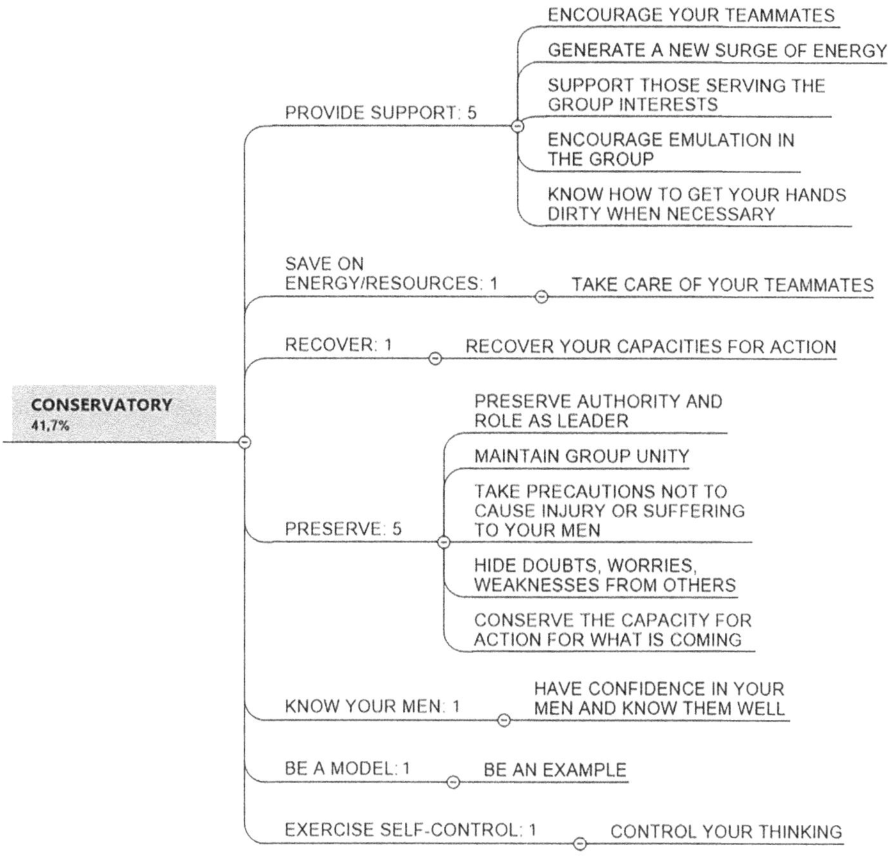

Fig. 2 The typical concerns as matters for conservatory engagement

5.2 *Six Design Principles for Simulated Training Programmes to Prepare Civil Protection Professionals to Know How to Act in Unknown, Unforeseeable, Uncertain and Even Unbearable Situations*

In addition to providing a more detailed understanding of how individuals immersed in risky environments manage to sustain their action, the results of this research are notable for their focus on fields of professional activity beyond the military world. The common denominator of these professions is the imperative of preserving the continuity of professional action even though the individuals are coping with multiple hindrances to their action and thus must figure out how to act at the limits of the known, the expected, the certain and even the tenable. Among these fields is of course civil protection, but the management field might be included as well, as under the pressure of management systems aimed at maximizing control and

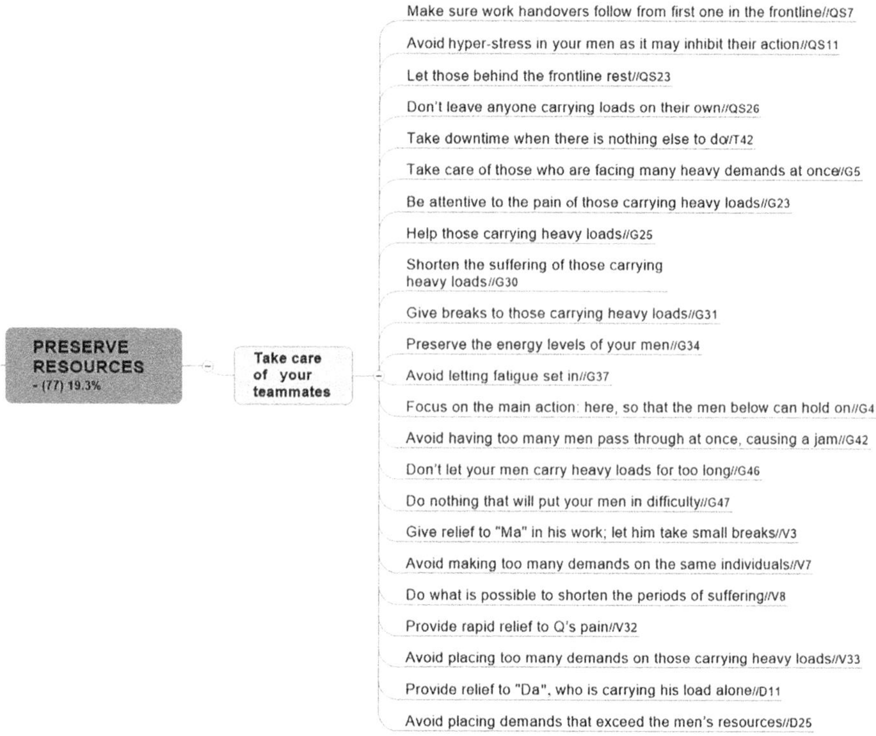

Fig. 3 The concerns as part of the typical concern of 'take care of your men'

performance, this field has seen managerial practice transformed from the 'governance of people' to the 'administration of things' (Boussard, 2008).

As our sample was made up of future officers in the military, firefighting and policework, our results can be applied to these professions of civil defence and protection, though future research might expand the scope of applicability. We therefore propose six principles for enhancing learning potential through the design of training programmes that prepare individuals to know how to act in the face of the unknown, the uncertain and the unforeseen.

5.2.1 Design High-Intensity Simulated Training Programmes That Disrupt the Trainees

Prompted by the reflection initiated by Schot et al. (2019) on events-driven adult training, we propose here a form of 'high-intensity' simulated training. Let us recall the four main criteria for specifying its nature.

First, these training programmes immerse individuals in environments that place great demands on them. Two dimensions are important here: immersion and environments that are aggressive for one's physical integrity. The first dimension is operationalized by the training duration, which covers several days that are long and therefore fatiguing. The second is due to the intrinsic characteristics of the training environment (here, high heat and humidity compounded by the density and dangerousness of the surrounding fauna and flora), which differs greatly from the one that the trainees are physically accustomed to. As a result, the activities carried out in this environment tend to deprive the trainees of their capacities.

Next, as these programmes are based on a positive conception of risk (Johnston & Paton, 2001), they are not designed to protect the trainees from the occurrence of the feared risks but are instead oriented towards training them to know how to preserve their capacities to act while in the middle of these threatening environments. In this case, individuals are trained to know how to cope with an overwhelming experience rather than avoiding it.

In addition, these programmes are designed as a seemingly endless series of simulated situations that leave trainees in the dark about the programme design. Finding themselves in this situation teaches them to modulate their level of investment in the exercises in such a way that they are constantly engaged in preserving the resources that will be necessary for them to continue to act.

Last, another factor that contributes to the high intensity of these simulated training programmes is the endless barrage of disturbances that become so many potential obstacles to action. Gorman et al. (2010) showed that when these disturbances are introduced into trainees' learning dynamics, they promote the adaptive processes that are crucial for action in uncertain and dynamic environments.

5.2.2 Give Preference to Events-Based Training Courses That Simulate Situations of Real Testing

When professionals are being prepared for situations that are unthinkable because they are unpredictable, the training curricula designed on the basis of predefined knowledge have limited effectiveness, as noted by Flandin et al. (2018). The results of our research were similar to their results and illustrate the benefits of simulated training programmes based on the occurrence of events that test the trainees to their limits.

Two notions are central here: the *event* and the *ordeal*.

An *event* breaks with the usual phenomena of everyday life. It disrupts the usual anticipatory processes, generating surprise and even astonishment. In this sense, an event is a resource for training as it is conducive to immersing learners in new situations. Zarifian (1995) distinguished two forms of event. The first is random and unexpected (an *aléas* event). The second is expected but its occurrence and modalities remain uncertain (a *rendezvous* event). Although a key element of programmes for preparedness training is the randomness of events, this does not preclude the introduction of *rendezvous* events in future programmes or a combination of the two.

As Baudoin reminded us (2014, p. 225), an ordeal refers to 'a certain number of decisive or critical moments in personal history that are salient, transitional, and life-changing'. The examination of how these officer cadets were tested revealed three phenomena that might be mobilized in other training courses: (i) the discovery of personal limits, (ii) a situated assessment that allowed them to test themselves, and (iii) the embodied experience of what their own bodies were able teach them about themselves and their environment. The trainees' ordeal was thus simultaneously:

- *What the ordeal is*; that is, what makes it a painful experience. This is the space of sanction, not in the sense of punishment, but as the discovery of personal limits and the ontological finitude of any individual as a vulnerable being.[13]
- Yet it is also *what has caused it to be an ordeal*. This refers to the personal evaluations that allow the trainees to test themselves. The ordeal thus has a revealing role because through it the trainees discover and assess the supports (artefacts or social) and resources (personal or social) that they possess or can manage to mobilize.
- Last, the ordeal is *what the trainees experience* as a place of the corporeality[14] of the activity, that is, the place of experience inscribed in the body that has both a physical and a lived structure.

5.2.3 Combine the Design of Spaces for Action That Are Both Encouraged and Prevented

In the chapter of this book titled 'Four lines of analysis for civil security crisis simulations: insights for training design', Flandin underlines the importance of disturbance in training because, among other things, disturbance makes it possible for trainees to test 'the robustness of their modalities of interpretation, action and collective configuration…'.

However, using disturbances as a teaching method is a delicate operation. Both designers and trainers must regulate a complicated mix of adjustments. Indeed, disturbances must generate enough surprise to shake the learners up and trigger new elaborations of meaning in order to shed light on the novelty of the situations. But at the same time, they must not destabilize the trainees to the point of generating forms of disengagement from the educational activity underway or of neutralizing their capacities.

Thus, to preserve the mediating character of training situations and promote transfers on the part of learners, preparedness training teaches us that educational programmes are called on to be both 'spaces of encouraged action (Durand, 2008; Reed & Bril, 1996) and spaces of impeded action'. 'Encouraged' refers to the sense

[13] As much for biological reasons as for dependence on the social environment. See Le Blanc (2011) and Maillard (2011).

[14] That is, the set of interconnections of sensory, sensorimotor and cognitive dimensions.

that they generate a feeling of ontological security in the trainees, which is expressed among other ways by the conviction that the trainers want what is 'good' for them and their success. 'Impeded' refers to the sense that the ordeal as described above offers them a potential to learn that generates the conservatory modes of engagement described in our results.

5.2.4 Encourage the Development of Modes of Contextual Engagement and Operational Engagement

The analysis of the officer cadets' modes of engagement in 'learning to lead' revealed an unexpected mode: conservatory. Let us recall its characteristics: when this mode is actualized, the trainees do not seek so much to execute an action or to seek information for doing so or to control what is being executed. Instead, they are engaged in preserving the favourable conditions for doing what needs to be done, for seeking information about doing what needs to be done or for monitoring what was done or is being done. In this sense, we describe this mode of engagement as contextual to distinguish it from the exploratory and executory modes that are described here as operational.

Contextual modes of engagement like the conservatory mode[15] contribute to creating, maintaining or developing the conditions that enable the trainees to carry out the tasks directly related to the productive part of the activity: in this case, carrying out the mission.

In these contextual modes, we see a competence for discrimination in risky environments: knowing how to preserve and maintain the conditions for task execution.

5.2.5 Seek Skill Acquisition Rather Than Knowledge or Know-How

As we noted above,[16] training programmes to prepare for action in unknown (and therefore unthinkable) situations cannot be designed on the basis of predefined knowledge. This does not mean that no knowledge is to be acquired, but rather that critical learning here is related to the development of dispositions to act in certain ways in certain circumstances (Muller & Plazaola Giger, 2014). Indeed, this research shows that trainees, by jointly developing exploratory and conservatory modes of engagement, are mainly called upon to transform their ways of being, acting and interacting with themselves and their peers, in other words, to transform their dispositions to act and interact in these two modes.

---

[15] We assume that other studies will uncover other forms of contextual engagement.

[16] See Sect. 5.2.2.

5.2.6 Focus on Developing Transformative Dispositions to Act as a Way of Being in the World

The distinction between doing and preserving the conditions for doing may seem simple, but from a learning perspective, it is not because it refers to two forms of relation to reality.

In the first, trainees focus on learning the pertinence of the decisions, actions or gestures to be made. In the second, the concerns revolve around the relationship that they have with what they are doing and what is being done. In other words, in this second case, they need to acquire another form of relation to reality in which their capacities are as much in the service of what is happening (in and around them) as they are in the service of what is to be done. It is about being open to or available to what is and what is coming.

Indeed, what unfolds between these two relations to reality is a shift between two ways of being in the world is: the trainees shift between an actively active posture and a passively active posture. In the second form of relation, the challenge for the trainees is learning how to be present and attentive to the relation they have with the phenomena within and around them. The first involves learning to do what is necessary to meet the demands of the task and the situation.

However, learning to be available to what is happening calls for a form of passivity and thus may at first glance be perceived as unnatural by those trainees who think (and rightly so, in part) that in risky environments they must be hyperactive to cope with the multiplicity of demands they are facing.

So here we have a double educational challenge. The first consists of ensuring that learners acquire a way of being passively active even though nearly everything in their environment is pushing them to an activity oriented towards 'doing' and not towards 'being available to what is being done'. The second challenge is to identify the pedagogical processes capable of supporting the trainees in knowing how to execute an action, but in such a way that these two modes are harmoniously coordinated in the action. This is vital, because obviously the goal is not for them to pass alternately from one mode to the other, but to be in the world through the two jointly.

6 Synthesis and Perspective

The objective of this research was twofold: (i) to describe how officer cadets experience their ability to maintain the resources of everyone involved in a situation of high-intensity simulated training and (ii) to derive principles that can guide the future design of these training programmes.

The findings on 'learning to lead' in a simulated high-intensity training situation showed that the officer cadets experienced their ability to maintain the resources of others through a counterintuitive process: the conservatory mode of engagement. They showed the same levels of executory and conservatory engagement in that they were equally intent on action and on preserving those conditions conducive to sustaining their own capacities and those of the individuals under their command. They also sought to preserve both individual and group capacities in physical, psychological and mental dimensions. The study further suggested six principles for the design of simulated training programmes dedicated to civil protection professionals learning to know how to act when they find themselves in unknown, unforeseeable, uncertain and even unbearable circumstances. The principles are based on the intensive testing of the trainees in spaces for action that jointly encouraged and prevented their action and that favoured the development of contextual modes of engagement and a transformation in their way of being in the world.

We would now like to emphasize a learning potential offered by this programme that was somewhat left aside in this article. Our study, however, suggests that it was an important, if not the major, part of what the officer cadets experienced as they worked to maintain the resources of the individuals under their command: This was the transformation in the nature of their attention which, little by little, shifted from an attention 'focused on' to an 'attentiveness' to the presence of oneself and others.

To clarify what we mean, we must recall that the trainees' third[17] typical concern was to 'capture and orient the cognitive capacities of their men' and call upon the work of Depraz et al. (2011) on a phenomenological reduction summarized as the suspension of judgement, which is described by a double movement of attentional conversion and receptiveness/letting go. We here hypothesize that the double movement—by which the cadets were constantly alert to the micro-indices that informed them about the state of their bodies and those of their men (the mode of conservatory engagement) and were also able to capture their men's attention (to ensure the effectiveness of their command)—contributed to the process of attentional conversion described by these authors.

The repetition of this mechanism seemed to lead to an experience that the trainees described as a widening of their field of consciousness, which we believe is an appropriate way to describe the transformation in their mode of attention. What took place when the officer cadets 'let go' was an opening to what could emerge at any moment in their bodies, minds or situations. They thus shifted from a conquering attitude directed by an outward-looking intentionality (objects of attention) to a posture of availability to whatever might happen, as it happens.

Finally, let us note that when this very particular disposition was shared by several members of the group, it then became what Depraz (2014, p. 399) called 'being attentionally together'. This then allowed the officer cadets to deploy a new form of coordination, dispositional, so called because it was based not so much on cognitive or operational coordination but on a new way of being together, with all attentive to what is happening within them, between them and around them.

In short, what initially appeared to be obstacles to the activity of the officer cadets (the multiple demands disrupting the courses of their experience) turned out to be learning factors capable of balancing their activity between executory and

[17] In terms of frequency of occurrence.

conservatory engagements and converting their attention towards an activity of vigilance for oneself and others.

References

Agresti, B. (2012). *In extremis – L'épopée du secours dans le massif du Mont-Blanc* (2e édition revue et corrigée). Guérin.
Amalberti, R. (2001). La maîtrise des situations dynamiques. *Psychologie Française, 46*(2), 107–118.
Baudouin, J.-M. (2014). La « Phrase qui tue » La notion d'épreuve, de la dissémination à la conceptualisation. In J. Friedrich & J.-C. P. Castro (Eds.), *Recherches en formation des adultes. Un dialogue entre concepts et réalité* (pp. 223–253). Raison et Passions.
Bechky, B. A., & Okhuysen, G. A. (2011). Expecting the unexpected ? How swat officers and film teams handle surprises. *Academy of Management Journal, 2*(54), 239–261.
Bigley, G. A., & Roberts, K. H. (2001). The incident command system: High-reliability organizing for complex and volatile task environments. *The Academy of Management Journal, 44*(6), 1281–1299.
Bion, W. R. (1991). *A memoir of the future*. Routledge.
Bourgeois, E., & Nizet, J. (1997). *Apprentissage et formation des adultes*. PUF.
Boussard, V. (2008). *Sociologie de la gestion: Les faiseurs de performance*. Belin.
Caroly, S., & Barcellini, F. (2013). *Le développement de l'activité collective*. PUF.
Catino, M., & Patriotta, G. (2013). Learning from errors: Cognition, emotions and safety culture in the Italian Air Force. *Organization Studies, 34*(4), 437–467.
Armée de Terre. (2017). *Politique pour l'aguerrissement au combat de l'Armée de Terre*. Ministère de la Défense.
Chauvin, B. (2014). *La perception des risques—Apports de la psychologie à l'identification des déterminants du risque perçu*. de boeck.
Dechy, N., Mortureux, Y., Planchette, G., Blatter, C., & Raffoux, J.-F. (2016). Explorer «l'imprévisible»: Comment et jusqu'où ? *Maîtriser les risques dans un monde en mouvement.* 20ième congrès de Maîtrise des Risques et de Sûreté de Fonctionnement, Saint-Malo.
Depraz, N. (2014). *Attention et vigilance-À la croisée de la phénoménologie et des sciences cognitives*. puf.
Depraz, N., Varela, F. J., & Vermersch, P. (2011). *À l'épreuve de l'expérience: Pour une pratique phénoménologique*. Zeta Books.
de Sardan, J. -P. O. (1995). La politique du terrain. Sur la production des données en anthropologie. *Enquête. Archives de la revue Enquête, 1*, 71–109.
Dieumegard, G., Nogry, S., Ollagnier-Beldame, M., & Perrin, N. (2019). Lived experience as a unit of analysis for the study of learning. *Learning, Culture and Social Interaction*, 100345. https://doi.org/10.1016/j.lcsi.2019.100345
Durand, M. (2008). Un programme de recherche technologique en formation des adultes. Une approche énactive de l'activité humaine et l'accompagnement de son apprentissage/développement. *Éducation et didactique, 2*(3), 97–121.
Durand, M., & Poizat, G. (2015). An activity-centred approach to work analysis and the design of vocational training situations. In L. Filliettaz & S. Billett (Eds.), *Francophone perspectives of learning through work* (pp. 221–224). Springer.
Durand, M., Saury, J., & Sève, C. (2006). Apprentissage et configuration d'activité: Une dynamique ouverte des rapports sujets-environnements. In I. J.-M. Barbier & M. Durand (Eds.), *Sujets, activités, environnements* (pp. 61–83). Presses Universitaires de France.
Faraj, S., & Xiao, Y. (2006). Coordination in fast-response organizations. *Management Science, 52*(8), 1155–1169.

Flandin, S., Poizat, G., & Durand, M. (2017). Développer la résilience en renouvelant la formation à et pour la sécurité: Une recherche en cours. *52 ième Congrès International Société d'Ergonomie de Langue Française*, 9.

Flandin, S., Poizat, G., & Durand, M. (2018). Improving resilience in high-risk organizations: Principles for the design of innovative training situations. *Development and Learning in Organizations: An International Journal, 32*, 9–12.

Gautier, A. (2010). Le management des situations extrêmes dans les organisations de secours: la complexité de l'implémentation du retour d'expérience dans la conduite des opérations. In P. Lievre & M. Aubry (Eds.), *Gestion de projet et expéditions polaires: que pouvons-nous apprendre?* (p. 12). Presses Universitaires Québécoises.

Godé, C., & Lebraty, J.-F. (2015). Experience feedback as an enabler of coordination: An aerobatic military team case. *Scandinavian Journal of Management, 3*(31), 324–336.

Gorman, J. C., Cooke, N. J., & Amazeen, P. G. (2010). Training adaptive teams. *Human Factors: The Journal of the Human Factors and Ergonomics Society, 52*(2), 295–307.

Hällgren, M., Rouleau, L., & de Rond, M. (2017). A matter of life or death: How extreme context research matters for management and organization studies. *Academy of Management Annals, 12*(1), 111–153.

Hannah, S. T., Uhl-Bien, M., Avolio, B. J., & Cavarretta, F. L. (2009). A framework for examining leadership in extreme contexts. *Leadership Quarterly, 20*(6), 897–919.

Hoc, J.-M., Amalberti, R., Cellier, J.-M., & Grosjean, V. (2004). Chapitre 2. Adaptation et gestion des risques en situation dynamique. In J.-M. Hoc & F. Darses (Eds.), *Psychologie ergonomique: Tendances actuelles* (pp. 15–48). PUF.

Horcik, Z., Savoldelli, G., Poizat, G., & Durand, M. (2014). A phenomenological approach to novice nurse anesthetists' experience during simulation-based training sessions. *Simulation in Healthcare: The Journal of the Society for Simulation in Healthcare, 9*(2), 94–101.

Johnston, D., & Paton, D. (2001). Disasters and communities: Vulnerability, resilience and preparedness. *Disaster Prevention and Management: An International Journal, 10*(4), 270–277.

Le Blanc, G. (2011). *Que faire de notre vulnérabilité?* Bayard.

Maillard, N. (2011). *La vulnérabilité, une nouvelle catégorie morale?* Labor et Fides.

Melkonian, T., & Picq, T. (2010). Opening the « black box » of collective competence in extreme projects: Lessons from the French special forces. *Project Management Journal, 3*(41), 79–90.

Muller, A., & Plazaola Giger, I. (2014). *Dispositions à agir, travail et formation* (p. 2014). Octarès Editions, DL.

Oget, D., & Audran, J. (2016). Autour des mots de la formation: « Simulation ». *Recherche & formation, 82*, 75–84.

Peirce, C. -S. (1931). *The collected papers of Charles Sanders Peirce, Vol. I and II: The principles of philosophy and element of logic*. Harvard University Press.

Piaget, J. (1945). *La formation du symbole chez l'enfant: Imitation, jeu et rêve, image et représentation*. Delachaux & Niestle.

Reed, E. S., & Bril, B. (1996). The primacy of action in development. In M. Latash & M. Turvey (Eds.), *Dexterity and its development* (pp. 431–451). Erlbaum Associates.

Rogalski, J., & Samurçay, R. (1993). Représentations de référence: Outils pour les contrôle d'environnements dynamiques. In A. Weill-Fassina, P. Rabardel, & D. Dubois (Eds.), *Représentations pour l'action*. Octares éd.

Samurçay, R. (2005). Concevoir des situations simulées pour la formation professionnelle: Une approche didactique. In P. Pastré (Ed.), *Apprendre par la simulation – De l'analyse du travail aux apprentissages professionnels* (pp. 221–239). Octares Editions.

Samurçay, R., & Rabardel, P. (2004). Modèles pour l'analyse de l'activité et des compétences, propositions. In R. Samurçay & P. Pastré (Eds.), *Recherches en didactique professionnelle* (pp. 163–180). Octarès.

Samurçay, R., & Rogalski, J. (1998). Exploitation didactique des situations de simulation. *Le Travail humain, 4*(61), 333–339.

Schakel, J.-K., van Fenema, P. C., & Faraj, S. (2016). Shots fired! Switching between practices in police work. *Organization Science, 27*(2), 391–410.

Schot, S., Flandin, S., Goudeaux, A., Seferdjeli, L., & Poizat, G. (2019). Formation basée sur la perturbation: Preuve de concept par la conception et le test d'un environnement numérique de formation en radiologie médicale. *Activites, 16*(2), 1–25.

Sève, C., & Leblanc, S. (2003). Exploration et exécution en situation: Singularité des actions, construction de types et apprentissage dans deux contextes différents. *Recherche & Formation, 42*(1), 63–74.

Theureau, J. (2003). Course of action analysis & course of action centered design. In E. Hollnagel (Ed.), *Handbook of cognitive task design* (pp. 55–81). Lawrence Erlbaum Ass.

Theureau, J. (2006). *Le cours d'action: méthode développée*. Octares.

Theureau, J. (2009). *Le cours d'action: méthode réfléchie*. Octarès.

Theureau, J. (2010). Les entretiens d'autoconfrontation et de remise en situation par les traces matérielles et le programme de recherche « cours d'action ». *Revue d'anthropologie des connaissances, 4-2*(2), 287–322.

Varela, F. J. (1979). *Principles of biological autonomy*. North Holland.

Vidal-Gomel, C., Fauquet-Alekhine, P., & Guibert, S. (2011). Réflexions et apports théoriques sur la pratique des formateurs et de la simulation. In I. P. Fauquet-Alekhine & N. Pehuet (Eds.), *Améliorer la pratique professionnelle par la simulation* (pp. 115–141). Octares Editions.

Wallon, H. (1941). *L'évolution psychologique de l'enfant*. A. Colin.

Walter, A. (2015). Le combat en forêt équatoriale. In I. D. Danet, R. Doaré, & C. Malis (Eds.), *L'action militaire terrestre de A....à....Z* (pp. 210–217). Economica.

Weick, K. E. (1993). The collapse of Sensemaking in organizations: The Mann Gulch disaster. *Administrative Science Quarterly, 38*(4), 628–652.

Williams, M. H. (2018). *The aesthetic development: The poetic Spirit of psychoanalysis: Essays on Bion, Meltzer, Keats* (1st ed.). (e-Book)—Routledge.

Zarifian, P. (1995). *Le travail et l'évènement*. L'Harmattan.

Zeitler, A., Guérin, J., Benghanem, S., & Jacquet, E. (2017). *Ergonomie des situations de formation (ESF): analyser l'apprentissage comme un travail*. Education permanente n°HS9–2017-1 – Hors série AFPA 2017.

On Care and the Sensitive Experience of Caregiver Activity in Simulation Situations: A Possible Model for Encounters Between Health Practitioners and Their Patients to Enhance Communication Training

Elodie Ciccone, Lucie Cuvelier, Anne Bationo-Tillon, Thomas Baugnon, and Françoise Decortis

Abstract According to the evolution of paradigms in medicine, we study the "care beyond cure" through the analysis of a medical simulation training named "communication skills". These simulation sessions train physicians to deliver difficult diagnoses to patients (who are children) and to their families (especially the parents). That singularity makes them very suitable for investigating the integration of sensitive dimensions of healthcare into practitioner training. Based on the observation of 16 simulations cases, the results focus the analysis of post-simulation debriefings. We analyze through the verbalizations the lived experience of participants during the simulation and the link with their professional lives In all the sessions observed, trainers had a facilitator role consisting in encouraging participants to speak about their subjective experience. However, results show a great variability in the way participants tell and share their simulation experiences. The results describe the dimensions of simulated and work activities that are discussed during debriefings, with a special focus on the sensitive dimensions addressed by

E. Ciccone (✉)
Université Paris 8, Saint-Denis, France

Université Clermont Auvergne, Clermont-Ferrand, France

L. Cuvelier · A. Bationo-Tillon · F. Decortis
Université Paris 8, Saint-Denis, France
e-mail: lucie.cuvelier@univ-paris8.fr; anne.bationo-tillon@univ-paris8.fr; francoise.decortis@univ-paris8.fr

T. Baugnon
Hôpital Universitaire Necker Enfants Malades – APHP, Paris, France

Université Paris Descartes, Paris, France
e-mail: Thomas.baugnon@nck.aphp.fr

S. Flandin et al. (eds.), *Simulation Training through the Lens of Experience and Activity Analysis*, Professional and Practice-based Learning 30,
https://doi.org/10.1007/978-3-030-89567-9_13

participants. These results suggest opportunities for future exploration of simulation models integrating the sensitive dimensions of healthcare activities. Sensitive dimensions can be integrated in scenarios or in the trainer's reminders.

Keywords Simulation · Sensitive dimensions · Lived experience · Activity discussion · Healthcare

1 Toward a Greater Understanding of Care Practices in Medicine

1.1 Beyond the "Cure" Mindset

The doctor was previously considered the sole custodian of medical knowledge, a knowledge today built on the foundations of evidence-based medicine (Bizouarn, 2007). Diagnosis in this approach is regarded as the objective and depends solely on patient symptoms, with cures being subsequently prescribed in accordance with a set of standards, or "golden rules," that apply to specific situations. Virtually all medical students today are trained in evidence-based medicine (Greenhalgh, 1999). However, in the face of the crisis of contemporary medicine, whether from the perspective of the physicians, who no longer identify with their work, or of the patients, who have become more involved in healthcare processes and who feel increasingly "neglected," Klein (2014) suggests that a reevaluation of the current and future role of the medical profession is necessary.

On the one hand, patient perspectives on illness have evolved; patient empowerment improves the patients' ability to understand and cope with medical conditions (Breton, 2019). On the other, "a narrative-based model of medicine" has emerged, providing a better understanding of both the carer's role and of caregiver-care receiver interactions. Diagnosis in the current healthcare process is no longer solely established on perceptible clinical symptoms but is likewise based on the respective histories of the patient and the physician. These developments have led to a greater understanding of *care* practices in medicine, in other words "the work carried out in response to the needs of others" (Molinier, 2006, p. 145). Traditionally defined as the application of knowledge to benefit individual patient needs without being limited by or merely complementary to the administering of treatments (cures), care practices in medicine can be regarded as invisible, since the actions carried out are not necessarily tangible (Hesbeen, 2002). Practicing care, in other words, involves treating the patient "as a whole" (Molinier, 2013) by employing such interpersonal means as eye contact, verbalization, touch, and other expressions of feelings and emotion (Hirata & Molinier, 2012; Pernet, 2013).

Ironically, despite the increased recognition of the impact of care on treatment quality and safety (Eyland, 2017; Pernet, 2013), and the multiplication in recent years of studies and theoretical models dealing with interpersonal relationships (patient participation, proper treatment, etc.), it is clear that "the link between the patient and the caregiver has gradually become frayed," with technique today prevailing over care (Eyland & Leblanc, 2019).

1.2 Care beyond Notions of Non-technical Skill

With these invisible facets of caregiving generally unaddressed in current medical school curricula, educators are searching for new care transmission methods (Eyland & Jean, 2016). In doing so, they often emphasize so-called "non-technical" skills, such as the improvement of interprofessional and doctor-patient communication capabilities (Bergström et al., 2008; Fletcher et al., 2003; Goupy et al., 2013). Such initiatives stem from an observation commonly reported in hospital departments: poor communication by healthcare professionals can directly result in negative care-related outcomes (Huet et al., 2016). In environments where care quality and safety are of constant concern, team leaders commonly make use of "communication facilitating" techniques, such as checklists, clear and concise language, active listening, reformulation, and leadership, in order to ensure "orchestrated" communication, even in emergency situations. In keeping with these methods, caregiver communication programs have been developed to improve carer-patient relations and, consequently, the quality of care. The basic premise here is that communicating with patients and families requires structured instruction, much the way interprofessional communication does.

Unfortunately, training programs like these tend to reduce job-specific competencies to transversal and general healthcare skills. Thus, while the use of simulators to train healthcare staff, especially during the post-simulation debriefing phase, has led to new methods of skills development and communication, simulation-based training is largely driven by technical expertise. Few studies to date have analyzed whether simulated learning programs improve participant learning efficacy, what is more (Pastré, 2005). The gray area is even greater here given the fact that simulation-based training is focused not on medical techniques (cure) and human factors skills (crew resource management) but on healthcare staff communications and relations with patients. These programs have come under fire in recent years (Bourquin & Stiefel, 2017; Flandin et al., 2019; Salmon & Young, 2011), the two main criticisms being:

1. Standardized communication methods (frameworks, scripts, and other prompts) can be an impediment to individual patient encounters.
2. Expert recommendations pertain to a fundamentally decontextualized form of communication, casting doubt on the very concept of improving *aptitude* or *ability to communicate* through training.

We believe that there is more at stake in these courses aimed at improving "communication skills" and, more broadly, "non-technical skills" than the instructors initially believe. "Because simulation training is a suitable framework for authentic, situated, embodied, and embedded experimentations for professionals, it seems to us that this type of training has much to offer." () In other words, other aspects of the caregivers' work activity are developed during the sessions, which cannot be reduced to targeted, non-technical skills acquisition. While several authors (Bationo-Tillon & Decortis, 2016; Bonnet, 2020; Cahour, 2010; Decortis et al., 2016) have demonstrated the complexity of the participants' experience, having revealed the so-called invisible aspects of care practices liable to be exposed, and even debated, in courses designed for communicating with patients, current models do not take these aspects into account. And yet a better understanding of the real activity that unfolds in such situations could provide leads for enhancing future training sessions.

2 Training Through Simulation, a Potential Space for Sensitive Expression

2.1 Analyzing the Simulated Activity

There are multiple theoretical models for the design of non-technical skills programs, as described by a good number of authors (Bouchot & Leblanc, 2019; Rudolph et al., 2007; Sawyer et al., 2016) (see introduction). Many of these training programs aim to provoke the development of professional experiences under safe and effective conditions using high-fidelity simulation (SHF), as recommended by the Haute Autorité de Santé (HAS, 2012) and the Direction Générale des Offres de Soins (DGOS, 2013). However, the representational design of these training programs, focused more on simulator lifelikeness and notions of workplace ecology than on the educational purposes and specific nature of the simulated situations, has been criticized by many schools of thought: simulation will never replace real experience, despite the significant advances of technology today (Béguin & Pastré, 2002; Cuvelier, 2018; Samurçay & Rogalski, 1998).

Thus, while these situations always refer to a real activity, they are first and foremost educational situations, i.e., situations designed, organized, and structured to meet predefined training course objectives (Ciccone et al., 2018; Cuvelier, 2018; Mayen, 2009). This observation led Horcik et al. (2014) to define this specific experience in simulation as "mimetic experience," i.e., an experience characterized by the double (or multiple) intentionality between the simulated work and the targeted work experience: the experience in simulation is both felt as an experience in itself (including the participants' awareness of the simulated situation as an enactment, an assessment, and a shooting) while being guided by "the real and embodied work activity upon which the simulation is based." Horcik's definition thereby emphasizes the importance of taking into account the activity that occurs during the simulated scenarios: as a rule, simulation procedures, and debriefing sessions in particular, are determined by predefined educational criteria (targeting regular work situations) that leave no room for discussions about the participants' lived experience in simulation.

And yet failure to account for the real experience of simulation is tantamount to neglecting experiential learning and potential inter-experience relations or "resonances" (Rosa, 2018). Supported by research conducted in cultural-historical activity theory (Clot & Leplat, 2005; Daniellou & Rabardel, 2005; Vermersch, 1994), we propose that the efficacy of simulation sessions for professional development depends on discussions focused on both the work experience being targeted and on the unique nature of the participants' activity in simulation, on the lived experience. Nevertheless, that unique activity of an encounter with a patient (or the patient's relatives) remains poorly understood, and current models for simulation training are founded on curricula that fail to factor in the multiple dimensions of the encounter.

2.2 Taking into Consideration "All" Dimensions of the Activity

Ergonomics and educational science have historically focused on the behavioral, physiological, biomechanical, and cognitive aspects of activity (Bourgeois & Hubault, 2005; Bourgeois et al., 2006). More recently, the importance of the dimensions of sensitivity inherent to activity has come to light, initially through studies on the role of emotions (Cahour, 2010; Cahour & Lancry, 2011), based, in part, on Damasio's work on how absence of emotion impedes decision-making (2010). Conversely, research in sociology-philosophy (Rosa, 2018), psychodynamics (Molinier, 2006), and the sociology of work (Böhle & Milkau, 1998) argues against assimilating sensitive aspects to emotional response. Building on these concepts, we maintain that the sensitive experience of the work activity emerges from physical involvement, i.e., from a concomitant participation of the body's senses and emotions.

Sensitive activity therefore infers a way of being in the world, whereby situations can be perceived using imagination, without being limited by a rational perspective. It can thus be differentiated from analytical activity, whereby the object of an activity is carefully examined, described, broken down, and studied, to be qualified and made categorizable (Bationo-Tillon et al., 2013). This definition, founded on the work of Bationo-Tillon et al. (2013) in the field of cultural mediation, whose MARO activity model offers a heuristic lens for assessing aspects of sensitivity in the activity of a museum visitor, makes it possible to consider the dynamics of the sensitive/analytical relationship while distinguishing the time period to which the experience refers: the present (the here and now), the past (the link to previous experiences), or the future (the forecasting of future experiences). Based on the singular nature of experience within the cultural sector, Bationo-Tillon's work challenges many of the concepts, methodological arguments, and epistemological bases of ergonomics and is therefore, we believe, a relevant conceptual tool for assessing the lived experience of activity in simulation situations.

3 Objectives and Methods

3.1 Hypotheses

The aim of the study described in this chapter was to enhance our understanding of the activity of caregivers engaged in a training simulation program designed by teaching physicians in pediatric anesthesia and critical care. The participants were observed over two training sessions. Our findings show that:

- The activity of an encounter between caregivers (doctors or health practitioners) and their patients is defined by therapeutic and medical (cure) concerns, as well as by caregiver response to the needs of the patients and families (care). The activity of a caregiving encounter targets four objects: treatments, patients/families, colleagues, and self (Flageul-Caroly, 2001).
- Response to the four aspects of the caregiving encounter can be sensitive and/or analytical (Bationo-Tillon, 2013).

The first type of response (the sensitive relationship) is distinguished by the emergence of the caregiver's sensations and impressions during the encounter with the patient. It infers a way of being in the world, whereby individuals and pathologies are perceived through the lens of imagination and emotions, without being limited by rational perspectives. The second, the so-called analytical relationship, is characterized by the caregiver taking a rational and analytical approach to the patient and the pathology. In such cases, concrete elements are factored in and carefully described, and the pathology/treatment is broken down and analyzed with the aim of better qualifying it for classification. When the object of the activity is seen through the lens of analysis, "[the patient], instead of being approached, understood, and embraced by the subject [the caregiver], is kept at a distance to be observed like a painting" (Bationo-Tillon, 2013, p. 88).

3.2 Description of the Observed "Communication" Training Simulation

Developed within a pediatric anesthesia and critical care department, the observed communication training simulation was designed to provide caregivers with tools for interacting with their patients (children from birth to the age of 18) and the patient families. The aim of the simulations is to teach participants to identify and respond to the defense mechanisms of the parents of sick children, such as denial. The team of teaching practitioners who conducted the study were veterans in patient safety training simulation. The earliest simulation-based courses designed by the team were part of a decade-old effort to improve safe practices in healthcare. The simulations in question fall into one of two overarching categories:

- **High-fidelity simulation for basic technical skills development.** These sessions were designed for novice physicians to ensure optimal preparation for a "first time" field experience and emergency care situations (sessions such as crew resource management).
- **Emergency care situation simulation, within the framework of obtaining an interuniversity qualification in traumatology.** These emergency care sessions were designed for experienced physicians. This course has since evolved to include a scenario simulating the announcement of news to a patient's parents.

More recently, in keeping with the above-described scenarios, the training simulations have been expanded to include communication situations with the parents of sick children. The program is built around two distinct sessions. The first, which is intended for junior pediatricians, stems from an observation made by caregivers and reported by teaching physicians over the course of their careers, with regard to **certain communication situations:** "Situations that involve the announcing of unexpected bad news or care-related complications are extremely difficult and are therefore a source of anxiety for the patients and caregivers alike" (Baugnon et al., 2015). The doctor's intervention in such cases is characterized by its suddenness. As the consequences of a "poorly made" announcement may be felt not just immediately but in the long term, a training simulation was consequently designed to provide inexperienced practitioners with tools for interacting with patient families in the best possible way. The second, more recent simulation session is specifically designed for healthcare staff working in pediatrics. Likewise, it is based on the observation that **certain interaction situations between caregivers (nurses, nurses' aides), but excluding doctors,** are *extremely difficult and are therefore a source of anxiety for patients and caregivers alike.* These health workers also frequently report feelings of being insufficiently prepared and trained, especially in skills specific to pediatric care. *A training session including experiences in simulation was therefore purposely designed to meet their needs. Since healthcare assistants are not responsible for announcing bad news to families, t*he cases simulated involve ordinary caregiving situations, but with the parents of the patient present in the room.

The course material for both sessions was designed and taught by a multidisciplinary team of instructors (anesthesiologists and psychologists) and is divided into two main parts:

- A theoretical foundation built on interactive sessions, focusing on specific themes such as structuring interviews, modes of communication, and the defense mechanisms of patients, patient families, and caregivers.
- Simulated interactions with the parents of a patient (child). The parents are played by professional clown actors from the association Le Rire Médecin trained to meet the specific needs of vulnerable populations in hospital environments. The simulated scenarios are filmed and last approximately 10 minutes; they are followed up by collective debriefings that last approximately 40 minutes.

The simulation scenarios for both sessions were inspired by existing cases (realistic situations) **and were developed to explore the defense mechanisms of patient parent(s). In other words, to provoke the development of the healthcare participants' non-technical skills in communication, the simulations address**

the interactional processes at work in the predefined defense mechanism(s) ascribed to the professional actors (denial, anger…). One specific aspect of this training program is the emphasis it places on mimetic experience, in that the group as a whole is invited to take part in the subsequent debriefing session (the participants and instructors, but also the actors who played the role(s) of the parent). The instructors, at the time of our initial meeting, had several years' experience in communication training simulation and were presently interested in assessing the relevance of the program. While steps including post-simulation questionnaires had been taken to evaluate the relevance of the training course, a more detailed analysis of the participants' experience inside the simulated scenarios and a better understanding of the skills potentially developed could provide leads for enhancing future training sessions.

3.3 Methods

An initial observation of the simulation center introduced us to the general principles of simulation-based education and to the specifics of the training course. This enabled us to situate the verbalizations and actions of the caregivers (anesthetists) and to establish the above-described hypotheses.

From this initial encounter, we also observed that, although the instructors were all trained in simulation debriefing, their methodology remains inchoate, i.e., it is based on the unfolding simulated procedure and not on an evaluation grid or checklist. At the start of the debriefing sessions, the instructors ask the participants to comment on the simulation experience: how they felt, the parts that most impressed them, and the difficulties encountered. The exchanges are focused on what the participants consider the most relevant aspects of the simulated situation. The analysis of verbalization data, recorded during the debriefing phase and then fully transcribed, is thus a key to understanding the participants' perspective and experience during the simulated activity. It makes it possible to frame the results from the participants' perspective (Daniellou & Rabardel, 2005).

3.3.1 Systematic Observations: Data Collection

A total of 4 days of training were observed, corresponding to four different groups. The groups of physicians in training were comprised of personnel who were not used to working together. The debriefing phase in this case was an exchange forum between colleagues who do not constitute a team. The caregiver groups were comprised of personnel from two departments who were used to working together. The debriefing phase in this case was seen as an exchange forum between colleagues who could potentially constitute a team (Caroly & Clot, 2004). Levels of seniority also differentiated the two groups, with the caregivers having 3 to 15 years of field experience and the doctors in training at the start of their careers.

Each of the 4 days of training was dedicated to four simulations. For each, we received copies of the recordings of the simulated activity (filmed by the instructors,

Table 1 Systematic overview of the simulated situations: group composition, situation description, length of recordings

Instructors/ occupation	Group composition	Scenario number	Description of announced medical condition	Scripted parent defense mechanism (actor's role)	Perceived level of difficulty	Length of simulation/ debriefing sessions (in minutes)
4 teaching physicians	Group 1: 10 doctors in training	M1C2	Case 2: polytrauma	Anger	Difficult	11/53
2 psychologists		M1C3	Case 3: bronchiolitis	Shock	Easy	11/47
3 teaching physicians	Group 2: 8 internes	M2C1	Case 1: bronchiolitis	Shock	Easy	6/33
3 psychologists		M2C4	Case 4: polytrauma:	Anger	Difficult	11/31
3 nurses	Group 3: 1 childcare assistant	P1C4	Case 2: a new cannula needs to be inserted	Parents in need of information	Easy	12/24
2 teaching physicians practitioners	10 nurses					
3 psychologists						
4 nurses	Group 4: 2 childcare assistants	P2C1	Case 1: bronchiolitis	Parents are affectionate	Easy	8/26
1 teaching physicians practitioner	6 nurses	P2C2	Case 2: a new cannula needs to be inserted	Parents in need of information	Easy	12/38
3 psychologists	1 assistant nurse					

as stipulated in the program); the debriefing sessions were filmed by us. Table 1 provides an overview of the composition of the groups and the length of the recordings.

3.3.2 Data Analysis

Our findings are based on the analysis of the audio-video recordings of the simulated situations and the subsequent simulation debriefings.

First, the a posteriori analysis of the films of the simulation situations enabled us to examine the behaviors of the participants (carers in training and actors) during the simulations. Next, by coupling our observations with the data from the debriefing sessions, we identified the objects of the participants' activity during the simulated situations, as well as the way they responded to the activity's goals. A similar classification was chronologically conducted for each of the simulated situations. A log was generated from the findings, as shown in the summary table below for the scenario M1C3 (Table 2).

Table 2 Report on the activity of an encounter with a patient – scenario M1C3

Length	The steps defined for making the announcement	Data from the simulation recordings (films)	Data from the debriefing recordings (films)	Object of the activity	Type of situation	Strategies (how)	Relationship to the identified object
3’20”	Preparing the right listening conditions	“Do you understand what they were doing in the emergency room?”	/	Treatment	Identifying what the parents know	Ask questions	
		Wait until the father arrives	“the mother, feeling of helplessness, we are there to give her the news, but we can’t do it […] we wanted to tell her ‘it’s going to be alright’”	Parents	Making sure you are being listened to	Wait	Sensitive
		Wait until the father asks to hear more	“The father, he was looking at his wife, so I couldn’t tell if he was listening to me too”	Support	Making sure you are being listened to	Wait	
3’40”	Announcing the news	“They put an oxygen mask on him in the emergency room to help him breathe”	/	Support	Explaining what has been done so far	Describe the situation, provide information	
		“It’s an infection caused by a virus, his airways are congested” “he is fine”	/	Support	Explaining the current condition of the child	Describe the situation, provide information	
		“It’s a common respiratory tract infection, children make a full recovery after having bronchiolitis”	“I think that most bronchiolitis patients suffering from pauses in breathing, once they are stabilized, they are fine [...] here, the doctor and the mother are not on the same page”	Parents	Reassuring the parents	Keep them at a distance, provide information	Analytical
		“He is breathing on his own, but with the help of a machine to prevent anymore pauses in breathing”	/	Parents	Reassuring the parents about their child’s condition	Describe the situation, provide information	

3’30”	Preparing the parents to see the child	“Right, before going in to see him, just so you know, he’s connected to a device with a little mask, and there’s a catheter in his arm to hydrate him because, for the moment, he can’t eat.”	“The mother, if she enters the room and we haven’t explained it all to her, and she sees her baby with all of those bruises…”	Parents	Breaking the news gently, to avoid giving the parents a shock	Describe the situation,	
						Explain that the child is instrumented	Sensitive, then analytical
		“The nurses are taking care of him right now.”	/	Parents	Reassuring the parents	Describe the situation, provide information	

4 Results

4.1 The Activity of Encountering Patients, an Activity Targeting Four Objects

The a posteriori observation of the training simulation videos in conjunction with the analysis of the debriefings enabled us to generate an activity log describing the encounters between the carers and the parents (actors). For each simulated case, the recurrent (prescribed) phases of the activity along with its associated objects were identified. The results showed four families of activities, classified according to the targeted objects:

- The first type, the "cure," refers to the technical and rational dimension of the caregiving activity (Lalau, 2021). The object here is patient treatment, which may be technical, therapeutic, or procedural.
- The second is related to care, i.e., the activities carried out "in response to the needs of others" consisting in "anticipating the difficulties and needs of others" (Molinier, 2006, p. 145). In this case, the object of the caregiving activity is the patient and his or her families; in pediatric care situations, it is very often the parents to whom the caregiver refers.
- The object of the activity of the third type is the carers themselves. This type of activity is related to actions of self-protection and personal development. The object is not to provide care, because other people are not the object here, but it is tied to the idea of taking care. In this case, it concerns notions of taking care of self, i.e., of the carers' integrating their own activities, resources (physical, cognitive, psychic, and emotional), and experiences into decision-making and analytical processes.
- The last family of activity pertains to the activity's collective dimensions. In this case, the object of the activity is the caregivers' colleagues, including their professional associates and all other staff members involved in the care process.

These findings substantiate our hypothesis drawn on the works of Caroly (Caroly & Weill-Fassina, 2004a, b; Flageul-Caroly, 2001). They enabled us to establish a model for the activity of encountering patients, with care and cure constituting two of the four objects involved in the activity of communication between caregivers and their patients (see Fig. 1).

4.2 A Sensitive or Analytical Relationship to the Objects

The findings, and the data from the debriefing sessions in particular, show two types of response to these objects, as well: sensitive and analytical (Bationo-Tillon, 2013). Sensitive relationships to the object of the activity are distinguished by the emergence of the caregiver's sensations and impressions during the encounter with the patient.

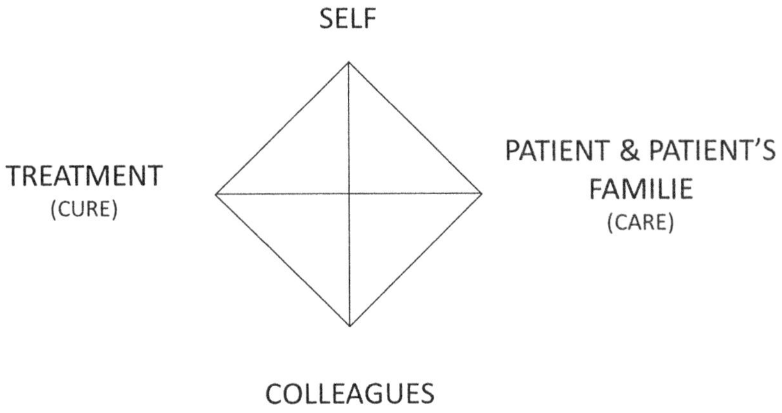

Fig. 1 A model of caregiver activity during encounters with patients. Based on Caroly's quadripolar model (Caroly & Weill-Fassina, 2004b; Flageul-Caroly, 2001)

The first type of response (the sensitive relationship) is distinguished by the emergence of the caregiver's sensations and impressions during the encounter with the patient. It infers a way of being in the world, whereby patients, families, and pathologies, and, more generally, the care situation involving the team, can be perceived through the lens of imagination and emotions without being limited by rational perspectives. This sensitive relationship to the object shows that the encounter with the patient cannot be reduced to the mere compilation and subsequent analysis of clinical symptoms and data from the different areas of work activity. On the contrary, the encounter activates the ability to "feel," activating, therefore, not just the caregiver's memories of previous experiences of relationships to the object but an overall physical and emotional response (Böhle & Milkau, 1998). The second response, the so-called analytic relationship, is characterized by the caregiver taking a rational and analytical approach to the patient and the pathology. In such cases, concrete elements are factored in and carefully described, and the pathology/treatment is broken down and analyzed with the aim of better qualifying it for classification. When the object of the activity is seen through the lens of analysis, "[the patient], instead of being approached, understood, and embraced by the subject [the caregiver], is kept at a distance to be observed like a painting" (Bationo-Tillon, 2013, p. 88).

This distinction between the two types of relationships to the object allows us to analyze and evaluate the sensitive experience in communication training. Current research and prospective future studies should look at the different ways these relationships can be developed and combined according to certain characteristics, such as the objects targeted, the caregiver's function (doctor or healthcare assistant), and seniority. Our ongoing cross analysis seems to indicate that sensitive relationships to the objects of the work activity were more prevalent among the nurses and care assistants observed during the simulations. Obviously, before making such a distinction, we need to bear in mind that in real situations, these two types of relationships are not mutually exclusive and are often consecutive and even simultaneous. It could even be suggested that the mutability of these two relationships makes it possible for the activity of encountering patients to unfold. In terms of training, this facet can be mobilized as a resource for understanding the way that the analytical and sensitive elements of an activity interact, with the purpose of verifying that each of the components can be developed without gaining ascendancy over the other and thus hindering the actors' ability to act.

5 Conclusion

The findings of our study seem to indicate new avenues in communication training. By considering all types of activity (care, patient and family, self, and others) and the way they interact in work situations, it is possible to ensure that critical dimensions of the activity are not overlooked.

Indeed, while providing care is the primary and most visible goal of the work activity (what caregivers are asked to do), other types of activity associated with caregiving are also part of the caregiving experience. In other words, the activity of the caregivers does not only consist in doing what they are asked to do; it is also a question of negotiating different work goals. One way to improve simulation training resources is to focus therefore on the ways in which this balance is achieved. In short, we believe that taking into consideration the care professionals' relationship to the work activity makes it possible to gain a better understanding of how they negotiate different goals. In this study, the participants' sensitive relationship to work activity objects consists in letting themselves be affected by them, in letting their feelings emerge when interacting with them.

This sensitive relationship does not only pertain to the objects related to "caring" but also to those more rational objects associated with "curing." Thus, the more ways subjects are able to relate to the object of their work activity, the more opportunities they have for developing their capacity for action. In other words, the twofold development of the analytical and sensitive dimensions of the work activity goes hand in hand with the development of the participants' power to act. Though the sensitive experience of the work activity seemed to be more common among the nurses who took part in the training sessions, we believe these dimensions of sensitivity are just as prevalent among the junior doctors who participated. They are simply less verbalized and, therefore, less visible. A debriefing session integrating the verbalization of the work activity in all of these areas is therefore a promising avenue for helping the participants develop a greater sense of agency at the workplace.

References

Bationo-Tillon, A. (2013). Ergonomie et domaine muséal. *Activités, 10*(2), 82–108. http://www.activites.org/v110n102/v110n102.pdf

Bationo-Tillon, A., & Decortis, F. (2016). Understanding museum activity to contribute to the design of tools for cultural mediation: New dimensions of activity? *Le travail humain, 1*(76), 53–70. https://doi.org/10.3917/th.791.0053

Bationo-Tillon, A., Lahoual, D., Alexandre, D., Mateev, C., Tichadou, C., & Decortis, F. (2013). Les activités muséales et les médiations culturelles: de nouveaux terrains d'études et de nouvelles collaborations pour l'ergonomie. *Article soumis au 48e Congrès de la Self 2013.*

Baugnon, T., Duracher, C., Jacquelet, E., Le Ficher, G., Perié, A. C., & Orliaguet, G. (2015). Communication et simulation en anesthésie-réanimation pédiatrique: retour d'une expérience pilote. *Anesthésie & Réanimation, 1*, A129. https://doi.org/10.1016/j.anrea.2015.07.199

Béguin, P., & Pastré, P. (2002). Working, learning and designing through simulation. In S. Bagnara, S. Pozzi, A. Rizzo, & R. Wright (Eds.), 11th European conference on cognitive ergonomics : Cognition, culture and design, (pp. 5–13). Catania, Italy.

Bergström, J., Petersen, K., & Dahlström, N. (2008, October 28–30). Securing organizational resilience in escalating situations. Development of skills for crisis and disaster management. In E. Hollnagel, F. Pieri, & E. Rigaud (Eds.), *3rd International symposium on resilience engineering* (pp. 11–17). Antibes - Juan-les-Pins, France.

Bizouarn, P. (2007). Evidence-based medicine: méthodes et critiques. *Annales Françaises d'Anesthésie et de Réanimation, 26*(4), 334–343.

Böhle, F., & Milkau, B. (1998). *De la manivelle à l'écran. L'évolution de l'expérience sensible des ouvriers lors des changements technologiques*. Eyrolles.

Bonnet, T. (2020). *La régulation sociale du risque émotionnel au travail*: Octarès Editions.

Bouchot, H., & Leblanc, S. (2019). Observer ses pairs lors de séances de simulation haute-fidélité: une activité de nature ludique portée par des en-jeux sérieux. *Activités*, (16–2).

Bourgeois, F., & Hubault, F. (2005). Prévenir les TMS. De la biomécanique à la revalorisation du travail, l'analyse du geste dans toutes ses dimensions. *Activités, 2*(1), 19–36. http://www.activites.org/v12n11/bourgeois.pdf

Bourgeois, F., Lemarchand, C., Hubault, F., Brun, C., Polin, A., Faucheux, J.-M., ... Albert, E. (2006). *Troubles musculosquelettiques et travail: Quand la santé interroge l'organisation.* Editions de l'ANACT.

Bourquin, C., & Stiefel, F. (2017). Formation à la communication clinique: malaise dans la médecine [Training in communication: medicine and its discontents]. *Revue Médicale Suisse, 13*(549), 350–352.

Breton, H. (2019). La reconnaissance des savoirs expérientiels du patient : Repenser les capacités narratives en éducation thérapeutique. *Reconnaissance, validation et certification des acquis de l'expérience au Portugal, France, Belgique et Italie, 2019.*

Cahour, B. (2010). Émotions, affects et confort comme nouveaux déterminants de l'activité et de l'usage. In G. Valléry, M.-C. Le Port, & M. Zouinar (Eds.), *Ergonomie, conception de produits et services médiatisés* (pp. 273–305). Presses Universitaires de France.

Cahour, B., & Lancry, A. (2011). Émotions et activités professionnelles et quotidiennes. *Le Travail Humain, 74*(2), 97. https://doi.org/10.3917/th.742.0097

Caroly, S., & Clot, Y. (2004). Du travail collectif au collectif de travail. Des conditions de développement des stratégies d'expérience. *Formation et Emploi, 88*, 43–55.

Caroly, S., & Weill-Fassina, A. (2004a). Développement des compétences professionnelles et collectif de travail aux guichets de la Poste. *Bulletin de psychologie, 57*(1, 469), 49–53.

Caroly, S., & Weill-Fassina, A. (2004b). Evolutions des régulations de situations critiques au cours de la vie professionnelle dans des activités de relations de service. *Le Travail Humain, 67*(4), 304–327.

Ciccone, E., Cuvelier, L., Baugnon, T., Orliaguet, G., & Decortis, F. (2018). Qu'apprenons-nous du travail à travers la formation: étude exploratoire sur une situation de communication difficile en pédiatrie. *TransFormations-Recherche en Education et Formation des Adultes*, (18).
Clot, Y., & Leplat, J. (2005). La méthode clinique en ergonomie et en psychologie du travail. *Le Travail Humain, 68*(4), 289–316. https://doi.org/10.3917/th.684.0289
Cuvelier, L. (2018). "Never the first time on a patient:" the stakes of high-fidelity simulation for safety training. *Development and Learning in Organizations: An International Journal, 32*(5), 23–25. https://doi.org/10.1108/DLO-09-2018-131
Damasio, A. R. (2010). *L'erreur de Descartes : La raison des émotions* (M. Blanc, Trad.). Odile Jacob.
Daniellou, F., & Rabardel, P. (2005). Activity-oriented approaches to ergonomics: Some traditions and communities. *Theoretical Issues in Ergonomics Science, 6*(5), 353–357.
Decortis, F., Bationo-Tillon, A., & Cuvelier, L. (2016). Penser et concevoir pour le développement du sujet tout au long de la vie: de l'enfant dans sa vie quotidienne à l'adulte en situation de travail. *Activités, 13*(2), mis en ligne le 15 octobre 2016, consulté le 2018 octobre 2016. doi:https://doi.org/10.4000/activites.2909.
Eyland, I. (2017). *Les savoirs professionnels liés au care chez les infirmiers libéraux: construction d'un outil d'analyse des gestes professionnels liés au care dans des situations de soins.* Université Montpellier.
Eyland, I., & Jean, A. (2016). Exercice et apprentissage du métier d'infirmier: à la recherche du Care. *Éducation et socialisation. Les Cahiers du CERFEE, 40.*
Eyland, I., & Leblanc, S. (2019). Comprendre l'activité des infirmiers libéraux: légitimation de gestes professionnels liés au care dans une visée formative. *Activités*, (16-1).
Flageul-Caroly, S. (2001). *Régulations individuelles et collectives des situations critiques dans un secteur des services: le guichet de la Poste.* Thèse de doctorat en ergonomie, EPHE- LEPC .
Flandin, S., Poizat, G., & Perinet, R. (2019). *Contribuer à la sécurité industrielle "par le facteur humain." Un regard pour aider à (re) penser la formation*: Regard, Foncsi.
Fletcher, G., Flin, R., McGeorge, P., Glavin, R., Maran, N., & Patey, R. (2003). Anaesthetists' Non-Technical Skills (ANTS): Evaluation of a behavioural marker system. *British Journal of Anaesthesia, 90*(5), 580–588. https://doi.org/10.1093/bja/aeg112
Goupy, F., Abgrall-Barbry, G., Aslangul, E., Chahwakilian, A., Delaitre, D., Girard, T., Lassaunière, J.-M., Roche, N., Szwebel, T.-A., Dantchev, N., Triadou, P., & Le Jeunne, C. (2013). L'enseignement de la médecine narrative peut-il être une réponse à l'attente de formation des étudiants à la relation médecin–malade ? *La Presse Médicale, 42*(1), e1–e8. https://doi.org/10.1016/j.lpm.2012.09.012
Greenhalgh, T. (1999). Narrative based medicine : Narrative based medicine in an evidence based world. *BMJ, 318*(7179), 323–325. https://doi.org/10.1136/bmj.318.7179.323
Haute Autorité de Santé. (2012). Rapport de mission. *État de l'art (national et international) en matière de pratiquesde simu-lation dans le domaine de la santé.* HAS.
Hesbeen, W. (2002). Care strategy. Care knowledge, between art and science. *Soins; la revue de reference infirmiere*, (666), 49–52.
Hirata, H., & Molinier, P. (2012). Les ambiguïtés du care. *Travailler*, (2), 9–13.
Horcik, Z., Savoldelli, G., Poizat, G., & Durand, M. (2014). A phenomenological approach to novice nurse anesthetists' experience during simulation-based training sessions: *Simulation in healthcare. The Journal of the Society for Simulation in Healthcare, 9*(2), 94–101. https://doi.org/10.1097/SIH.0000000000000021
Huet, D. G., Rosenstrauch, C., & Carlier, D. (2016). *Communication avec les soignants et les familles.*
Klein, A. (2014). La figure du bon médecin : Du rôle des mythes épistémologiques dans le processus de professionnalisation de la médecine française. *Recherche & formation, 76*, 61–78. https://doi.org/10.4000/rechercheformation.2236
Lalau, J.-D. (2021). Le cure et le care. *Médecine des Maladies Métaboliques, 15*(1), 99–103.

Ministre des affaires sociales et de la santé. (2013). Rappport d'activité 2013. Direction générale de l'offre de soin 2013

Mayen, P. (2009). Activité et individualisation. *Savoirs*, (3), 53–64.

Molinier, P. (2006). *Les enjeux psychiques du travail. Introduction à la psychodynamique du travail*. Petite Bibliothèque Payot.

Molinier, P. (2013). *Le travail du care*. Dispute (La).

Pastré, P. (2005). Apprendre par la simulation: de l'analyse du travail aux apprentissages professionnels.. Octarès éditions.

Pernet, A. (2013). *Coproduire un soin sûr et efficace: le développement des capabilités des patients en radiothérapie*. CNAM.

Rosa, H. (2018). *Résonance: Une sociologie de la relation au monde*. La Découverte.

Rudolph, J. W., Simon, R., Rivard, P., Dufresne, R. L., & Raemer, D. B. (2007). Debriefing with good judgment: Combining rigorous feedback with genuine inquiry. *Anesthesiology Clinics, 25*(2), 361–376.

Salmon, P., & Young, B. (2011). Creativity in clinical communication: From communication skills to skilled communication. *Medical Education, 45*(3), 217–226.

Samurçay, R., & Rogalski, J. (1998). Exploitation didactique des situations de simulation. *Le Travail Humain, 61*(4), 333–359.

Sawyer, T., Eppich, W., Brett-Fleegler, M., Grant, V., & Cheng, A. (2016). More than one way to debrief: A critical review of healthcare simulation debriefing methods. *Simulation in Healthcare, 11*(3), 209–217.

Vermersch, P. (1994). *L'entretien d'explicitation*. 7ème édition (2011). ESF.

Part III
Promising Avenues for Simulation Training Design and Research

The third and last part is a prospective discussion and extension to the preceding chapters. The authors have been asked to react to the chapters, to expose complementary views, and/or to establish the connections between the content of the book and its implications for simulation training research and design.

New Questions for Interventions and Research in Simulation Training Based on Actors' Activity

Janine Rogalski

Abstract This chapter stresses specificities of care situations for designing simulations for training caregivers. Caregiving is considered as a particular case of dynamic management, where the activity is oriented toward other human subjects and is also "distributed" in temporal and organizational dimensions. Leplat's model of "double regulation of activity" is used as a key framework. It is extended beyond the initial focus on individual activity and takes into account the various temporalities of caregivers' actions. Rasmussen's three levels of functioning are considered: skill-based (routine situations, linked to caregivers' experiences), rule-based (applying predefined rules of action) and knowledge-based (when facing unusual cases). This analysis is then used for transposing the care-related dimensions from situations of action to training situations via simulation. Several challenges are stressed for their design: beyond the construction of "empathic" representations of the other who is the "object" of care they include the acquisition of a flexibility in caregivers' levels of functioning, both for adapting to their "patient" and for preserving their own health. Broad avenues remain open to research and action in this complex issue of simulation in the care domain.

Keywords Design of training simulations · Transposition · Double regulation of activity · Levels of functioning · Caregivers

J. Rogalski (✉)
André Revuz Didactics Laboratory (LADR), Université de Paris, Univ Paris Est Creteil, CY Cergy Paris Université, Univ. Lille, UNIROUEN, Paris, France

S. Flandin et al. (eds.), *Simulation Training through the Lens of Experience and Activity Analysis*, Professional and Practice-based Learning 30,
https://doi.org/10.1007/978-3-030-89567-9_14

1 Introduction

It was from a double point of view that I read the publication coordinated by Simon Flandrin, Christine Vidal-Gomel, and Raquel Becerril Ortega: the point of view of the French-speaking ergonomics psychology community – in the footsteps of Jacques Leplat and that of professional didactics – in line with the works of Pierre Pastré in which analyzing the activity of a subject already on the job is used to organize the interventions for training new actors. This point of view differs from the CHAT (*cultural-historical activity theory*) developed by Engeström who used it to analyze learning (Engeström & Sannino, 2010), since we focus on individual actors instead of a more complex system of activity in which they would be integrated, as well as on situations seen as crucial determining factors of the activity, without getting centered on the instruments of action. Simulation situations appear to be good candidates to help trainees develop skills, as well as situations of action, which are also potential means to develop skills (Savoyant, 2010b/2005).

The aforementioned work had me raise some questions about simulation used for training purposes, around which this paper is organized. A very important specificity of those situations is the fact that some individual is intervening both as the object of the action (for care, help, etc.) and as the active and interactive subject in relation to other participants. Models of activity, designed in cognitive ergonomics, were initially elaborated to analyze situations in the field of industry: they must thus be subjected to a significant transposition process. The same can be said of the design and making of professional training sessions or sequences and all the more so of the design and use of simulation situations as analyzed by this school of thought. We will start with presenting the directions in which the categories of situations that could be grounds for simulation-based training have been broadened. We will outline the adaptation of Leplat's framework model (1981) to the objectives of care training, acknowledging factors that are important for that transposition. They are mostly organizational factors, in what context do care activities occur – in an institution or at the "patient's" home – and temporal factors: is it a one-off intervention such as the accompaniment of a nursing act with appeasing words or gestures? Is it the care activity that a care professional or family member acting as a caregiver performs throughout their working day or week or even their whole career? Finally, we will question the diverse modalities of transposition of the target situations – which should be mastered by the end of the training course – into simulation situations for training, in order to take into account the care-related dimension of an activity that is directed toward another person (from hospital care to home support).

2 Evolution of the Categories of Simulation-Based Training Situations

For very many years, simulation has been used as a double-edged tool: for researchers and for trainers who analyze the activity of professionals on the job with a view to design training courses (Béguin & Weill-Fassina, 1997). Regarding this particular use of simulation for training purposes, works in the field of ergonomics psychology (or cognitive ergonomics) have initially dealt with material situations, primarily in the aviation sector, and related to industrial processes and other similar dynamic processes (Bainbridge & Quintanilla, 1989). Process management analysis was also transposed into specific human interaction situations. It has been the case with the activity of teachers in class (Rogalski, 2013; Goigoux et al., 2015). Clearly, this was not enough to go beyond the analysis of activity and think out a transposition in terms of simulation for teachers' training. We can point out in particular that in a "strict" – or blind! – transposition, we are faced with the following problem: "Is it possible – and if so, how – to transpose pupils, who are at once the objects of the teachers' actions, and subjects of their own learning processes?" This difficulty is somewhat subdued if we integrate the fact that the objective is not to simulate "the object of the action" but "the situation of action." This shift in perspective was developed in the special issue of the journal *Le travail humain*, coordinated by Samurçay and De Keyser (1998). It consists in questioning the extent to which the activity in a simulation situation represents the activity in the target situation and prepares trainees to handle it. In the field of teachers' training, the most accurate simulation situation seems to be the one in which teachers take on the role of pupils. It is the case, for instance, when a new content is integrated to the curriculum they are in charge of. Trainers help teachers familiarize themselves with this new content, and the teachers – possibly with the trainers' help – must transpose this situation that they have experienced as students into the teaching they will provide to their own pupils. It is that very same perspective that was favored in Lang's research (2001), whose objective was to introduce ergonomics in initial professional training courses, so that the students, as future operators, could become ergonomics-savvy stakeholders and thus contribute to the prevention of occupational risks. Teachers were put in the position of students: after being taught about the concepts by teachers-researchers, they had to conduct an analysis of the activity of operators in situation and report the results found. After this experience, they were required to prepare their future teachings. In didactical mathematics, this type of simulation has been called "homology-based training" (Robert & Vivier, 2013); it can thus also be used in professional training.

A similar simulation situation can exist, but only under specific conditions of activity: it is called "modeling-based" training. The trainer works "as closely as possible" with the student or apprentice and makes the content of his activity explicit; the student/apprentice follows and reproduces the trainer's actions, which models their own actions.

We can interpret in terms of "modeling" a situation where a trainer films a lecture given in front of simulated students/apprentices, so that teachers-in-training can later reproduce in their actual work situations what the "model" has done in the recording, which they get to watch and analyze. Here, notably, some properties of video recording are exploited: the possibility to freeze the image or go backward allows for a detailed observation and a finer analysis. We personally participated in one of those training sessions, acting as a trainee (Janine Rogalski and Renan Samurçay). A video recording focusing on the trainer was taken in order to be used as a model by the next trainer. In this particular case, the trainer must mobilize their acting skills, since they must consider the simulation in front of them as an actual group of professionals attending a training course.

This modeling-based training can be seen as a derived form of "teach your twin" training (Oddone et al., 1981; Saujat, 2004). We chose to allude briefly to those examples, since care situations share an essential property with training situations: the object of the action is another human subject with their own autonomy, and simulation situations for training purposes thus pose partly similar problems.

We are now going to present a framework for analysis that will allow us to orient and specify the questions that can be raised in these types of simulation-based training courses: i.e., the model of double regulation of activity proposed by Leplat (1981, 1997). We will then propose a list of questions that should be answered in the study, design and use of such simulation situations.

3 A Framework Model for Analyzing Care-Related Activity and Designing Simulation Situations: Leplat's Double Regulation of Activity Model

In the collective work he published, *Apprendre par la simulation. De l'analyse du travail aux apprentissages professionnels* (*Learning through simulation. From work analysis to professional training,* 2015), Pastré develops the idea that the link between the analysis of activity and the use of work situations for training purposes is at the core of professional didactics,[1] these two dimensions walking hand in hand. Daniellou and Rabardel (Daniellou, 2005; Daniellou & Rabardel, 2005) restated the key principles of the French-speaking world's ergonomics tradition and specified the links between this tradition and the input contributed by the theories of activity developed in Russia in the footsteps of Vygotski (1978) and Leontiev (1979). Here we will use one of the components of this very same research tradition, initiated by Leplat: the double regulation of activity model (1997).

[1] Professional didactics is a school of thought that allies research and intervention in professional training and relies at once on the contributions of Leplat's cognitive ergonomics and Vergnaud's model of conceptualization in action (2009). Mayen (2015) gives a detailed presentation of it.

This model, introduced and developed in work psychology by Leplat (1997), is a conceptual tool which we are going to use to present the dynamics of activity in a care-related situation.[2] The analysis of activity, its conditions, and the professional skills involved were first brought into play for studying the security of systems (Leplat, 1981) and human-machine interactions (Leplat, 1989; de Montmollin, 1991) and then for designing computer systems. We will then propose a model for care-related activity, drawing inspiration from the work done in the studies related to teachers' activity.

Leplat's model is built around two main ideas: the double determination of the activity and the effects produced by it being carried out. This model can be directly transposed in the case of collective activity (Leplat, 1994, p. 213), which allows for the analysis to go beyond individual stakeholders. On the one hand, the activity is determined by factors that are related to both the situation which the activity responds to and the subject who develops it; on the other hand, a subject's action has effects both on the object targeted by this action (the target-state) and on the subject themselves. Darses presents the state of the works relying on activity analysis: "[...] from a psychological point of view, as the product of a coupling between a task (which provides external determinants), and a subject (who provides internal determinants)" (Darses, 2016, p. 193). The activity in itself is motivated by personal and social factors (it is always "addressed" to another person – or several other people); it aims at reaching goals and organizes operations to achieve them (Leontiev, 1979; Savoyant, 2010a/1979).

The regulation of the activity is due to the fact that it changes over time according to two types of effects produced depending on the subject's intentions. The first dimension of this regulation is taking into account the state in which the action has put the object, compared to what the goal of the action was. This regulation is well-known in learning psychology, but also as an effect of professional experience. The second dimension of the regulation is the adaptation of the activity according to its impact on the stakeholder themselves (their tiredness, their interest, their emotions, their social relationships at work, etc.). It can lead them, for instance, to carry out the most complicated operations first: this is called regulation by anticipation and helps prevent risks (see, e.g., Clot & Simonet, 2015).

The initial double regulation model does not specify over what time span the action is being considered, but it can be completed and adapted to various temporalities. In the field of work, we can distinguish three main time spans that are relevant; they correspond to three levels of "granularity" in the analysis of the subject's activity (be it individual or collective). At *micro* level, the activity is analyzed over a "short" time span (depending on the object of the action and the dynamics at play: it can be only a few seconds long in the case of plane piloting). For people-oriented tasks, it can be a specific intervention for a patient in an institution or at home (helping the patient shower, doing the dishes, tidying up the room, etc.). For training

[2] We use the term "situation" to refer to the task system, with a system of resources and constraints, within an organization of stakeholders and prescribers. We can see this term as a development of Leplat's definition of task (following Leontiev, op. cit.): a goal to reach under certain conditions.

situations, it can be a practical exercise that the trainee must carry out. At *meso*-level, the whole duration of the activity in a specific work position is being considered: for a trainer, it corresponds to 1 day of training course or even a whole session and, for care professionals, to their entire working period in one position (or 1 day with the professional's own "patients"). At *macro*-level, we consider the longest time span associated with each kind of task: the school year of a teacher in charge of organizing the implementation of the curriculum in a certain class; a professional training course in the long run; and the long-term activity – depending on the results – of therapists, for example, physiotherapists or speech pathologists.

4 The Regulation of the Care-Related Dimension in a People-Oriented Activity

As far as care is concerned, two different situations must a priori be distinguished. In the first type of situation, the care professionals act within the context of an organization such as that of a hospital or an establishment for dependent people. In the second case, they work with patients who are independent enough to live at home but need help in their day-to-day life.

Two dimensions then take on different values: the temporal dimension of the organization of the activity and the social dimension of collective action. Indeed, within the context of an institution, on the one hand, a group of care professionals is in charge of a number of patients, all in the same location, for the duration of the working day. On the other hand, they have the possibility to help each other perform some care-related actions and must "physically" cooperate with each other (to turn over a bedridden patient, change sheets, help a patient move from their bed to their wheelchair, etc.). The move from one patient to another happens over a short time span, since they all are in the same functional space.

In a work situation at the patient's home, the constraints are different: they are related to the organization and layout of the person's place, the number of at-home visits that must be carried out in a day, the trips that must be taken, the administrative follow-up of the patients, etc. In most cases, professionals who work at the patients' home have comparatively less people in their care than those who work in institutions, but the travel time needed to carry out the necessary visits is a limiting factor and can be stress-inducing. Moreover, those stakeholders cannot get immediate help when an unplanned difficulty arises. The working collective is also more "distant" which makes it more complicated to discuss patients and their care routines as well as talk about various work-related difficulties and exchange views on the way to deal with them. In this case too, albeit not for the same reasons than in institutions, the knowledge that "time is running out" is a factor that puts pressure on the relationship between the professional and the patient and causes tensions in the caregivers' activity. Indeed, care is centered on the interpersonal dimension of the "patient's" well-being. The positive impact of affective social interactions on mental and physical health has been proven: such interactions may need time to develop and produce an effect. Furthermore, the cooperation with other stakeholders mostly takes place remotely, which increases the need for anticipation and, potentially, the caregivers' decision-taking responsibility (we can think of pain management, which depends on a medical decision but is implemented by nurses – in particular when the painkillers can have serious side effects).

5 What Model(s) of Activity Apply for Care Stakeholders?

The question of simulation for training purposes is not limited to the determining elements that we have just gone back over. It calls for an analysis of the activity itself as it is being carried out. One of the goals of training is indeed to outline a reference activity for trainees. The analysis makes it possible to mark out the elements of the activity which care stakeholders are going to be trained for or that will contribute to their development as professionals. The distinction between technical and non-technical skills is well-known in the field of collective work situations analysis: in this case, the non-technical skills are those that are directed toward human interaction during a specific task, as shown by Salas et al. (Bedwell et al., 2014). Here, we focus on those that are at stake in care-related situations that occur between the actors and their "patient."

This analysis can be conducted from two different perspectives: either it is centered on the activity of the "caregiver" actor, who takes another human subject as the object of his action, or it concerns the interaction between two stakeholders, who are in an *request and answer* situation where the caregiver carries out actions that the person cared for cannot perform on their own. From the theoretical point of view of cognitive ergonomics, the first perspective is that of an individual action, whereas the second perspective takes into consideration the activity of a collective, in a strongly dissymmetrical relationship. We chose here to take the first approach in order to analyze the care stakeholders' activity (vis-à-vis those in need of care), taking into account their training goals.[3] Several aspects of the activity can be integrated in the training course.

For instance, a review of questions about care for seriously ill people highlights the expectations related to care: "[it] encompasses the patient and family being respected, given complete information, involved in decision-making and supported in their physical, psychological, social and existential needs. The studies highlight the importance of [...] structuring service organization to enable care continuity" (authors' abstract, Giusti et al., 2020).

We also keep in mind the works of Naweed, Stahlut, and Keeffe (2021) whose detailed analyses are consistent with Leplat's model (op. cit.) and allow us to

[3] We nevertheless also mention here the specific situations created by long-term illnesses or pathologies, where the patients can become "expert patients" and interact with care professionals on an equal footing.

identify a number of avenues for reflection about stakeholders' training. They bring to light determining factors of the situation that can have negative effects on the activity being carried out and its results on the patient's care, their well-being, or even that of the care professionals themselves: "contextual factors in scenarios highlighted inadequate staffing and procedures, inadequate training, challenging residents, time poverty, and low support." From the perspective of the caregivers' activity, they underline the development of "close relationships with residents, influencing care provision but blurring personal boundaries" (which, by contrast, highlights the necessity to maintain professional detachment). The results of these works (op. cit.) bring to light the occurrence of adaptation processes in the course of the activity: "individually directed adaptive strategies [...] used to alleviate dissonance and maintain emotional resilience" and the place of diagnosis and prognosis processes, "including dynamic risk assessment involving rule breaking." Their analyses were conducted at the *macro-* or *meso*-levels of analysis of the activity (expected or carried out).

One element that seems to have been left out of the studies in this questions' review is the management of the tension that exists between the various goals related to the same "patient," i.e., carrying out a care or help-related action for the patient's benefit while also interacting with them in a quality way. Achieving this type of joined objectives is an integral part of the short-term activity of caregivers (at the *meso*-level of granularity in the analysis of activity). This type of goal can give rise to the elaboration of collective strategies. For instance, in an ongoing research survey, we can identify a strategy for managing aggressiveness in elderly patients suffering from cognitive impairments during their washing routine.[4] This particularly complicated and hazardous moment relies on a specific distribution of tasks: one of the caregivers attentively interacts with the patient in order to divert their attention from the ongoing washing, while the other caregiver carries out the washing gestures. The interaction becomes more intensive at the trickiest moments. Strategies of that kind are precious for initial and ongoing training. They can be analyzed, debated, and improved. They participate at once in the prevention of occupational risks and the fostering of the patient's well-being. Those compromises that can be identified in the analysis of activity at micro-level can occur in every type of care or home support organization.

In the paragraphs above, we have oriented our questioning toward the care-related dimension of an activity directed toward another person. This dimension can also be present in collective actions between co-workers (in "horizontal cooperation" as in the example mentioned) or between stakeholders in a hierarchical relationship (in "vertical cooperation"). Examples of this have been given in this book, about stakeholders in civil security or police forces, highlighting the possibility to design simulations for their training (see Dubois, Vandertrate, & Van Daele's chapter). Furthermore, the hierarchical relationship can also be used for care-related purposes in order to circumvent defensive behaviors; for instance, a rescue

[4] R. Renaudin, Master student, University of Nantes, personal communication

operations chief systematically requests the services of a hospital psychiatrist for first-responder firefighters under his command when they have been confronted to tragic situations affecting people, thus avoiding possible denial regarding the psychological impact of their intervention.[5] In this case, it is not easy to see how the situation could be transposed and integrated in a relevant manner into the training of new chief first responders.

6 Transposing the Care-Related Dimension from Situations of Action to Training Situations via Simulation

The model of activity analysis we worked on shows the diversity of perspectives that can be considered and makes it possible to orient the transposition of those objectives and the characteristics of the target situations toward simulation-based training. It allows us to see the impact of the choice of components and the relationships at play in the target situations that will be reproduced in a simulation situation according to the goals of the training course.

Another dimension of the analysis of activity for training purposes, and its transposition into didactic simulations, is that of the three levels of functioning in a work situation, developed by J. Rasmussen (1983), i.e., respectively, the skill-based, rule-based, and knowledge-based levels. At skill-based level, routines of professional functioning and automatisms are at play; at rule-based level, the stakeholder draws from a basis of action processes that can be expressed in terms of involvement: "in case of situation S1, carry out action A1." At a knowledge-based level, the stakeholder is faced with a problem of which he must design the resolution (or to which he must find an acceptable enough solution). It is easy to see that the level that is most easily transposed into training is the one that aims at assimilating rules (rule-based level) by adapting into simulations a series of cases in which this or that rule will be applicable. It seems to us that it is this level that is at stake, for instance, in Naweed, Stahlut, and 0'Keeffe's analyses (2021), which consider that "versatility as an adaptive response to challenges [...]" in elderly people's care is the "essence of care."

The skill-based level is very strongly linked to the multiplicity of experiences that have thus become sedimented (Rogalski & Leplat, 2011): in initial training, it can thus be aimed at for professional development, relying on oriented simulations called "drills" – i.e., learning through rehearsal, repetition, and practice of a task – based on repeated interactions with a high-physical-fidelity simulator.

A simulator with a high functional fidelity but a low physical one will only be appropriate for knowledge-based processes, while a simulation that is faithful on a conceptual level but modifies the conditions of information gathering and action in

[5] Personal communication. Anonymity was requested.

the target situation will pose problems with regard to the processes of representation of the situation (indispensable for functioning at rule-based level).

In the field of care, simulation can, for instance, aim at building up a representation of this "other, sick or elderly" who is the object of a trainees' action. Thus, Eost-Telling et al. (2021) present "ageing *simulation equipment*" (impeding movements and walk, affecting sight and hearing, etc.) to enable caregivers in training "to undergo experiences which potentially affect older patients and by asking the learner to act the role of patient this may be more effective in developing greater empathy [...]." The authors, however, do not underestimate conceptual and theoretical training (which aims at reaching knowledge-based level) but use that simulation "to challenge ageist attitudes and behaviour."

The question of taking into account the three levels of functioning in the prospect of designing and performing simulation situations, which has already been raised in Rogalski (1997), brings up another, much trickier question: what role can simulations play in the process of acquiring a particular component of professional skill, i.e., the possibility to switch from one level of functioning to another over the course of the activity? It seems to us that this last question has hardly been explored by research in the field of professional activity analysis and that it is particularly crucial in situations of action exerted "on" or directed "toward" another person, when it comes to training professionals to take into account the care-related dimension of such situations.

We hope to show that broad avenues are still open to research and action in the schools of thought that mobilize theories on activity, with a both an epistemic and a pragmatic dimension.

References

Bedwell, W. L., Fiore, S. M., & Salas, E. (2014). Developing the future workforce: An approach for integrating interpersonal skills into the MBA classroom. *Academy of Management Learning & Education, 13*, 171–186. https://doi.org/10.5465/amle.2011.0138

Clot, Y., & Simonet, P. (2015). Pouvoirs d'agir et marges de manœuvre. *Le travail humain, 1*(1), 31–52.

Daniellou, F. (2005). The French-speaking ergonomists' approach to work activity: Cross-influences of field intervention and conceptual models. *Theoretical Issues in Ergonomics Science, 6*(5), 409–427.

Daniellou, F., & Rabardel, P. (2005). Activity-oriented approaches to ergonomics: Some traditions and communities. *Theoretical Issues in Ergonomics Science, 6*(5), 353–357.

Darses, F. (2016). Activity analysis: Not what it was! *Le travail humain, 79*(3), 193–208.

de Montmollin, M. (1991). Analysis and modelling of operators' activities. In J. Rasmussen, H. B. Andersen, & N. O. Bernsen (Eds.), *Human-computer interaction (Research direction in cognitive science, European perspective)* (Vol. 3, pp. 95–112). Lawrence Erlbaum.

Engeström, Y., & Sannino, A. (2010). Studies of expansive learning: Foundations, findings and future challenges. *Educational Research Review, 5*(1), 1–24. https://doi.org/10.1016/j.edurev.2009.12.002.

Eost-Telling, C., Kingston, P., Taylor, L., & Emmerson, L. (2021). Ageing simulation in health and social care education: A mixed methods systematic review. *Journal of Advanced Nursing, 27*(1), 23–46.
Giusti, A., Nkhoma, K., Petrus, R., et al. (2020). The empirical evidence underpinning the concept and practice of person-centred care for serious illness: A systematic review. *BMJ Global Health, 5*, e003330.
Goigoux, R., Riou, J., & Serres, G. (2015). La régulation de l'action des enseignants. *Travail et Apprentissages, 1*(1), 66–83.
Lang, N. (2001). Comprendre et transformer les situations de travail quand on est enseignant en lycée professionnel ? Les apports d'une formation à l'analyse ergonomique. *Formation Emploi, 74*, 37–52.
Leontiev, A. (1979). The problem of activity in psychology. In J. V. Wertsch (Ed.), *The concept of activity in Soviet psychology* (pp. 37–71). M.E. Sharpe.
Leplat J. (1981) Task analysis and activity analysis in situations of field diagnosis. In: J. Rasmussen, & W. B.Rouse (Eds.), *Human detection and diagnosis of system failures* (Vol. 15, pp. 287–300). NATO Conference Series. Springer.
Leplat, J. (1989). Simulation and simulators in training: Some comments. In L. Bainbridge & S. A. Ruiz Quintanilla (Eds.), *Developing skills with information technology* (pp. 277–292). Wiley.
Leplat, J. (1994). Collective activity in work: Some lines of research. *Le travail humain, 57*(3), 209–226.
Mayen, P. (2015). Vocational didactics: Work, learning, and conceptualization. In L. Filletaz & S. Billet (Eds.), *Francophone perspectives of learning through work: Conceptions, traditions and practices* (pp. 201–219). Springer International Publishing.
Naweed, A., Stahlut, J., & 0'Keeffe, V. (2021). The essence of care: Versability as an adaptive response to challenges in the delivery of quality aged care by personal care attendants. *Human Factors*. https://journals.sagepub.com/doi/pdf/10.1177/00187208211010962
Oddone, I., Re, A., & Briante, G. (1981). *Redécouvrir l'expérience ouvrière*. Éditions sociales.
Rasmussen, J. (1983). Skills, rules and knowledge; signals, signs, and symbols, and other distinctions in human performance models. *IEEE Transactions on Systems, Man, and Cybernetics, 3*, 257–266.
Robert, A., & Vivier, L. (2013). Analyser des vidéos sur les pratiques des enseignants du second degré en mathématiques: des utilisations contrastées en recherche en didactique et en formation de formateurs – quelle transposition ? *Éducation et didactique, 7*(2), 115–144.
Rogalski, J. (2013). Theory of activity and developmental approaches for an analysis of teachers' practices and students' activities. In F. Vandebrouck (Ed.), *Mathematics classrooms. Students' activities and teachers' practices* (pp. 3-22). Sense Publishers.
Rogalski, J. (1997). Simulation dans la formation à la gestion d'environnement dynamique: approche de didactique professionnelle. In M. Baron, P. Mendelsohn, & J.-F. Nicaud (Eds.), *EIAO'97 Environnements Interactifs d'Apprentissage avec Ordinateur* (pp. 25–36). Hermès.
Rogalski, J., & Leplat, J. (2011). L'expérience professionnelle: expériences sédimentées et expériences épisodiques. *Activités, 8*(2), 4–31.
Samurçay, R., & de Keyser, V. (Eds.). (1998). Théorie de l'activité, action située et simulateurs. *Le Travail humain, 61*(4), 305–312.
Saujat, F. (2004). Comment les enseignants débutants entrent dans le métier. *Formation et pratiques d'enseignement en questions, 1*, 97–106.
Savoyant, A. (2010a/1979). Éléments d'un cadre d'analyse de l'activité: quelques conceptions essentielles de la psychologie soviétique. *Travail et Apprentissages, 1*(1), 91–107.
Savoyant, A. (2010b/2005). L'activité en situation de simulation: objet d'analyse et moyen de développement. *Travail et Apprentissages, 1*(1), 125–142.
Vergnaud, G. (2009). The theory of conceptual fields. *Human Development, 52*, 83–94.

Simulation in Healthcare, a Resource in Times of Crisis. A Look Back and a Look Forward

Eliana Escudero

Abstract The use of CRM-based curriculum has been implemented in the field of health education and training, and evidence shows that there are changes in behavior and improvements in teamwork performance; however, it is necessary to continue researching their impact on the organization and patient safety (Levine et al (eds), The comprehensive textbook of healthcare simulation. Springer, New York, 2013; Salas et al, J Hum Factors Ergonom Soc 48(2): 392–412, 2006). The Covid-19 crisis has affected patient safety that of clinical teams, and healthcare organizations, leading to reflections on outstanding challenges in the use of simulation as a standard in healthcare training that should lead to a safety culture (Park et al, Manifesto for healthcare simulation practice. BMJ Simulation and Technology Enhanced Learning. Published Online First: 04 September 2020, 2020; Hardeep Singh et al, BMJ Qual Safety 30: 141–145, 2020). Simulation modalities provide answers to many different objectives, and professionals must get trained to make the best use of this powerful education tool through different modalities that make it possible to harness its strengths (Levine et al (eds), The comprehensive textbook of healthcare simulation. Springer, New York, 2013; Posner et al, Adv Simul 2: 1–5, 2017). SBE and training-based simulation will solve many existing problems in the healthcare field that were mentioned since Kohn's publication more than 20 years ago (Kohn et al., (eds), To err is human: building safer healthcare system. National Academy Press, Washington, DC, 2000).

Keywords Simulation · Training · Healthcare · Crisis · Patient safety

E. Escudero (✉)
Facultad de Salud y Odontologia, Universidad Diego Portales, Santiago, Chile
e-mail: eliana.escudero@udp.cl

S. Flandin et al. (eds.), *Simulation Training through the Lens of Experience and Activity Analysis*, Professional and Practice-based Learning 30,
https://doi.org/10.1007/978-3-030-89567-9_15

1 Introduction

The book publication from 2000 entitled *To Err is Human* (Kohn et al., 2000) suggested that medical errors can occur in any medical service process. These errors are committed by individuals or teams and can lead to harm or death. Statistics on these errors reach levels from other high-risk industries or even surpass them (Ibid, p. 67). Simulation has emerged as a method to improve the performance of clinical teams and prevent medical errors (Ibid, p. 78, 79). Several authors recognize this publication as the starting point for the current perspective of simulation-based education (SBE) (Foysi-Doll & Leighton, 2018). In 2007, the Latin American Association for Clinical Simulation (ALASIC) was established as a network of educators, researchers, and professionals from different disciplines working on issues related to patient safety. It then became a federation in 2019 to be able to be an entity that accepts societies from countries in the region (FLASIC, 2020). A boost from the World Health Organization (WHO) since 2004 has formalized research attention in patient safety (World Health Organization, Patient Safety, 2021).

Two types of errors co-exist within healthcare teams: technical errors and non-technical errors. Non-technical errors are most frequent, primarily due to mistakes related to communication, teamwork, division of tasks, leadership, etc. These errors increase during crisis situations along with human factor errors (Rall & Dieckmann, 2005). Crisis resource management models have been practiced in healthcare based on proposals from the anesthesiologist Gaba. This proposal, termed crisis resource management (CRM), is employed as part of the simulation-based education method (Rall & Dieckmann, 2005). Simulation is a training tool used in industries involving human activity, such as aeronautic, nuclear, military, etc., and it has entered the healthcare industry with the aviation model (Gaba, 2004). However, in healthcare, certification of skills is not required prior to the first patient encounter. In other industries, professionals must attain the corresponding certifications or accredit certain skills to be able to practice in their respective occupational field (Sujin Shin et al., 2015). For example, in the field of commercial, tourism, and military aviation, a pilot is not authorized to fly unless he/she has guaranteed flight hours under different scenarios in a flight simulator. In the world of healthcare, certification of proficiencies is done with human beings and not through simulation.

SBE is considered to be an andragogic model for adult learning in a protected, controlled, and designed environment, according to requirements, and for it to be applicable (Corvetto et al., 2013; Levine et al., 2013). It allows the learner to control and plan their achievements from the novice stage up until attaining certain proficiencies or ultimately an expert status. The teacher takes on a role of facilitator and provides support for the student to make progress by using the deliberate practice model (Gonzalez & Edgren, 2017), for example.

Scientific societies and associations that work for patient safety promote and suggest incorporating this method for undergraduate and graduate education (Foysi-Doll & Leighton, 2018). According to this same outlook, arguments are made for it to be integrated into continuing education, the purpose of which is to achieve patient safety and a culture of safety in healthcare (Park et al., 2020). Training healthcare professionals in simulated scenarios is part of lifelong learning in some health institutions and has successfully contributed to reducing errors (Weinger & Gaba, 2014).

Remote learning is being encouraged within the context of crisis brought about by the COVID pandemic. The notion of using simulation in different modalities is also being promoted (Kronick, 2014). During the 2014 Ebola pandemic, Kronick, the Director of the Agency for Health Care Research and Quality (AHQS) at the time, confirmed the importance of having guidelines in place and training on protocols for the healthcare team based on simulation to control the health problem. Identifying cracks in the safety chain is critical, and simulation is the tool for this, both for recognizing individual and team breaches (Kronick, 2014). Other arguments for expanding SBE are the need to practice, correct, and prepare for a similar or new situation (Kronick, 2014).

The issue of clinical team training has now reappeared during the SARS COVID-19 pandemic, with the entire world having been affected and human skills overwhelmed (Donaldson & Neelam, 2020). COVID-19 has also revealed the flaws in undergraduate education and sparked a number of debates surrounding the future planning of curricula (Donaldson & Neelam, 2020). Simulation-based education and training have undoubtedly generated new proposals. Although previously only of interest to some, they are currently growing across the board in education and in clinical care (Park et al., 2020). A different attitude is being seen that is willing to incorporate simulation into undergraduate and graduate education, with an emphasis on interdisciplinarity that brings about challenges and new risks (Park et al., 2020; McNaughton & Gormley, 2021).

Simulation awakens expectations and ghosts of the past; it needs to be targeted and developed with a different focus, with new dimensions and new techniques and goals, while creating scenarios that consider ethical issues (Tritrakarn et al., 2014), greater respect, diversity, emotions, new conditions, and early, quick, and simultaneous responses for the most diverse contexts (McNaughton & Gormley, 2021; Park et al. 2020; World Health Organization, Patient Safety, 2021). On the other side, the simulator industry is developing innovative options and educational technologies with the purpose of providing greater support to academia and continuing education, and our present challenge is to learn how to incorporate this very quickly.

Throughout this chapter, we will be able to observe that the educational theories applied by this method and the existing models are very relevant in attaining learning outcomes and different constructs or deconstructs of cognitive processes where we intervene via guided reflection and debriefing techniques, thus producing significant behavioral changes in individuals working in healthcare (Sabei & Lasater, 2016; INACSL Standards Committee, 2016a, b, c, d).

2 Concept of Error and Patient Safety

Over the last 20 years, training of healthcare professionals has undergone changes in curricular designs; it considers interdisciplinarity and incorporates results-oriented learning in public health or that contributes to the community (Davis et al., 2005). Student-centered teaching models aim to develop technical, non-technical, and cross-disciplinary skills focused on achieving collaborative work, effective communication, leadership, and teamwork (INACSL Standards Committee, 2016a, b, c, d). Cross-disciplinary skills are not currently part of undergraduate education. Nevertheless, absence of these skills is what leads to recurring errors that occur when caring for the patient upon entering the workforce (Guinez-Molinos et al., 2017). This issue, which is a central theme in the book *To Err is Human*, points to the complexity of the work system as a generating source of errors, causing much harm, the death of patients, and high costs for the system (Kohn et al., 2000). All of this involves great economic loss, legal problems, and loss in the self-confidence of healthcare personnel, among other issues. The research conducted in this report highlights the foreseeable nature of some of the errors that can in fact be prevented (Ibid p. 78, 79). This book advances the thesis of coordination within simulation training as a way of preventing medical errors and improving patient safety (Escudero et al., 2018). From this standpoint, simulation is incorporated as a tool for generating "good practices" while following the model of "crew resource management" from aeronautics. This makes it possible to develop team training programs and test out methods for improving team management (Guinez-Molinos et al., 2017; Rall & Dieckmann, 2005).

The book has undeniably left a legacy of great contribution and an invitation to reflect on healthcare team practices, but it also opens up many questions and creates opportunities for other organizations to expand on knowledge.

2.1 World Alliance for Patient Safety, WHO

In 2004, the World Health Organization (WHO) created the World Alliance for Patient Safety, headed by Dr. Liam Donaldson. The primary aim was to develop a universal taxonomy with the purpose of sharing the same lexicon, concepts, and definitions so as to join forces to achieve the same goal (World Health Organization, Patient Safety, 2021). The intended purpose of this organization is for the member countries to work in collaboration to improve patient safety (WHO, 2021). Its main activities involve producing guidelines, standards, and tools that are implemented throughout the world. An example of this is the protocol for "5 Moments for Hand Hygiene" and the "Surgical Time-Out," which help to decrease surgery-related harm by 40% (Lara, 2018).

In 2009, the proposal of the World Alliance for Patient Safety, headed once again by Donaldson, integrated another area and offered the "Curriculum Guide for

Medical Schools" (World Health Organization, 2009a, b). This was a proposal for modifying the curriculum for medical students. Considering these students to be leaders in healthcare, the aim was to achieve essential learning outcomes in patient safety. In this regard, contents and pedagogical methods were included such as simulation for practicing skills and developing clinical scenarios that enable training and student immersion into realistic and controlled settings (World Health Organization, 2009a, b). In 2011, the proposal was expanded with the guidelines for the healthcare team (World Health Organization, 2011). In this most recent proposal, the objectives were broadened to training the educator on issues related to patient safety, and the clinical simulation method was examined further (World Health Organization, 2011). Strategic objectives were also added that include the patient with an active role on issues related to their own safety and with a role that accompanies the healthcare team more closely (Donaldson & Neelam, 2020).

In 2018, the World Alliance for Patient Safety agreed on a new definition: "Patient safety is the absence of preventable harm to a patient during the process of health care and reduction of risk of unnecessary harm associated with health care to an acceptable minimum. An acceptable minimum refers to the collective notions of given current knowledge, resources available and the context in which care was delivered weighed against the risk of non-treatment or other treatment." A world day of patient safety was created in 2019 and has been commemorated ever since.

2.2 *Data and Evidence on Patient Safety*

An increase in the risk to patient safety caused by the SARS COVID-19 virus has produced new challenges, given that this pandemic has introduced greater risk into patient safety (Donaldson & Neelam, 2020). A new problem has emerged because healthcare worker safety is undergoing an enormous crisis (Hardeep Singh et al., 2020). Healthcare professionals have fallen ill and many have passed away. This is a situation that has never been seen before in any other health emergency (Singh et al., 2020). As per indicated by Donaldson, between 14% and 35% of healthcare workers in various countries have been infected (Donaldson & Neelam, 2020). Thus, the issue has taken on new dimensions that require the development of proposals. However, before taking a closer look at these new challenges, data and scientific evidence need to be analyzed to understand why the situation with safety failures continues to be a considerable problem, and global in nature, which has been exacerbated with this crisis.

The publication entitled *To Err is Human* addresses the fact that in 1 year alone, around 100,000 Americans admitted to hospitals died due to preventable medical errors and that the probability of exposure to an error increases by 6% during each day of hospitalization (Kohn et al., 2000). Twenty years later, the numbers have not significantly changed, and by contrast, there has been an increase in safety problems as a result of COVID-19 (Singh et al., 2020).

A 2008 WHO report entitled "Learning from Errors" provided statistics on patient hospital admissions. Between 5% and 15% experienced an error in medication. If the problem is analyzed based on medication errors with the example of vincristine, which was wrongly administered intrathecally and not intravenously, this same report promotes accepting the error and using it to seek out the underlying causes, thus aiming for finding solutions rather than handing out penalties. The report also states that the healthcare work system involves constant risk and proposes working models for prevention to the institution, thus accepting this as an institutional and not an individual problem. From this standpoint, the concept of "Safe Medication and the Human Factor" emerged, which promotes the need to create operating protocols and training mechanisms with technical and non-technical simulation.

The lack of data for each country means that WHO research studies continue to be an important benchmark for information and proposals, some numbers from 2021: one out of every ten patients admitted into a hospital suffers some kind of harm in the care provided. The global cost for medication errors is USD 42 billion annually. Four out of every ten patients are harmed in primary care, and over 80% of harm in these settings could be avoided (World Health Organization, Patient Safety, 2021).

In 2017, Martin Makary et al. presented new data on medical errors as a third leading cause of death in the United States (Makary & Michael, 2016). Possible errors are deduced based on statistical reports for reporting deaths from the country. Nevertheless, the authors propose implementing other reporting models with more sources, so as to delve deeper into the knowledge on errors and design prevention strategies (Makary et al., 2016).

Employing a European perspective, the Centre for Clinical Risk Management and Patient Safety in Tuscany, Italy, contributes to this issue through multidisciplinarity (Tartaglia et al., 2008). This center, a collaborator of the WHO World Alliance for Patient Safety, works in a transdisciplinary fashion while aiming to implement the best practices. Thus, the behavioral patterns of healthcare professionals are analyzed that result in errors or adverse events, and solutions are created based on this (Tartaglia et al., 2008; Bellandi et al., 2007). One of the research studies reports how doctors and nurses are interrupted 13 times per hour in the operating room, or every 4.5 min, thus increasing the risk of adverse events as a consequence of suspending the task at hand and resuming after the interruption (Bellandi et al., 2018). Interrupting healthcare professionals is a regular event; however, it causes there to be a loss in concentration on the task at hand and sometimes results in an error or adverse event (Romero-Ruiza & Gómez-Salgadoc, 2015).

Another safety problem mentioned by WHO and linked to interruptions, among other things, is in medication (World Health Organization, 2008). This task is frequently associated with the role of nursing, although these are not the only professionals who participate in this process. Medication starts as of the moment of prescription; thus, there are many potential breakdowns in the quality of this process, which makes it difficult to intervene and improve it up until the end with the assessment (Dominguez-Cancino et al., 2020). The possibility of training the multiple sub-processes in simulation, with controlled environments and realistic scenarios, will allow students to face situations like those in real life and acquire skills through experiencing their own stress and the interruptions that occur in clinical settings (Ameer et al., 2015; Dominguez-Cancino et al., 2020).

Not all countries have statistical information available on errors and adverse events due to a fear of penalty. This is a barrier to progress and means there is a high level of underreporting (Tartaglia et al., 2008). Only some countries have advanced in integrating safety into curricula; therefore, the lack of knowledge on this issue in future healthcare professionals continues to be an enigma.

In 2017, the target of "Medication Without Harm" was approved at the Second Global Ministerial Patient Safety Summit in Bonn with data from WHO and its collaborating teams. The purpose of this was to reduce serious and avoidable harm by 50% over the next 5 years (World Health Organization, Global Patient Safety, 2017). However, the pandemic has placed other targets on the agenda, present in the Global Patient Safety Action Plan 2021–2030, indicating "engage patients and families as partners in safe care, achieve results through collaborative working, analyze and share data to generate learning, translate evidence into actionable and measurable improvement, base policies and action on the nature of the care setting, use both scientific expertise and patient experience to improve safety, and instill a safety culture in the design and delivery of health care" (World Health Organization, Patient Safety, 2021). To carry out all these proposals, a working framework is proposed with a rubric containing seven strategic objectives. The creation of high-confidence systems is suggested, with strategies related to human factor ergonomics, collaborative inter-professional education, and simulation with the development of education and training centers that spearhead the development of processes (World Health Organization, Patient Safety, 2021). Thus, with this statement, SBE could make progress in education and healthcare with very steady support.

2.3 Human Factor and Patient Safety: A Dialogue Between Concepts

The Society for Simulation in Health Care (SSH) is a scientific society of administrative and technical personnel and researchers in simulation, whose role is essential for the development of the SBE model. Their aim is to use globalized participation to improve the performance of whomever carries out simulation activities (Foysi-Doll & Leighton, 2017). Around 4500 members participate in SSH, and since 2004 they have held the largest global conference in the United States, the International Meeting for Simulation in Healthcare (IMSH). This is a global meeting with over 3000 participants that enables collaboration and networking through committees and groups of interest (Ibid, p. 54). Basic and simple solutions up to the most innovative and sophisticated technologies can be found at IMSH, which provides a one-of-a-kind space for creativity. SSH has always contributed with educational tools that help to develop simulation with quality while certifying educators and accrediting simulation programs inside and outside of the United States (SSH, 2021; Ibid, p. 56.x). The simulation dictionary, already in its second edition and translated into several languages, has allowed the taxonomy of simulationists to have a unique standard of communication (Lioce et al., 2020). One concept from this dictionary is human factor (HF). It is defined using the SBE approach to understand its relationship with patient safety and how it applies to scenarios (Lioce et al., 2020). We find two definitions in the dictionary: both refer to human interactions and highlight the cultural, psychological, and social aspects of individuals that have an influence on decision-making, but also their interaction with technology and the systems that impact work performance (Lioce et al., 2020).

The concept of HF is a term with historic use in other professional fields or cultural contexts. For Europeans, HF is related to ergonomics, and the concept is associated with labor laws and, thus, with conditions affecting workers (Patricia et al., 2016). For the United States, the term HF is related to the system, meaning to teams, technology, and the work environment. Currently, both visions co-exist and are used interchangeably (Patricia et al., 2016).

The World Alliance for Patient Safety also incorporates HF by proposing learning and using it in professional education and lifelong learning (World Health Organization, 2008, 2011). HF must be understood in its elements and trained in different clinical simulation scenarios to improve patient safety (World Health Organization, 2011, 2021; Weinger & Gaba, 2014).

The role of HF continues to be elaborated on, and in 2009, the WHO Patient Safety group prepared a report with definitions, approaches, and applied methods in high-risk industries that achieve safety (World Health Organization, WHO, 2009a, b). There are proposals for methods and tools for clinical guidelines, thus providing a referential framework for issues, without disregarding the concern for workers and risks they could experience (World Health Organization, WHO, 2009a, b). It is proposed that errors by healthcare professionals are linked to the type of organization and how this organization manages its processes, leadership models, communication, etc., thereby impacting patient safety. The concept of safety culture emerges as a principle associated with patient outcomes (World Health Organization, WHO, 2009a, b). The proposal it makes regarding developing simulation is tangential, but the issues and problems analyzed are transferable to simulated scenarios.

Going back to the book *To Err is Human*, first in recognizing the errors of healthcare teams, it examines HF to research why they occur and not who is guilty (Kohn et al., 2000). It analyzes the complexity of the healthcare system and the difficulties of the interfaces that are produced. It is important to identify the points of breaches in safety, the design of processes, and to assess every stage, thereby helping out in researching the circumstances for failures of the devices (Ibid, p. 64). Something simple like labeling syringes in anesthesia, which was not implemented during the 1990s, is now a standard. Another critical aspect of the clinical setting is the noise, time limits, simultaneity of tasks, diversity of flows, etc. and a healthcare team that does not know each other and is not trained under these conditions, unlike firefighters, who are able to prevent and improve performance by recreating lived experiences (Kohn et al., 2000).

Gaba publishes with Dr. Weinger, both anesthesiologists, about the movement of the concept of human factor engineering (HFE) to the field of healthcare (Weinger & Gaba, 2014). The concepts of quality and safety in the healthcare field are used indistinctly. Nevertheless, quality is associated with aiming for results in confidence and efficiency, while safety is related to resolving latent threats of a system that fails and must improve confidence (Ibid, p. 1). The authors promote multidisciplinary studies based on HFE. It indicates that engineers, computer scientists, sociologists, psychologists, ergonomists, or others will be able to identify zones of breaches in the system through observation and provide feedback and support the clinical team in making proposals for improvements in strategies and measurements of impact (Ibid, p. 2). HFE implies that the organization must consider integrating a permanent work group to contribute to a safety culture (Weinger & Gaba, 2014).

Healthcare professionals and educators in SBE must have knowledge of HFE if the objective is patient safety. Integrating HFE into transdisciplinary work will make it possible to reduce risks in healthcare and for there to be a real culture of safety. The healthcare team and their leaders must apply pressure for the government to incorporate and develop laws that promote the creation of multidisciplinary bodies with clear and non-punitive policies that strive for the safety of patients and to improve the clinical and service working systems (Kohn et al., 2000).

3 Simulation-Based Education

3.1 History and Beginnings of Clinical Simulation: Between Technological Advances and Societies

The use of simulators in healthcare dates back to the past and even many centuries ago, with findings of very basic obstetric mannequins that were most likely used to practice skills or techniques (Levine et al., 2013). It would be difficult to specify details and dates, and their impact on the training of healthcare professionals is also unknown. Hence, this analysis will be aimed at the time when simulation was implemented in clinical use and in education with clear objectives related to educational processes and theories seeking to improve the quality of healthcare and the best professional training.

The first models appeared between the 1950s and 1980s, and some of them have endured until the present day, such as the Resuscy Anne model for cardiopulmonary resuscitation (Tjomsland et al., 2021; Levine et al., 2013). These were simple models, task simulators, but the value of this training that makes it possible to save lives is understood through their use (Tjomsland et al., 2021). Another model was developed in the 1960s by Doctors Abrahamson and Denson with the support of the aeronautics industry. It was sophisticated and quite costly, with potential use in anesthesia through their physiological response software, all of which made widespread use impossible (Corvetto et al., 2013; Levine et al., 2013).

Clinical simulation drew upon the principles of aeronautic simulation; however, the development of industry, technologies, and the Internet enabled its expansion and the creation of mannequins with software and a massiveness that facilitated access into clinical and educational institutions (Levine et al., 2013). There are also other factors that have contributed to the use of simulation, such as the development of bioethics based on the Declaration of Helsinki regarding human experimentation (Manzini, 2000) and also a change in paradigm in education, focusing education on the student and outcomes, as well as in changes in methods and assessment (Corvetto et al., 2013; INACSL 2016a, b, c, d). Concern over patient safety as it was previously analyzed was also a dominant factor (Levine et al., 2013; Corvetto et al., 2013).

Simulation in education is supported by educational theories, and there is abundant research on this that addresses general issues and other very specific ones. Simulation still presents an extensive field yet to be explored, but the contributions made by researchers over the last 20 years have been significant (Park et al., 2020).

Those who have defined SBE have proposed a very broad description that includes technical and non-technical aspects, definitions that can be found in various book publications and in the SSH dictionary (Lioce et al., 2020). Simulation is a way of educating, practicing, assessing, testing, correcting, and measuring a certain performance or task in a protected setting with a high degree of realism (National League for Nursing, 2008; INACSL Standards, 2016a, b, c, d). One of the most frequently quoted definitions is from Gaba, an anesthesiologist from Stanford, educator, and researcher, renowned by scientific societies and for his tremendous work in simulation-based research (Levine et al., 2013; Gaba, 2004). This definition clearly establishes simulation in the field of educators and not in industry or technology.

Breakthroughs in simulation would have been difficult without technological developments; however, it likely would not have prospered had it not been for the work of scientific societies and their leaders. In 2007, Gaba pointed out that the future of simulation and its development for achieving patient safety would only be possible with the ingenuity and commitment of the healthcare simulation community (Gaba, 2004). The possibilities for networking and collaboration offered by societies are fundamental for the development of simulation in healthcare. They promote participating in various disciplines and do not question cultural differences, strengths, or weaknesses of institutions and even less so regarding their available resources.

The National League for Nursing (NLN) stands out as a collaborating society and for its contribution to the development of simulation in the United States. It is also one of the most long-standing societies in the discipline. In 2003, the NLN and the company Laerdal started a project that would lead to development of the first theoretical model for teaching in simulation (Susan Gross Forneris et al., 2018). Dr. Pamela Jeffries was chosen as the leader of this research study, which would be conducted for 3 years (Susan Gross Forneris et al., 2018). Jeffries is a huge global reference for SBE and research, and she has held prominent academic positions in universities and as the President of SSH in 2015. Jeffries' and the NLN's creation of the first educational model in simulation was a guide for the following challenge, and as a leader, her next task would be to create the Simulation Resource Center (SIRC) (Gross Forneris et al., 2018; Hovancsek et al., 2009). The SIRC project began in 2007 with 9 experts out of 169 who were brought together to represent different geographic regions and educational institutions in the United States, as well as 8 educators in simulation from Australia, Canada, Chile, China, Japan, Norway, and Scotland. This work was finalized with courses on a website for simulation educators with educational topics establishing quality standards and criteria and contributing to dissemination of knowledge in the world (Hovancsek et al., 2009). Faculty development in simulation began (National League for Nursing, 2008). The outcome demonstrated the high level of impact and contribution for nursing educators (Foysi-Doll & Leighton, 2017; Gross Forneris et al., 2018).

SBE enhanced its quality through support from the International Nursing Association for Clinical Simulation and Learning (INACSL), whose mission is "The global leader in the art and science of healthcare simulation through excellence in nursing education, practice, and research" (International Nursing Association for Clinical Simulation and Learning, INACSL). INACSL originated in Texas in 2003 and primarily stands out for its research and release of the Standards of Best Practice. There have been ten up to the present date, and they allow the simulation educator to incorporate clearly described criteria into their educational practice, which contribute to conducting quality simulation and for attaining the proposed objectives (INACSL Standards Committee, 2016a, b, c, d). The standards undergo constant development and have been translated into nine different languages. They are useful for educators in SBE and will allow beginners to learn and get motivated to continue examining the rest and reflect on the need to get trained and stay up-to-date as an educator (INACSL Standards Committee, 2016a, b, c, d).

3.2 Educator in Simulation: Simulationist

Being a specialist or simulationist entails fully complying with the INACSL standards or becoming certified as an educator or simulationist by SSH, with great dedication of time and lifelong learning (Lioce et al., 2020).

Being a simulation educator may appear to be simple; he/she must be young, tech-savvy, and a specialist in clinical topics on the case being developed in simulation. However, time has shown that this teaching model requires a profound change of the educator (Issenberg, 2006; INACSL, 2016a, b, c, d). The educator in simulation must understand the curriculum, educational theories, assessment, and feedback, among other things (Issenberg, 2006). They must accept their weaknesses and constantly reflect on their own educational practice. Teaching is done by being a facilitator, meaning a coach for students. They allow them to make mistakes, provide feedback, observe them, and help them to come up with improvements and to build their learning outcomes (INACSL, 2016a, b, c, d). They always guide and respect each participant according to their level and experience, without making any judgments, but placing limits and exploring their thoughts to resolve problems that will enable developing critical thinking and clinical judgment to apply with future patients (INACSL, 2016a, b, c, d). In addition to these skills, there are other requirements that define a simulationist. During her tenure as President of SSH, Christine Park invited world leaders at the IMSH 2018 in Los Angeles, USA, to participate in a brainstorming activity. Together with experts in ethics and with the subsequent approval from 25 simulation societies, they created "The Healthcare Simulationist Code of Ethics" (Park et al., 2018). The code, which has been translated into 15 languages, states six values: integrity, transparency, mutual respect, professionalism, accountability, and results orientation, all with their descriptions that provide clear signs of the importance of training the educator in simulation (Park et al., 2018).

Clinical and educational institutions that have simulation centers or departments set a high standard for the facilitator or simulationist in charge. It is required for them to be specialists, and this is why there is a wide offering of courses. There are various conferences that make it possible to stay up-to-date in the field, and they give credits for participating. There are also training programs such as professional certificate programs and fellows lasting from 1 to 3 years that are equivalent to any clinical specialty or graduate program (Levine et al., 2013). The book entitled *The Comprehensive Textbook of Healthcare Simulation* dedicates a chapter to the analysis of "Professional Development in Simulation" (Levine et al., 2013).

New knowledge and new demands for simulation are growing. During 2020, at the peak of the COVID-19 pandemic, SBE was implemented in the world with greater stamina than ever before (Park et al., 2020). Simulation is considered to be a unique resource for making progress with student training in healthcare to replace practical hours with remote simulation. This is observed in an SSH and INACSL statement providing relevant support to academia with this communication (SSH-INACSL, March 31, 2020). On the other hand, simulation is being expanded for training clinical teams in the use of standard precautions, putting on and removing personal protection equipment (PPE), and supporting clinical safety (Vera et al., 2021).

3.3 Curricular Integration and Educational Theories

Healthcare requires a paradigm change in education from a behavioral model to a constructivist model, given that learning based on practical experiences with training and feedback fosters more significant achievements (Levine et al., 2013). The clinical professional must be trained as an educator and transform the curricula saturated with contents into comprehensive models that will provide solutions for the patient, the physician, and societal changes (Issenberg, 2006; Patricia et al., 2016). Over two decades ago, Knowles described the concept of andragogy and pointed out the characteristics of adult learning, which will lead to a different manner of teaching, where the role of the educator must consider the experience, needs, and the motivation of the student (Patricia et al., 2016). Considering other issues, educators from Johns Hopkins University propose development of Kern's curriculum model, which has been accepted by educators from different regions around the world (Ibid, p ix). It is defined for proposing six steps to develop an educational experience plan, whether these are abbreviated or complete programs of an academic track or specialty, thus requiring a change of the educator (Ibid, p. 5, 12). The six steps are presented in a circle, whose elements are interrelated, dynamic, and interdependent; these are problem identification and needs, targeted group and assessment, goals and objectives, educational strategies, implementation, and evaluation and feedback (Ibid, p. 6, 7, 8). The curriculum may have changes and must be constantly being improved upon from the educational methods, contents, and educational strategies, and assessment always implemented (Ibid, p. 178). Kern's model makes it possible to coordinate with the integration of SBE, and for many simulationists, these six steps are the base foundation in constructing the curricula, for which there is evidence validating replacing clinical practice hours with simulation and with successful learning outcomes (Ibid, p. 2; Maryann Alexander et al., 2015).

SBE requires the educator to be proficient in the principles of the constructivist educational theories that will make it possible to change knowledge with metacognitive processes while considering the adult learning indicated by Knowles (Patricia et al., 2016). There are different theories present which contribute to SBE and enable constructing the learning process of each student with a certain degree of flexibility (Levine et al., 2013). To this effect, the most important thing is to know how to coordinate and connect the perspectives of each theory so as to produce the expected outcome (Ibid, p. 51). With the social learning theory, Bandura is present in the simulation of tasks or low fidelity, through modeling, self-regulation, and immersion in the simulation setting where the student incorporates language, attitudes, and behaviors based on their own experience, which are effective forms in adult learning and grant meaning to what is learned (Ibid, p. 52). Kolb and his experiential learning cycle are applied in simulation in its four stages: a concrete event is experienced, and then there is reflective observation, abstract conceptualization, and meaning learning that is conceptualized to apply or modify for a future experience, which can be real or simulated (Ibid, p. 52). The teacher must motivate, understand, and respect every student, thus encouraging the progress of every learner based on what happens to them during the process and not based on what they do as an educator; this converts them into a facilitator (Patricia, et al., 2016; Levine et al., 2013). However, the most complex part of SBE is what is developed in high-fidelity scenarios, where the students apply knowledge in their complex performance in a setting with a high degree of realism and which ends with the debriefing. This is the instance that integrates everything prior and where the facilitator participates in a process where they must compile and analyze information with different strategies and lead toward meeting proposed objectives (Ibid, p. 52). Debriefing is defined as "an activity that follows a simulation experience and where the students and the facilitator examine the experience lived within the scenario both formally and collaboratively" (Lioce et al., 2020). In this stage of the simulation, the facilitator uses Schön's model, reflection in and on action for the construction or modification of the participant's learning based on the lived experience (Ibid, p. 75; INACSL Standards Committee, 2016a, b, c, d). At this moment, the experiences are considered, as well as the participation of all, and although there are different ways of conducting or organizing the debriefing, there are key elements or stages: research of the learner's mental model, observation, and performing different forms and types of questions that enable identifying new learning (Dieckmann, 2009). Collecting information, analysis, and the conclusion are also elements that are present in the debriefing and will result in proposals and new knowledge to apply in future situations in the real world (Dieckmann, 2009).

3.4 Challenges of SBE for Crisis Management, a Look Forward

CRM had its origins in aeronautics, and Gaba transferred it to training in simulation in anesthesia and later generalized it to be applied in all spheres of healthcare intervention (Rall & Dieckmann, 2005). CRM is a training system in simulation so that teams can practice, incorporate the resources and protocols, and optimize them for patient safety (Levine et al., 2013). Its widespread use and application for preventing errors or identifying errors before damages associated with human factor problems are caused are proposed in Gaba's model with 15 key points (Rall & Dieckmann, 2005). Gaba's observation on clinical teams at Stanford University enabled associating adverse events with mistakes related to decision-making, communication, or securing errors in problem situations, and it has been the object of study, creation of courses, and research on simulationists ever since (Levine et al., 2013).

The use of CRM-based curriculum has been deployed in the field of healthcare training, and evidence shows there are changes in behavior and improvements in performance on the work teams; however, it is necessary to continue researching their impact on the organization and patient safety (Levine et al., 2013; Salas et al., 2006). The COVID-19 crisis has affected patient safety and that of clinical teams and organizations, leading to reflections on outstanding challenges in the use of simulation as a standard in healthcare training that will lead to a culture of safety (Park et al., 2020; Hardeep Singh et al., 2020).

Simulation modalities provide answers for many different objectives, and professionals must get trained to make the best use of this powerful tool through different modalities that make it possible to harness its strengths (Levine et al., 2013; Posner et al. 2017). SBE and training-based simulation will resolve many existing problems in the field of healthcare, and they have been mentioned since Kohn's publication over 20 years ago (Kohn et al., 2000).

The time has arrived to see what lessons we are learning during the pandemic and how we will move forward to overcome this crisis that is affecting the entire world, countries, governments, and, thus, their populations, the safety of patients and healthcare workers. The consequences of this have presented challenges for us

(World Health Organization, Patient Safety, 2021; Donaldson & Neelam, 2020; Singh et al., 2020). Nothing has been exempted from this crisis. Technologies, computer science, and SBE itself that were available and greatly underused have now become very essential and have reemerged with great potential and proposals such as tele-healthcare, remote learning, hybrid education, robotics, IT healthcare systems, interdisciplinary training, and networking and collaborative synergies (Donaldson & Neelam, 2020: Singh et al., 2020; Paige, 2021).

SSH and INACSL are providing ongoing solutions and continue to support institutions in decision-making and in changing in-person modalities or clinical hours for simulation and thus finalizing or moving forward with training processes (SSH-INACSL, March 31, 2020). SSH has supplemented the second edition of the dictionary with an addendum on terms related to distance simulation, thus explaining the different ways that simulation has reinvented itself to support educators and physicians in training interdisciplinary teams in specific healthcare units that are working with COVID-19 patients (SSH, 2020).

Hospitals, rescue workers, and universities, among others, trained in simulation to prepare people with no prior experience to become part of the front line immediately, to master air transfer of critical patients submerged in pods, and, lastly, for training on specific skills: intubation, pronation of patients on ventilators, and putting on and removing personal protection equipment (PPE) (Vera et al., 2021).

We are able to conclude that SBE is being increasingly validated by society and suggested within the context of medical education or education in healthcare (Davis et al., 2005). The emergence of societies that take care to standardize and improve educational processes in training doctors and other careers in healthcare is a fundamental pillar for integrating simulation into curricular projects, as well as requiring the training of educators (Wojtczak, 2013). It is necessary to prepare responsible teams, because with the high level of requirements mentioned, it is not possible to be an expert in all areas and aspects existing today in SBE, and centers must comply with a certain level of quality (Escudero et al., 2017). One piece of knowledge that is cross-cutting for any educator or simulationist is to be proficient in educational theories and curricular integration (Standards, December 2016).

The simulation community implores reexamining SBE and simulation centers and reviewing these spaces and the work done there, so they once again become safe places, with healthcare professionals trained with high-quality standards who develop an ethical and inclusive practice with real accountability toward our patients and their surroundings (Park et al., 2020).

SBE research and evidence still have much yet to define and justify, but to date, its merits and contributions seem to be beneficial and this provides encouragement to continue applying it in our educational and training activities (Jeffries et al., 2015). Our patients deserve it, because they are always going to have expectations and trust in the work of the healthcare team.

1. Simulation is a technique—not a technology—to replace or amplify real experiences with guided experiences that evoke or replicate substantial aspects of the real world in a fully interactive manner.

2. National League for Nursing SIRC http://www.nln.org/sirc/about-sirc
3. Mission Nursing Association for Clinical Simulation and Learning https://www.inacsl.org/about/mission-vision-values/
4. Position Statement on Use of Virtual Simulation during the Pandemic March 30, 2020. Synopsis. The International Nursing Association of Clinical Simulation and Learning (INACSL, www.inacsl.org) and the Society for Simulation in Healthcare (SSH, www.ssih.org) support the use of virtual simulation as a replacement for clinical hours for students currently enrolled in health sciences professions (i.e., nursing students, medical students) during the current public health crisis caused by COVID-19.

Bibliography

Alexander, P., Durham, P., Hooper, J., Jeffries, P., Goldman, N., Kardong-Edgren, S., Kesten, K., Spector, N., Tagliareni, E., Radtke, B., & Tillman, C. (2015). National Council of State Boards of Nursing (NCSBN) simulation guidelines for Prelicensure nursing programs. *Journal of Nursing Regulation, 3*(6), 39–42.

Ameer, A., Dhillon, S., Peters, M., & Ghaleb, M. (2015). Systematic literature review of hospital medication administration errors in children. *Integrated Pharmacy Research and Practice, 4*, 153–165.

Bellandi, T., Albolino, S., & Tomassini, C.-S. (2007). How to create a safety culture in the healthcare system: The experience of the Tuscany Region. *Theoretical Issues in Ergonomics Science, 8*(5), 495–507.

Bellandi, T., Cerri, A., Carreras, G., Walter, S., Mengozz, I. C., Albolino, S., Mastrominico, E., Renzetti, F., Tartaglia, R., & Westbrook, J. (2018). Interruptions and multitasking in surgery: A multicentre observational study of the daily work patterns of doctors and nurses. *Ergonomics, 61*(1), 40–47.

Corvetto, M., Bravo, M.-P., Montaña, R., Utili, F., Escudero, E., Boza, C., Varas, J., & Dagnino, J. (2013). Simulation in medical education: A synopsis. *Revista Medica de Chile, 141*, 70–77.

Davis, M., Karunathilake, I., & Harden, R. (2005). AMEE education guide no. 28: The development and role of departments of medical education. *Medical Teacher, 27*(8), 665–675.

Dieckmann, P. (Ed.). (2009). *Using simulation for education, training and research*. Pabst Science Publishers.

Dominguez-Cancino, K., Bravo-Tare, C., Vergara-Arias, K., & Escudero, E. (2020). Transgresiones y errores potenciales de medicación en estudiantes de enfermería en ambiente simulado. *Revista De Investigación (de La Universidad Norbert Wiener), 8*(1).

Donaldson, L., & Neelam, D. (2020). World patient safety day: A call for action on health worker safety. *Journal of Patient Safety and Risk Management, 25*(5), 171–173.

Escudero, E., Fuentes, C. M., Gonzalez, V., & Corvetto, A. (2017). Simulación en educación para ciencias de la Salud: ¿Qué calidad hemos alcanzado en Chile? *ARS MEDICA Revista De Ciencias Médicas, 26*(2), 16–20.

Escudero, E., Avendaño Ben-Azul, M., & Domínguez, C. K. (2018). Simulación clínica y seguridad del paciente: integración en el currículo de enfermería. *Scientia Medica, 28*(1). https://doi.org/10.15448/1980-6108.2018.1.28853

Federación Latinoamericana de Simulación Clínica y Seguridad del Paciente (FLASIC). (2020). *Historia de la Federación Latinoamericana de Simulación Clínica y Seguridad del Paciente*. Retrieved from https://www.flasic.org/historia

Foysi-Doll, C., & Leighton, K. (Eds.). (2017). *Simulation champions: Fostering courage, caring and connection*. Nederland Wolters Kluwer Ed.

Foysi-Doll, C., & Leighton, K. (Eds.). (2018). *Simulation champions: Fostering courage, caring and connection*. Nederland Wolters Kluwer Ed.

Gaba, D. M. (Ed.). (2004). The future vision of simulation in health care. *BMJ Quality & Safety, 13*, i2–i10.

Gonzalez, L., & Edgren, K. (2017). Deliberate practice for mastering learning in nursing. *Clinical Simulation in Nursing, 13*(1), 10–14.

Gross Forneris, S., Tagliareni, M.-E., Jeffries, P., & Rizzolo, M.-A. (Eds.). (2018). *Simulation champions, fostering courage, caring and connection*. National league for nursing and Simulation Innovation Resource, Nederland Wolters Kluwer Ed.

Guinez-Molinos, S., Martínez-Molina, A., Gomar-Sancho, C., Arias-González, V. B., Szyld, D., García-Garrido, E., & Maragaño-Lizama, P. (2017). A collaborative clinical simulation model for the development of competencies by medical students. *Medical Teacher, 39*(2), 195–202.

Hovancsek, M., Jeffries, P. R., Escudero, E., Foulds, B. J., Husebo, S. E., Iwamoto, Y., Kelly, M., Petrini, M., & Wang, A. (2009). Creating simulation communities of practice: An international perspective. *Nursing Education Perspectives, 30*(2), 121–125.

INACSL Standards Committee. (2016a, December). INACSL standards of best practice: Simulation SM debriefing. *Clinical Simulation in Nursing, 12*(S), S21–S25.

INACSL Standards Committee. (2016b, December). INACSL standards of best practice: Simulation design. *Clinical Simulation in Nursing, 12*, S5–S12.

INACSL Standards Committee. (2016c, December). INACSL standards of best practice: Simulation: Facilitation. *Clinical Simulation in Nursing, 12*, S16–S20.

INACSL Standards Committee. (2016d, December). INACSL standards of best practice: Simulation-enhanced interprofessional education (Sim IPE). *Clinical Simulation in Nursing, 12*(S), S34–S38.

Issenberg, S.-B. (2006). The scope of simulation-based healthcare education. *Simulation for Healthcare, 1*(4), 203–208.

Jeffries, P., Rodgers, B., & Adamson, K. (2015). NLN Jeffries simulation theory: Brief narrative description. *Nursing Education Perspectives, 6*(5), 291–293.

Kohn, L. T., Corrigan, J. M., & Donaldson, M. S. (Eds.). (2000). *To err is human: Building safer healthcare system*. National Academy Press.

Kronick, R. (2014). *Health care simulation to advance safety: Responding to Ebola and other threats*. Agency for Health Care Research and Quality (AHQS). https://www.ahrq.gov/research/findings/factsheets/errors-safety/simulproj15/index.html#contents

Lara, C. (2018). Importancia de la Pausa de Seguridad Quirúrgica. *Actualizaciones Clínica MEDS, 2*(2), 40–48.

Levine, A. I., De Maria, S., Jr., Schwartz, A. D., & Sim, A. J. (Eds.). (2013). *The comprehensive textbook of healthcare simulation*. Springer.

Lioce, L. (Ed.), & Lopreiato, J. (Founding Ed.). (2020, September). In D. Downing, T. P. Chang, J. M. Robertson, M. Anderson, D. A. Diaz, Spain, A. E. (Assoc. Eds.), & the Terminology and Concepts Working Group (Eds.), *Healthcare simulation dictionary* (AHRQ publication no. 20–0019) (2nd ed.). Agency for Healthcare Research and Quality.

Makary, M., & Michael, D. (2016). Medical error – The third leading cause of death in the US. *BMJ, 355*, 2–5.

Manzini, J.-L. (2000). Declaration of Helsinki: Ethical principles for medical research involving human subjects. *Acta Bioethica, 6*(2). On-line version ISSN 1726-569X. https://doi.org/10.4067/S1726-569X2000000200010

McNaughton, N., & Gormley, G. (2021). From manifestos to praxis: Developing criticality in healthcare simulation. *BMJ Simulation & Technology Enhanced Learning, 7*(3), 123–125.

National League for Nursing. (2008). About SIRC. http://www.nln.org/sirc/about-sirc

Paige, J.-T. (2021). What's in a name? Simulation and technology enhanced learning uses and opportunities in the era of COVID-19. *BMJ Simulation & Technology Enhanced Learning, 7*, 1–2.

Park, C. S., & Murphy, T. F. et al. (2018). *Healthcare simulationist code of ethics*. SSIH.org. Retrieved from: https://inspiresim.org/wp-content/uploads/2019/01/CodeOfEthics-web-FINAL.pdf
Park, C. S., Clark, L., Gephardt, G., et al. (2020). Manifesto for healthcare simulation practice. *BMJ Simulation and Technology Enhanced Learning*. Published Online First: 04 September 2020.
Patricia, A., Thomas, D., Kern, M.-T., Hughes, B., & Chen, Y. (Eds.). (2016). *Curriculum development for medical education: A six-step approach* (3rd ed.). The Johns Hopkins University School of Medicine.
Posner, G. D., Clark, M. L., & Grant, V. J. (2017). Simulation in the clinical setting: Towards a standard lexicon. *Advances in Simulation, 2*, 1–5.
Rall, M., & Dieckmann, P. (2005). *Crisis resource management to improve patient safety*. European Society of Anesthesiology.
Romero-Ruiza, A., & Gómez-Salgadoc, J. (2015). Enfermería y seguridad clínica: ¿Cuál es el camino? *Rev Enfermeria clínica, 25*(4), 155–157.
Sabei, S., & Lasater, K. (2016). Simulation debriefing for clinical judgment development: A concept analysis. *Nurse Education Today, 45*, 42–47.
Salas, E., Wilson, K.-A., Burke, S.-C., & Wightman, D.-C. (2006). Does crew resource management training work? An update, an extension, and some critical. *The Journal of the Human Factors and Ergonomics Society, 48*(2), 392–412.
Shin, S., Park, J.-H., & Kim, J.-H. (2015). Effectiveness of patient simulation in nursing education: Meta-analysis. *Nurse Education Today, 35*(1), 176–182.
Singh, H., Sittig, D.-F., & Gandhi, T.-J. (2020). Fighting a common enemy: A catalyst to close intractable safety gaps. *BMJ Quality and Safety, 30*, 141–145.
Society for Simulation in Healthcare (SSH)- INACSL. (2020, 31 March). *COVID-19: Position statement on use of virtual simulation during the pandemic*. https://www.ssih.org/COVID-19-Updates/ID/2237/COVID-19-SSHINACSL-Position-Statement-on-Use-of-Virtual-Simulation-during-the-Pandemic
SSH. (2020). *Healthcare simulation dictionary. V2.0 ADDENDUM: Terms related to simulation at a distance*. https://www.ssih.org/Dictionary
SSH. Accreditation of Healthcare Simulation Programs. https://www.ssih.org/Credentialing. Retrieved in January 2021.
Tartaglia, T., Bellandi, T., & Albolino, S. (2008). *Organizing patient safety: The experience of Tuscany's clinical risk management centre*. Researchgate. https://www.academia.edu/22732452/Organizing_patient_safety_the_experience_of_the_Tuscanys_Clinical_Risk_Management_centre
Tritrakarn, P., Berg, B., Kasuya, P., & Sakai, D. (2014). Medical school hotline: Can we use simulation to teach medical ethics? *Hawaii Journal of Medicine & Public Health, 73*(8), 262–264.
Vera, M., Kattan, E., Cerda, T., Niklitshek, J., Montaña, R., Varas, J., & Corvetto, M. (2021). Implementation Distance-Based Simulation Training Programs for Healthcare Professionals. *Simulation in Healthcare: The Journal of the Society for Simulation in Healthcare*: January 27, 2021 – Volume Publish Ahead of Print – Issue. https://doi.org/10.1097/SIH.0000000000000550
Weinger, M., & Gaba, D. (2014, April). Human factor engineering in patient safety human factors engineering in patient safety. *Anesthesiology, 120*, 801–806.
Wojtczak, A. (2013). *History of AMEE 1972–2009* (AMEE Occasional Paper 5). Association for Medical Education in Europe.
Word Health Organization (WHO). (2011). *Patient safety curriculum guide for multi-professional*. WHO Library Cataloguing-in-Publication Data. https://www.who.int/patientsafety/education/mp_curriculum_guide/en/. Retrieved in January 2021.
World Health Organization (WHO). (2004). *World Alliance for patient safety, forward programme*. WHO Library Cataloguing-in-Publication Data. https://www.who.int/patientsafety/worldalliance/alliance/en/#:~:text=The%20fundamental%20purpose%20of%20the,in%20an%20annual%20work%20programme. Retrieved in January 2021.

World Health Organization (WHO). (2009a). *Curriculum guide for medical schools 2009*. WHO Library Cataloguing-in-Publication Data. https://www.who.int/patientsafety/education/curriculum_guide_medical_schools/en/. Retrieved in January 2021.
World Health Organization (WHO). (2009b). *Human factors in patient safety: Review of topics and tools*. WHO Library Cataloguing-in-Publication Data.
World Health Organization (WHO). (2017). *Global patient safety. Medication without harm 2017*. WHO. https://www.who.int/initiatives/medication-without-harm. Retrieved in January 2021.
World Health Organization (WHO). (2021). *Global patient safety action plan 2021–2030. Toward eliminating avoidable harm in health care*. WHO Library Cataloguing-in-Publication Data. https://www.who.int/teams/integrated-health-services/patient-safety/policy/global-patient-safety-action-plan. Retrieved in January 2021.

Index

S. Flandin et al. (eds.), *Simulation Training through the Lens of Experience and Activity Analysis*, Professional and Practice-based Learning 30,
https://doi.org/10.1007/978-3-030-89567-9

The manufacturer's authorised representative in the EU is Springer Nature Customer Service Centre GmbH, Europaplatz 3, 69115 Heidelberg, Germany. If you have any concerns regarding our products, please contact ProductSafety@springernature.com

Printed and bound by CPI Group (UK) Ltd, Croydon, CR0 4YY
30/09/2026
02225491-0009